TRAGEDY & TRIUMPH:
Ruby & Thomas B. McQuesten

RUBY BAKER MCQUESTEN   THOMAS BAKER MCQUESTEN

1879-1911   1882-1948

TRAGEDY & TRIUMPH:
Ruby & Thomas B. McQuesten

By Mary J. Anderson, PhD

Tierceron Press

ACKNOWLEDGMENTS

I am profoundly indebted to Eleanore and Richard Kosydar of Tierceron Press for the confidence they have shown in this book, and for their generous assistance in editing, design, photography and photo-placement throughout. As we approach the 100th anniversary of Ruby McQuesten's tragic death (April 9, 1911), I can think of no finer tribute than her inclusion in a celebration of Thomas B. McQuesten's triumphs. I am grateful to the Hamilton Historical Board for declaring 2011 as "McQuesten Year." I thank Tom Minnes and the staff at Whitehern Historic House and Garden for their expert help, and the Hamilton Public Library for providing space and technical expertise for the continuing expansion of the Whitehern Museum Archives website, www.whitehern.ca. My children, Mark and Janelle, have been a constant source of advice and encouragement. My three grandchildren, Jessica, Sarah and Rebecca, have shown great interest in the progress of this book, and Jessica and Rebecca have worked on the website digitization team along with many others. I am grateful to Therese Charbonneau of the City of Hamilton, who has been extremely helpful in the conservation of Ruby McQuesten's paintings, and to Jeff Tessier, whose expert photography has brought Ruby's paintings to the gallery-show stage, and will allow her to emerge from obscurity into the annals of Canadian Art History. Julie Nash and Melissa LaPorte, Master's students in Art History, provided much expert assistance with the photographs, and Julie has given me some insights into Thomas B. McQuesten's aesthetics in architecture and landscape design. The five poets whose eight perceptive poems enrich the text will live forever on these pages, on the Whitehern website, and in my gratitude.

Mary J. Anderson

Copyright © Mary J. Anderson, 2011
ISBN 978-0-9867583-0-0

All photographs are courtesy of Whitehern Museum Archives, www.whitehern.ca, unless otherwise specified. Care has been taken to trace the ownership of copyright material used in this book. The author and the publisher welcome any information enabling them to rectify any references or credits in subsequent editions.

No part of this publication may be reproduced, stored in a retrieval system or transmitted, in any form or by any means, without the prior written consent of the author.

Published in Canada by Tierceron Press   Printed in Canada by Friesens
                        Dundas, Ontario
                        tiercpress@cogeco.ca

Library and Archives Canada Cataloguing in Publication

Anderson, Mary J. (Mary Johanna), 1931-
Tragedy & triumph : Ruby & Thomas B.
McQuesten / by Mary J. Anderson.

Includes bibliographical references and index.
ISBN 978-0-9867583-0-0

1. McQuesten, Ruby B. (Ruby Baker), 1879-1911.
2. McQuesten, Thomas B. (Thomas Baker), 1882-1948.
3. McQuesten family. 4. Public works--Ontario--History--20th century. 5. Public works--Ontario--Hamilton--History--20th century. 6. Ontario--Politics and government--1923-1943.
7. Teachers--Ontario--Biography. 8. Politicians--Ontario--Biography. 9. Lawyers--Ontario--Biography. 10. Hamilton (Ont.)--Biography. I. Title. II. Title: Tragedy and triumph.

FC3075.1.M33A54 2011   971.3'030922   C2011-900279-5

Dedicated to my husband,
James John Anderson (now deceased)
for enduring inspiration

CONTENTS

PAINTINGS & PYROGRAPHY BY RUBY B. MCQUESTEN
Colour Plates 1 - 19

PART THREE

TRIUMPH: Thomas Baker McQuesten (1882-1948)

REPRESENTATIVE ACCOMPLISHMENTS OF THOMAS B. MCQUESTEN
Selected Colour Photographs

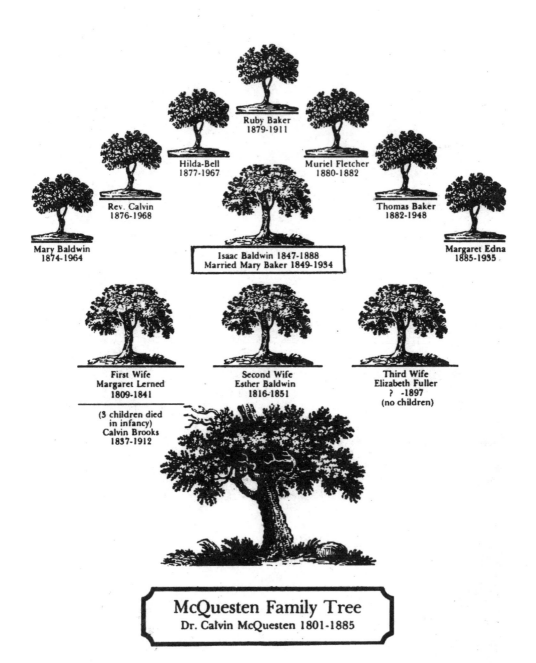

Mary Baldwin
1874-1964

Rev. Calvin
1876-1968

Hilda-Bell
1877-1967

Ruby Baker
1879-1911

Muriel Fletcher
1880-1882

Thomas Baker
1882-1948

Margaret Edna
1885-1935

Isaac Baldwin 1847-1888
Married Mary Baker 1849-1934

First Wife
Margaret Lerned
1809-1841

Second Wife
Esther Baldwin
1816-1851

Third Wife
Elizabeth Fuller
? -1897
(no children)

(3 children died
in infancy)
Calvin Brooks
1837-1912

McQuesten Family Tree
Dr. Calvin McQuesten 1801-1885

WHITEHERN HISTORIC HOUSE
AND GARDEN

Whitehern Historic House,
a City of Hamilton Museum
since 1971, as it appears today

Richard Kosydar

Both the garden gazebo and
MacNab Street Presbyterian
Church are visible from
the west walkway

Whitehern today:

The house today reflects the alterations made by three generations of the McQuesten family. It contains elements from many time periods – Georgian, Victorian and Edwardian – all overlaid with original possessions dating up to 1968 when the last remaining member of the family, Rev. Calvin McQuesten, died. None of the six children married.

The gracious DINING ROOM at Whitehern

Whitehern Hamilton

Richard Kosydar

Below:
The pianoforte in the parlour, purchased in 1855 by Mrs. Dr. Calvin McQuesten (see W8278)

Richard Kosydar

Whitehern LIBRARY

The library at Whitehern consists of more than 3500 books, the oldest of which is dated 1569.

Thomas kept a reading diary from 1918-33 that includes several books about the War of 1812 (Best 51).

T.B. McQuesten's LOUNGE

Note the Royal Chairs used by King George VI and Queen Elizabeth during their Canadian Tour in 1939 (see P234)

Richard Kosydar

Ruby's and Hilda's *Xmas* dolls *(p.36)*,
on display for Christmas at Whitehern

Inscription in a book
for eight-year-old Ruby
from her *Papa & Mama*

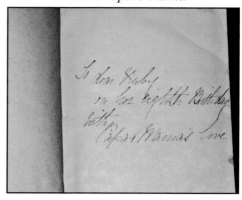

The Girls' Bedroom: Note Ruby's paintings

Richard Kosydar

Richard Kosydar

The MORNING ROOM or Family Room at Whitehern

Richard Kosydar

STAIRWELL, 2nd floor, with stained glass window at back of house

Vignettes of **WHITEHERN INTERIORS**

Richard Kosydar

FRONT ENTRY HALL, detail

Richard Kosydar

Vignettes of
WHITEHERN EXTERIORS

The exceptionally fine massing of forms
at Whitehern is enhanced by
the beautiful stonework

Richard Kosydar

The lovely **REAR GARDEN**
at Whitehern

Left:

Path to the Stable

Below:
View of Stable from
the west end of the garden

View of MacNab Street Presbyterian Church from the rear garden at Whitehern

Public picnic in Whitehern garden, with music in the gazebo (c.2000)

Richard Kosydar

The REAR GARDEN in autumn

Garden design by the Dunington-Grubbs

The GAZEBO in summer

Note the ornate iron fence post at right

Richard Kosydar

Vignettes from
the **REAR GARDEN**
in autumn

Richard Kosydar

Richard Kosydar

Jeff Tessier

Above:

Sunflowers in Iron

One of the Iron Flowers
gracing the stone wall in the
garden at Whitehern, made by
Fred Flatman, artist in iron.
MacNab Street Presbyterian
Church is visible at back.

T.B. McQUESTEN®

Lovely large amber blossoms. Grows to
.6m tall. A beautiful award winning rose!

*T.B. McQuesten founded the Royal Botanical Gardens
in Burlington, Ont. and originated Ontario Parks and
Recreation.*

Right:
The T.B. McQUESTEN Rose,
dedicated by MacNab Presbyterian Church
to Thomas B. McQuesten and his family

THE McQUESTEN PLOT at the Hamilton Cemetery on York Blvd.
Note the two large memorial monuments, and the small individual gravestones

Ruby McQuesten's gravestone, foreground

Thomas B. McQuesten's gravestone, rear left

WHITEHERN HISTORIC HOUSE AND GARDEN in Autumn

Richard Kosydar

The garden with a fall blanket of leaves

Part One

THE MCQUESTEN FAMILY:
PRELUDE TO TRAGEDY

HISTORY

**Dr. Calvin
McQuesten**

**Dr. Calvin Brooks
McQuesten**

**Rev. Thomas
Baker**

**Isaac B.
McQuesten**

**(left to right) Hilda, Tom, Mary, Mary (Jr.)
Edna, Ruby, Calvin**

(C. 1890)

RUBY BAKER McQUESTEN (1879-1911)

Ruby at age two, four and eight

THOMAS BAKER McQUESTEN (1882-1948)

Thomas at age two with his
grandfather and namesake,
Rev. Thomas Baker

Thomas as a dignified
four-year-old

Thomas at age six

Chapter 1

INTRODUCTION

The McQuesten family of Whitehern underwent several periods of adversity during their three generations in Hamilton. Despite their often severe tribulations, however, the Honourable Thomas Baker McQuesten emerged a triumphant hero for the family and for Ontario. He was a man of vision who accomplished more for the modernization and beautification of roads, bridges and parks, than has any other person before or since. His work brought prosperity to the province, including the north. However, little is known about the sacrifices that Tom's sister Ruby made for his education and welfare. The story of Ruby's vital role in Tom's remarkable accomplishments has never previously been told. Ruby, a beautiful Victorian maiden, died tragically at the age of thirty-one, and was soon forgotten.

Ruby Baker McQuesten was only nine years old when her father, Isaac Baldwin McQuesten, died suddenly and unexpectedly. Her brother, Thomas Baker McQuesten was five years old at the time. Their father's untimely death at the age of forty-one occurred after taking a combination of sleeping medication and alcohol. Isaac had been an alcoholic from an early age, though he swore to give up alcohol twice in order to win the hand of Mary Baker in 1873. In the years leading up to his death, Isaac suffered several mental breakdowns and had spent regular sessions at the Homewood Retreat[1] in Guelph. He was being treated for insomnia, melancholia, alcoholism, and dependence on *stimulants*. Isaac admitted, *it is one long continuous want or craving* (W2511, Oct 1 1887). Because of the circumstances surrounding Isaac's death, it was widely rumoured to be a suicide.

To make matters worse, Isaac died bankrupt. Consequently, on that day, March 7, 1888, the world changed for the McQuesten family. Isaac's wife, Mary Baker McQuesten was left widowed *and* impoverished, with six children between the ages of two and fourteen *(see family photo on p. 19)*. Isaac had the forethought to leave Whitehern in trust for Mary, but the house was sadly in need of repair and many years would pass before the necessary work could be undertaken.

Ruby and Thomas were born into a privileged upper-class family in Victorian Ontario. Ruby was the fourth child and Tom the sixth of seven children born within the first twelve years of their parents' marriage. Both were attractive, intelligent, healthy children. Ruby was born in Hamilton; Tom was born in Hespeler where their father had opened a woollen mill. In Hamilton they lived in an attached house

---

[1] In 1883 the **Homewood Retreat** was founded by John W. Langmuir and Dr. Stephen E. Lett. In 1902 it became the **Homewood Sanitarium**. Note spelling: **Sanitarium** is from the Latin noun *sanitas* meaning health, so a kind of health resort; while **sanatorium** is derived from the Latin verb *sano* meaning to heal, so a medical establishment. (See www.homewood.org/history)

**MacNab Street Presbyterian Church,
beyond the Whitehern Garden Gazebo**

at 1 Bold Street, and their maternal grandparents, the Rev. Thomas and Mrs. Baker, lived in the other half. Their paternal grandparents, Dr. and Mrs. Calvin McQuesten, lived just a short block away at Willowbanks (later named Whitehern), a stately mansion on the corner of Jackson and MacNab Streets. Between these two locations stood the monumental MacNab Street Presbyterian Church. Their grandfather, Dr. Calvin McQuesten had financed the church, and continued to support it as an elder and benefactor. The children's father, Isaac, a lawyer was also an elder of the church. Their mother, Mary Baker McQuesten—a minister's daughter—was a charter member of the Women's Foreign Missionary Society (WFMS), established in 1876. She was its president for twenty-five years (1893-1918), and was an active member for fifty years. Mary's continuing dedication to the Presbyterian Missionary cause is remarkable considering that she became a single mother of six children prior to assuming the presidency, and had many personal and financial cares and woes.

Ruby and Tom's world was defined by wealth, stability, the Presbyterian Church and social prestige, and their early prospects for a privileged life were excellent. Ruby was beautiful, charming and artistic; Tom was handsome and robust, and both were

Central Public School

Canada Life Bldg. (later Birks Bldg.), James St. S.
Hamilton Art School (1886-90), 3rd floor

scholastically inclined. They attended Central Public School, just a block away from home. Within Ruby's first year she had already skipped a grade. She also attended the Hamilton Art School from an early age and won praise for her art.

This comfortable world disintegrated with their father's sudden death and bankruptcy. From that day forward the McQuesten family was forced to confront an uncertain future, and more tragedy would yet befall them. Ruby is the most tragic figure among the McQuesten children. She grew up to be beautiful, charming, articulate, intelligent, artistic, and very loving and caring, but was sacrificed for the betterment of the family.

Of the six children, Ruby Baker and Thomas Baker showed the greatest potential for an education and career. One is tempted to speculate that Mary may have perceived something of this special promise at birth, and so blessed each of them with the name of her revered father: Baker. Although Thomas was the younger of the two

Mary Baker McQuesten

by three years, his prospects as a man in the Victorian Age[2] were better for earning a professional salary and thereby restoring the family to solvency and social status. Unfortunately his impoverished mother had no money to send him to school. In response to these realities, Mary gradually conceived a complex plan that would take years to come to fruition. She determined that Ruby would become a teacher, and found her a position at Ottawa Ladies' College. There she would be provided room and board, and could send her salary home to pay for Tom's university education and law degree. The details of the family's tight finances are related in the family letters, and are at the crux of the story.

Ruby continued teaching in Ottawa long after she developed a chronic cough. Shortly after Tom graduated she succumbed to her illness; she died of consumption (tuberculosis) four years later. Ruby was sacrificed to the family cause, but she bore her lot heroically. She is the "Tragic Victorian Heroine" of their story. In spite of

---

[2] The "Victorian Age" is used throughout in the sense of its continued influence into the twentieth century. Royce MacGillivray comments in *The Mind of Ontario*: "Explanation is needed for the late introduction of Victorianism to Ontario, and for its late departure. . . . The educated Presbyterian clergy with their Scottish associations . . . and rationalism appropriate to their intellectually-oriented religion, prolonged . . . the dominance of the Scottish Enlightenment." One of the reasons he offers is that it promoted a settled way of life rather than the disorder and fluidity of pioneering conditions and immigration. It provided a network of congregations for the dissemination of ideas, moral standards, literacy, higher education, family values, and the work ethic based on a British model (51-52).

**Ruby Baker McQuesten (1879-1911)
whose sacrifice made possible
the eventual success of her brother,
Thomas Baker McQuesten**

poor health and her burden of work, Ruby's letters are always warm and witty, full of interesting details about visits to Parliament, lectures on many themes, social events, sports, and her paintings.

Tom graduated in 1907, becoming a successful lawyer and politician, a Member of Provincial Parliament, and Minister of several important cabinet posts. He initiated and developed many public works and beautification projects for Hamilton and for Ontario. He is gradually being recognized for his achievements as a master builder, whereas Ruby has been virtually forgotten. Tom was always grateful to his mother for her guidance and vision, and he implemented his "City Beautiful" projects in accordance with a shared family vision. Ruby is rarely mentioned after her death in 1911, and there is no record that Tom ever acknowledged in writing her crucial contribution to his success. Nevertheless, her story demonstrates that Ruby played a major role in bringing Tom's vision to fruition, and that her sacrifice was not in vain.

THE THREE-PART FAMILY SAGA

Dr. Calvin McQuesten (1801-85)

Isaac Baldwin McQuesten (1847-88)

Hon. Thomas B. McQuesten (1882-1948)

Chapter 2

THE RISE OF THE McQUESTEN FAMILY

The story leading up to Ruby's tragedy and Tom's triumph is a three-part and three-generational saga: THE RISE, THE FALL, AND THE RESTORATION OF THE McQUESTEN FAMILY. The rise occurred with the children's grandfather, Dr. Calvin McQuesten, who came to Canada from New England in the 1830s to open Hamilton's first foundry. Although he had been educated as a medical doctor, he found the prospects much better in industry, and chose to settle at the head of Lake Ontario for the shipping advantages it offered. From this humble beginning in the foundry industry Hamilton eventually became known as the "Birmingham of Canada."[3]

Dr. Calvin McQuesten made a fortune in threshing machines, stoves, and various metal products, and retired in 1865 with a fortune of $500,000, along with other investments and real estate. He was an evangelical Presbyterian and, after retirement, he devoted himself to the design and building of various Presbyterian churches in Canada and the U.S., including MacNab Street Presbyterian Church in Hamilton.

Dr. Calvin McQuesten was an astute business man but he made two serious mistakes in his life. His first mistake occurred when he took Elizabeth Fuller as his third wife in 1853. His first and second wives had died in childbirth leaving him with three living sons: Calvin Brooks (later Dr.) and his half-brothers, Isaac Baldwin and David (who died in a fire in 1854 at the age of five). Dr. Calvin McQuesten married

Elizabeth Fuller McQuesten (b.1816, m.1853, d. 1897): **"The Wicked Stepmother"**

---

[3] The story of the early foundry business in Hamilton during the 1830s can be read in the *Whitehern Museum Archives*: www.whitehern.ca (see W-MCP5-6.240n).

Miss Fuller so that his children would have a mother. Unfortunately, Elizabeth Fuller did not like children. She sent the boys away to school and instructed them to call her Mrs. McQuesten. In retaliation, they secretly called her the "O.L." (Old Lady). She is "The Wicked Stepmother" of the McQuesten saga.

Elizabeth Fuller McQuesten's hobby was shopping and she frequently traveled to Boston and New York to purchase expensive clothing and furnishings. She also ordered goods from Paris and London. In one of her letters home to her husband she decides that she will stay in Boston to shop longer because, *it would be a pity not to spend a little more money, since I came **so rich**; so I must spend a few days here in order to lighten my purse* (W1213). Elizabeth gradually became estranged from her husband because of her extravagance and her poor relationship with his sons. Nevertheless, she is responsible for the many beautiful Victorian furnishings that are on display at the Whitehern Museum today.

Dr. Calvin McQuesten's second mistake was to entrust his son Isaac with the administration of his finances following Isaac's graduation in law. Isaac and his stepmother engaged in a long and bitter battle over control of Dr. Calvin's fortune and estate. In collusion with his father and his half-brother, Dr. Calvin Brooks McQuesten, Isaac finally managed to arrange for a secret will that left Elizabeth with an annuity after Dr. Calvin's death in 1885. Grudgingly, she accepted her lot and retreated to the U.S., never to be heard from again.

Isaac and Mary Baker were married in 1873, and had seven children in twelve years: Mary, Calvin, Hilda, Ruby, Muriel, Tom, and Edna. Unfortunately, Muriel died before the age of two. After Dr. Calvin McQuesten died, Isaac and his wife

Isaac McQuesten & Mary Baker on Their Wedding Day June 18, 1873

Mary and their large family of six children moved into Willowbank, the stately home on Jackson Street. Mary promptly renamed it "Whitehern."

Isaac died very suddenly on March 7, 1888. The reports of Isaac's death vary, but the most reliable account states that late one evening in the library at Whitehern, Isaac took a sleeping potion (or several), generously laced with alcohol, and fell into a stupor. His wife, Mary, who had just retired after returning from a missionary society meeting, rushed to his aid and called Dr. Mullin, the family physician. Isaac rallied briefly but relapsed again, and by morning he was dead. This urgent telegram from Isaac's law partner, James Chisholm, to his half-brother Calvin, reflects the sudden nature of Isaac's death:

WESTERN UNION TELEGRAPH COMPANY

TO DR. CALVIN BROOKS MCQUESTEN, New York
From James Chisholm, Hamilton, Ontario
May 7 1888

Isaac Died This Morning. Come At Once.

[Signed] James Chisholm [W2520]

Isaac Baldwin McQuesten (1847-88)

Chapter 3

THE FALL OF THE MCQUESTEN FAMILY
OH, ISAAC, HOW COULD YOU?

WHAT REMAINS?

Oh, Isaac, how could you have squandered so
Much fortune? Cash, trust, real estate and health
All dissipated, blown apart. Although
Your father Calvin steamed his way to wealth
Your frittering addiction soon outran
The sturdy chambered comfort he secured.
It seems your paregoric was more than
Mere tincture—dilution shunned, strength assured.
I could weep like a willow on the bank
That named the house—but there is no bank, and
Scant vestige of the funds your habits sank.
New generations take the task in hand,
And now it will be for others to learn
What chance, what hope remains to keep Whitehern.

by **G. W. Down** (2005, Box 14-112)

Isaac's place in the family saga represents THE FALL OF THE McQUESTEN FAMILY, which was sudden and catastrophic. Isaac's condition leading up to his death is well-documented in the Whitehern correspondence. Mary wrote several anxious letters to Isaac's half-brother, Dr. Calvin Brooks McQuesten in New York, seeking his help for Isaac's "nervous condition":

> *I had resolved that I would never again mention the subject of Isaac's health but my anxiety about him is so great, that I must beg of you one favour and that is to tell me, if you would recommend him trying a specialist on nervous disease and who is the best. My greatest difficulty is that Isaac does not feel he has a cent to spare except on necessities, and he has no faith in any man being able to help him. However if you could hold out any inducements as to the skill of any physician in New York, perhaps I could coax him. I asked you once, but you forgot to answer me if you thought there was any virtue in this "Compound oxygen" prepared by a Philadelphia firm. Will you be so very kind as to answer me as soon as you received this, for I am very anxious and if anything can be done the sooner the better.* (W4327, Jul 8 1885)

The cause of Mary's great anxiety is further explained in a letter written by Isaac to Calvin on October 1, 1887 after Isaac's return from a course of treatment at the

Homewood Retreat in Guelph. Isaac had been suffering from alcoholism and severe depression, insomnia, frequent breakdowns and he underwent several periods of treatment at the Guelph Sanatorium.

In this last letter (extant) from Isaac to his brother, he describes his condition as an *unhealthful excitement, and afterwards came the reaction*; he suffered periods of *sluggishness* and insomnia. Isaac is frank about his guilt and despair over his *responsibility* in the use of *stimulants*. Isaac also provides a cryptic and somewhat incoherent message about a *mystery* and a potentially violent course of action that he was contemplating:

> *I am fully aware that I and I only am to blame as far as responsibility. Nor think that I will allow feelings to permit me to do a foolish thing that could benefit nobody, and simply injure all concerned. And while I cannot tell what the exact step to be taken—as yet—is . . . . Don't think I am making any mystery now. I am not. But I want you simply to be prepared, when such occasion may occur, to quickly and calmly use your best judgement, and not by my leaving the possible consideration of steps that may not be necessitated, until such time or action has to be taken, then be flurried by being taken unexpectedly. . . . I have made no attempt at concealment and have so informed those who have spoken with me. It may be very painful and humiliating, but nothing is gained by an attempt at evading it. . . . And it is these sudden impulses that I must look out for. It is one long continuous want or craving.* (W2511, Oct 1 1887)

Isaac's comments here are difficult to interpret but his despair is palpable. His preoccupation with death and suicide is further indicated in a rather poignant underscoring in one of the books in his library entitled: *Responsibility in Mental Illness* (London, 1874). Isaac's neatly underlined passage reads:

> let him then suppose it to be no dream, but conceive himself to be overwhelmed by the horrible nightmare day after day, and to be, as he surely would be, incapable of the hope of relief; what cry would then suffice to express his agony and despair save the cry of supreme agony, 'My God, My God, why hast thou forsaken me?'—what act save an act of suicide? (p. 240).

To make matters worse, Isaac's death was accompanied by bankruptcy. The circumstances surrounding his death, his mental health and bankruptcy, inevitably generated rumours of suicide. As a result, the family suffered much social stigma, and became increasingly insular and guarded. The children were cautioned not to speak of family matters.

THE MCQUESTENS' *"INHERITED"* MENTAL DISEASE

Isaac's long battle with his stepmother, Elizabeth Fuller, over the family finances had worn him down, and his habitual dependency on alcohol and stimulants took their toll on his mental health. He regularly took various medications containing opium, laudanum, morphine and mercury, such as paregoric, chlorodyne, belladonna and calomel. Isaac spent regular periods at the Homewood Retreat, a mental institution at Guelph, Ontario, under the care of Dr. Lett, a specialist in the treatment of alcoholism, opium neurosis and other addictions.

Isaac wrote a brief and almost illegible letter from his office in 1880 in which he admits: *this morning I have taken a good dose of HEALTH LIFE & [?] pills. Result is my hand is so unsteady that I can scarce write* (W-MCP2-4.029). Isaac is likely referring to a patent medicine or combination of medicines, such as those commonly advertised as "Healthy Life" by a Dr. Scudder in the newspapers in the 1870s. The combination often consisted of Belladonna for congestive headaches, Macrotys for muscular pains, and various other substances such as opium or morphine for "specific ailments," all mixed with alcohol. Belladonna, or deadly nightshade, is a narcotic, sedative, antispasmodic—and a strong poison; it can cause paralysis and can affect the central nervous system.

Several members of the McQuesten family suffered from mental illness in varying degrees, and Isaac's wife Mary referred to it as an inherited condition: *a nervous temperament like we have* (W5665) *at the very center of the nervous system* (W8734). She also observes that, *Unfortunately, all the McQuestens seem more or less nervously excitable* (Box 12-501). It is difficult to say whether this truly was an inherited condition, or whether it may have been induced or exacerbated by some of the many medications that the family used regularly, many of which are now known to have an adverse effect on one's mental health and nervous system.

In the Victorian age little was known about the toxicity of various medications. Chlorodyne, paregoric and laudanum are all opium-based, and calomel is mercury-based. Dr. Calvin McQuesten in his article on *Dyspepsia* recommends: *The compound calomel Pill . . . may be given at night from 5 to 10 grains . . . followed the next morning with a small dose of rhubarb* (W0410). Later, Mary is prescribed ½ grain calomel and is told to take twice that amount. Calomel was a powerful purgative. These were common prescribed and patent medicines of the day, and were used by the McQuestens even for children and during pregnancy, often in large doses. They were usually prepared with an alcohol base of as much as 40 to 50 percent. When Ruby was being treated for chronic cough, and later in the sanatoria, she, too, was administered calomel regularly as a purgative, supposedly to bring her fever down.

There were two doctors in the McQuesten family and many of these medications were prescribed or recommended by them. Isaac reports to his brother, Dr. Calvin Brooks McQuesten about treating their sleepless child, baby Mary:

> *All well at home. But we are all about played out with that youngster's sleeplessness. Whoever has her must make up the mind to not more than a couple of hours sleep. So we have to take it turn about. Chlorodyne was effective twice—taken at intervals of about a week—but no longer, Paregoric [Cherry or Chivas?] whisky &c., are more likely to put her wide awake than asleep, so the only thing is to grin & bear it.* (W2469)

Isaac also made his own wine and beer and hard cider and was exceedingly proud of its alcoholic quality: *Am going to have this year some of the finest wine you ever tasted. Believe if I bottled our kind it would be equal to a very fine champagne— none of the heavy, cloggy taste of most of the rest* (W2467). There are several instances in the letters in which various types of wine are mentioned as being enjoyed. In 1908, Edna writes: *Mrs. Stuart brought us another bottle of dandelion wine so I had a swig to keep out the cold.* Mary and her family fought hard during the Temperance Referendum on liquor in 1902 to close the saloons. In her home, alcohol and liquor were not tolerated. However, wine appears to have been acceptable—and, of course, even the teetotallers, either unsuspecting or otherwise, used the patent medicines that were generously laced with alcohol.

THE ARISTOCRATIC VICE

In 1881, "opium eating" was viewed as "The Aristocratic Vice," as it was extensive and more prevalent among the wealthy and educated classes than among those of lower social position. Homewood's patients in the nineteenth century were physicians and barristers, housewives and politicians—individuals of high social standing who were able to maintain their status after institutionalization, and who alternately tried asylums, travel and tonics to break their habits. The use of narcotics and stimulants was so common that drug addiction was seen as unfortunate but unexceptional, similar to the current view of alcoholism.[4]

ISAAC'S BANKRUPTCY

On the financial issue, Isaac had invested substantially in railroad patents with a William Dunn who proved to be a charlatan (W2554a). He also partnered with a John Harvey in a woollen mill in Hespeler which failed, partly by poor management, and partly by the economic circumstances of the textile industry at the time. Isaac

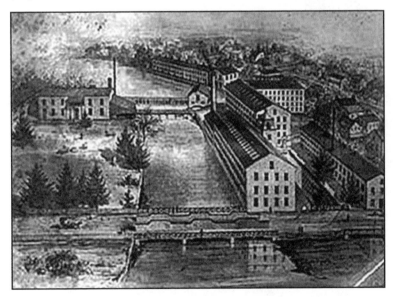

Isaac McQuesten's Mill at Hespeler (Whitehern drawing)

---

[4] "The Aristocratic Vice: The Medical Treatment of Drug Addiction at the Homewood Retreat, 1883-1900," by Cheryl L. Krasnick *ONTARIO HISTORY*, the quarterly journal of the Ontario Historical Society. Volume LXXV, NO, 4, December 1983, Pages 403 to 427.

also enjoyed Tiffany watches at $240 each. By 1888 Isaac had lost his father's fortune, his half-brother's share of the estate, *and* most of his wife's inheritance from her father, Rev. Thomas Baker, who had died in 1887. Isaac's liabilities amounted to $900,000 and his assets were approximately $9,000.

As a lawyer, Isaac would have known that there were no bankruptcy laws in effect in 1888.[5] His partner, James Chisholm acted as trustee to settle the claims. Mary was left with the house, Whitehern, which needed repairs and a new roof. She was also granted the two attached houses on Bold Street—one that she and Isaac had owned, and one that her parents had owned. These two houses had been badly neglected: they also needed new roofs, and it was many years before Mary could make the repairs and gain any rental income from them.

No social safety nets such as welfare and medical care existed then, and even public schools charged tuition. Upon Isaac's death, Mary B. McQuesten was devastated. She had six children to raise and educate on a very limited income and no social assistance of *any* kind. Fourteen years after the bankruptcy, Mary explained her financial situation to her son Calvin when writing about making her will. During those fourteen years she had been paying for repairs and new roofs on Whitehern, and on the Bold Street houses, which were not generating any income during this period:

**Mary Baker McQuesten,
the Victorian Matriarch**

To begin with the present income is about $1700, out of that Tom could not receive $350 a year and leave enough for the girls to live on. Ruby has really paid his way. . . . You see the interest from present investments is about $950. Bk. of Montreal stock $400, and rent from Bold St. after taxes, repairs, insurance are deducted is about $350. . . . but of course during the last 3 yrs we have been paying for roofs, but it certainly is marvellous how much it takes to live even with greatest economy. . . . The taxes on homestead are $226 & water rates $48. (W4544, Feb 10 1902)

This does not take into account the cost of coal and all utilities, nor of food and clothing. Practicalities aside, the family additionally suffered the stigma of bankruptcy, poverty, and the family's history of mental illness.

After a period of mourning and a breakdown, Mary grew stronger and gradually assumed a strong matriarchal role. She is the "Victorian Matriarch" of the McQuesten saga. She was able to rally her children around her, assign them their life-tasks and, especially

---

[5] Although the Bankruptcy Act "was amended in 1876 and 1877, the Act was repealed in 1880 and for forty years there was no general bankruptcy law in force in Canada." ("Canadian Corporate Bankruptcy Law," www.aucc.ca, p. 8)

with the help of Ruby and Tom, was eventually able to restore the family's honour and prestige, if not their wealth.

THE VICTORIAN MATRIARCH—MARY BAKER MCQUESTEN

When the children were away from home, Mary maintained her matriarchal control by regular letter-writing, and the letters were circulated among them so that all could receive the same news along with her instructions and admonitions. Her letters, rarely subtle, often describe the poor behaviour of other children as negative examples or warnings for her own children. Letter writing was a duty, and a full reply required filling the whole page with text as an economy measure. The family complied with all of these rules—but letter writing was forbidden on the Sabbath. The precedent for saving and circulating the letters was set by the previous McQuesten generations, who had carefully preserved many letters from the nineteenth century that were brought to Whitehern from New England.

**Women's Foreign Missionary Society, 1897
(Mary Baker McQuesten, right foreground)**

Considering all of her duties and cares with her six children, it is surprising that Mary was also able to continue her executive work with the Women's Foreign Missionary Societies (WFMS). She even travelled throughout Ontario to lecture to the women's groups and to form new auxiliary branches. As part of her executive duties, she visited the west in 1906 to inspect the Native Missionary Schools at Winnipeg and at Birtle Hills (W5470, W5487).[6]

The remarkable Mary, a tiny widowed and impoverished woman from a privileged background, somehow managed to do all of this and more.

---

[6] For Mary's story, see *The Life Writings of Mary Baker McQuesten: Victorian Matriarch* (WLUP 2004) and/or www.whitehern.ca. For some samples of Mary's missionary society lectures, see (W8447, W7172, W7181, W8432).

THE SIX McQUESTEN CHILDREN *(all photos Whitehern)*

Mary Baldwin McQuesten, 1874-1964

Rev. Calvin McQuesten, 1876-1968

Hilda Belle McQuesten, 1877-1967

Ruby Baker McQuesten, 1879-1911

Thomas Baker McQuesten, 1882-1948

Marguerette Edna McQuesten, 1884-1935

Chapter 4

THE LONG ROAD TO RESTORATION BEGINS

**Back row L to R: Mary, Thomas, Hilda, Ruby, Calvin
Front row: Mary (mother), Edna (c.1890)**

Two years after Isaac's death Mary had this family portrait taken. Ruby and Thomas represent THE RESTORATION OF THE MCQUESTEN FAMILY, but without Mary's matriarchal guidance, Ruby's sacrifice, and Tom's dedication to the family cause, the restoration could not have been accomplished. Ruby's role is central to the restoration, since there was *absolutely no* other source of income for Tom's education. It could not have been achieved without the sacrifice of her salary, and of herself, to this end. The process was lengthy and painfully slow, and the family lived in genteel poverty for twenty years before any relief was felt. Finances are often discussed in the McQuesten letters as they struggle with their limited budget.

After she was widowed, Mary gradually assessed each child for his or her potential to help the family. First she considered her two sons, Calvin and Thomas, for in the Victorian age only a man would have the earning potential to support a family. Mary observed that her eldest son, Calvin, had a congenital disability in his left hand and arm and some weakness on his left side. He also suffered from the family's "inherited" mental fragility especially under stress, such as at exam time. Mary perceived that Calvin did not have the potential for financial success, and she was right. Although Calvin did achieve some limited success in several careers, including journalism, homesteading, and the ministry, he was never able to earn more than a stipend for himself and was not able to assist the family with any regular income.

Mary's second son, Thomas, was only eight years old when the family portrait was taken. He was robust, handsome, athletic and scholarly, and showed no sign of emotional illness. He was already his mother's favourite. Mary realized that there was hope in Tom. He had good potential, but he would need to be educated in a profession, and that would take a great deal of money which they clearly did not have.

Mary then looked to her daughters. The two eldest, Mary and Hilda, were healthy and attractive but not interested in books and learning, so Mary assigned them to take care of the house, since she could no longer afford to keep servants. The youngest daughter, (Margarette) Edna was attractive and clever; but she was only five years old when the photo was taken, and had already demonstrated signs of some mental imbalance. She was highly emotional and her moods were erratic.

Mary then focused on Ruby and knew that this daughter showed promise. At only eleven years of age when the family portrait was taken, Mary saw that Ruby was scholarly, artistic, witty, charming, beautiful, and showed no sign of mental fragility. So Mary determined that Ruby should be educated as a teacher; she could then reserve her daughter's salary for Tom's education. This plan would take many years, but ultimately Ruby was the *only* hope for the restoration of the family.

Mary concentrated some money and effort on Ruby and arranged for her to be educated as a teacher at Ontario Normal College in Hamilton. She then found a

Hamilton Collegiate Institute, Ontario Normal College attached in one wing

job for her at Ottawa Ladies' College, a Presbyterian institution, where she began to teach in 1899. Ruby subsequently sent most of her income home for Tom's education, and for some household expenses.

There was no one else to whom they could turn for assistance—not even Isaac's half-brother, the children's uncle, Dr. Calvin Brooks McQuesten. He was still bitter because he felt that Mary had received a more generous settlement in the bankruptcy than he had. However, Mary had six children to raise; whereas Calvin was a doctor and a bachelor, and he remained so.

For twenty years after Isaac's death, from 1888 to 1908, the family scrimped along and attempted to maintain their social standing, at least in the Church. They maintained their dignity in society and in the MacNab Street Presbyterian Church by regular attendance, twice on Sunday, and by strict adherence to religious observances such as the Sabbath. Mary's continuing role as president of the Women's Foreign Missionary Society also provided some prestige for the family. Their strong convictions provided a moral superiority that encompassed pride and even arrogance. Mary never lowered her aristocratic standards of a classical education, good breeding and moral integrity. In fact their poverty made it easier for Mary to control her children, and to deny them any frivolous *temptations*. She admitted that the *shortness of money had really developed the family* (W5297).

This proud public stance lent the family a kind of "Southern Ontario Gothic"[7] aura of mystery that is evident to this day in the comments and questions from visitors to Whitehern Museum. One of the family's greatest mysteries is the fact that none of the six children ever married, despite the fact that all were attractive and intelligent. Mary's matriarchal interference in the three broken engagements for Hilda, Tom and Ruby, is often cited as a cause. There can be little doubt that the stigma of the father's possible suicide and bankruptcy, poverty and mental illness was a factor in their remaining single. The family grew increasingly insular as a result of that stigma, and the strict Calvinist religious repression was an additional factor in discouraging possible suitors. The McQuesten letters provide some verification for the various rumours. At one point, Mary bemoans her children's lack of chances to meet anyone from a *really nice home*. By her definition that would have been an upper-class and wealthy family such as they had been before their impoverishment. Mary lamented their lack of opportunities:

> *I hope Ruby is not freezing at that college. What troubles me about her too is that she never gets an invitation to a really nice home or has a chance to meet any one. Although she sees more than the girls at home do, it is very monotonous for them tho' they never complain. However some day, something may turn up for them.* (W4549)

---

[7] Alice Monro uses the term "Southern Ontario Gothic" to describe a similar kind of repressive Presbyterianism in small-town Ontario.

Chapter 5

RUBY'S LETTERS FROM OTTAWA LADIES' COLLEGE

We won't count this a letter . . . but tho't Tom might need his money.
(W4440)

The Scholarly Ruby Baker McQuesten

Ruby became a teacher at the age of twenty. She took a position at Ottawa Ladies' College, a Presbyterian boarding and day school, at a salary of $5.99 per week, most of which was sent home to pay for Tom's education (W4877; W4544). For many years, Ruby was the *only* person in the family who was earning a salary. Sometimes she sent money directly to Tom and at other times she sent it home and her mother would then send it on to Tom. Ruby also paid for some household expenses, such as a new sewing machine and general repairs. Mary writes to Tom in 1906: *We have had to buy a new sewing machine, but what Ruby sends will nearly pay for it. When is your room rent due? Am afraid to risk it in a letter but will send postal note* (W-MCP1-3a.020).

Ruby's letters to the family from the college between 1899 and 1907 describe her homesickness, the draughty old school, the epidemic outbreak of illnesses, her own deterioration in health, the long hours of teaching and the meagre pay. Nevertheless, her letters are always cheerful, even when her health is failing (W4709). Ruby's charming personality and loving nature always shine through. Her plaint to Calvin at the end of 1909, *I who Love in letters,* recalls the words of Hamlet: "I must unpack my heart in words" (W6555; *Hamlet*, scene II).

Ruby writes to both Calvin and Tom when they are boarding together in Toronto while Calvin works as a journalist with Copp Clark on the *Toronto News* in 1900. In the following letter, Ruby discusses a postal money note that she had sent to Tom and gently chastises him for his lack of response; then she promptly sends him another postal note. Why does she write to Calvin and not to Tom directly? Perhaps she may have thought that coming through Calvin it would convey a softer reprimand. The family always seem to favour Tom and to protect his dignity.

TO CALVIN MCQUESTEN [REV.][8] from his sister Ruby (W4440)

Toronto, Ontario   Presbyterian Ladies' College
                                                    [Ottawa Ladies' College]
                                                    Ottawa, Ontario

My dearest Cal,

You don't know how glad I was to get your letter for I had begun to feel rather low, it had seemed such a long time since I had heard from either of you. But your fine long letter & then Tom's quite cheered me up. You poor fellows certainly have been busy I don't wonder in the least.

It was at the <u>boy Tom</u> that my <u>hint</u> was aimed "to drop a fellow a line" & I was really provoked to think he couldn't have sent me a card sooner, for I worried about the money from Monday as various people had told me about losing money thro' the post & when each day went by & Thursday night came I couldn't wait any longer so sent the card & such a card back as the cheeky young dog sent me. However I've forgiven him, as he wrote a fine long letter & give him my love & say I'll answer soon.

I'm glad you had such a pleasant time at the Gartshores. [It] seems a thing of the far past for we have had sleighing for the last couple of days & seems regular winter.

The elections certainly went finely & we had some fun here over it. Tho' the excitement over the return of the troops was not so great as at home I fancy.

I really don't know what I have been doing—nothing particular, the only thing I know is that I have a whole set of reports for the term to make up which will keep me busy to-night & to-morrow.

We won't count this a letter now as I'm going out to tea & just had ten minutes to write, but tho't Tom might need his money.

Take care of yourself & let things go if you can. With much love my dear old brother.

                                        Your ever affec'ate sister,
                                        Ruby McQuesten

Ruby, far right, with women at Ottawa Ladies' College

---

[8] The **[REV.]** is inserted here in square brackets because Calvin is not yet a minister, and he has no middle name. We have inserted same in order to distinguish him from his grandfather and his uncle, both named Calvin. When Calvin is ordained in May 1909 the letter title changes to **Rev. Calvin McQuesten.**

Ottawa Ladies' College or Presbyterian Ladies' College (c.1900)
(Library & Archives, Canada)

Ruby regularly continues to send postal notes directly to Tom. At times she also sends money home for repairs. Gradually, Ruby's first reports of illness appear. Within her first two years at the college she begins to show signs of illness, although she usually minimizes the severity, and tries to continue with her work and activities such as snow-shoeing and Field-Naturalists' excursions. She describes an epidemic of grippe among the girls at the school, in which she becomes one of the duty nurses who cares for them. Grippe is a catarrhal and influenza-type of disease characterized by inflammation and cough. It is possible that Ruby was first exposed to the tuberculosis germ at this time, as she continued to have bouts of illness, *grippe* and *cough* from time to time. But her letters remain cheerful and full of news about the school and the students.

TO CALVIN MCQUESTEN [REV.][9] **from his sister Ruby McQuesten** (W4454)
[Toronto, Ontario]   [Ottawa Ladies' College]
                                                      Feb 1 1901, Friday noon

My Dearest Cal,
It was so good to get your letter—I really had been quite hungry for a word from you, tho' I knew you would be busy as ever. We always expect more time after Xmas & there are always more things going on to take up time. You must have had a lovely time at your boarding house. I wish you could have got a couple of rooms at your old place. I hope the good people won't go to anymore balls & sprees, or you will be expected to get your own dinners.
This week has been a long slow one to me. Tho' I didn't really have the grippe; on Sunday & Monday was pretty sick & rather under the weather the rest of the time. But I'm all right now & have an invitation to go out snow shoeing to-morrow night which I've accepted if nothing interferes.

Such a family as we've had between grippe & colds here. No less than twenty girls had to have hot drinks last night, so we have a cup brigade & the teacher on duty carries around a tray of cups & dispenses drinks to all the dry ones. It is really funny to call out, "Who wants a drink!" However most of the girls are better now, tho' thirteen were down at one time. Grippe is very prevalent here as I suppose it is elsewhere.

Last Friday night the whole household was suddenly awakened at 2 o'clock by the ringing of the electric bell through the whole house. It rang thru all the flats & the girls thought it was a fire alarm. I did not know what it was but wasn't frightened. Miss Browne came in in quite a panic. No one knew why the bell was ringing & still it rang. The girls were all in the hall with white faces asking each other in ghostly tones, "what is it?" Miss B & I hurried downstairs & found Mrs. Ross & Miss Boyd looking at the button. But no one was pressing it. Mr. Grierson was the only one asleep. We came up & met the head laundress followed by her maids hurrying down to see if the laundry was on fire. Finally Grierson was aroused to take the battery to pieces & the noise stopped. Whatever possessed the bell to ring of its own accord no one knows. It will remain a mystery unless you could suggest, but it gave the house a lively scare by way of variety.

There goes dinner bell so will leave this for the present.

1:15 pm: Dinner rather Friday lunch is over & have just a few minutes to scribble. I'm sending you this letter of Uncle Calvin's—it's too good to keep to myself—but be sure you don't lose it & after you are thru please send it back to me for, wouldn't lose it for the world.

Next week is the last of the term so we've been giving the luckless youngsters exams to write & now it is luckless me to examine them. Tomorrow we'll have special services in the churches & then it'll be all over.

The question of mourning here produced quite a discussion. [Queen Victoria died on January 22, 1901] *The government people of course went into mourning & all the government clerks however poor & all the people who go in the government set, or want to be considered in it, e.g. Mrs. Herridge at her dear Lord's wish.*

Well we here had no money to spend on new dresses & we wouldn't feel any more sorry if we had, so we're wearing our colors & of course are very common & unfeeling among all the black gowned St. Andrews people. However it doesn't worry me in the least, only it makes me provoked to see the number of people who will do anything to be considered in the fashion.

Well dear old boy must close. I hope you'll be invited again to Eglinton & have some fun. I've just finished your book & really it has been quite a change from ordinary things. It is very well written all thro'!

With very much love, hoping you'll take good care of yourself,

Your affectionate sister, Ruby

Calvin had written a large article for the paper on the death of Queen Victoria in January of 1901, describing the banners and the black draping. Ruby's comments on the Queen's death make clear that the funeral fashions of the day would have been too expensive for the teachers or the students to manage. Ruby's usual attire was a plain shirtdress in white or coloured duck.

The letter *of Uncle Calvin's* to which Ruby refers is, indeed, very strange and eccentric, and *too good to keep to [herself]*. It may have been written under the influence of alcohol or other stimulants, such as the *Pure Crystal Beverage* upon which he is *sailing*. The letter is quite long, but is abbreviated here. Obviously, Uncle

Calvin Brooks McQuesten, often called *Unc*, is visiting the family on one of his rare visits. This may have been an extended visit after Christmas, as he usually resided in New York where he practiced medicine.

> *To the School Marm: I was told to write—I am writing—I hate to write. Love is born of a good disposition so hate is not to love—A good disposition— love—therefore I am loving to write. Next—give it up—don't know—am doing my duty—am collecting my thoughts—they, the thoughts, are wandering—one just came—saw Sardi on the fence with a black cat. Black cat struck at Sardi—Sardi retaliated. Black cat retreated, Sardi followed, not retreat, but black cat. Black cat jumped Sardi jumped—tableau closes. Next—Sparrow in the tree, crumbs on the pi-az-za—Sparrow in pi-az-za— crumbs gone—Sparrow gone—exeunt tableau. . . . I have lost my thoughts and am sailing out to sea on the "Pure Crystal Beverage" wagon. (W4451)*

For her summer vacation, Ruby is excited about taking the scenic route home by train and by boat, including sleeping quarters, a bath and meals. She writes a particularly *chatty* letter and would like to accompany Calvin on his assignment to cover the Pan-American Exposition that was held in Buffalo, New York from May 1 to November 2, 1901. The fair covered a 342-acre site and featured the latest technologies. The Electric Tower was illuminated nightly by thousands of coloured bulbs and floodlights and attracted nearly eight million people. Nikola Tesla's alternating-current electrical supply system allowed designers to light the Exposition using power generated 25 miles (40 kilometres) away at Niagara Falls.

Electric Tower, Pan-American Exposition, Buffalo 1901

TO CALVIN MCQUESTEN [REV.] from his sister Ruby McQuesten (W4496)
[Toronto, Ontario]　　　　　　　　　　　　Ottawa Ladies' College
　　　　　　　　　　　　　　　　　　　　Jun 20 1901

My dearest Cal,

I'm just going to scribble a line on this paper I've torn out of my note book. It's such a delightful feeling that I might as well use up my old book as I'll need it no more—Hurrah! I've just made out my marks for the various classes & now we're ready for the reports & years honor cards etc. We'll hardly suffer from ennui these last days. I must tell you my latest plan about coming home. You know I had tho't of coming by boat & then I tho't I couldn't without staying in Kingston over Sunday, so had resolved to take the train. However I found out, & we've looked into the matter pretty carefully, that we can arrange it all right by boat

A train leaves here at 8.10 on Friday morning & reaches Prescott at 10.30 in time for the boat at 11.15. Miss Boyd will be with me & we'll take the boat to Kingston together reaching there by night & thus having the sail thro' the Thousand Islands in the day. There I'll have my bath & come along to Toronto, reaching it Sat. morning at six o'clock. The trip by boat is about a dollar cheaper than train, including meals & bath. So I'm quite pleased to think of seeing something & having such a nice little trip for no extra expense, & reaching home on Sat. too. Of course it isn't quite decided, but I don't think there will be anything to hinder.

By the way you spoke of going to the Pan on Monday 1ˢᵗ. I'd love to go with you, if you'll take me, & have no other arrangements.

You see I was interrupted in my epistle. One after another of the teachers strolled in till finally Mrs. Ross also came & we had a regular teachers' meeting which lasted till tea time—then after tea we had another affair which lasted till there was no time to send off this scribble as Miss Boyd & I were invited out for the evening & had to rush & dress. I'm ashamed of myself for never writing before.

It has been quite a treat having your paper arrive each day. We've enjoyed reading your account of the coup each day after class. I think they're splendidly written, so bright & comical. That last one was a good one on Gen. O'Grady Haley. I hope he enjoyed it, but it is just good for him. It's a good thing you're not one of the soldiers or I'm afraid you'd have to be reprimanded for disrespectful allusions to his August person & character. I can't help laughing whenever I read that article & I'm going to take the various papers & read them to the Rosses. I've been too busy to see them lately.

We had a great time of it here with the minister. I don't think I can begin to tell you the various ones I met. I'll have to reserve it for the future. I met Mr. MacDonald of the Westminster who is always so jolly & spoke so kindly of you & also Charles Gordon, just as lovely as ever. He is one of the most loveable men & spoke so kindly of his visit to our place & about you & Tom. And I met Dr. MacTavish & little Mr. Mackay

Ruby, centre front *(Library & Archives, Canada)*

Ruby to Calvin: *You really are a duck to offer me your snowshoes.* (W4546) *of [Madock?] & big Mr. MacMillan, & Mr. Love of Quebec, & our ministers Dr. Fletcher & Mr. Colin [Fletcher] & Dr. Lyle, & various young ministers around here. But I'll tell you all when see you.*

To-night we're going out for the evening again & next week will be closing etc. I hardly know whether to send this to Niagara or not but think I'll risk it.

This is a most scrappy good-for-nothing letter but I feel too unsettled to do anything well, so you'll have to forgive me & we'll make it up I hope at no very distant period.

With much love,
Your loving sister, Ruby

Ruby's reference to the various Presbyterian ministers and dignitaries that she meets in Ottawa includes Charles Gordon, a family friend and missionary to the miners in Alberta and lumbermen in the North West Territories. Gordon was a model minister and was a colourful and articulate speaker on the "Social Gospel," which was allied with the "City Beautiful" movement that was sweeping the Victorian world, and which the McQuestens espoused. In fact, both movements were a guiding principle of Tom's vision when he became a politician.

Gordon wrote many articles for newspapers and for the Presbyterian Church. *The Toronto News* of May 15, 1905 reports a speech/sermon by Charles Gordon with the headlines: "Attacks Evils of Society" and "Revelations Which Have Come to Him Have Filled Him With Sorrow and Shame." Gordon also wrote novels under the pseudonym of Ralph Connor; he wrote at least twenty-eight adventure stories with a strong moral tone. His first three books sold five million copies: *Black Rock* (1898), *The Man from Glengarry* (1901), and *Glengarry School Days* (1902). The latter became a minor classic in the United States and Britain. Many of Gordon's books are in the Whitehern library and have been well-used.

Ottawa Ladies' College Hockey Game 1906, Ruby 4ᵗʰ from right
(Library & Archives, Canada)

Chapter 6

TOM WORKS HIS WAY TO ENGLAND

I have spared her [Mamma] the description of the voyage over,
but will describe it to you. (W4490)

In the summer of 1901, Thomas wished to take a job surveying for the new railroads as some of his friends were doing; however, his mother refused to allow him to go because of the danger. She advises Tom through Calvin:

> *I now think I will not let him go surveying, I have heard from several that it does not pay in any way. Gordon MacKay has suffered from neuralgia in his back more or less ever since, the result of standing for hours up to the waist in water, & Mrs. Lyle does not think it good at all, so let Tom try and think of something else.* (W4436)

The *something else* for which *Mamma* obviously did give her approval, was for Tom to work his way to England on a cattle boat. Tom decided to go to Scotland to search his family roots and to find the family homestead there, but he had no money with which to do so. So he did what many young men did at the time; he rode a freight train to Montreal, and then applied to work on a cattle boat to make his way over. At Aberdeen, Scotland, he writes to Calvin and describes the dreadful conditions he endured, but he notes that he will spare his mother these details.

TO CALVIN MCQUESTEN [REV.] from his brother Thomas B. McQuesten (W4490)
[Toronto, Ontario]   155 Crown [?], Aberdeen, Scotland
                                              Jun 16 1901

Dear Cal,
    This is Sunday and I arrived here yesterday morning at 7:30 from Manchester where I started at 11 o'clock the night before. Here I am comfortable for the first time since I left Toronto. Will write Mamma a description of the place and you can see it from her. I have spared her the description of the voyage over, but will describe it to you. By the way have just seen the results but there is nothing about the honour list.
    We did not eventually leave Toronto until 9 o'clock and we arrived in Montreal about 3 o'clock the next afternoon. The journey was not bad. During the day we spent most of our time seated in a row on top of the freight train and so we enjoyed the scenery better. When I arrived at Montreal I found the two MacDougalls waiting. They had been there for two days and had made all kinds of inquiries about the ships.
    We were to sail on the <u>SS Concordia</u> and so we all went down to the docks to see it. It certainly was the most wretched looking craft you ever set eyes on, the dirtiest-looking boat we saw there as well as the smallest. We said there and then that we would not sail on her, so set out to look for another one. We picked out the best boat we could see, and set about getting on her which proved to be the easiest job in the

SS Manchester City, **1901**

world. This was the <u>Manchester City</u>, belonging to the Manchester line. She is one of the largest and best tramp ships on the North Atlantik [sic], 8500 tons burthen.

    And so our trip in this particular was much ahead of the rest of the bunch 5 in number who preferred to stick to the Concordia. The trip across was the hardest thing I have ever had to endure and I hope I will never have to do it again, altho' I don't regret having done it. I am not going to tell people how hard it was for they will be sure to say I told you so.

    Well, we went aboard on Saturday night. Commenced to work, tying up the cattle at 8:15 after having had 15 minutes sleep and worked steady getting up hay and watering until 6 o'clock Sunday night with no rest and nothing that I could really eat. I thought after I had been at camp that I could stomach almost everything but what we got there was luxurious compared to this. The whole journey across I never got even one square meal.

    For breakfast there would be skilly which consisted of potatoes and vegetables all stirred up in some kind of gravy. I never ate that once—could not do it. The potatoes were always absolutely rotten. Dinner would be salt horse and potatoes. I made three attempts at this during the trip and then I would only eat [?] and bits of meat it was so tough and salty and half a potato. The tea was all the meal we got, it consisted in one cob (a loaf about 4 inches square), & sometimes we got butter generally we did not. For the most part we lived on hard rock biscuits and water. We tipped the Steward $2 each and got from him 2 loaves a day except for the last two days when we got nothing. He cheated us and we could do nothing. This, we learned afterwards was the general thing in Stewards. I lost from 14 to 20 lbs in weight altho' I am now as hard as nails and I think the trip did me good.

    We arrived at Salford the port of Manchester at 1 o'clock on Friday after having gone up the canal past Liverpool a distance of 35 miles. Salford is the wickedest *looking place I ever saw and we lost no time in getting out of it to Manchester, two or 3 miles away.*

Manchester was a miserable sort of a place so we set out that night for Aberdeen. I have not seen a house yet here which is not made of grey granite. It is the most magnificent city, I was ever in. It is spotlessly clean. It is a very queer place very often the street will be on a level with the third story of the house and you will look over a fence and there away below is a bright little garden. I guess I will grow rather tired of the place for there is absolutely no lawn in sight, everything of that sort being behind the houses. There are blocks and blocks of lodging houses such as I am in when you [?] and home.

By the way, [Mullin & Lazier?] surprised me last night as I was getting undressed. They want a room in the same house, so we have a jolly party, a sitting room amongst two or three where meals are served. It is certainly very comfortable. Everything is spotlessly clean and the meals are cooked to a turn just as you get them at home. We will start work tomorrow. We have only a very little paper, so can only afford you this much.

With regard to my fellow-cattlemen they were the toughest men you could imagine. There was only one of them who had not served his turn in jail and they certainly looked it. On board ship a cattleman is looked upon as just a little lower than the stoker and you can imagine how low that is, so we certainly learned humility. However, those things are done with. I'm now feeling fine and ready for anything and would not sell my experience for the world.

Your loving brother
Tom

It is not known if Tom's mother ever read this letter or ever found out about Tom's adventurous voyage; however, the letter was preserved along with other family letters of the same period. The milder descriptive letter that Tom wrote to his mother is not extant; it would have made an interesting comparison. If Mary had known of

Thomas McQuesten in Scotland, age 19, 1901

the dangers, she certainly would not have allowed Tom to make the trip. She may have thought it would be good for him to see something of the Old Country; finding work on a ship seemed like a good idea to her.

Tom does not mention finding or visiting relatives in Scotland, but he may have located some distant relatives. The McQuestens had emigrated from Scotland by way of Ireland in the 1730s and then settled in New England. Tom's paternal grandfather, Dr. Calvin McQuesten, was born in New Hampshire and immigrated to Canada in the 1830s. Thomas and his siblings represent the sixth generation to have lived in North America. However, none of the McQuesten children at Whitehern married or had issue so the Canadian branch of the family died out. The mystery of why the children never married will become clear as our tale progresses.

The next summer, 1902, Tom considered work with a Geological Survey that would have paid $45 per month for five months, a total of $225 that would have made a huge difference in paying for his next year's tuition. In spite of his mother's efforts in writing letters on his behalf, however, he did not get the job (W4582). Instead, Tom joined the militia and became a non-commissioned officer in the 4th Field Battery, Royal Canadian Artillery, under Major John S. Hendrie (Minnes 5, 12), and became an expert marksman. Ruby provides a graphic and humorous description of the *warrior's* return after a three-day exercise:

> *Then shortly after Mary & Edna appeared & after dinner Tom, lean and brown with a white stripe around his face where his strap came. Then came the tug of war with his boots which hadn't been off for three days & were too small for him anyway. He sat on the sofa & hung on & Edna & I sat on the floor & braced our feet against the side of the sofa & tugged till the warrior's feet were left behind.* (W4595)

Tom (3rd row, 2nd from left) in Militia, 4th Field Battery, Royal Canadian Artillery

Chapter 7

HILDA'S THWARTED ENGAGEMENT

I always heard a traveller's life was one of great temptation. . . . So
I said I could never consent. On explaining the state of affairs
to H. [Hilda] she agreed with me. (W4635)

Hilda-Belle McQuesten   Kenelm Trigge

Hilda McQuesten was intelligent and beautiful. Not especially scholarly, she had been assigned by her mother to help her sister Mary take care of the household duties. She became quite proficient in sewing and cooking, but was *not of the reading kind*, as Ruby puts it.

Kenelm Trigge lived in the same boarding house with Calvin in Montreal and the two became good friends. Ken Trigge was the son of Captain and Mrs. Trigge of the "Auchmar" estate in Hamilton. Calvin and Ruby promoted the growing relationship between Ken and Hilda. Ruby urges, *Tell Ken to hurry up the moves* (W4546).

Ken proposed marriage to Hilda in September 1902. However, her mother discovered that Ken was a traveling sales representative and that he not only drank alcohol himself, but he also *treated* others to drink, and to smoke. Considering the memory of her husband's alcoholism, that was just too much for Mary and she insisted that Ken find other work. Ken refused, and she prevailed upon Hilda to reject him, which Hilda did, although reluctantly at first. Mary was adamant:

> *So I said I could never consent. . . . But Hilda I must say was wonderfully*
> *brave and conscientious and though she had quite determined to take him,*
> *she withstood him and said no, she would not marry a man whose living*

was made in such a way. . . . I spoke to Ken about being a teetotaller. I am very very sorry, for I think he would have suited Hilda very well & she seemed quite heart broken but we must hope that it may all be overruled for their lasting good. All this fuss quite spoiled the last week of R. [Ruby's] visit.
(W4635)

When Ken became angry and difficult, Hilda came to feel justified in her refusal. Unfortunately for Hilda and Ken, the temperance referendum was being hotly debated just at that time and the McQuestens were actively campaigning for the vote against the *saloons*, to be held in December 1902. There can be little doubt that this was a factor in her mother's and Hilda's refusal of Ken, and they would have felt righteously justified in doing so. The family's experience with Isaac's alcoholism, which contributed to his death, had created an ardent temperance commitment in the household. Much later Mary speculates that she may have been *self-seeking* in some of her judgements (W5654). Ruby is sympathetic as she comments on the broken affair in confidence to Calvin.

TO CALVIN MCQUESTEN [REV.] from his sister Ruby (W4657)
Montreal, Quebec　　　　　　　　　　　Ottawa Ladies' College
　　　　　　　　　　　　　　　　　　　Sep 26 1902, Friday afternoon, 3:30

My dearest Cal,
　　There's a few minutes to spare, so tho't I would drop you a line. Many thanks for your papers. Your last letter was fine. I liked particularly your article about the doing away of the sword.[9] It seems to me an article like that would be splendid for a magazine. I think it is beautifully written. You certainly should get more for your ideas and your way of expressing them.
　　I had a letter from the Mither [sic] today and from Hilda the beginning of the week. In Hilda's letter she showed just good spirit. She is thoroughly angry with Ken & was going to tell him that his affections weren't worth much if he couldn't give up that much for her sake. I quite agree with her that she would never feel safe & happy once Ken was away, knowing he took anything. We're really thankful to you for finding out the truth so well and now that he has told Hilda he can't give up spirits, it has given her an opportunity of settling matters.
　　Because though Ken is a nice, manly, gentlemanly, kind fellow—he really is not a fine enough character for Hilda. He hasn't enough strength of will, I'm sure and his moral senses—if you call them that—are not just keen because we are from the Plum style of religious training. And so if Ken has to keep on his way—I just trust that this offer will soon be of the past & Tousie [Hilda] will not worry over it. She says she's not going to bother her head about it.
　　Because Tousie is a thoroughly fine character. She's not of the reading kind like us old boy—but she's such a thoroughly unselfish one and that I often wish I were like her. And she is a real Christian too and would be unhappy to be continuously having to live on a lower level.
　　Well old boy this week has flown like last year's weeks went. On Sat. I had a good game of tennis at a Miss Duff's a friend of the MacLarens. On Sunday I went as usual to church and [to teach] my Chinamen. My Chinaman presented me with a fine photo

---

[9] Box 13-011, Apr 26 1902, "THE TATLER," *The Montreal Herald,* written by Calvin McQuesten.

of himself and nine others. It is really good and I wish I could show you it. He is evidently very proud of it. Miss Johnson a missionary from China addressed them in their own language.

Monday was my duty day & Tues. afternoon I called on Marion Marsh—you know Judge Proudfoot's grandfather who is in the [Govt.] Buildings.

On spare evenings I've been making myself a pair of those cloth curtains. I think they're very pretty & total cost is 35 cents—7 yds. at 5 cents. I'm getting practical, hoorah!

Today I've invited Emily McLaren to a little five o'clock tea the girls are having & she's going to sing. Well my dear old boy I must close. I know you're very busy so don't mind not having a letter but I'll be very glad when it comes.

In the Art Room I'm doing a little study of phlox drummondii, *pink, dark red & white. I hope it turns out decently. Every time I start a study I feel like simply giving up it looks so hopeless but I stick at it. Well old chap, don't work too hard. "Enjoy yourself."*

With much love and a good old hug.
Your affectionate sister, Ruby

P.S. *You'd better burn this letter.*

In family matters, Ruby is able to discuss confidential private events with Calvin; in this case it is the breakup of Hilda's engagement to Kenelm Trigge. It might

have been embarrassing for Hilda if the rest of the family heard her being discussed, so Ruby cautioned Calvin to *burn this letter*, which he obviously <u>did not do</u>. Such requests occasionally appear in the letters, yet many have been preserved in spite of the warning. Of course, we do not know how many were actually destroyed.

Ruby often comments on her paintings referring to style, colour and subject matter. She usually sends them home as gifts for family members. There are at least sixty-five of Ruby's paintings at Whitehern, as well as some of her pygrography (wood burning art). *[See colour insert following Part Two for examples of Ruby's paintings and pyrography.]*

Hilda never married, and we have no record of any other proposals;

Hilda-Belle McQuesten

no doubt word of the strict family matriarch and her morals forestalled any other suitors. When the time came for the family to have an automobile, Hilda was the first to learn to drive, even before Tom. She was very charming and often acted as Tom's hostess after he entered politics. She lived at Whitehern into her ninety-first year and is buried in the family plot at the Hamilton Cemetery.

The dolls in the photo below are on display at Whitehern with a collection of children's toys. Mary writes before Christmas 1882: *I have been very busy dressing two dolls for Ruby and Hilda, they don't know any thing about it. They are to have them for Xmas and I think they will be delighted for the dolls have beautiful long hair* (W4309). The girls obviously treasured them and took good care of them, so they have been carefully preserved.

Hilda and Ruby and their *Xmas* dolls, 1882

Hilda and Ruby were close in age, just seventeen months apart and were good friends and often exchanged confidences. It must have been difficult for them to be separated for so many years. It was Hilda who took care of Ruby when she was ill, and it was Hilda who became Calvin's housekeeper when he had his own manse.

The poem that follows, written more than a century later, might reflect Kenelm's sentiments regarding Mrs. McQuesten.

Hilda's Scorned Lover Makes a Toast

A toast to Mrs. McQuesten,
She is the ice that cools my glass,
whose frosty edict swayed my lass
before our hearts could join together.

A toast to my lost, tender Hilda
whose face swims within my whiskey.
With each sip, her liquid lips kiss me,
as ice cubes creak and shiver.

She has abstained from my heart
for it has absorbed the Devil's drink;
and my soul does surely shrink
each time I raise my glass.

I, the once loved Kenelm Trigge,
courted darling Hilda a full year,
I proved my heart true and dear,
Until Mother and sobriety clashed.

For though God approves of wine,
'tis a mortal sin to distill rye
When I asked the Matriarch why
she said 'The answer is clear as day.'

Mary Baker McQuesten

'Tis as clear as the barons and titans
who drink hard at the gentlemen's club,
who've never received a McQuesten snub
as Whitehern galas seek men of fame.

Hilda shall live as mere lonely spinster
I saw this truth in her mother's eyes
She shall remain an unclaimed prize,
shall never know the laugh of her child.

A final toast to Mrs. McQuesten,
who interfered before daughter could wed,
whose words dripped with feigned regret,
as Her Ladyship, the ice cube, smiled.

by Chris Butler, 2006 (Box 14-115)

Chapter 8

AN EPIDEMIC AT THE COLLEGE

And be sure & don't let the family know. (W4680)

It is significant that Ruby and Calvin's close relationship allowed them to share secrets with one another. When Ruby is ill, she can confide in Calvin, and can ask him not to tell *the Mither* or the rest of the family. If she wrote the same letter to one of her sisters at home, it would have been most difficult to conceal the fact of her illness. In October, 1902, Ruby admits to having the grippe and dizzy turns for a week, and this may have been an indication of the onset of her later illness.

TO CALVIN MCQUESTEN [REV.] from his sister Ruby (W4680)
Montreal, Quebec   [Ottawa Ladies' College]
                                                        Oct 28 1902, Tuesday night

My dear old Cal,
*   I'm writing propped up in bed from pure laziness so you mustn't mind scrawls.*
These last couple of weeks have been queer ones for me—the week before last on
Sunday night I had an attack of the old grippe—the real article & no mistake—but
I fought it off & taught all week & went out on Thanksgiving to dinner at the
Armstrong's and to tea at the Milne's where was also our little friend Mr. Smith & his
wife & thoroughly enjoyed the day & felt so well in the evening that I was up watching
the eclipse till morning.
*   But the beginning of the next week didn't I have a couple of my old dizzy turns &*
couldn't do anything, so had to have the doctor & he said it was just the effect of the
grippe in my system & gave me powders & medicine etc., & didn't I have to stay in
bed on my own all week. I felt thoroughly disgusted with myself in addition to feeling
pretty miserable.
*   On Sat. evening I went out a little & have gone out a little each day since, but*
I don't feel a bit brilliant. Don't you get the grippe, Cal—it's a horrible wretch—
underhand you know—and I vow I'll appreciate it when I feel myself again. But
they've been as good to me as possible here & I'll pick up soon now. <u>And be sure &</u>
<u>don't let the family know. It would just worry the Mither.</u> [emphasis added]
*   And I wrote a fine long letter on general things last week. And I did get such a*
cheerful letter from the Mither about you. It did my heart good. You cheered her up &
looked so well she said that I know she feels happy in her mind about you.
*   It was delightful to get your fine old letter—it really seemed as if so many letters*
came the week I was sick. I'm glad the poor syndicate has some strawberry jam
with strawberries. Fancy tempting down your bread & butter with that other awful
mixture; and "the Lord help the poor lad he comes from a good home."
*   By the way, last Thanksgiving I met your friend Robinson on the car here—I*
suppose he told you. But Cal I don't like his looks at all—he's getting so fat & puffy & he'd been

having just a little bit too much that day, tho' it was only noon. I smelt it strongly & his manner was not quite naturally gay. It may have been imagination but it repulsed me.

Well various people on Thanksgiving Day were inquiring after you & the first chance I have I'm to let Dr. A. [Arnott] see some of your writing. Mr. Smith is also most anxious to see them. He takes a great interest in you. He does so thoroughly love and admire papa & he was interested in you for his sake and now for your own. He said he saw very little of you of course as a boy but he hardly expected you to grow into such a fine strong character and so strong physically as you seemed. So put that in your pipe and smoke it, Lad. But he is fine little man, little Mr. Smith & there is no one I enjoy more & he's going to see you the first time he goes to Montreal. He seemed quite aggrieved when I said you'll see Cal if you go to Montreal. [He replied:] O, Yes, Yes, certainly.

Your paper came today, and your articles are fine. You make one perfectly long to read some of the books you describe. I think the authors should be mighty grateful to you. Your article on Booth is strong & suggestive, I think, & your other one was good too and what an unearthly home you must have been at. It gave me the creeps.

Well dear old boy my point [nib] *is entirely gone. I'm going to send on Mike's [Edna's] letter—I think it is comical. Don't work too hard & take care of yourself. I'm invited out to Mrs. Hay's for Hallowe'en & to stay all night if I care to.*

With much love, Ruby

[P.S.] Tom gets a bad reputation from Edna's letter.

In the early twentieth century, before immunization, many communicable diseases were rampant, especially in groups living together such as boarding schools, and the Ottawa Ladies' College was no exception. Shortly after the above episode of Ruby's illness there was another outbreak at the college and a quarantine was ordered. Ruby's letter describes the seriousness of this latest epidemic and again, it was the teachers who were required to do the nursing.

TO CALVIN MCQUESTEN [REV.] from his sister Ruby (W4690)

c/o *Montreal Herald*	[Ottawa Ladies' College]
Montreal, Quebec	Nov 3 1902, Monday night

My dear old Cal,

I had a very proper parental rebuke you have administered me. You done your duty I assure you [sic]—I quite approve of you and probably I agree with you but it would never do to say. However the rest of your letter was very fine & like a breath of outdoor life. For my illness is a thing of the past & lately other things have taken our minds.

Last week an epidemic of "grippe" laid low eighteen patients by Sat. & four cases of scarlet fever had developed from it & two more on Sunday. So you can imagine the consternation & upsetting—everything was turned out of Miss Curry's Art Room & it made ready for the six patients and nurses. It is a large sunny room & it was thought better to put them all together & sheets with carbolic acid are stretched across the door & the nurses have a stove & bathroom & everything they need. They can wash their own dishes & towels etc. & things are taken to the top of the stairs. Well, who do you think the girls are—Eleanor and Jean Ross—another Ross—Marion, no relation— Ethel Crombie—Maggie Fulton & Ethel Paul from Montreal—the latter's father has a large grocery I understand.

Well these poor unfortunates have to stay up six weeks—there is nothing slower & of which you have to be more careful than scarlet fever. We are quarantined for ten days—no one can go in or out & when that time is up we think all the girls will want to go home and we fear no day pupils would dare to come in. So Mrs. Ross is seriously considering at the end of ten days letting everyone go home & then starting at best after Xmas.

But it is so disappointing—our classes were just doing so nicely & this was the finest year for some time with such a bright outlook. And now it is knocked on the head. Well if we go home—the teachers will have to be paid for all the time I fancy— I can't say that I could really mourn at the thought of getting home a month before the Xmas holiday—my, it would be jolly. Such a thing I may have longed for in my first selfish year like I really cared for the college but I couldn't wish it now. But if it comes I'm young enough to thoroughly appreciate holidays. However we don't know anything yet but I'll let you know if anything more occurs.

Friday has been my busy day ordering meals for twelve, three times, and getting them ready myself at tea. However, the doctor says they may be up to-morrow & we'll be sincerely thankful for the cook has no more patience poor thing & the little boy Hector—we have boys with fine names—Clyde, Napoleon, Hector must have trotted his poor legs off taking up trays & the teachers are tired of taking around gargles and medicines five times a day. The nurse of course attended to these girls till she went above with scarlet fever patients. The doctor ordered pailfuls [sic] of gargle & medicine as if for a prison. Really these things are funny.

Well old boy—I have been writing home explaining and I'm quite exhausted. You were a dear to write to me, for I know you're awfully busy. With very much love my dear old boy,   *Your ever affectionate sister,*
                                                               Ruby
[P.S.] Probably there is a dear little germ sitting on this letter waiting to jump at you.

Fortunately, the college undertook antiseptic measures to isolate the sick during epidemics and used carbolic acid as a disinfectant. They were aware of the "germ theory," which had been pioneered in Scotland by Drs. Malloch, Lister and Osler and brought to Hamilton <u>and</u> North America by Dr. Malloch (W4582). Despite Ruby's jest about a *germ* lurking on the letter, they might not have known about the airborne nature of the tuberculosis bacteria. The teachers usually did duty as nurses and, in spite of the antiseptic measures, Ruby often became ill. She had just recovered from one of these bouts when the epidemic of November 1902 broke out.

Occasionally, Ruby's personal expenses prevent her from sending all of her money to Tom for his tuition; however, she sends what she can and, if she is short, then the family must come to Tom's aid. Now, because of the epidemic, the College was forced to close early before the Christmas holidays and Ruby's salary was cut.

TO THOMAS B. MCQUESTEN from his sister Ruby (W-MCP3-5.041)
38 Alexander St.,   Ottawa Ladies' College
Toronto, Ontario   Nov 20 1902 [Postmark] Thursday

My dear Tim [Tom],
Just a note as I'm very busy getting ready expecting to go home to-morrow. A card from Mither just told me not to expect you at the station as you were invited to the Proudfoot's for the evening.

I was going to give you your money—at least a little when I saw you, but now I'll send it off in this letter. We only, of course, got our one term's salary and I had boots and rubbers and my ticket & drug bill and art bill and numerous other wicked little bills so that I can't spare a bit more than a paltry $7—but I'll report at home and they'll have to come to your aid.

We had so hoped to be paid up till Xmas & had sent in a petition that if they deduct a half term's salary they would give us the amount up to Xmas & take it—a little each time—from our payments to after Xmas. I'm just hoping that they'll let us have our salary—It means so much, $34 & it seems as if some of the rich people on the Board could afford it better—and it isn't our fault.

However the Board have put up with a good deal already I fancy. Well must run out for I have an hundred and one things to finish. Thankful to say I looked up books and got my paper on Moravians satisfactorily finished all in one day & the day before I sat up till three and finished my other essays so I'll not worry the family with my writings.

Well dear old boy, Good-Bye.

With much love. Ruby

P.S. I'll find out if your order can't be made out for a branch post & if it comes otherwise, you'll know I couldn't. This is a postal note so can be cashed at any branch post.

In Mary's letter to Calvin of November 26, 1902 (W4709), she comments on the financial situation and the politics at the college, but she does not mention Ruby's illness. Probably Ruby has not informed her. The children often try to protect their mother, or in some instances she is not informed because they fear her wrath. Nevertheless, she often has the uncanny power of finding out their secrets, and seems to know that Ruby *needs a rest.*

We had quite a disappointment on Friday evening, when the train came in, without Ruby, found that the Montreal Express was 1 1/2 hours late at Toronto, so she had to go up & spend the night at Mrs. Mackay's & [corner missing]. *It is good for her to get a rest, for I think the sickness at the college had meant a lot of extra evenings, besides the worry of it. You see they had only 25 boarders, but several were coming at the beginning of November term, these had to be told not to come, so that the finances of the school were so low, that there was a discussion amongst the directors whether to continue the school at all. Dr. Armstrong and Mr. Paul of Montreal put up a strong fight for it and the teachers offered to give up their half-term's salary. The trouble is there is such a debt on the building and as Mr. Paul said, "if the Presbyterians would only stand by their own, but they are fools, they give large sums to outside things and let their own institutions want." Well, in the meantime it makes the work lighter for the girls to have Ruby at home.*

It had been fourteen years since Isaac's death and bankruptcy in 1888, and the family continued to suffer impoverishment. The Christmas of 1902 was a particularly meagre holiday for the McQuestens, and Ruby clearly expresses the family's poverty through their attempts to find, or to make, gifts for one another. Although Ruby's salary has been reduced by the epidemic at the school, her good humour and joy at being home still shine through. Ruby makes plans and catalogues a series of inexpensive gifts for members of the family:

TO CALVIN MCQUESTEN [REV.] from his sister Ruby (W4263)
Montreal, Quebec   Ottawa Ladies' College
                                           Dec 3 1902 [dated by context]

My dearest Cal,

The Mither is writing & wanting to know what she'll tell you about Xmas as presents—Well really we're not going to spend any money on each other this year. But the Mither, we think, must have glasses, so if you will chip in with me for them, Hilda & I will trot her down to have her eyes examined. We're scaring her that you'll do all kinds of things if you come home & find she hasn't obeyed your orders.

Hilda has a five o'clock tea table—of drawn work that will be lovely for the Mither & I'll have a carving cloth, also a pleasure work started before last Xmas done in time, & with her glasses—she'll count them a present & a little plant.

I fancy you needn't think about any other way of getting rid of your [fees?].

We really don't think any member of the family should spend much money for we have what we really need.

I had thought of getting Edna a pair of manicure scissors & Mama says she'll chip in. Edna can't cut her right hand nails with the ones we have & I don't blame her. So if you have extra cash going, you can chip in, it all goes to the family after all.

I suppose the Mither told you I'm minus 6 weeks pay $34 but it is to be taken off, part off of each payment after Xmas & we are to have all our money up to Xmas. So I expect a $34 coming in—but after I've taken out fare back to Ottawa & something to keep me going till Feb. there will be only about $20—however it will help us along.

As to Hilda, Mary is giving her a hat pin holder & I have nothing for either. But we'll probably think of some article each needs & get it later on. Really I get as excited as ever when I think of Xmas coming & you coming home, Hurrah!—Won't it be jolly? We are poor but I guess it must be the Irish in us that makes us most joyful & hilarious on occasions!

In spite of being short so much it is really fine having such a long holiday and I can help the girls & we'll be having really a jolly time. Last week we were quite gay, going to three "Teas," Wed, Thurs, & Friday. And this week we've made calls & done fancy work. Hilda has started me on drawn work mats that cost nothing & are very pretty & not hard to do.

I was up on Monday to see Emily MacLaren & she said Jean had been suffering tortures from an ulcerated tooth, but it had been lanced & she was better, tho' very much pulled down.

The little Mither got her meeting over yesterday. She was almost ill beforehand, but as soon as it was off her mind she was as gay as could be & trotted me down town to look at—well, perhaps you'll see later, if Santa comes to bad boys.

This morning I walked down to Brown's to have him doctor a fern & up to the James's where I sat on the table & was regaled with eleven o'clock tea & chocolate cake. By the way it would almost pay you to get your boot laces as we do from Willie James. He is getting us a gross for 62c, that is 144 for 62c & usually pay 50c for 24 or 12 pairs.

I expect Annie Anderson, you know, Mrs. Ross's niece, to stay with us on the 10th on her way to her brother Harry (Arry) at Chatham. Well, my dear old boy, had better stop.   *Your affec'ate sister, Ruby*

[P.S.] I'm telling the Mither she must hurry & practice her piece. I bought her a song "My Rosary" & the family like encouraging her to sing.

Chapter 9

MORE ILLNESS AND FINANCIAL WOES

I've not been having a bad time of it though lately. (W4893)

TO CALVIN MCQUESTEN [REV.] from his sister Ruby (W4753)
Montreal, Quebec
[Ottawa Ladies' College]
Jan 27 1903, Tuesday afternoon
[estimated date]

My dear old Cal,

Just a note as it seems a long time since I wrote. Mama told me in her letter how busy you were and why, so I quite understand and you needn't worry trying to steal time to drop me a line. I'll content myself with a one-sided correspondence though it isn't awfully high living, feeding on the imagination, so to speak.

Ruby McQuesten

It was good to get your paper and I enjoyed your articles ever so much. How many you had! It must indeed have kept you busy doing so much extra.

I hope you're not tired out for it must be hard work finding out all about your subjects besides the writing part. You have to understand things so thoroughly to write clearly that it must be a strain.

Well we've had our own times lately. Last Thursday another case of scarlet fever breakout. The child was taken immediately to the new contagious hospital & school continued as usual.

But of course it frightened away some of our day pupils—too precious to lose—and has kept away a half dozen girls just coming in to board. We can only hope that these girls will just wait to see that nothing more occurs for a few days and will then come on. Three of them had their trunks already packed & Mrs. Ross had to notify them.

We felt it would be only right tho' the doctor has not quarantined us at all and says there is no danger. But of course people ask how this case occurred and it is a mystery. The place was so thoroughly fumigated, but it was most discouraging. We expected a Board Meeting but it has not met yet. Perhaps it is just as well not to discuss the situation now & later it may have improved.

I've not been having a bad time of it though lately. Last Friday night I took eight girls to the rink & we had quite a good skate. Lolly MacLaren is the sole man I always see at the rink. I wanted him to be introduced to the girls but he said he was afraid his programme was full—the sinner. We had cocoa & bread & butter on our return.

Then Sat. I spent trying to see how little I could do & pretend to be working in the Art Room. I'm doing one of those studies I know you admire—biscuits & cheese &

*teapot & cream jug (I suppose you think a mug of beer would be more appropriate)
well I'll do one with that one of these days when the cheese has a stronger look—as
long as it will stand steady long enough to be painted. It's unfortunate you can't
paint things moving—think of the sentiment.*

*Then on Sat. evening Miss Curry & I went out for tea to the Tuckers—not little
Tommy Tucker but another—a very kind little couple, brother, sister who keep house &
always give us a most hearty welcome. On Sunday I went to [teach] my Chinamen as
usual and went to the MacLaren's for tea.*

*Monday was my duty day & in the evening Mrs. Fraser the elocution teacher gave
us an evening on Whitcombe Riley, his life and a number of selections. I do enjoy
some of his things. By the way—Riley is a bachelor—I've always laboured under the
delusion that "To an Old Sweet Heart of Mine" was dedicated to his wife.*

*Last night we went to an illustrated lecture of Prof. Penfellow's on the wood-pulp
industry of Canada. It was very good.*

*To-night I'm invited to tea to Sace Robertson's—if that's how you spell her name.
The rest of the people are going to hear [Albert?] but I heard her & wish to keep the
glorious memory of her tonight. Hilda & I sat up in the Gods chaperoned by lady Bell.
To-morrow night is teachers' meeting & then comes Friday and the end of another
week & we'll be into Feb. How the time flies.*

*Well my dear old boy, take care of yourself and have some fun. I hope you're
having some snow-shoeing this winter.*

With very much love, Ruby

Ruby's description of this painting is echoed by her mother in a letter to Calvin
as she compliments Ruby's art: *She has brought home some lovely pictures. One of a
tea pot, sugar bowl and tea cup with biscuits and cheese on a fringed napkin. They are
really lovely, and some daffodils in a ginger pot, but my table is wonderful* (W5002, Jun
27 1903). Many of Ruby's paintings hang in her bedroom at Whitehern today, and several
are featured in the Colour Section of her Paintings & Pyrography *(see list, p. 322)*.

Ruby was a good artist and won acclaim at a Hamilton Art School exhibit when
she was quite young: *In sepia work the best thing shown for years is a castor plant leaf
by Ruby McQuesten* (News clipping n.d., Box 8). This work, or one very similar, is on
display at Whitehern. At a more recent Art Show of her paintings, an art critic stated
that Ruby would have been a "significant woman artist," if she had had the leisure
and health to pursue her talent (Regina Haggo, *Hamilton Spectator*, Oct 25 2006).

In spite of some illness, 1903 is a good year for Ruby. Her happiness is evident
in the following letter to Calvin; she is delighted at the prospect of seeing him in
Ottawa, and she indulges in some daydreaming about being wealthy. Her description
of large houses is a reflection of her mother's considerations about selling Whitehern.
Mary rejected this idea several times because the house remained badly in need of
repair. Also, she would still need a sizeable home for her large family, and their
beautiful things would be dispersed with little monetary gain. Their stately home
and furnishings were invested with a great deal of social prestige that they were all
loath to give up, as is demonstrated by Ruby's musings.

Ruby conveys news to Calvin of some extra money expected soon from the rental
of the attached Bold Street houses that had been salvaged from the bankrupt estate.

This rental income is the first indication of any financial relief for the family in fifteen years since Isaac died. Unfortunately, more hard times still lay ahead.

TO CALVIN MCQUESTEN [REV.] from his sister Ruby (W4777)

Montreal Herald,   Ottawa Ladies' College
Montreal, Quebec   Feb 9 1903, Monday morning

My dearest Cal,

I must really send you a scowl this morning. My little devils—when the Irish use it, it is an affectionate term, isn't it—are memorizing the "Last Rose of Summer"! It is so nice to start them on something they have to do all by themselves. It is good to be a teacher at such times. Poor little wretches! But they do not look at all miserable.

I was so delighted to get your fine cheery letter. It quite cheered me up. I wish my snow shoes were magic ones & would transport me some night to go out with your party. And it is good that the Creelmans are living in Montreal. How fortunate that you happened to meet Mrs. C. & in your best frock too. That was your lucky day.

I quite appreciate your sentiments on large houses. We've all been spoilt in that direction, I fancy. It simply seems homelike and natural to be in a large, fine house. These little modern houses, even fair sized ones haven't room enough. One really can't expand sufficiently. It seems to make you feel free and easy and quite in your element—you can draw a large breath, so to speak, in a large house. One can get along well enough in small rooms but when you get into large ones you feel as if you know what it is to live.

You are meant to have been left a large house & fortune, my dear, and you could buy the most expensive pictures and all kinds of rare things, for you're blessed with extravagant tastes. And so long as no missionaries come along and other troublesome elements wanting help you could have plenty of enjoyment in spending money. However, I always fancied that we could spend our money and enjoy spending it on various people & causes as well as ourselves if we had it. We'd have a splendid house & entertain deserving people right royally. Wouldn't it be jolly! We'd have a chef & everything swell & stuff the duffers. Oh we'll know how to do it when the spar [ship] comes in.

By the way, sonny, the fortunes of this family are on the rise. Mama was telling that her Bold St. houses would both be taken in March by Mrs. Hill. Isn't it a blessing to have them rented to such a capable woman? And then our Montreal stock has behaved quite decently of late hasn't it? The same day that this news came in Mama's letter we got our checks & instead of having anything deducted as we had agreed on account of five weeks missed, we were given the full amount.

Your letter just came—Hurrah! <u>Would</u> I like you to run up to Ottawa? It is too good to be true. I feel too cheerful to live soberly. This is the final piece of good news. It will be good to see you, you dear old fellow. About the snow shoes, I'd like ever so much to go out and I was wondering if I could think of anyone to go out with us. The people I used to go out with are away. None of the teachers have snow shoes except Miss Ross & hers are almost no good. The MacLarens might go out with us—the boys have snow shoes, if Jean could get a pair. However I'll see & if you can bring your snow shoes without too much trouble, do it. I'd love a tramp. And to go to a hockey match too—such dissipation.

And then to have you over Sunday—you'll see our Chinese School. I'll introduce you to my man & I'll be glad to have Mr. Nosse meet you. He is the superintendent & both he and his wife are so kind. And you'll see St. Andrews & as many things and people as we can manage. And you'll see my room which is fixed up. You'll be sharing your attentions with the Robinson family, of course, but we can have you, I expect for Sunday dinner & Saturday. Oh! We'll just see later on. Well, old boy must run and post this. With much love, hoping you can manage it all right.

Yours expectantly,
Ruby

P.S. Did I tell you I had met the three Robinson sisters & thought them nice girls? I'm glad you are to stay with them since I can't keep you at the College.

Ruby's news about the Bold Street houses would be welcome financial news for the whole family. The houses had brought in very little income, since they were so badly in need of repair when Isaac died in 1888. Slowly, Mary had been able to have some repairs done on them, including new roofs. Finally after fifteen years, they will be in capable hands and earning an income. Mary writes to Calvin with the news: *Have rented both the Bold Street houses to Mrs. Hill at $40 and water rates, for three years and option of five years. Was sorry to let them go so low but Mr. C. [Chisholm] thought perhaps it was best . . . and if she does as well as she hoped will give me $45 on first of January* (W4769). However, it will be four more years (1907) before Mary can make further repairs and realize an increase in rent for them (W5898).

VISITS TO PARLIAMENT

Ruby often attends lectures and visits Parliament to hear the speeches. She describes some of her activities to Calvin, and comments on a particular speech:

> *Just a note on foolscap while I sit with the girls at study. I exchanged my Monday duty with Daisy Racey & went to hear L. M. King's lecture on Social Settlements. It was really well worth hearing & he had good lantern views. He showed us an ordinary tenement block such as might be seen many places in New York & in Chicago containing 48 houses—many storied & 2800 people nearly 3000 & not undeserving people, but those working hard for a livelihood. In such a block there would be 4 or 5 hundred rooms with no window at all, only opening off a room with one, & 600 rooms opening on to walls opposite with only a narrow shaft between. A man, he said, would pay $15 a month for two front rooms with windows and two back rooms & these about the size of my bedroom.*
>
> *He showed us pictures of the Hull House Settlement in Chicago superintended by a Miss Adams, a graduate of some University who has given her life to the work which has grown enormously. He also showed us Toynbee House in London, started by an Oxford student, Toynbee, & now supported by a number of students. Mr. King spoke for two hours in the most utterly unabashed manner for a youth.* (W4785, Feb 18 1903)

It is obvious that Ruby made special arrangements so that she could hear William Lyon Mackenzie King and his lecture, and she is impressed by him partly for his youthful manner and partly because he was espousing the philosophy of the Social Gospel movement that was sweeping Britain and North America. King was a Presbyterian and a social activist, like the McQuestens. He was approximately twenty-nine years of age at this time. He entered politics when he was twenty-five as Deputy Minister of Labour, and was elected Prime Minister for three periods between 1921 and 1948 totaling twenty-two years.

The activities at Parliament are important events for the ladies at the Ottawa Ladies' College. Ruby describes taking her class to see the opening of Parliament. Some of the parliamentarians are invited to the school for tea. Ottawa Ladies' College, a Presbyterian establishment, had regular contact with Parliament and was considered the most superior in Canada for young women both as a school and as a home. Ruby often writes about attending lectures and meeting some of the dignitaries. The teachers were regularly invited to tea or to dinner at Dr. Macdonald's, the Deputy Speaker of the House, who was notably generous with candy and gifts for the staff (W4893, W4908). Ruby's letters were circulated among family members and Ruby may also have sent a similar report to Tom.

1910 Portrait of the Hon. William Lyon Mackenzie King (1874-1950)
Minister of Labour *(National Archives of Canada, Topley Collection)*

TO CALVIN MCQUESTEN [REV.] from his sister Ruby (W4832)
Montreal, Quebec   Ottawa Ladies' College
                                                           Mar 13 1903

My dearest Cal,

Just a note I'm in a furious hurry. I'm sending on Hilda's letters which Mama sent me and a letter of Tom's which you mustn't lose but return to the Mither. This letter of Tom's I should have sent you long ago. I was delighted to get your jolly little letter—it was very cheering. Your Mephistos have been entertaining characters.

We are to have our Saturday "At Home" to-morrow & members of Par. [Parliament] are invited—that is some of them, I'm not inviting dear Pa Bruce. And tonight we have to decorate & I'm getting this affection for them all. This has been a busy week, but fairly gay.

Yesterday afternoon was the great crush at the opening of Par. I and my flock looked down condescendingly at the gay ladies below. Laurier is his same sweet self— the new gentleman of the blackened locks, the elegant bows of the [former?]. We saw the performance well, were nearly roasted etc., returned home to rest till tea.

On Tues. afternoon went to a committee meeting of the Field Naturalists & in the evening to one of their lectures on whales. We had a whale of a time. On Wed. I went to Miss Sutherlands, met a Mr. Green who knew of you at Varsity.

Well my dear boy, take care of yourself with much love. Ruby

"Mephistos" refers to a Graduate Student Conference on the History, Philosophy, and Sociology of Science, Technology, and Medicine. The conferences often included refereed debates on relevant issues of the day, and they sometimes became raucous affairs.

Also, Ruby often goes on outings with the Field Naturalists. She attended their functions, and accepted a position on the executive. The McQuestens were avid naturalists; Calvin was President of the Hamilton Bird Protection Society for many years.

The financial problems continue for the family during the spring of 1903, and Ruby lists some of her own expenses in a letter to Calvin, including medical expenses pertaining to her illness in November (W-MCP3-5.041). She also describes her efforts at sewing her own clothes. Hilda was the more accomplished seamstress; but Ruby also demonstrates some capability. On one occasion Ruby was able to send the money home for a new sewing machine (W-MCP1-3a.020). When the family could afford to do so, they had a seamstress come in for several days to do the family sewing, altering and mending (Box 12-179, April 1912).

As she reports on her financial situation, Ruby apologizes to Calvin because she is unable to send any money to him at present. She also states that her money *is due now.* She likely would have sent some of that to Calvin and to Tom when she received her pay. This is one of those indications that she occasionally sent money to Calvin as well as to Tom. Even though he was working at the *Montreal Herald*, his journalist salary was pitifully low. It is obvious that the later part of the year had been difficult for Ruby and for the family, medically and financially. Yet she remains remarkably positive, loving and cheerful: *of course, we've had our fun too.*

TO [REV.] CALVIN MCQUESTEN from his sister Ruby (W4893)
Montreal, Quebec   Ottawa Ladies' College
                                                  Apr 19 1903

My dear old Cal,
    I wonder what has been the matter with us lately. I really feel as if my reputation for letter writing must be entirely ruined. I don't think I ever left you so long before. Somehow one feels restless in the Spring and it seems hard to settle down and collect one's thoughts. I have been so wondering about you, whether you have changed or any of the others, your boarding house. And I wondered if you were going to get a chance for N.Y. at Easter time & I thought at one time I might have some spare cash to help you out, but some of it vanished and I have two five cents for collection to-morrow till my money comes which is due now.
    The doctor whom I had in November when I was sick sent in his bill of $3 for 2 visits. I owe the dentist for past and present $2.50. And on such insignificant things my money vanishes. However pay day is at hand and the full dinner pail.
    Well I've really been having a pretty good time lately. Of course we had our holidays from Thursday night till Tuesday afternoon. And we had a very pleasant time. We were very busy, sewing on the machine we had rented, as we were anxious to get all our stitching done before it left. And I succeeded in making and finishing up quite satisfactorily two shirt waists,—tho' I did take the band off of the neck of one six times. I'm sure Miss Middleton also had her troubles & for a full day was

quite depressed over the wrinkles on the shoulder of hers. Shirt waists are sometimes very troublesome my dear, tho' you don't know very much about them from personal experience. They are one of the things that try people's character and I'm quite sure you wouldn't worry about such trifling affairs as your country and its government if you were fitting a shirt waist into its place about your neck. Besides that I bound a skirt and mended an underskirt and fixed up a list of things that I had written down to make sure of remembering.

Of course we had our fun too. We were out for tea one evening at MacLaren's. Our Field Naturalist excursion was on Sat. and a perfect day it was. Part of the time I helped the bug-man lift up stones and pop into his bottle all kinds of little crawly things & hoppers. It was quite exciting. I'll be really getting bold enough to lift up snakes one of these days with only one or two quivers down my spine and no one could ever see those. Did you know that the copper snakes here are not poisonous? Dr. Fletcher had them crawling over his hand this afternoon when we went out to the Aylmer and gathered the trailing arbutus. He says the black snake will attack you but it is not venomous. Then on Sunday I went to Dr. Armstrong's for dinner and out to the Willie Smith's for tea.

The week before the holidays I had on my mind the getting of the girls off. I was given the full charge of seeing about their tickets and finding what time each ones train left and arranging with the baggage man to have the trunks down to the stations in time. There were about twenty-five going off and I felt it quite a responsibility, for I don't think I'm naturally much good in that line. However everything went off without a hitch in spite of crowds at holiday time. The last batch of six went off to Lachute on the 6:20 p.m train & I was so anxious to have them off safely as the others, that they had their tea at five and were started off & had their baggage checked & their seats in the car at five minutes to six. So they had a clear 25 minutes to wait—poor brutes! However they were quite cheerful and seemed to think there was nothing strange about it.

Then since the holidays it has been examination papers ending with the making out of reports until eleven to-night. I really don't intend to look at the time to-night. But of course we might have worked last night. Instead we were invited by Dr. Macdonald, the deputy speaker, to dine at "The House" with him. He has a lovely little suite of rooms there, his butler who served us a most elegant dinner. At half past eight we went up to hear the speeches but it was very dry so Dr. Mac[donald]. took us down and treated us to ice cream & cake and bought us an elegant box of candy which we indulged in, not just hungrily in his room, while he told us a couple of creepy tales to dream on & then he escorted us & the candy home. Isn't he a fine gentleman, the old doctor?

The night before, Thursday, I had a kind of feeling of hopefulness in my bones, that perhaps you might be up for the "Budge" [Budget at Parliament] but when I tho't of your long tiresome return journey, I was glad for your sake you hadn't to come. You're quite a notorious villain taking up the words of your superiors in this strike. And the worst of it is that Mr. Monk supported you in your evil doing.

It must be very interesting meeting the Japanese Consul. I'd love to hide in a corner of his beautiful drawing room and listen to your talk. It is a fine opportunity for you.

Well dear old boy, you'll think this is an endless letter once I'm started. But I really had to explain my various doings. I hope old boy, you'll be having some good walks—I wish Johnston were not engaged so you could go together.

What is Ken [Trigge] *making of himself these days? I wish you were away from him altogether, you poor old fellow. You have to put up with it all for the family.*

Well dear old boy, good-night. I'd like to give you a good old hug but we'll just imagine it.   *With very much love.*

Your affec'ate sister, Ruby

Ruby's letter provides an indication of the cost of medical and dental visits. According to a previous letter Ruby was earning approximately $5.99 per week: *I suppose the Mither told you I'm minus six weeks pay, $34* (W4263). Ruby's doctor and dental bills add up to almost a week's salary.

In the following letter, Ruby excuses Tom from acknowledging the money she is sending, and also gently chastises him, for not having heard *how the last one worked.* Later in the letter she also apologizes to Tom for not sending something *extra.* Clearly, Ruby feels it is her duty to pay for Tom's education, and wishes to *stalk* his *brain,* so as to have some effect on his development. Yet she does it as tactfully as possible and often with some humour.

TO THOMAS B. MCQUESTEN from his sister Ruby (W4908)
Toronto, Ontario   [Ottawa Ladies' College]
                                              Apr 24 1903, Friday afternoon

My dear old Tom,

You'll be cramming your poor cranium with all kinds of learned lore, so I don't expect you to answer this. But I'm just sending you a little of that poor stuff necessary sometimes, as the brain cannot stalk along by itself, no matter how fine it be. It is just made out for the ordinary post I fancy as I never heard how the last one worked.

Well my old brain has been on a mixture of things lately frivolous and otherwise. On Monday night there was the Musical "Festival" here and it was very fine. The Oratorio of Hiawatha was given from the part with the death of Minnehaha beginning with "Oh! the bitter, bitter winter! Oh! the cruel biting winter!" or something of that kind, and the orchestra started in with a weird wail. It is a most beautiful thing. I had heard it given before but not with such fine chorus and orchestra and really it is the finest thing in the Oratorio line I've ever heard. We had Mackenzie's "Dream of Jubal" too and the "Coronation March."

Then we had our feast of art on Wednesday afternoon. The Art Exhibition is held every three years and there was really a fine collection of pictures. I can recognize my old favourites now and it is very interesting to see a style of painting I like and that looks very familiar and find on looking at my catalogue it is the artist I guessed. Bell-Smith's were there, beautiful misty pictures with purple tints, of street scenes and churches and water. McGillivray Knowles has fine ones too particularly her water colors, and Colin Forbes, Manly and Hammond and Laura Muntz are my favourites. Of course there are others I like too but it is hard to really take them in though we did stay for more than two hours. Well those are our parts of soul.

You should only talk of such high things but I'm going to make your little mouth water with other kind of parts. I don't know whether your eyes watered at my description of the paintings and your ears tingled at the musical sounds described but certainly your mouth must be affected by this.

On Friday afternoon last we—Miss Bennett and myself went over to "The House" and had dinner with Dr. MacDonald, the deputy speaker. You've heard me speak of the old gentleman? There were just the three of us and the butler served us an elegant little dinner—soup, roast duck and jelly, hot roast tongue, peas, little white butter beans, potatoes. Then there was a very fine pudding, then peach pie, tea, fruit, nuts and raisons [sic]. We didn't do badly did we. Then we went upstairs to hear the speeches, but Dr. M. tho't there would be nothing good so in about twenty minutes, it was about nine o'clock by then, we were taken out and treated to ice cream and cake. Then we wandered back to his room & chatted till time to go home when we were left with a fine box of candy and told we'd be treated better every time we came.

And on Tuesday night, as the House was adjourned on account of Sir Oliver Mowat, we were invited by phone to go over, and we're again treated to ice cream and cake and a larger box of candy. The people here tell us to go often by all means. Poor little chappie, you're only a boy and men don't treat you to ice cream. But you'll have to treat yourself to keep up your spirits in these exams.

I'd send you a little extra but there is 2.50 for dentist bill & 3 for an old doctor's bill before Xmas and various other sundries run away with treat money.

We've been having some pleasant Sat. afternoons, Field Naturalist Excursions. We've had perfect weather here lately only things are really so dry and there is so much dust that everything feels gritty even my clothes and hair. So we are really longing for rain as there is no growth.

Well my dear, I think I've done pretty well in the news line. David Ross started for Montreal where he was to wait for a couple of days before starting for the Old Country. He told his mother he might work his way to India before coming back. But it may have been only in fun. Take care of yourself and don't kill yourself studying.

With much love,
Your affectionate sister, Ruby

As an accomplished artist herself, Ruby enjoyed the *feast of art* at the exhibition of Canadian artists, and she recognized many of the artists and their work. Frederic Marlett Bell-Smith (1846-1923) was an art teacher in Hamilton and in Toronto, and he may have been one of Ruby's art teachers at the Hamilton Art School. Colin Forbes (1846-1925) was a North American artist who was noted for his portraits, and, in another letter, Ruby remarks on his painting, *Riling Clouds* (W4916). Ruby also selected several women artists: Elizabeth A. McGillivray Knowles (1866-1928) was a Canadian landscape and figure painter; Laura Muntz Lyall (1860-1930) was an Impressionist painter, probably the first Canadian woman artist to be recognized in France with the *Societe des artistes Francais*, 1894, and she is also the first woman asked to exhibit with the Canadian Art Club in 1909.[10] Ruby's love of art is evident in her closing comment about the paintings and the artists: *Well those are our parts of soul.*

TO CALVIN MCQUESTEN [REV.] from his sister Ruby (W4936)
Montreal, Quebec   Ottawa Ladies' College
                                                        Apr 30 1903

Many Happy Returns of the Day my dear old boy. The New Year is coming with all sorts of fine things in store for you, you thing of the May. It was a shame of you to oust your sister off the throne and seat yourself thereon and smile blandly when she came

---

[10] www.artcyclopedia.com/general/alphabetic.html

along a couple of days later. Never mind we shared up our Birthday parties and we'll share up other things too.

I'm just sending along a photo frame I did for you. The daffodils should suit the month. It's nothing much but there's lots of love and a big hug with it, my old Sweet Heart of a brother.   *Your loving sister,*
                                                                Ruby

The photo frame decked with daffodils is an example of Ruby's pyrography, or wood-burning art. It is in the Whitehern collection, and can be viewed in the colour section of her *Paintings & Pyrography* following Part Two.

As previously indicated, Ruby is occasionally able to send some money to Calvin as well as to Tom. Calvin was planning a trip to the McQuesten family homestead in New Hampshire and Ruby sends him money to help with the trip.

TO CALVIN McQUESTEN [REV.] from his sister Ruby (W4981)
c/o *Montreal Herald,*   Ottawa Ladies' College
    Montreal, Quebec   Jun 12 1903

My dear old Cal,

The Mither has told me of your expected trip to the old McQuesten country [New Hampshire]. *It is fine to think of one member of the family getting down to see our relatives. I hope you'll have a good time. By the way I wasn't sure of your address from the last letter so have to send your letters to your office, so there is really no news particularly and am about to get this off by post to tonight. So excuse scribble.*

                          With much love, my dear old brother.
                          Your loving sister, Ruby

[P.S.] Tell me in your next letter and I'll send it to your flat. I was at the Robinsons for tea last Sunday night and they told me Burnside had said your room was tidy for once. Isn't it fine that Tom has done so well and got his scholarship? Really it has cheered us all. By the way, don't be stuck up if I send you a little money. I have plenty to spare and Tom didn't need any and here I don't know what to do with my 'mon.' So you may as well take some to take you on your trip.

The family were all cheered at the prospect of a having their financial struggles ease a little. Tom had won the Alexander Mackenzie Scholarship for Political Science in 1903, which brought a small cash prize. Tom also wrote to his brother Calvin to tell him that he had been able to secure the job as manager of *The Varsity* magazine for the next term: *It will be something two hundred so that will help some, altho' there is a good deal of work in connection with it. . . . Just now I am working 12 hours a day and my exams begin the day after to-morrow on the second* (W4933). Tom was able to hold this job for only one year, after which time the faculty took over and *The Varsity* was no longer a student-run publication. Mary objected to the faculty involvement: *It is not supposed to be of the same order as a paper edited by experienced and paid men. . . . I think the object of the paper is lost if it is not kept as the students' organ* (W-MCP3-5.018).

Chapter 10

TOM WORKS AT THE LUMBER CAMP

I will let mama think I am clerking or it will worry her to death.
(W8160)

During the months of June to August 1903, Tom took a job as a lumber man on the Ottawa River. It paid $22 a month plus board. Tom warned Calvin several times not to tell their mother, because it would worry her. The real reason is that she would not have allowed Tom to take the job if she had known the danger involved. Tom wrote several letters to Calvin about this position, excerpted here:

I think I will go up the Ottawa this year as a river rat. I will let mama think I am clerking or it will worry her to death (W8160). *. . . . I am not letting the Mother know the nature of the work I am doing which is common log-driving. It is pretty hard work for ten hours a day but I will get used to it and the air is fine. The food is enough but very good and that is the most important thing. A person can stand hard work if the food is good. As yet I am not very expert at running on the loose timber but there is not very much danger as the men, who are on the whole a fine set of fellows, are careful to watch a green hand* (W8164). *. . . . The crew too are the wildest looking men. A great many of them are Indians and they are all lousy; Indians and white men both. . . .*

Illustration of early 20th Century log driving in North America
(photo courtesy of The Forest History Society)

One of the lads had a fiddle and when we came over a big buck Indian did a dance for us. The mosquitos are pretty bad yet but there is pretty good money in it. At least, comparatively so. The highest wages given here are $26 a month

*and board, I am getting $22. It is very decent of the foreman, Courtney
Hutchinson, to give me that because better men are getting less, but none of
the men know it.* (W8166)

Tom went back to this lumber camp in the summer of 1904 and for a brief time in
the late fall of 1905, after receiving a letter from his foreman, Courtney Hutchinson:
*I hope you will be back to see us this Season again. I expect to be back at Mohr's Island
again & would like to see your worship then* (W-MCP1-3a.028, W5410). The money Tom
earned at the lumber camp, although it was not a great deal, did help to relieve
matters at home. When Tom returned from the lumber camp, Mary reports that Tom
is literally the colour of mahogany and shows his muscle with great pride. However,
Mary still did not know the nature (the danger) of Tom's work at the lumber camp,
but he loved it and enjoyed the company of the rugged workmen.

Tom did have an adventurous nature. In 1902 while he was at the logging camp,
he devised a "scheme" with his brother Calvin to purchase a canoe. He asked Cal in
Montreal to write to their mother about the canoe because she might be more willing
for Cal to have one (W4592, Jul 2 1902). His mother refused: *Now as to the canoe, I have
tried to make up my mind to stand it, but simply cannot; the anxiety is more than I can
stand. . . . Besides I know you need all your money* (W4601, Jul 4 1902).

In 1904 Tom wrote to Cal from the logging camp to say that he had a canoe,
and recounted a dangerous adventure. He did not write of this to his mother, but the
letter to Cal is extant and she may have seen it after the fact:

*I got a little bark canoe from Aylmer that you can lift with one hand. It just
holds one nicely. It is a great thing for running around in, although alone in
a wind they are useless still they can stand a far larger wave than a Peterboro
and are safer in a big sea if not too heavily loaded. The other night we had a
rather squeak. Two of us were out on it. . . . He is as big as I am and it was
just a little too much for the canoe. . . . By the time we started back there
was quite a wind and a good sea. Still we went ahead, but we made the
mistake of paddling so that we shipped water when we cut through a wave.
Before we knew it we were pretty nearly half full and with our small canoe it
meant that we were close to swamping. I had to stop paddling and bale with
my hat for dear life and we finally got in, a fellow learns a lot from a little
experience.* (W8176, July 17, 1904)

Although Calvin had a congenital defect in his left arm and side, he, like his
brother, was an avid canoeist and no stranger to the potential difficulties and dangers
of the sport (see his article, "Canoeing at Gaspe," Box 08-001).

The family was very happy about Tom's success with winning the small
scholarship, and his income from the lumber camp work. Yet, in spite of these
additional funds and Ruby's steady income, the McQuestens were still exceedingly
poor. In the summer of 1903, Calvin was able to send home ten dollars ($10) so
they could manage a vacation away from the heat of the city. In her reply to Calvin,
Mary gives some indication of their financial situation, including household costs,
bolstered by Ruby's continuing contributions and Mary's careful management of
finances (W5012, Jul 9 1903):

Your letter has just come with its generous enclosure and it was most *acceptable. It will just pay Edna's board for the two weeks. . . . We found out from Helen that very good boarding houses are there at $5.00 a week, so we have written to secure rooms for Mary for three weeks and Edna for two weeks. Mary gets so thin and tired out with the heat and work that I had determined to give her a change though I could really scarcely manage it.*

In addition to the extra bills for Bold St. houses which I have yet to make up, I had $25 to pay for cement walks and sodding at Bold St. (<u>Ruby brought home just enough for that</u>) (emphasis added). *And also had to get my coal in April in order to secure reduced rates, but still it was high, making my coal bill $114. I have only paid $60, but the Capt. is very lenient. Then some of my money on mortgage came in and in re-investing I found by making a push and keeping some of my creditors waiting I could pay off a $1050. mortgage on Webber property held by North Scottish Life Ass. For I find if I do not watch carefully, I am tempted to use principal, if it comes in small sums & there were two or three odd sums waiting at Ham. Prov. for re-investment. I could only get 12 shares of the Ham. Prov. for which I paid $122. but as they pay 6 per cent I get 5 per cent on money invested and can get no more on mortgage.*

They always laugh at me, when I say that we shall be much better off next summer but if nothing happens to Mrs. Hill, it seems as if we must be, for to have one of the [Bold Street] houses vacant a whole year is a very great loss, & it takes me a while to catch up, having water-rates to pay too besides all the repainting & plumber's bills, the latter a hundred dollars & Ross the same, besides $200 for electric light. I think it is just a wonder, we are as well off as we are. <u>I am telling you all this to show how much help your ten dollars is</u> [emphasis added].

Calvin's, Ruby's and Tom's combined financial contributions indicate how the family worked together to help their mother, and how they felt a responsibility for one another. In the summer of 1903 the girls, Hilda, Mary and Edna, spent some time with their friends, the Gartshores, at Roach's Point and at Orchard Beach on Lake Simcoe. Mary remarked on the social difference between the two vacation spots: *You might call Roach's Point the aristocracy and Orchard Beach the commoners* (W5053). It may have been a vacation in which the McQuesten girls assisted with the care of the Gartshore children.

At the same time Mary took Ruby to Port Carling for a rest. She found accommodation at $5.00 per week with room and board; however, while they were there she found it necessary to write to Calvin to send a little money to help bring them home: *afraid I have run myself a little short, so if you could send me in a letter a two dollar bill . . . would be very much obliged, or perhaps a <u>V</u> [$5.00] if you can spare it, we may have to buy our dinners on the way home* (W5059, Aug 5 1903). No doubt, this necessity reinforced for Ruby the family's poverty and the need for her salary.

Chapter 11

CALVIN: RUBY'S KINDRED SPIRIT

My old Sweet Heart of a brother. (W4936)

Many of Ruby's extant letters are written to her brother Calvin. Sister and brother were deeply fond of one another; both were literary, intellectual, sensitive and artistic. Calvin was born with a slightly withered left hand and some disability on his left side. By his own description he had *emotional problems,* and he was *crippled in body* and *without the physical and nervous stamina for continuous mental effort.* In September of 1920, he informed the Principal Gandier of Knox College that:

> *I . . . continue to be dependent on the charity of my mother and brother. And although this charity is always tendered me with the most cordial generosity, and the most exquisite delicacy, this position of dependency is one which would not allow any man to maintain his self-respect, if there was any other course open to him.* (W-MCP2-3b.035)

Calvin suffered from the family's tendency toward mental instability, characterized by periods of excitement, optimism and great productivity, followed by periods of insomnia, lassitude and depression (W-MCP2-3b.035). The Victorian term for this condition was nervous prostration. This may have been what is known today as manic-depression, or bi-polar disorder. Calvin suffered periodic breakdowns, usually in connection with the stress of examinations during school, or overwork during periods of journalism or the ministry. As mentioned earlier, several other members of the family suffered in varying degrees from a similar mental disorder.

Calvin is a particularly interesting character in the McQuesten story. In spite of his disabilities he had a variety of careers, but achieved little success in monetary terms. He worked as an editor and a journalist from 1899 to 1903. For *The Toronto News,* Calvin wrote a column for women readers under the pseudonym of Nina Vivian—a name that he had appropriated from a female impersonator of the day. For the *Montreal Herald* he wrote a column named "The Tatler" in the style of the Addison and Steele "Tatler" in *The Spectator,* England (1712-15). Like its namesake, the column was full of items of history, politics, literature, and humour.[11]

Unfortunately, the newspaper work and deadlines proved too stressful for Calvin. He had a breakdown during the railroad strike of 1903 just as he was earning a small but steady income at the *Montreal Herald.* He found that he had to give up his journalism position. The editor regretted losing him, and invited him to return at any time. Calvin wrote to his mother that year on the anniversary of his father's

---

[11] Many of these columns are available on the Whitehern website: **www.whitehern.ca**

death. It is obvious from his mother's reply of March 13, 1903 that he had apologized to her for his failures, physical, financial and mental:

> *You praise me far too much my dear and make far too little of yourself.*
> *Though I have had to manage on a limited income and had some reverses*
> *& difficulties to meet, I have never been worried with my children's bad*
> *conduct. That is the thing which would have killed me. You are not to abuse*
> *yourself and call yourself slow & stupid. You were <u>never either,</u> you were*
> *sadly handicapped physically, poor fellow, from the start, and met with some*
> *disappointments in your plans, but you bore it heroically and have had to*
> *push your way along without assistance from any one.*
>
> *Your employers, who have hinted at your slowness, have simply used*
> *that as an excuse for not paying you your rightful reward. You have fallen*
> *into the hands of poor men, one would think unfortunately, but I cannot but*
> *believe in the guiding hand of a Heavenly Father, who is fitting you for some*
> *better work; though you may not have attained to a higher salary, you have*
> *certainly to a higher character and is not that the greatest thing in the world.*
> *I am always proud of you, for what you are. My only regret is, that you should*
> *be writing so little, that you do not see any prospect ahead of enjoying a home*
> *of your own for a long time and also that you do so much good work, for*
> *which you get no credit whatever. But still, we can only believe that is all a*
> *preparation for something in the future. But please, do not speak to me of your*
> *stupidness & slowness, for it is not true and makes me feel very badly.* (W4835)

Rev. Calvin McQuesten, Glenhurst Saskatchewan (c. 1907)
(Whitehern Museum Archives)

After leaving his position at the *Montreal Herald*, Calvin took a job as a missionary preacher and was sent out west to MacLeod and Stand Off, Alberta, where he travelled on horseback between three churches. About a year later, he decided to go back to university to become a minister. His mother made it clear that he would need to pay for his own tuition; there was no other way since all of the financial resources (Ruby's salary) were being channeled toward Tom's education. His mother explained: *Do you think of going back to University? If so, how do you mean to manage it? Tom's law-fees have made me so short; I can scarcely know what to do. . . . I seem tied hand and foot* (W5271, Jul 25 1904).

Calvin received a meagre stipend as a missionary preacher but managed to save enough money to take himself to Knox College in the fall of 1905, to begin his studies toward the ministry. He continued to work during the summers as an

Knox College on Spadina Crescent, completed in 1875

Calvin McQuesten (upper left)   Calvin ordained in 1909 at age thirty-three
at Knox College, 1909

itinerant preacher and missionary in the west, and attended school in the fall. In this way he slowly managed to pay for his education.

When Calvin was working, he was occasionally able to provide some modest financial assistance to his mother. For instance, when he was preaching at Staney Brae, Muskoka in 1905, he sent an unspecified amount to his mother. Mary is most grateful to be able to pay off a debt that she had been carrying for more than seven months: *Your enclosure reached me on Saturday and I was delighted to go out and pay some bills. It enabled me amongst other things to pay for the gas grate which was put in before Xmas which was quite a relief. It does seem perfectly astonishing where money goes* (W5359, Jul 17 1904).

Calvin was thirty-three years of age when he was ordained as a minister in the Presbyterian Church at Glenhurst, Saskatchewan. Mary was disappointed that his ordination was such a cursory affair:

> *It just seemed too bad that your ordination should have been performed in just such a hole in corner sort of style. Does Dr. Carmichael ever appear when expected! I had hoped by the paper you were to have something of a service. It does seem poor Calvin as if you were kept in the background a good deal, but we do not know what you may do some-day.* (W6419, May 15 1909)

Although Calvin was ordained in 1909, he did not finish all of his exams until the next April. He had received no financial help but had earned his own way through school. It is admirable that with all his limitations he still had the determination and even the stamina to complete his university education. When at the age of thirty-four he successfully completed his exams, Ruby was very ill. His mother wrote to him:

> *Amidst all my cares, I feel I am not half thankful enough for your health. It really is such a great blessing and such a comfort to send you off in perfect health, and after all the disappointments it is a most wonderful achievement to have finally passed all your examinations and be finally launched, for which we have great reason to thank God. One cannot forget the time, when we both decided that nevermore must you attempt examinations. It is truly wonderful, the goodness of God!* (W9033, Apr 26 1910)

Unfortunately, Calvin was never strong enough to hold a church for very long before the stress wore him down. Calvin acknowledged that he was *crippled* to some extent, both physically and mentally. Calvin also tried homesteading in Saskatchewan, living in a *shack*. He had to rely on his neighbours to seed and harvest and, just as he was on the brink of selling a good crop in 1910, it was destroyed by hail (W-MCP6-1.408, W-MCP6-1.410, W8944). He spent some time in Quebec as a minister and as a naturalist, and held executive positions for the Hamilton Bird Protection Society. He met with Jack Miner on several occasions in connection with the bird preserve at Cootes Paradise in Hamilton[12] (W8084). He loved his canoe and took many photographs,

---

[12] Calvin was president of the Hamilton Bird Protection Society in the 1930s (W8084) and was an active member until his death in 1968. Several photos on the Whitehern web site (www. whitehern.ca) include Jack Miner, the famous bird conservationist, IMG050, IMG053, IMG071, IMG124, IMG139, IMG140. The McQuestens were avid naturalists and Ruby often writes of the Field-Naturalists' outings; she was on the executive in Ottawa.

Rev. Calvin McQuesten in his birch bark canoe

including interesting native photos to accompany his article: "The Sun-Dance of the Blackfeet" (Box 14-099).[13]

From 1920 to 1950 Calvin was the much-loved chaplain of the Hamilton Mountain Sanatorium (tuberculosis), a semi-volunteer position. Was it the tragic memory of his beloved Ruby's death that motivated him to volunteer for the San? Calvin never earned more than a stipend with which to keep himself. He ran for Hamilton Alderman once but was not successful. He did, however, assist his brother Tom with his political campaigns, civic and provincial.

Calvin, like his brothers and sisters, never married. He outlived them all and, before he died in 1968 at age ninety-two, he arranged with his sisters to leave Whitehern to the city, intact with *all* family possessions, including thousands of letters, documents and photographs dating from 1819 to 1968.[14]

Jack Miner (L.) and
Rev. Calvin McQuesten (Rt.)
at Cootes Paradise
in Hamilton

[13] "The Sun-dance of the Blackfeet" was published with Calvin's photographs in *The Canadian Magazine*, Vol. XXXVII, No. 5, September 1911, (403-412); however, it may have been written in 1904. See: Box 14-040, Box 14-018, W-MCP2-3b.055, W-MCP2-3b.053, W-MCP2-3b.054, W5261. Calvin was an avid photographer; many of his photographs are available on the Whitehern web site including several photos of native Canadians: IMG030, IMG081, IMG082.
[14] Whitehern opened as a museum in 1971. It is now a National Historic Site. (see www. whitehern.ca)

Chapter 12

THOMAS NOMINATED FOR RHODES SCHOLARSHIP

What makes me feel so sore is to think of the injustice of the whole thing.
(Mary Baker McQuesten, W5199)

The Rhodes Scholarship was the major subject in the McQuesten letters in the early part of 1904 (W5199). There was great excitement at the prospect that Tom might receive it. Tom wrote to Calvin on April 24: *As to the Rhodes Scholarship, it needs a lot of grafting . . . I have a fighting chance. . . . and I am working all the pull I can. . . . Don't say much to momma about Hutton because she would be calculated to do anything if she got mad with him. It's just a toss-up if I win or not* (W8171). As there were only two candidates Tom had a strong chance of winning.

The Rhodes Scholarship was newly instituted in 1904 according to the Last Will and Testament of Cecil John Rhodes (1853-1902), the Prime Minister of Cape Colony who had earned his fortune in diamonds. In a codicil, he declared his reasons for the scholarship: "[because] a good understanding between England, Germany and the United States will secure the peace of the world, and educational relations form the strongest tie."

But Tom did not win. He would have been the first recipient of the Rhodes Scholarship, which would have been a great honour. The scholarship would have provided $1,500 per year for Tom's education at Oxford, and that would have relieved *all* of the family's financial problems, especially Ruby's as she was dedicating most of her wages to his tuition. Also his mother's income was only $1,700 per year, just $200 more than the scholarship would have been and she was responsible for a large family and house. The wait to hear the results seemed interminable for the family. Mary wrote to Calvin on April 11:

> *I scarcely dare hope and am so foolishly anxious, though I know perfectly well, that it may not be the best thing for him to have it, and I have put the matter in God's hands day after day but just like a silly mortal cannot leave it there, but carry the burden with me night and day. . . . I am just so unsettled in mind I cannot write* (W5122). *. . . . I have really got over worrying about it. The idea of Tom's going away for three years so over-burdens the honour of getting it.* (W5183)

After Tom lost the bid, it is not surprising that Mary was deeply disappointed. On May 23, 1904, she wrote to Calvin expressing her distress at the loss:

> *When one has not got good news to tell, one does not enjoy letter writing. Perhaps you will have seen the* News *before this that the Rhodes Scholarship did not come to Tom. I can scarcely believe it and must say it has given me quite a shock. Though I endeavoured to prepare myself for the worst,*

*still I could not help building on it, and I am afraid it is a very sore
disappointment to Tom, have not heard a word from him. . . . We cannot but
believe it was a most unjust decision. . . . We are quite sure that P. [Paterson]
was not Tom's equal at all. Mr. C. [Chisholm] said it was just another
instance of favouring Toronto. . . . What makes me feel so sore is to think of
the injustice of the whole thing. . . . It makes me sick to think of it, though I
know that God over rules all things and I put it into his hands and yet here I
am fretting about it, it is so wrong of me, but it seems as if I can not forget it.
Mrs. James tries to console us by telling us of the awful wickedness of Oxford,
filled with bad women.*

*But I would just have been too proud, I feel myself swelling at the
prospect and I think Tom was almost sure of getting it. I feel so anxious as to
how he comes out, after such a distracting time, poor old chap, he has really
had a hard year of it. To show you how these Toronto men act, Mr. C. told
me they actually object to Hamilton having two members on the Senate. . . .
It is all so terribly unjust that one feels hopeless. . . . It seems as if something
really ought to be done if one had some strong friend to take it up & fight it.*
(W5199)

Ruby also comments on the Rhodes Scholarship and *poor Tom's* disappointment
in her letter to Calvin. She directs her anger at the professors and reasserts her faith in
Tom and his ability. She thoughtfully does not mention the fact that the scholarship
money would have been a great personal relief for her, since her teaching salary
would no longer have been needed for Tom's education.

TO CALVIN MCQUESTEN [REV.] from his sister Ruby (W5191)
Standoff, Alberta   Ottawa Ladies' College
                                                     May 19 1904, Thursday evening

My Dearest Cal,
*It seems ages since I'd written to you and yet the days fly past so quickly. Here it
is actually near Queen's Birthday and then only a month till holiday time.*
*I was so glad to get your fine letter last week and that letter of John [Knox]
McQuesten's is certainly rich. I'll take care and send it back to you. I'm glad you had
a happy Birthday tho'. You did celebrate it on my day. It's provoking my small sketch
didn't reach you—it must have been playing a game on the way. Oh you needn't be
afraid it is too good to use.*
*And so poor Tim didn't get the scholarship. Well I feel thoroughly angry which
shows good Christian spirit but keeps me from being dejected. They had no right to
give it to anyone in preference to our Tom & I soothe myself with thinking it will be
sort of consolation to the other fellow who certainly is not nearly equal to our Tom.
But he had no right to get it when he finished his course two years ago. I don't think
it's fair. And so I feel angry at the other fellow professors and all. But I really do
believe that it must be right for Tom when it has happened thus and there is something
better in store for him. But it would have pleased the little Mither so and poor Tom!
and I guess we all feel badly—but then that is our Nature.*
*Well to-day was Mrs. Ross's Birthday and in the afternoon we had teachers'
meeting and a party afterwards. I've suddenly acquired a taste for teachers' meetings.
We had ice-cream and cake. You see we all put in ten cents as Mike [Edna] says and*

treat ourselves to keep the lady in whose honor the feast is from eating too much. It somehow seems wrong in theory but it's all right in practice.

By the way, have you read the book <u>Tom Moore</u>. *It is about the real Tom Moore and so comical and interesting. If you haven't read it I think I must send it to you. It would do you good to read it and give you a good laugh. And you could lend it to any friends out there. Let me know whether you've read it?*

And so the Mewburns are in Calgary now. I had a note from May and they like the air and feel well and May is pleased with their new home and is busy with her mother settling affairs. She sent me a pretty little cut glass affair for smelling salts to hang on my chain. So when you see me next I'll have developed a languid, faint-like air and will be constantly raising the article with all the style of the professor and his one eye-glass. . . .

Did I tell you that Margaret Ross has gone to a Sanatarium in Cambridge near Boston for treatment? It is Osteopathic treatment and Miss Hardy who has been treating Margaret here hopes it may do her good. She is to be away for six weeks so will be back here just before the Closing.

Well dear old boy, I've really exhausted my news. I'm glad you like the books the Mither sent you. I enjoy mine more and more.

By the way, on the 24th I'm invited to go with Mr. & Mrs. Rose in their gasoline launch up the canal to Long Island. They say it is a lovely trip & I only wish you were along. I'm quite looking forward to it. Well dearest take care of your self with ever so much love.   *Your Loving sister,*

Ruby

[P.S.] Friday—Dearest Cal—your letter has just come—My! how I love to hear from you—My mother says "My!" is a vulgar exclamation.

I'm so glad you like your picture—I wondered whether it was as refreshing as the brown & yellow scene, but the people here all thought you'd approve of it. I'd love to have seen that picture the day of the rainbow. It must be lovely the wide fresh view you get. It makes my mouth water.

My twin sister Tous [Tousie, Hilda] sent me a lovely green linen dress she made. You should see how elegant I look. It suits my tawny wool & Irish mug.

[Note: Ruby and Hilda are eighteen months apart in age]

                                    With lots of love. Ruby

In spite of the disappointment of losing the scholarship, Tom still had the prospect of his earnings from the lumber camp which was twenty-two dollars ($22) a month for three months or sixty-six dollars ($66). He also arranged with his professor to take the month of September off to take a job as a military surveyor before returning to university, for which he earned seventy-five dollars ($75), an amount that he thought was just too good to pass up (W5313, W-MCP3-5.057). The total for these earnings would be $143.00. However, it was still not enough for his tuition and costs, which came to $350.00 annually.

As a result of the scholarship disappointment, Ruby continues to send money to Tom for his education. In November 1904 she sent another money order: *This isn't a letter but only a scrawl with my blessing to take your money order. I was afraid you might be in need so hurried off to get it* (W-MCP2-4.096, Nov 17 1904). Ruby also is planning to send a painting to Tom that she has just finished, *a copy of a Turner* and if Tom *is good, he might just get it* (W-MCP2-4.018, Apr 11 1904).

Sample of Ruby's handwriting (W-MCP2-4.055)

Ruby sometimes follows her mother's instructions in sending money to Tom, and in this instance, to Calvin also: *Mama said that if I sent you $26 you would give Cal $15 & next time you would need more money yourself. So you can see Cal & give him his and tell him he will get a letter very soon, probably by Monday* (W-MCP2-4.055, Mar 10 1905).

If we recall that Ruby was earning $5.99 per week, the $26 represents more than a month's wages. Ruby occasionally mentions that she is doing extra tutoring in Latin and Greek to add to her income: *"it takes time though it pays better than ever so many class lectures"* (W-MCP2-4.032). Mary's insistence on a classical education is now paying off.

Ruby never shows resentment about the extra work or about sending all of her money to Tom and her family. Her good humour is often evident in her ability to recall witty excerpts for her reader:

> *By the way, I had a letter from a Mr. Doherty in China. . . . a very fine Irishman from the North of Ireland. . . . & he's speaking of the difficulty in stirring up Chinese workmen to hasten the building of a Sunday school. He says it reminded him of Kipling's lines from his experience with the Hindoos:*
>
> **It is not good for the Xtian's health to hustle the Ayrian brown.**
> **For the Xtian riles & the Ayrian smiles, & he weareth the Xtian down.**
> **For the end of the fight is a tombstone white, with the name of the late deceased.**
> **And an epitaph drear, 'A fool lies here who tried to hustle the East.'**
>
> (W-MCP2-4.032)

On another occasion Ruby repeated a limerick that she learned from a friend who thought that Calvin might find it edifying:

> *There was an old monk of Siberia*
> *Whose life became drearier, drearier*
> *Till he broke down from his cell with*
> *a h'm of a yell*
> **And eloped with the Mother Superior.**
>
> (W5208, May 27 1904)

Chapter 13

EDNA'S ABORTED SCHOLARSHIP

I really was terrified that her brain had given way. (W5398)

Margarette Edna [Ted, Oddy, Mike] McQuesten (1885-1935)

The McQuestens suffered two scholarship disappointments in 1904, with sad results for their finances. First came Tom's unsuccessful bid for the Rhodes scholarship in the spring, followed by Edna's aborted scholarship to Queen's University in August. Margarette Edna, the youngest child, was unable to attend the University because she had a mental breakdown. Edna had always demonstrated mental fragility in times of stress.

Both scholarship losses must have been sad disappointments for the McQuesten family, especially so for Ruby, because after the initial optimism that both scholarships promised, she resumed her role as the sole family member with any real earning power. To add to their poverty, Edna's medical care became an additional burden on the family. Edna's decline into madness is a particularly sad story.

In August of 1904 Edna was initially overlooked for the Scholarship in Classics to Queen's University. It was first granted to another student but Edna's mother Mary became incensed when she learned that the other student had not taken Greek and was generally less proficient in Classics. She promptly wrote to the Registrar at Queen's and when the error was corrected, she was jubilant:

> *Imagine our feelings when the reply came on Friday that it was a mistake &*
> *my daughter had won __The Governor-General's__ Scholarship in Classics. . . .*
> *Our heads were nearly turned. Just to think of little Edna. . . . She has been*
> *receiving congratulations on all sides, people have been so kind about it.*
> *Edna thinks now that after this year's rest, she will try Queen's next year, if*

she only goes a year. In fact she is full of projects. She is going to try for pupils to coach and thus make a little towards paying her music lessons. . . . Success is certainly very cheering. (W5297)

The scholarship provided a money prize and exemption from "class fees":

TO (MARGARETTE) EDNA MCQUESTEN from Queen's University (W7169)

QUEEN'S UNIVERSITY
The......Governor General's
Scholarship, value.....$75.00....and exemption
from class fees for four Sessions,
tenable during Session 1904-1905 and
three succeeding Sessions, is awarded to
...Margarette Edna. McQuesten........

...............................Registrar

Kingston......August 12th 1904.........

It is tragic that even though Mary was delighted to have secured the award for Edna, she also acknowledged from the start that Edna may be incapable of finishing even one year at Queen's University. Early in September, shortly after her daughter's breakdown, Mary wrote to Calvin at Standoff, Alberta, describing Edna's condition:

We received your letter on Saturday, Edna was very pleased to receive your hearty congratulations; it was indeed a great event in the family history. Poor Edna at present is under doctor's orders; she has been troubled with headache a long time and so as it continued after she was studying, she went to Dr. Osborne to see if it was her eyes, but he said no her eyes were all right, so then we consulted Heurner, so he ordered her to rest all the time and not go about at all; so she has the camp bed on the verandah and spends the day there and we try to nourish her in every way with raw eggs &c. It is very trying, when she wanted to enjoy her freedom from school. (W5307, Sept 6 1904)

Mary had hoped that if Edna rested for a year she might be able to attend Queen's. But the next summer in August 1905, Edna was *in such a miserable state of nervousness and weakness* that Mary did not know what to do with her, so she sent her to John Puckridge Baker, Mary's nephew by her half-brother James Alfred Baker. However, John had a *violent temper* and argued a great deal about religion, and upset Edna so much that she left abruptly and in a very poor state of mind. Mary writes to Calvin:

I have been really quite upset with Edna's letters, such long ones written in such an excitable way. She had made up her mind to leave John's. . . . Accordingly what did she do but stay at the Hicks. . . . You can imagine my feelings when a long letter came Tuesday, telling where she was, how it had rained so on Saturday. . .she had got into a fearful state of nervousness, had gone to Dr. Arnott up there. . . . O, I cannot begin to tell you all, but I really was terrified that her brain had given way. (W5398, Sep 6 1905)

Unfortunately, Edna was <u>never</u> able to take advantage of the scholarship because of her mental condition. In the fall of 1905 Edna's mental health continued to deteriorate, and finally she was taken to Montreal by a nurse. Because of the stigma against mental illness, Hilda wrote to Calvin about the need for secrecy. Edna is the "the madwoman in the attic" in the family story (see W5382 & fn).

> *In Tom's letter I warned him that if people become too inquisitive about Edna to say that the nurse came from Montreal and that Edna went back with her as the doctor advised change of scenery and invigorating air, <u>we do not mention her name unless people ask about her particularly</u>* (W5430, emphasis added). . . . *We had word from the Doctor to-day, 'Miss McQuesten has been quieter to-day (Wednesday) and has taken her nourishment fairly well.' To me, this is very encouraging, as she had taken nothing for days and we were powerless to make her. . . . Have not yet heard if we may write her. . . .*
>
> [P.S.] *<u>Pray earnestly</u>.* (W5434)

It is not known how long Edna stayed in Montreal, but she did recover somewhat over time. Ruby looked after her at the college in April and into June 1906, while her mother went to the West to inspect the missionary schools there. The family was greatly concerned about the cost of medical care for Edna. In a letter to Tom of October 1906, Mary notes that Dr. Clark charged $25 for consultation in the home, the doctor at a Mimico asylum was charging $100, and that a Mrs. B. was paying $50 a week for her daughter's care at the Guelph institution (W-MCP2-3b.047).

Edna recovered but remained fragile and suffered several more episodes. When a friend, Mrs. James came to visit, she upset Edna with her incessant talking, so that Edna never slept at all one whole night, and subsequently suffered a turn of nervous prostration (W5867, Jun 10 1907, see also W6630).

Edna remained unstable and eccentric even at her best (one of her nicknames was "Oddy") and the family always treated her with deference. In September 1920, *Edna* [was] *restless and she could do nothing but play the piano; we do not generally suffer as we did that night* (W7006). She was finally hospitalized at Homewood Sanitarium in Guelph in October, 1920, with *irrational and hysterical behaviour.* There she underwent some treatment and surgery, possibly electric shock therapy, a hysterectomy to cure the hysteria, and a lobotomy, after which she grew very quiet and tractable. Calvin states in his diary: **Oct. 10,** [I pray] *That Edna may be healed and enjoy peace of mind in Jesus Christ & family may not make remarks.* **July 12,** *Operation successfully performed.* **Oct. 26,** [Edna] *Happy at Guelph.* Edna died at the age of fifty-one at Guelph in November 1935, just one year after her mother's death.

It is undoubtedly significant that the McQuesten family used medications that later were known to induce mental illness. Whether that was the cause of Edna's condition or if it exacerbated an existing inherited condition is not known. The letters specify the medications that they used even for the children: paregoric, chlorodyne, belladonna, and calomel, which consisted of opium, morphine, laudanum, and/or mercury, in an alcohol base. Isaac's half-brother, Dr. Calvin Brooks McQuesten was their medical adviser, and he freely prescribed these medications for all members of the family. Edna demonstrated sleeplessness even as a small child and it was common practice in those days to give paregoric (opium) and whiskey to babies to quiet them (W2511n, W2469). Some doctors at the time warned against their use but they were readily available as patent medicines.

A final note on Edna's mental health: Edna was born just three days after her grandfather's death in 1855. The months preceding her birth were a time of great stress for the family. Isaac was in a financial struggle with his step-mother and was negotiating desperately with her and his father and half-brother to secure the estate, which he did. Unfortunately, he later lost the fortune in bankruptcy. Isaac was an alcoholic and was taking *stimulants* and medications for insomnia and depression, which were opium-based, and Mary was concerned about his mental health. It is not known what medications Mary took during her pregnancy with Edna, her seventh child. She complained during pregnancy of heartburn and possibly took calomel; Dr. Calvin McQuesten had recommended it for dyspepsia in one of his medical papers (W0410). There is evidence that she also drank wine during pregnancy (W2440). The effects of alcohol on the foetus were not known at that time. However, if there were foetal effects from these medications and circumstances, they were not present in all of the children and certainly Ruby and Tom appear to have been mentally robust and healthy even as children.

Margaret Edna McQuesten
(1885-1935)

Your portrait draws me to you—
that wild blonde hair, constricted
into pompadour and ringlets
frames a fine-boned face,
presents a perfect image to the world.
But tragedy shadows your eyes,
poses you, sets you apart;
one more victim of Victorian privilege.

They called you 'Oddy,' or Edna,
when they spoke of you at all.
I nickname you Sandy,
see you laughing free,
skipping barefoot
across the spreading lawns;
the walls of Whitehern
the first to shut you up.

So bright for your age,
too eager to strain against
tight and fundamental bonds
that gagged and choked you—
you, an intellect in a family
shrouded by too many cobwebs;

a family that loved you
through all the bewilderment.

Only fifty when you died,
locked away in a Guelph asylum,
when the attic no longer sufficed.
Medical gurus of the day
took your womb, part of your brain,
to 'cure your hysterics,'
left you hollow as an ivory box—
until you just closed up.

I will remember you as a faerie child,
an Isadora who never needed shoes
for dancing.

by Becky Alexander (2007, Box 14-116)

Chapter 14

TUBERCULOSIS AT THE COLLEGE

Margaret Ross dies of the *"dreaded Inflammation of the Lungs."*
(W-MCP1-3b.013, Jan 1905)

In a previous letter (W5191, May 19 1904) Ruby stated that Margaret Ross, daughter of Mrs. Ross, was being sent away for *osteopathic treatment* for her lungs. However, the treatment was not successful and Margaret died of the *dreaded inflammation of the lungs* in January of 1905. Her illness and death are significant if we recall Ruby's letters about the epidemics at the college and the repeated episodes of *grippe and scarlet fever* such as in 1902 (W4454), when Jean and Eleanor Ross were also ill (W4690). The patients did a great deal of coughing and they were placed under quarantine. It is impossible to know for certain but Margaret may have contracted the illness at that time, or she may have already been suffering from it, or she may have been a carrier. Ruby, too, may have become infected during the epidemic, although it is impossible to determine when exactly this occurred.

The *osteopathic* treatment mentioned by Ruby consisted in stimulating blood flow to the lung area. Ruby may also have been referring to a homeopathic procedure which was an early treatment for tuberculosis. Developed by Dr. Robert Koch in Germany in 1882, it was continuing in use in Canada.

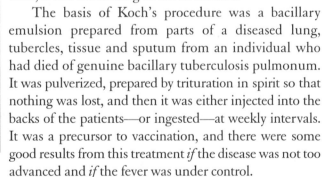

Dr. Robert Koch

The basis of Koch's procedure was a bacillary emulsion prepared from parts of a diseased lung, tubercles, tissue and sputum from an individual who had died of genuine bacillary tuberculosis pulmonum. It was pulverized, prepared by trituration in spirit so that nothing was lost, and then it was either injected into the backs of the patients—or ingested—at weekly intervals. It was a precursor to vaccination, and there were some good results from this treatment *if* the disease was not too advanced and *if* the fever was under control.

The use of that dreaded term, *inflammation of the lungs*, meant that Margaret was seriously ill and that she likely suffered from tuberculosis; yet the word "tuberculosis" is avoided in the letters, either out of fear, stigma or lack of knowledge. Certainly they knew the term and its possible consequences, because when Ruby was in Calgary, she referred to a young boy as a *hopeless tubercular invalid* (W6355). The term "consumption" was also feared and is mentioned only briefly as *the Con*.

In 1905 tuberculosis was considered "the great white plague." In Dr. Koch's Nobel Prize speech, he pointed out that "one in seven of all human beings dies from tuberculosis. If one only considers the productive middle-age groups, tuberculosis carries away one-third, and often more." The "overall Canadian tuberculosis mortality rate was around 200 deaths per 100,000 population in 1880 and . . . it did not decrease in the next 20 years."[15]

Ruby reports Margaret Ross's death to Calvin and asks him to get some flowers for her funeral in Toronto:

TO CALVIN MCQUESTEN [REV.] from his sister Ruby (W-MCP1-3b.013)
Knox College,   Ottawa Ladies' College
Toronto, Ontario   Jan 1 1905, Thursday afternoon
                                [Postmark 1905, but date illegible]

My dearest Cal,

We have just had a telegram saying that Margaret Ross passed away peacefully this morning. We knew she was very ill for on Saturday Eleanor heard she had <u>inflammation of the lungs</u> and then on Monday came the word that Margaret was very low & Eleanor was to take the morning train. We waited then for word from Eleanor which came yesterday Wednesday, and said Margaret was a little better but not to ask to have her stay, she wanted to go. So we were really prepared for the word that has just come. You can understand how they will feel about it. They will miss Margaret perhaps more than any other member of the family for she has needed so much care but they will feel resigned to have her go. She was so brave and sweet & cheerful but she suffered so much.

Yesterday when I was out, a Mrs. Kidd, the mother of a little day-pupil, Claudia Kidd, was speaking of Margaret. This Mrs. Kidd was very fond of the Ross's and has been at death's door with inflammation of the lungs herself but she wanted to do something for Margaret & thought she would like to send her some flowers. However, she did not know how to do it & I said that if she gave me the money I thought you would get some flowers for her. I know you are busy but thought you might get some flowers or whatever you think & tell them whom they are from.

Mrs. Ross always likes to see you. Even now I think they would all like to see you. The funeral is on Saturday but if you could get the flowers to them on Friday it would be better. I hope it doesn't upset some plan. With much love, dearie.

                           Your loving sister, Ruby

[P.S.] *We are going to send some flowers from the school because we think they'd like it, but Mrs. Ross doesn't believe in spending money on flowers and I don't think you need think of buying any yourself. . . . The teachers have decided to send flowers too, so here is $5 if you would order a shower bouquet of white roses tied with white satin ribbon. In these envelopes are the cards to go with our flowers and Claudia's name on those from Mrs. Kidd. It is too bad to cause you so much trouble but it was the only way we could think of.*

The curious phrase in the letter that states that Margaret did not want others *to ask to have her stay, she wanted to go* refers to the prayers being offered up for her life. She would have been experiencing prolonged pain and obviously no longer wished to live.

---

[15] (www.lung.ca/tb/tbhistory/timeline) Dr. Robert Koch (1843-1910) is regarded as one of the three main founders of microbiology, together with Louis Pasteur and Ferdinand Cohn. In 1882, Koch, a German physician and scientist, presented his discovery of *Mycobacterium tuberculosis,* the bacterium that causes tuberculosis (TB). www.historylearningsite.co.uk/robert_koch.htm

Chapter 15

RUBY AS MUSE AND MENTOR FOR CALVIN & TOM

Tom, I have often . . . wondered if in the course of time
you mighn't become a Member of Parliament. (W-MCP2-4.053)

Cal dear, I know you have some grand qualities
that God is just waiting to use greatly. (W5126)

Margaret Ross's prolonged illness, her eventual hospitalization, and later her
death had a profound effect on Ruby, as demonstrated by a deepening religious
commitment. She assumes a muse-mentor relationship with her two brothers and
attempts to guide their moral and religious life. Calvin is older than Ruby by three
years and Tom is younger by the same number, but she admonishes them both as a
"big sister." Ruby does not usually lecture her brothers or belabour any religious points,
and there are only two letters in the Whitehern archive that she writes on this theme.

A philosophical and more deeply religious turn is evident in her birthday letter
to Calvin in April 1904 when he is in Standoff, Alberta working as an itinerant
preacher. On the eve of his birthday, Ruby attempts to counter his negative thoughts
about himself. For Calvin, who obviously has expressed some doubts about his
faith, she guides him in his chosen field as a minister. She indulges in some lengthy
religious introspection and personal struggle and analysis, and ends in a kind of
religious conversion or affirmation, and a deepening of faith. The letter is longer
than her usual writing, but has been reproduced here in its entirety to demonstrate
her own struggle with her faith and her eventual spiritual commitment. The letter
also coincides with the Easter season as Easter Sunday was on April 3 in 1904.

TO CALVIN MCQUESTEN [REV.] from his sister Ruby (W5126)
Standoff, Alberta   Presbyterian [Ottawa] Ladies' College
                                                   Ottawa, Ontario
                                                   Apr 22 1904, Friday
                                                   [date listed in Whitehern Calendar]

My dearest Cal,
    You are an awful boy and I really think you need just a real scolding to cheer
you up. That other scolding seemed to have the wrong effect and didn't do a bit of
good. Oh I'll have to think of an awful one to give you someday. You may not get it for
some years, for I'll be scratching my unfortunate brains to think of something to wax
worthy on.
    My dear old Cal—to think of your giving it to yourself in that way! But I know
how you feel. Sometimes it seems to me so hopeless to think of changing my own
natural wicked self. And don't think you're the only member of our family naturally
lazy as you say. It has been a perfect struggle with me all along. The thought of
anything extra coming to be done always caused an inward groan and I'd be so

Excerpts from Ruby's letter of Apr. 22, 1904 to her brother Calvin (W5126)

ashamed of myself for kicking about things to be done and feeling awfully injured at extra demands because one had to do things.

And really Cal I used to try and pray and I just seemed to be getting more careless and more unhappy. It seemed to me I was on the wrong track someway and I didn't enjoy my Bible and found so little in it and often only read a scrap and sometimes when I was very busy I didn't read any, because it seemed such hypocrisy. And when I would read or sing "I love to go into Thy House" etc., it seemed something I didn't feel. And Sunday was a dreary sort of day—I wanted to read story books and because I felt that was too far I shoved myself out Sunday after Sunday to teach my Chinamen and so at first I couldn't teach them the gospel anyway. I hope I didn't do them any harm.

And then it came to me just how I was going, not forward, but slipping backwards and all my professions of Christianity and all my good thoughts and hopes and I felt how much superior so many people were who had no such professions and I thought, What is my hope after all—I'm just a poor, weak character, and will never do anything and will grow old and awfully fat and heavy like some of these enormous women you see and I'll be a burden to myself and to those around me.

And I just prayed to God and said that I had tried and tried and could do nothing and that I was his creature and he had made me and didn't make me for a curse but for a blessing and he must make me a servant for Him for I could do nothing. And I felt it so strongly that I was utterly past helping myself that I think for the first time, I yielded myself wholly to God. And I prayed that God, not for anything I had done, but because Christ had died for sinners not for just people but sinners and I knew I was one. And I prayed that God according as he valued his Son and Christ's blood shed for us so he would not for my sake or anything I had done, but because I was one of the sinners for whom Christ's precious blood was shed, that he would save me and use me and make me to understand the love of God and Christ Jesus, and that he would give me the Holy Spirit in my heart and that it might take possession of my heart and teach me about God and lead me and guide me.

For I felt so powerless and yet I felt that if He was God it was not beyond Him to really give me a new heart. And I prayed that he would fulfill his promise in Ezekiel 36:26, 27—"And I will put my spirit within you and cause (make) you to walk in my statutes, and ye shall keep my judgements and do them." And in Ezekiel 11:19 & Jeremiah 24:4 and in another place, "I will put my laws in the minds & write them upon the tables of their hearts." And then we are told that all the promises of God in Him are [?] and in Him, Amen.

And what appealed to me was that God had promised to make us to walk in his Commandments & to himself put a new heart within us and I took hold of it and tho' it didn't come to me all in one day, yet the whole meaning seemed to dawn on me with consciousness that that [sic] I was one of God's creatures and I had given myself to Him & the responsibility of my own sinful nature Christ had taken off from me and God's Spirit would guide me now and keep me in God's way, and I could trust him to teach me as rapidly as possible.

So often I realize how much of my life has been wasted and so little real study of the Bible done. You have all along been engaged in some real Bible study or work but I haven't and I have so very much to learn that it is enough to discourage me. But He can help me and He is going to make something of both of us—I don't mean something the world calls great—but he is going to make us so that we can be of service to him so that he can send his light through us.

And Cal dear I feel it even more strongly for you, far more strong & I don't think I am saying it because I think too much of you. I know you have some grand qualities that God is just waiting to use greatly for his work on earth. He has some way and we cannot see his guiding but he is going to "make you perfect in every good work to do his will, working in you that which is well pleasing in his sight."

Sometimes it seems as if we advance so gradually in the Christian life, and we ask for things we cannot accept. For instance, a child asks her music teacher to teach her to play & interpret Beethoven. The music teacher promises she will but she starts at the beginning, at the exercises and it takes years before the child learns Mozart or Beethoven , but the teacher is fulfilling her promise. And so it is I think with us—we'll have to do start

Reverend Calvin McQuesten
(seated, upper left) with members
of his congregation c.1906

& keep on and go back & learn and look forward & not backward. The seed grows slowly but it grows. It comforts one Cal that we hear nothing of the "hidden years of Nazareth." Christ, the perfect man, was thirty years of age before we hear of the great work done. All that time he was growing in wisdom and stature and in favor with God & man.

And Cal dear, this is only your 27th birthday and will be my 25th.[16] *We're not any older than lots of people about our age who have lived life easily. We haven't—lived life easily and we shouldn't consequently pull ourselves more to pieces and feel far more responsibility than others. So let us both set aside "the weight that doth so easily oppress us and run with patience the race that is set before us, looking unto Jesus, the author and finisher of our faith."*

I have found the regular Bible study for each day is helpful. I'm glad Mama is sending you the books. Sometimes when things were crowded I would find it hard to really fix my mind on something I was reading but with these questions I felt I must honestly answer them to the best of my ability, and so would keep my mind fixed and would pray the Holy Spirit to teach me things I couldn't understand & every lesson has seemed more helpful. There are books out teaching in a similar way the other books of the New Testament & also the Old Testament parts of it—And only wish it didn't take so long to go thro' one set. It would be nice if we could be going thro' these books at the same time. I'll be glad to get you any of these books when you want them and send them to you.

Well, this is a powerfully long letter and I must send your Birthday note on another sheet. I'll be utterly broken if I have to use four double sheets of paper on you often, Mr. McQ.

Very Many Happy Returns of the Day, my very dear brother. May this Birthday be a very happy opening for a very happy New Year. The sun's shining, the first real spring sunshine and I've taken it as a sign for the coming years.

---

[16] Ruby may have mis-calculated: Calvin was born May 1, 1876 and Ruby was born May 3, 1879. Yet the letter is dated 1904 which would make Calvin 28 and Ruby 25 in May, 1904.

The little water color I'm sending you is only a little thing a copy of one of Turner's but it has heaps of love with it.

Your Birthday is a sort of thanksgiving for me also, honey, for I thank God that I have a brother whom I can love and understand and trust and who has the same feelings for me. It isn't every girl who has a brother she can be so fond of dear, and it is something to be thankful for.

I'm sending this mounted this way, for Jarmann who does the College mounting & art work etc., did it for me and assured me it would be no more difficult to do up than sending it in a roll and it would be safe [even] to England. So be sure and tell me if the mounting is cracked or anything wrong for really I'd almost like [it] if it were, he was so dreadfully confident. I would have liked to send you several water colors and I have some fresh breezy looking ones I'll send you later but you know all art work we're supposed to keep till June for the sake of Miss Curry's exhibit, and so many have been taking [classes in] what she considers the lower branches of [art] china painting and wood work, and so few oils and water colors, that I really didn't dare to suggest sending more than one. It is such a wee one too but the various people here liked it better than the larger ones and it has a cheery little sunset. I took a great fancy for it and then I was quite interested to see it was one of Turner's. Think of me attempting to copy Turner!

By the way, did you get the cartoon of Thomas? If you didn't I'll send you mine to see. It is very comical.

Well, Sonny dear, my tongue must stop wagging, tho' it does wag on so easily to you. Don't worry yourself that it is wholly laziness that makes you dislike doing things. I know, even tho' you say you're fat & well—I'm always fat—and there is often real physical weariness & I think it is that tho' we look well, we're not really robust & all the more honor to us if we do something.

Hurrah, Sonny, it's time I stopped.

With heaps of love, a good hug & Birthday best wishes. Ruby

As usual, Ruby manages to end her rather weighty epistle with some light humour. The painting that she sent to Calvin for his birthday—her copy of a Turner with a sunset—is presently on display at Whitehern.

Ruby loved to visit art galleries, and her newly renewed faith and devotion is evident in her approach to the new Holman Hunt painting "The Light of the World." Just completed in 1904, it was on show in Canada. Her description for Tom is deeply moving and reflects an affirmation of her faith.

TO THOMAS B. MCQUESTEN from his sister, Ruby (W-MCP2-4.043)

22 Grosvenor St.,	Ottawa Ladies' College
Toronto, Ontario	Apr 15 1905 Friday [Postmark]

My dear Tim,

It seems a long time since I had written or heard from you and yet the time has been flying along.

I can't say that I have been doing anything special since I last wrote & I expect you haven't been doing anything special either studying for old exams. I'm sure you're tired of them so many years of it. Well we're finished our exam papers for the third term and are starting reports, and I'm pretty sick of those old things. But then there is no anxiety about them as there is about exams, so I shouldn't complain.

The Light of the World, **by Holman Hunt, 1904**

*On Monday night we went to the House [of Parliament]
but there was nothing on except that Mr. Barker seems
to be talking a lot about what I couldn't hear.*

    *On Tuesday we went to see Holman Hunt's picture
"The Light of the World." It represents Christ standing
knocking at the door. The door is covered with vines,
the branches of which are thick and solid from years
of growth, and weeds are growing up from the bottom,
& the hinges and nails rusty with age and the door
looks as if it were hopeless to think of opening it and
yet Christ still knocks. There is a beautiful light from
His crown over His face and down the front of his
robe & on His hand, and then in His left hand is the
lantern of conscience which shines on the door & on the
weeds (the sins that have grown) and on some apples
(which represent hereditary sin). There is so much in
the picture you have to let it grow on you for you don't
care for it much at first sight.*

    *But if it comes to Toronto & it is to go to all the cities—you & Cal must go and see
it & give it an hour if you can.*

    *David Ross was here on Tuesday, on his way back to B.C. He saw you both he said.
This isn't much of a letter but I'll write a better one later when exams & reports are done.*

    Hoping you are keeping well in spite of exams.

    With much love, Your loving sister

        Ruby McQuesten

Shortly after viewing the Holman Hunt painting, Ruby again writes to Tom
and this epistle can be seen as a companion to her letter to Calvin in which she
announces her awakening religious convictions. For Tom, Ruby acts as his muse-
mentor and declares her moral aspirations for him in law and politics. Ruby's
thoughts for Tom were stimulated by a lecture by Dr. Grenfell, a medical missionary
and a Canadian hero of the north. At this point in 1905, Tom was still two years away
from graduation; however, Ruby's *sermon* had such a profound effect upon him that
many years later he fulfilled it *to the letter*.

TO THOMAS B. MCQUESTEN from his sister Ruby (W-MCP2-4.053)
22 Grosvenor St.,   Ottawa Ladies' College
Toronto, Ontario   May 8 1905, Monday afternoon

My dearest Tom,

    *Your birthday letter was very acceptable indeed. I appreciated your remembering
the day all the more when I knew how many other things the poor old brain was
trying to keep on hand. It was a regular treat that morning to get the home letter with
letters in it from Mary, Hilda & even young Mike [Edna], and then letters from you
and Cal. I had a spare in the morning and found my letters in the mail pile and made
straight for my room to open one after another of the supply. I had a mighty good time.*

Then came a box from home, the greatest surprise with two whole new summer dresses, a blue sailor suit and a muslin and two new blouses, a couple of belts, a kerchief and a lump of maple sugar. I wondered when I would come to the end of it all,—it was far too much.

I'm glad you heard Dr. Grenfell. We have him in town now and yesterday he preached in the morning in Dominion Methodist and in the evening in the English

Sir Wilfred Thomason Grenfell,
1865-1940
(painting by Bernard Gribble)

Church and to-night we are to see his views and hear him speak in St. Andrew's. I did enjoy his sermons yesterday. I followed him around to both churches. I haven't for a long time heard a man I admired more. As you say his words all are from his real experiences in life whether outward experiences or inner ones. He is such a genuine Christian—not an intellectual Christian—but a real liver and worker like Christ, teaching while he works and heals.

And he speaks out so plainly against thinking we can be Christians in one part of our life and yet not descend to anything, to anything the world considers indecorous, too far. He brought out where Christ was telling Peter that He would go to Jerusalem, & be tried and so on and at last die and Peter said "Not so Lord" (that is going too far) and the Lord said "Get thee behind me Satan."

There are so many people who would like you to be Christians if you would only not do anything in real earnest. If you do that they think you are losing yourself, you are going too far,—they don't realize that in the Christian life as in any other life if you are to get the real meaning and the beauty and the happiness out of it you must go as far as you can and be willing to do and go further, just any place. There are lots of people who think it is all right to teach so long as you do a little painting or learn some fine art when they consider it the main thing. They don't seem to realize that it is only as you consider that teaching is for character building and that as one tries by every means in teaching to give the very best and to be the very best that it is only in this way as a life of service that there is the real pleasure.

So many people would teach a Chinaman once a Sunday, would think it extreme to teach twice and when it comes to holding a prayer meeting for more blessing, they think that is going quite too far, and so about six out of our twenty-six teachers stay for ten minutes after the class in the afternoon. And as Dr. Grenfell said so many men think medical missionaries the most unhappy of men, away off without all their fine medical instruments and appliances. "Why," he said, "we are the happiest men in the world, we wouldn't exchange for anything."

I often think, you cannot but feel when you read Christ's life how infinitely peaceful he was, what calm control, so filled with the purpose of his Father and so conscious that he was doing his will that feared no one, he had an answer always ready for any question, never flurried or hasty with crowds coming, feeling always that each thing that came was another opportunity and gladly welcoming it.

I think if people could only see this! But really Tom it is only Christ's spirit that can make people feel this. It is a strange thing and yet it is a wonderfully real time thing that Christ can and does give this Spirit that makes a monotonous round of life a whole world of opportunity,—that makes one feel the sin they have often glanced at carelessly and long to have it righted.

You know Tom I have often, tho' I have never told you, wondered what you were going to make of your life. I have wondered if in the course of time you mightn't become a Member of Parliament. I just thought about it lightly but now I can't help thinking of you and longing and praying that God in mercy to a country that has so many blind (sin-blind) leaders may in His time raise up a saviour.

You think you are young, and so you are, but one needs to begin early. It seems as if in the study of the Old Testament one cannot but see how God chose leaders, (kings and prophets) and just as these kept themselves pure and obeyed God so the people followed them and were pleasing to God and were blessed accordingly.

Tom McQuesten, 1899

Now I don't know what God may have in store for you but this I know, and it is as real as life, that God will give his Spirit, the Spirit of Christ to those who earnestly and persistently ask it. And this Spirit will enable you to separate between good and evil as you never did before, it will help you as a lawyer to distinguish that faint line between right and wrong and it will make you pray earnestly and fearfully lest you ever be allowed to get on the wrong side and lose your keen sense of the right. I think Tom this alone could keep a man pure in politics now and make him so strong that he would keep above the tide of wrong-doing and stand firm and help up others.

And you might be a statesman like Lord Shaftesbury who was the most useful and highly honored man in his time by wealthy and educated and nobility and poor alike. But this was not his aim,—it was as he himself said "In ending my life I desire only that it may be said of me that, I have served man with a patience and resignation like unto this faithful beast." This was a donkey some poor slum children had presented to him.

You know Tom though I joined the church at home and for three years taught here and tried to live a Christian life yet I got so indifferent, I really didn't enjoy reading my Bible and on Sunday I sometimes thought I'd just like to read the novels of the day and I wondered if it mightn't be a good thing to learn to dance, & play cards as nearly everybody else did and I felt pretty unhappy. I felt tho' I could hardly express it even to myself that in some way I was drifting; I was not improving and I just prayed that God would give me something in some way that I might feel if only for a short time the real joy I knew some Christians had and that I might be given some power that I might love to read my Bible. And Tom I was answered and have been happier ever since and anything I give up I have repaid to me a hundred fold.

I've never since been really unhappy—I keep studying my Bible studies, for about forty-five minutes every morning from breakfast to school and the quiet time for thought and prayer gives me a confidence and courage to enter into my day's teaching determined to let nothing be done carelessly and yet to win all I can from

Excerpts from Ruby's letter of May 8, 1905 to her brother Tom (W-MCP2-4.053)

the girls by cheerfulness and brightness, not to scold it out of them. And my life is really very happy tho' very busy. And like Dr. Grenfell I know it is just the Spirit of Christ that has made all the difference. As he said, you could try to improve the people by making regulations against drink & by building hospitals but the only real blessing that utterly changed their lives and made them new men was the Spirit of Christ. And it is just as real for us tho' Satan tries to make us think there is nothing more in Christian life than we have in these civilized times & places. Don't you believe it & let Satan spoil your chance of a grand life.

Well dear, you'll think this is a sermon but I've so often thought of you & felt I owed it to you my own brother for I want you to have the very best. With very much love and thanks for your letter.

Your loving sister, Ruby

Ruby's *grand* aspirations for Tom actually amounted to a prophecy, since that is precisely what Tom *made of his life.* He demonstrated strong moral character as a lawyer, a politician and a person. Ruby's own example and dedication to him and to the family doubtlessly had a profound effect on his character and on his remarkable career.

In October 1905, Tom had an urgent need for money and Mary wrote to Ruby to ask for her help. Ruby arranged with Mrs. Ross for an advance in wages and immediately sent it off. This is a good indication that Ruby was the only wage earner and consistent source of funds for the family, even if it required incurring a debt on her future wages. Mary is sometimes very frank about having assigned Ruby's total wages for Tom until he is established: *I hope to have her* [Ruby] *put by her salary for a trip, when Tom keeps himself* (W5002, Jun 27 1903). In another letter, Mary bemoans the fact that, *poor dear Ruby. . . . I really never thought she would have had to teach so many years and that she received so little rest while she was home in the summer* (W5307, Sep 6 1904).

Ruby's letter accompanying the money for Tom clearly expresses her selflessness and how much she misses her family.

TO MARY BAKER MCQUESTEN from her daughter Ruby (W5996)
Whitehern, Hamilton, Ontario   Ottawa Ladies' College, Ottawa, Ontario
                                                Oct 8 1905 [Estimated date]

My own darling Mitherkins,

Just a good old talk for your birthday. And this time you have a still smaller family to celebrate it at home. Nevermind! your branches though away will try not to disgrace their little Mither.

How we would all love to fight over you, Tom, Cal and I, but we can only think jealously of those who have you and look forward to the holidays. Sometimes when Miss Gallaher speaks of going home I do so long to see you just to have a good hug. I feel as if I couldn't squeeze you hard enough my own best Sweet Heart.

And then I feel thankful that I can do a little to help things along. Your letter came at noon & I was so glad to get it. I will explain to Mrs. Ross and see what can be arranged right away. Poor old Tom! I'm sure he understands how things are & it truly made me feel quite happy to think I could be of some use, though really Mother dearest I'm not doing more than you all, for you save money if I make it and Hilda and Mary are as hard working as I.

Haven't you a big, strong kind of family for such a little person? But then it's the quality! You told me not to send you anything but a letter. Well I'm really not, for the little thing to put around your shoulders when you do your hair cost next to nothing, as I had the yellow cotton from a bit of ribbon. The towel is just a cheap one & I rather liked the idea & thought perhaps Hilda might like a couple for bazaar.

It is awful the way I have to give away the value of things when I send to the family! I'm scared of scoldings! Now seeing it's such a [?] elegant thing I'm sure you must have thought it worth a fortune. Never mind dearest, you would be rich if you could reckon in money all the love of the family, and we care for that most, don't we?

Well dearest I hear one of the girls coming for the letter so must hurry up. I've been very busy yesterday & today or would have started before. So can only send

My own darling Mitherkins
...
Your letter came at noon & I was _so_ glad to get it. I will explain to Mrs. Ross and see what can be arranged right away. Poor old Tom! I'm sure he understands how things are & it really made me feel quite happy to think I could be of some use, though really Mither dearest I'm not doing more than you all,—for you save money if I make it & Hilda and Mary are as hard working as I.

Haven't you a big, strong kind of family for such a little person? But then it's the quality! ...

With hugs & kisses & loving loving thoughts to you my dear dear best of Mothers
Your affec–ate child
Ruby McQuesten

Excerpts from Ruby's letter of Oct. 8, 1905 to her mother (W5996)

my own dearest Mother my very best love and wishes for you & many more happy birthdays to come.
  With hugs & kisses & loving loving thoughts to you my dear dear best of Mothers.
                    Your affectionate child
                    Ruby McQuesten

Ruby's curious comment about Tom, **I'm sure he understands how things are**, suggests that some of the financial difficulties in the family are being kept from him and that perhaps he does not fully realize the extent of Ruby's contribution to his university education.

The McQuesten family in the garden at Whitehern, c.1893

Below:
Ruby, holding a tennis racket
is seated at front left.
Hilda wears a hat
and sits next to her.
Tom stands directly behind them.
Edna is at the far right
on the tennis court.

Above:
Calvin, tennis racket in hand,
sits at the bottom of the stairs.
His sister, Mary is standing.
Mary Baker McQuesten sits
at the top of the stairs.

Part Two

TRAGEDY:
RUBY BAKER McQUESTEN
(1879-1911)

Chapter 16

RUBY'S THWARTED ENGAGEMENT

[David] is to be told to wait till his prospects have developed. (W5622)

David Ross, Age 24   **Ruby McQuesten, Age 27**

In July and August, 1906, after Mrs. Mary McQuesten's trip west to inspect the Presbyterian Missionary posts and the Residential Schools, she and daughters Edna and Ruby took a holiday at Bay View Farm, Muskoka. The other girls, Hilda and Mary, went to stay with friends. They all knew that Ruby was exhausted and needed a quiet rest and, although Edna's mental condition had stabilized somewhat, her behaviour was so erratic that she needed to remain with her family. Always mindful of costs, Mary described the lodgings and the price: *We feel ourselves to be most fortunate, the table is very cleanly and nicely set and the food very good, plenty of cream and milk and terms moderate for Muskoka, two in the room are $5.00 each and seven the other, but they are good sized* (W5538).

While they were vacationing in Muskoka they had a visit from David Ross, son of Mrs. Anna Ross, the principal of Ottawa Ladies' College where Ruby was teaching. He was also the brother of Ruby's fellow teachers, Eleanor and Jean Ross, and of Margaret Ross who had died of tuberculosis in the previous year. At first Mary enjoyed David's visit—but we will let Mary tell the tale to Calvin:

TO [REV.] CALVIN MCQUESTEN from his mother, Mary Baker McQuesten (W5622)
Macleod, Alberta   Bayview Farm, Dorset, Ontario
                                    Aug 20 1906

My dearest Cal,
     I was glad to see by weather probs that it was cooler in Alberta, for you would feel the heat very trying; it was extremely warm here on Saturday but is somewhat

*cooler. On Wednesday we had a great surprise in the shape of David Ross. His story
at first was that he had been at home with a sore leg and before going back to his
surveying job on the C.P.R. had come up to recruit. At first I quite enjoyed his visit,
he got a canoe and we went out paddling and one day I actually started to paddle
having got on a stream so shallow that we were in danger of grounding. But alas! it
was all a sham.*

*Would you believe it he had come to propose to Ruby! It was last night she told
me, and you can imagine I scarcely slept a wink all night. It was a complete surprise
to her too, for she had never dreamed of it, he is only 24, Tom's age, is three years
younger than R. Of course I know that he is a fine tempered Christian lad, and as R.
says they have much in common, she is fond of all the Rosses, but we both think he
must wait a while till his prospects are more settled.*

*I felt rather cross with him thinking about it at all with his mother and sisters all
working for a living, but of course he tells R. that he would not be ready for two years.
He is working with the head engineer on the double track of the C.P.R. between Fort
William and Winnipeg, gets $100 a month and expects soon $125.*

*[He] Has a man working his homestead, which is 50 miles north of Regina: his
plan is to build a home there for his mother and Jean, they expect also to have Bessie's
children to bring up. But it seems to me that R. ought to do better than this, she is a
very attractive girl and it has always been a grievous disappointment that she never
seems to meet any one worth looking at.*

*Then too I do not know whether David's view of things is to be trusted, the Rosses
are as a family easily satisfied (I fancy) for they have been brought up very plainly,
and what D. [David] might consider a very comfortable home I would not at all. R. is
not worldly wise enough either.*

*He looks such a boy too and has a weak face sometimes I feel angry at his
presumption; he speaks of the wife of one of the engineers, the only lady living in a car
and I believe they both think this would not be so bad, poor simpletons. The more I
think of it the less I favour it. Sometimes I know I am thoroughly irked, for R. suggests
that they might do much home mission work there and I know that is true, but it
seems as if R. were fitted to take a fine place in a higher sphere.*

*When you write me about this do so on a separate sheet. In the meantime D.
[David] is to be told to wait till his prospects have developed. Edna is writing. Write to
Hamilton next time. With much love from all.*

> *Your mother*
> *M.B. McQuesten*

David wrote from the west to Ruby's brother, Tom, on October 9, 1906 about his
engineering job with the railroad, and he mentioned his *week in Muskoka. . . . Your
mother let me take her out in the canoe once-and once-only—for, the very next day I
upset myself close to shore and so ruined my reputation* (W-MCP2-3b.048).

It is important to realize that Ruby was twenty-seven years of age at the time.
She was already considered to be a spinster by Victorian standards and in two years
she would be twenty-nine. Mary gave a further objection on August 27, again in a
letter to Calvin:

*David Ross went off on Thursday, he is such a restless jump-about, it was
quite a relief. I feel thoroughly cross, every time I think of him, speaking to
any girl before he had any settled living at all with his mother a poor worn*

out looking woman. It is a crazy idea too, that they have of Mrs. Ross and Jean settling out on a homestead 50 miles north of Regina on which a house has to be built. But then I am afraid, I am too worldly wise, it troubles me very much too, to think that I am. (W5630)

Mary had some good reason for viewing David as *restless* for in October 1906, she reports to Calvin that *Tom had a letter from David Ross, he is with a contractor in Saskatchewan, another change* (W5697). Tom did not totally approve of David either and a few years earlier he had conveyed his opinion of David to his mother.

Tom writes that David Ross is in Toronto, getting together another party of students to sell Views [photos]; he is to be as manager and starts in the spring. I cannot understand it at all, I thought the whole thing was a failure and when Annie Anderson was here she gave us to understand that David lived on his mother for ever so long and she was tired out going with him to her friends to buy the Views. Tom says David's eyes are so bad he cannot do anything else scarcely. It is very sad. (W4815, March 1903)

These cumulative comments about David over a few years showed him to be altogether too unsettled, uneducated and unprofessional for Mary's aristocratic taste. She was not about to encourage a relationship with one of her daughters, especially Ruby who was educated, intelligent, beautiful, and *fitted to take a fine place in a higher sphere* (W5622).

Mary extracted a promise from Ruby that she and David would not engage in a courtship for two years, to which Ruby agreed. This Victorian restriction entailed neither meeting nor corresponding. In spite of her promise, Ruby and David continued their relationship secretly during that time, and her mother was very angry when she learned of the deception:

What does irritate me is, that it was all brought on by her determination to stay at Ottawa; and I do not think she realizes at all, that she brought on this heart trouble with me. I never had that at all until after I discovered she had carried out her own way with that young man and broken her word to me. (W6135)

Mary gave several reasons in her letters for a delay in the marriage; but she does not mention the most compelling reason. Her objection must have been primarily motivated by the fact that Ruby's salary was still needed for Tom's university tuition for another two years, which was *a heavy fee* (W5744). Tom would not graduate until June 1907 and his future was not even then secure, since he would require a year of articling. Perhaps Mary did not wish to admit that Ruby was the sole source of funds for Tom's education. Mary did recognize that Ruby was already frail in September 1906, when she stated to Calvin: *I do hope this will be the last year for Ottawa* (W5636).

Ruby continued teaching but was ill during much of that last year in Ottawa and throughout the following year. By the summer of 1908, she had to be sent away for treatment. Perhaps, if Ruby could have rested rather than teaching that final year, she might not have succumbed to her illness.

Chapter 17

RUBY'S HEALTH DECLINES: SHE LEAVES THE COLLEGE

[Ruby] was troubled with headaches, which did not seem to get better.
(W-MCP2-4.033)

Ruby's decline in health is recorded in the letters; it is a long slow descent with many vacillations between hope and despair but, remarkably, Ruby's letters remain cheerful throughout. In November 1906, Eleanor Ross at the Ottawa Ladies' College was so ill with *pneumonia* that she required a night nurse. Her sister Margaret had died of the dreaded *inflammation of the lungs* in early 1905. The McQuesten family feared for Ruby's health, as she was displaying some of the same symptoms. So, Hilda wrote secretly to Ruby's friend at the college, Miss Boyd, to inquire about Ruby. Miss Boyd replied revealing details about Ruby's illness, as well as the working conditions and *worries* at *a school like this:*

TO HILDA MCQUESTEN from Ruby's friend at OLC, Miss M. E. Boyd (W-MCP2-4.033)
Whitehern   Ottawa Ladies' College
Hamilton, Ontario   Nov 19 1906 Monday noon

Dear Hilda,
    Your letter got here in this morning's mail, and I cannot tell you how glad I am that you wrote to me. I felt like writing to you several times, but was afraid I might alarm you.
    You must not imagine Ruby is dreadfully ill, for she is not, and you are quite mistaken in thinking it is for Mrs. Ross and her family that she decided to take this step. She had quite made up her mind to go [home] before Jean's [Ross] name was mentioned at all. It was I who thought of Jean for I felt that she would understand so well our system of duty. Of course she cannot begin to fill Ruby's place but she will be able to keep the girls working just for this four weeks.
    I do not know just what Ruby said to you, but I am going to tell you the whole trouble, as I understand it. Soon after school was in working order for this term, she was troubled with headaches, which did not seem to get better. She went several times to Dr. Shillington and he tried various medicines but none seemed to have any effect.
    You know how noisy this place is Hilda, and when I tell you that we have some particularly noisy girls this year you will understand what a person with a headache feels like.
    The May Queen who is rooming just next to me has had the same sort of headache and has almost decided to give up for this year.
    I do think that Ruby felt more worried when she saw how quickly Eleanor [Ross] was pulled down, and when Dr. Shillington told her last Wednesday that her temperature was a few degrees above normal and that she must come back & go to bed, she decided to go home.
    On Thursday night she had no fever at all and she felt decidedly better, but on Friday she was bilious and could not eat anything at all. She was up for a while

yesterday and to-day insists upon taking some of her classes and correcting the examination papers from last week.

I hope she will continue feeling better and I believe with her, that if she can be away from the noise and confusion for a while, her headaches may leave her.

There are worries and worries in a school like this and unless we are really well, it is almost impossible to endure the strain.

Persuade her to rest at home, and above all, I would say keep from her anything which might make her worry. Avoid letting her see that you are anxious about her, and I believe with five weeks quiet she will be ready for the rest of the year.

You have no idea how I will miss her, but I feel that unless she gets completely rid of her headaches now, she will surely break down before the end of the year.

Eleanor Ross has been keeping better since last Thursday. The doctor said they might let the special night nurse go yesterday. Of course she is still very ill but we feel now that she is going to get better.

This is a dreadful scribble Hilda dear, but it is now or never for to-day, for I am on duty.   *With much love,*

                                                     M. E. Boyd

Ruby did, indeed, have many worries and responsibilities, notably earning her salary, which was the only means by which to pay for Tom's university fees. The plan, as we have seen, was that Tom might be able to earn a lawyer's salary and thereby restore the family's status and prestige. He was due to graduate from law school in June of 1907 and could then begin articling (W5868). Until then, it was Ruby who carried the burden for the possible restoration of the McQuesten family.

Ruby went home to Whitehern for a rest until the new term in January 1907. When she returned to finish the year, Jean Ross assisted with the teaching duties (W5758). In spite of being ill for at least the past year, Ruby continued working long enough to see Tom graduate. It was the last teaching she was ever able to do (W5865).

In February, while still teaching, Ruby wrote a chatty letter to Tom, describing activities at the college. No doubt she enclosed a money order, although she does not state this directly.

TO THOMAS B. MCQUESTEN from his sister Ruby (W-MCP2-4.048)

22 Grosvenor St.   Ottawa Ladies' College
Toronto, Ontario   Feb 25 1907

My dear Tom,

Silence reigns along the halls though it is only 9:10 p.m. But the children are to be out late to-morrow to a symphony concert & Dame Needham sent word to have the bells rung early. And it suits me all right.

Now that our second terms' reports are over we seem sailing in a smooth sea. And it gives me a chance to write some of the letters so long on my mind.

Mama has been sending on to me some of your and Cal's letters so it doesn't seem as if you were quite so far away. I didn't think I ever congratulated you on passing your exams. It was a poem from the Bard that first acquainted me with the fact. But you're a fine boy Tom to have passed and I hope you'll soon have all exams over for it certainly has been a very [ink blot] of study and exams.

I'm rejoicing in the fact that February is nearly over. It has really been a very cold winter here—much less outdoor sport such as snow-shoeing than usual. And though our rink was finally ready for skating by the end of January the girls have not been able to use it very much. The Civil Servants have an outdoor rink to which are welcome all who buy their coupons 4 for a quarter.

I had a lingering idea that children might not be there but they seem to have many small descendants these Civil Servants. And since Rideau Rink has been burned they and others swarm to the open rink.

A week ago Saturday Thompson-Seton was in the city & the president of our Field Naturalist Club secured him to give a lecture in the Normal. It was on "Minds of animals and Heroes" & so interesting. He spoke steadily for fully two hours & kept up our interest without the least flag. I thought he was fine when I heard him five years ago but he had certainly improved. After it was over nothing would do but I must be introduced to him—Dr. Ami and Mr. Haskett hauled me up,—& Miss Scott also who is a member of the council & we were introduced to him. Wily man! He said he remembered my name on the back of the Field Naturalist paper. But he was very genial. I think Cal met him didn't he?

Then after that I went & stayed with Miss Scott one Sunday. Miss Berry who lives there & is a music teacher & a connection I think of the Greens was out riding with Mr. Green Senior & he was asking about you & told [me]: "He is a fine fellow, that Tom McQuesten!" But I guess he didn't mean it.

Ernest Thompson Seton 1860-1946
(Photo Courtesy of the Archives of Manitoba)

I'm hoping now that your Xmas exams are over it may be a little easier. But I suppose spring exams are ahead. Well, my dear, my time is done. Take care of yourself & don't bump your head against the ceiling of that lofty mansion of yours.

With much love,
Ruby

Ruby's time in Ottawa provided a cultural richness for her by which she influenced her whole family—another of her legacies to them. In addition to her Parliamentary visits and contacts, she attended many diverse lectures, and enjoyed the society of the Field Naturalists. Ruby had a passion for nature, as did all of the McQuestens, and while at the college, she was on the executive of the Field Naturalists' Club. There, as her letter to Tom indicates, she was introduced to the renowned author, wildlife artist and naturalist, Ernest Thompson Seton.

Several of Ruby's paintings are landscapes, and she loved to tramp the outdoors, sometimes digging for fossils, which was a popular Victorian pursuit. She also did some sketching on these outings. In April of 1907, Ruby sent a landscape painting to Calvin for his birthday, and her description of the *wee scene* is both playful and poetic:

TO CALVIN MCQUESTEN [REV.] from his sister Ruby (W5828)
[Toronto, Ontario]   Ottawa Ladies' College
                                                          Apr 30 1907

My dearest Cal,

Many Happy Returns of this May Day to you. The sky has been pouring down rain all day to clear away things for a fresh beginning.

Don't you think this wee scene is a cheerful little fellow even though he is blue? There is something fresh about it to match your Irish freshness my dear. And as for the windmills—they suggest a breeze that blows away the clouds. I've done pretty well for you my boy for I think I've put in five windmills. You may possibly only be able to see three. The other two form the poetic touch and are understood. They're in there though someplace to the left of the big boat. When you look at the arms of the windmills you're to see them waving good luck to you. And with twenty arms old Zeus himself will be moved.[17]

Yes for sure piles of good fortune are on your side of the scales. You're a foolish boy, you know & I suppose you feel old because you happen to be with a lot of kids. You're only a kid yourself & when this exam is over & you've had some holidays you'll feel like one & sorely need your sedate sister to keep you in order. With very best wishes my dearest Cal. Thanks for your fine letter I'm going to answer soon. And with much love.

                                        Ever your affectionate sister,
                                        Ruby

Ruby's penultimate letter from the college to Calvin five weeks later is jolly, full of news and gossip, and she expresses no regret at giving up teaching. The letter suggests that she would like to be going west herself, and is hopeful that she'll *be happy ever after.* Ruby and David Ross have now waited out one of their prescribed two years and there is some indication that she is anticipating a continuing relationship. Ruby jokes about going west to be with Calvin and taking care of his *shack* that he has built on his homestead in Saskatchewan. But she may also be thinking of keeping house for David on <u>his</u> homestead:

By now you'll be at Glenhurst [Saskatchewan]. I can't say the name suggests anything special. You'll have to describe it to me. But now when weather is fine & the school room's dusty, the idea of any country is most attractive. Yes if there were nothing but prairie & sky, I'd like to be out with you. You'll have to take me out with you some time & I'll keep your shack. . . .

Just think, son of a gun, only three weeks till holidays then, as the fairy tale goes, <u>I'll be happy ever after</u>. I'm afraid I'm not pining at all over giving up my noble profession. Perhaps in the future I'll teach a country school for fun out in the West near your charge & you can come & teach them scripture my love & anything else you like, provided you don't flirt with the older girls. . . . Well dear old boy—it is dinner time & I must run. It's horrid; I won't be able to tell you things when I get home. I just wish you were to be in Oakville with us. But I'll see you when you come back that is one comfort. Be good to yourself. (W5865, Jun 6 1907)

---

[17] See *Colour Plate 12* of Ruby's Paintings & Pyrography for her *Windmill* painting.

Calvin's "Shack"
on his Homestead
in Saskatchewan,
1908 (IMG169)

Characteristically, Ruby is cheerful in her writing and she does not admit any illness, but her mother reports that: *Ruby . . . came home from Ottawa thoroughly worn out with a bad cough. Glad she is not returning* (W5932). Ruby did go west for treatment in 1908, but her trip did not have the *fairy tale* outcome that she wished for.

Ruby's comment about Oakville refers to the cottage where Mary took the family for nine months in 1907 when she rented Whitehern to the Hamilton Club. The Hamilton Club roof had blown off in a hurricane and the Club required a temporary replacement. The rental money of $900 came at an opportune time for the McQuestens as it helped to provide some much-needed income for overdue repairs to their home, as well as to the two attached Bold Street houses that Mary had inherited but were in serious disrepair.

> *The bills for Bold St. improvements are coming in and though large, think they can be met in course of time without taking more of my principal than $500 of the money coming from the club. I cannot forget the wonderful provision made for us this year. I am so glad to get Bold St. in such shape as to obtain the increased rental but I would have been very loath to use over a $1000 of my principal; and then to think the Club was sent along to provide the extra money; just the year when Tom needed $200 in one sum and Edna needed to be in the country. It all seems just such a wonderful and kind provision of our Heavenly Father. And this place is so delightful and not too quiet.* (W5898, Jul 5 1907)

The family's return to Whitehern after the Hamilton Club vacated was devastating: *Those wretches* had left *"wine stains"* on the mantles and, when the McQuestens finally tracked down the offensive odours, they found:

> *5 kegs of rotten oysters in the coal room. . . . Then in the ice under refrigerator was a lot of rotten fish. But with it all think we have reason to be very thankful that no real injury has been done to the house. They certainly did very stupid things.* (W6012)

Mary insisted on further compensation and they also used part of the rental income for some re-decorating.

Ruby returned home from the college just in time for Tom's graduation, an event that held a major surprise for the whole family.

Chapter 18

TOM'S THWARTED ENGAGEMENT

Tom is engaged . . . to whom is not mentioned. (W5868)

| Isabel Elliot, | Thomas Baker McQuesten, |
| U of T Graduation (1907) | U of T Graduation (1907) |

At Tom's convocation in June 1907 at the University of Toronto, his mother heard a rumour, and we can imagine her surprise and shock: *We have also heard from Mrs. Culhain that our Tom is engaged and that the whole thing is settled, to whom is not mentioned.* Earlier in the letter she notes that Tom's close friend *Grey came in escorting Miss Elliott [sic]* (W5868). This is the first mention of Miss Elliot in the letters, and Tom was, indeed, engaged to her, but had not told his mother. Mother, of course, was not pleased, but she had to handle Tom a little more diplomatically than the other children. As she and the family had been in Oakville since April 1907 and would be there until January 1908, Tom had the free time and the opportunity to pursue a relationship with Isabel.

Miss Isabel Elliot was a classmate of Tom's and may have lived in the same boarding house. She soon found out about Tom's mother's objections and attempted to gain favour by having a miniature painted of Mary by a Miss Ramsay. Mary objected to this miniature and repeatedly found fault with each stage of the painting *and* of the retouching. Finally in February 1908 she expressed her displeasure pointedly to Tom:

> *I was afraid you would not be satisfied with the miniature. At one time thought it was fair except lower part of face, too heavy altogether and*

Miss Ramsay's Miniature of Mary Baker McQuesten

then at the last I found she had worked at the lips and spoiled the eyes and spoiled that. I would not care, if she had been practicing for her own benefit, but I am more than sorry to have you disappointed. I should have stood firm by my former experience of artists and not allowed you to be drawn in. How long will Miss Ramsay stay? You had better let Miss Elliot know you are not yet pleased with it. With much love, dearie. (W6012)

Mary was not one to be seduced so easily and Miss Elliot was no match for the matriarch's wiles (W5868, W6012). The romance continued in secret for a time. Miss Elliot wrote several affectionate letters to Tom between October 1906 and April 1907. She wrote them *in a masculine hand* on office stationery, but Mary was not deceived (W-MCP3-5.077).

Precisely why Mary objected to Miss Elliot is never fully explained in the letters. However, it is not difficult to surmise that Thomas had been groomed by his mother and by his whole family to replace his father as the successful lawyer and provider who would restore the family to its former honour and dignity. Tom was their only hope; now that he had just graduated and was on the brink of becoming their saviour, it seemed he was preparing to abandon them.

Mary became anxious, having *heart palpitations,* a *nervous heart* and *blind turns.* No doubt she was very worried; Ruby and Edna were not well. She and the family had so much invested in Tom, and now she feared that she was about to lose him.

Tom certainly felt an obligation to take financial responsibility for the support of his mother and sisters, which he did after he went into law practice. He would not have earned enough money for many years to support a wife as well. To bring Isabel in to live with his mother and sisters would have been unthinkable and, as far as the letters reveal, this was never discussed as a possibility. Mary had already established, in her objection to David Ross's engagement to Ruby, that it was a disgrace for a man to consider marriage until his duty to his own family had been fulfilled. The family had made many sacrifices for Tom's education, and Ruby especially had worked herself into exhaustion and possibly worse, to enable his success. Tom was twenty-five years of age at graduation and only just beginning to show promise of providing some financial relief for the family.

Isabel Elliot wrote to Tom:
"Love me, Love my dog"

How long the relationship continued is not known, but after the fall of 1908 Tom went off to Elk Lake and Cobalt with a Toronto law firm, and there is no more record of Miss Isabel Elliot in the archives. It is not known what changed Tom's mind. Perhaps the romance paled, but he may also have realized that he could not abandon his family. Although there is no direct evidence in writing that Mary actively broke up Tom's relationship with Isabel, it did not come to fruition, and Tom continued to fulfill his duties to his family.

Some of Tom's friends were getting married and having children, but Tom stated as early as the spring of 1906 that he was *not at all anxious to follow [their] example* (W5477, May 29 1906). Tom never married although he was handsome, charming and popular. He had other relationships with women, but these were very discreet (Best 205n1). Tom's secretary, Miss Yorston, reported that she shopped for him every Christmas to purchase gifts for certain women.

Tom was invited to article at $75 per month with Royce and Henderson in Toronto after graduation. The firm was pleased with his work and even paid him while he took his exams. In July 1907, Tom's prospects with Masten, Starr and Spence in Toronto became definite and he was invited to *go in* with Masten beginning that fall at $1,000 per year.

From January to June 1909, he took charge of the firm's new law office in Elk Lake at the hub of the silver mining boom (W5990&n, Sep 21 1907). Tom's letters home to his family record frontier life, and his mother repeats portions of the letters to Calvin:

> *Place very busy, as roads are only passable whilst there is sleighing, 75 teams a day going in, of machinery, etc. Gillies with his wife is living there in a shack. . . . Houses go up in a day. Plenty of wood to burn and the weather not too cold, as it is so dry, do not feel it. He enjoyed the drive through spruce woods, as his fur coat made him utterly <u>impervious</u> to the cold, path just wide enough for team, with here & there a place for passing.* (W6327, Jan 16 1909)

> *Heard from Tom to-day, he had just returned (on the 20th) from Gowganda having walked there and back <u>66 miles</u>. A pretty rough trip and lots of lice, it is a beastly hole. Wasn't that a terrible experience? Do not know how he did it, but that is all he says.* (W6398, Apr 24 1909)

> *Tom finally turned up on Tuesday morning. . . . He was as brown as an Indian nearly and weighs 196 lbs. evidently had been leading a very lazy life, they all do up there he says. By that trip to Gowganda he expected $200,*

Gowganda, west side Pop. <100
(www.geocities.com/foxfirecan/museum.jpg)

but he is not very explicit, he has a third interest in a line of gasoline boats.
(W6436, Jun 4 1909)

Silver had been discovered in the Cobalt district in the fall of 1907, and prospectors had rushed to stake claims. Tom's arduous trip to Gowganda in April 1909 would have involved legal work connected with the staking rush. The trip must have been urgent since he travelled on foot; the area was passable only in winter when sleds could traverse the frozen swamps. However, Tom enjoyed the woods and frontier life and did not shirk from the rugged outdoors. A description of the area states:

> From Elk Lake there was another 28 miles struggling through the bush and swamps teeming with black flies, deer flies and mosquitos. Camping where they stopped at night under the trees and stars exhausted. Soon all the area was staked and men were mining for silver. The town sprang up on Gowganda's north shore overnight. Recording office, banks, homes and stores became very busy and prosperous. (www.geocities.com/foxfirecan/museum.jpg)

Tom at Elk Lake, seated, far right

Tom enjoyed his experience at Elk Lake, and he finally had a steady salary. Mary was relieved: *I feel very thankful as it seems to be an excellent opening, and they are not always obtainable* (W5912).

Tragically, just as Tom graduated in law and began working, Ruby had to give up teaching because she was exhausted and began showing signs of serious debility. At that precise point the fates of Ruby and Tom cross. By the time Tom went to Elk Lake, Ruby was regularly *having her throat sprayed.*

Chapter 19

FURTHER DECLINE IN HEALTH: RUBY SENT TO CALGARY

Dr. Arnott: *Ruby's bronchitis is almost chronic.*
(W-MCP2-4.070, Jun 17 1908)

Dr. McDonnough: *. . . there was not a thing the matter,
no bronchitis at all.* (W6169, Jun 25 1908)

*Those doctors don't know what is the matter with me
any more than I do myself.* (W6188, Jul 11 1908)

The McQuesten family finished out their rental term at Oakville and moved back into Whitehern in late December 1907 or early January 1908. They did as much re-decorating and renovating as the rental income would allow. The repairs did renew the house after so many years of neglect due to lack of funds; it had been twenty years since Isaac's death, and the only steady income during that time had been Ruby's salary while she was teaching in Ottawa from 1899 to 1907.

During their time in Oakville in the summer of 1907, Ruby's condition had improved somewhat, but she could not get rid of the cough. In May 1908, Mary wrote a rather heartless letter to Calvin, blaming Ruby for the onset of her own *heart trouble.*

> *Ruby is going twice a week to the doctor to have her throat healed she got so very worse and coughed too, that I at last took her down and doctor said it was Bronchitis, and she must come twice a week to have it sprayed, and when the warm weather comes, we hope she will get rid of it. We are trying to find a place at Ancaster to send her, it is high and dry there. I am not worrying but [sic] because her general health is so greatly improved and she says she feels a different person.*
>
> *But what does irritate me is that it was all brought on by her determination to stay at Ottawa; and I do not think she realizes at all, that she brought on this heart trouble with me. I never had that at all until after I discovered she had carried out her own way with that young man and broken her word to me. However, in your letter do not say anything about her throat.* (W6135)

Mary reveals that Ruby had *carried out her own way* with David Ross which indicates that they defied the matriarch and did not wait the prescribed two years. There is no evidence in the Whitehern archives of how the romance was continued during this time, but initially it would have been in person since David was living in Ottawa at the time. By June 1907, he, his mother and sisters were already settled on his homestead fifty miles north of Regina, so the relationship would have been continued by correspondence which Ruby later destroyed.

Ruby did not recover completely and in June 1908, Dr. Arnott examined her again. This time he diagnosed her condition as chronic bronchitis and recommended that she be sent to Calgary, Alberta for rest in cleaner air. Mary was alarmed by the report and wrote a brief letter to Tom to inform him of the bad news and the added expense:

TO THOMAS B. MCQUESTEN, ESQ., L.L.B. from his mother, Mary Baker McQuesten
(W-MCP2-4.070)

41 Isabella St.	Whitehern
Toronto, Ont.	Hamilton, Ontario
	Jun 17 1908, Wednesday
	[approximate date, postmark]

My dearest Tom,
Today I sent Hilda down to Dr. Arnott for something for myself I was needing, and he then spoke to her about Ruby. He said that Ruby's Bronchitis is almost Chronic and her hoarseness shows signs she is often asthmatic. He might go on dosing and spraying as he has been doing, but he would not take the responsibility.
The one and best thing was to send her to Calgary, he thought two or three months of rest and clean atmosphere would completely clear it up. Of course this is very upsetting but it might be worse and I am trying not to be nervous about it. I only wish the doctor had told us sooner as we may have sent her off beginning of the month.
Have written to Mrs. Whittemore as to when she is going and Hilda has written to Florrie Whittemore as to a boarding place. Of course I know the expense will be great but I trust we shall be brought through this, as we have been brought through past difficulties. With much love, dearie.   *Your Loving Mother*
                                                    M. B. McQuesten

Mary determined to have a second opinion, and consulted a Dr. McDonnough, who was reassuring. The family naturally was relieved; however, he had provided false hope. Mary informs Calvin of this *most satisfactory* news:

> *He said it was just a muscular affection of the throat brought on by teaching, using her voice when she was tired. Dr. Caven says that Dr. McD. is one of the very rare men who knows the throat so it was worth a great deal to go and hear from him that there was not a thing the matter, no bronchitis at all, but just run down a little and she needed a good change.*
> *So you may just imagine how happy we all are to-night. I had got so nervous about her lungs, but both the doctors said there was not a single symptom. You see Dr. Arnott said it was difficult to tell as the trouble was in bronchial tube but Dr. McD. knew exactly what it was, as I have explained.*
> (W6169, Jun 25 1908)

Dr. McDonnough agreed that Ruby should still go west, as she needed a *good change*. Dr. Arnott had said that it would be for two or three months, but once she was there this was gradually extended to nine months, from June 1908 to the end of March 1909. Mary confides her concerns to Calvin about the cost for Calgary:

> *Of course we expect to have high rates of board to pay and the return travelling expenses will be nearly $100, but we shall not mind if she truly comes home strong and well, as we pray God she may. You must not think*

*that she seems any worse than when you saw her, for she is not <u>now</u>, but at
end of April it was damp and raw and she was worse so then I determined
to have no more nonsense and take her to the doctor. She had a little fever
then but that passed away and now seems really much better, but the doctor
thought it best to be on the safe side and try to get completely rid of the
trouble instead of allowing it to become fixed.* (W6161, Jun 19 1908)

Mary had reason to be concerned about the expense. Ruby was no longer working
and Tom had just begun articling and earning an income, but his job as a lawyer
was not yet secure. Most of the money from the rental of Whitehern to the Hamilton
Club had been used to catch up on repairs and renovations, but there were still
several accounts owing to tradesmen and still more work to be done: *In time we shall
get them [paid] off and our house is in good shape for a long time [now] all but the
verandah, the club took every vestige of paint off and it looks very bad* (W6135, May 22
1908). Also in May, Mary had to ask Tom for a *little monetary help. . . . If you could
just send me $5.00 or $2.00 **now**, it is all I require, and I **might** need another five before
end of month. . . . I have to send Ruby away and have no money to do so* (W-MCP3-5.004,
May 16 1908).

In 1908 Ruby was sent to Calgary for a rest-cure, and her travel and medical
expenses were high. Mary acknowledges her gratitude to Tom for his help with
Ruby's trip to Calgary: *So poor Tom again came to the rescue with $90 towards her
expenses. . . . I scarcely see how I am to get through* (W6173, Jul 2 1908). A few weeks
later, Tom also promised Ruby *$30 on the first of the month* (W6236, Jul 24 1908). At a
salary of $1,000 per year, $90 represents more than a month's earnings. Even if Tom
had still been considering marriage to Isabel Elliot, he would have realized that
his whole family was now dependent upon him; Ruby was ill, and Edna's mental
condition also entailed expenses.

RUBY'S TREATMENT AT CALGARY
These troublesome men—they didn't help me a bit. (W6188)

When Ruby first arrived at Calgary she was confused about her condition and
the conflicting reports from the doctors. She thought she might be able to teach part-
time but did not yet feel able. When she found out that she was to be treated for the
Con (consumption) she became very concerned. She asked Calvin repeatedly not to
tell their mother:

TO REV. CALVIN MCQUESTEN from his sister Ruby McQuesten (W6188)
Glenhurst, Saskatchewan   1510 Fourth St. West
                                                  Calgary, Alberta
                                                  Jul 11 1908, Saturday
My dearest Cal,
    *This is not a real letter but just a line before Sunday. I reached here safely on
Monday night but didn't get my room for a couple of days so couldn't unpack and so
it was Thursday before I got at my note paper to write a line.*
    *Then yesterday I wrote a regular staver home of how nicely every thing turned out
and I told them to send it on to you so brace up to stand the strain.*

It was fine to get your letter, the first one I read, almost immediately after reaching here. And then Mama sent on your letter about 'old man Dola' and the breaking in of your land. He is a dear and it is fine news. Shure's [sic] I'll be touring the country in a private car at your expense.

It seems very queer to find myself here—I hadn't the faintest idea of it. Sometimes I feel very puzzled by the thought of the future and then I try to trust and not to worry. Sometimes I hate the thought of teaching again and don't feel a bit able for it and then again I think I might be better if I were settled at something not too hard that interested me. Those old doctors, nice as they are, I don't believe know what is the matter with me any more than I do myself.

You know that Dr. Caven both [sic] pronounced me sound, but then Dr. Caven sort of bothers me—though you mustn't tell Mama this—because from the fact that I had some temperature and I told him I had had some off & on for the last couple of months & from my general sort of weariness (probably original sin in the form of laziness) he seemed to think there might be some latent trouble and seemed to think Calgary was the place and told me I should live and rest and feed up just as if I had the "Con" [consumption].

I'm to keep [taking] my temperature. Wasn't Dr. Caven kind, he gave me his own little thermometer—and probably he will give me further advice. Mama of course doesn't know about my thermometer, so don't give me away. But I'm first going to rest and go quietly to my meals and take my two glasses of milk & a little cream & one egg between meals as Dr. Caven said and go to bed early and see if in a week, I can't get quite rid of my fever. I'm sure it is just a kind of weakness. For my temperature isn't very high and Uncle says lots of people get a temperature if they raise their little finger.

But then Uncle spoiled that nice remark by saying that I'd better prepare to stay two years out here, which I couldn't and I couldn't tell Mama. And so these troublesome men—they didn't help me a bit, though Dr. Arnott & Dr. Caven were both so kind that I feel guilty about calling them names.

Only it makes me wonder about taking a school. Country schools start beginning of Aug. & I won't dare to start then and wouldn't want a town school particularly. But it would do no harm to try & find your friend Mr. Scully—I remember the picture & explain to him I was a little run down & taking a holiday & was there a school that might have no teacher & so take me any time.

Well dear old boy I must be off now or I'll miss the mail. Don't bother about me—I'm sure I've had spells of fever all my life only I've never had a doctor bothering before. And I'll escape out of their clutches soon, never fear. It is lovely here & I'm near the Whittemores & Mary & the hills & Elbow River—it couldn't be nicer. But you'll hear all that in my letter soon.

> *With much love*
> *Ruby*

A note is required here about Ruby's stay in Calgary and why she was sent there. It is difficult to piece together just where Ruby stayed and how, or if, she received any medical treatment in Calgary. With the help of the Calgary Central Library, we have been able to piece together a composite of Ruby's stay.

Ruby's first letters from Calgary, dated July and August 1908 are from 1510 Fourth St. West, which was in the Mount Royal district and near the *hills and the Elbow River.* There was not yet a sanatorium or an official YWCA building in Calgary so she stayed in a boarding house with a Mrs. Pavey, and took her meals at the YWCA which was in a temporary house nearby. The YWCA Board had raised funds of $1,500 and had rented and furnished a house on 15th Avenue S.W. which would have been near Ruby's boarding house. The streets were not yet paved, and walking any distance in a long skirt would have been difficult.

In early November 1908, Ruby moved into a room at 316 Fifteenth Ave West, Calgary, where she boarded with a Mrs. Motter and was still *near the hills and the river.* Ruby notes that she has meal tickets and takes her meals at the YWCA. The 1908 Henderson's Directory in Calgary confirms these names and addresses, and in 1909 the YWCA is listed as being at 222 Fifteenth Ave. W., which would be near where Ruby was boarding.[18]

Unfortunately for Ruby, the new YWCA was not built until 1911, and the Calgary Sanatorium was not built until 1913, all after she left Calgary. The important point

YWCA Calgary, 223 12th Avenue S.W.
Built in 1911, <u>AFTER</u> Ruby left Calgary

here is that there was no formal medical treatment for tuberculosis or chronic bronchitis while Ruby was in Calgary in 1908 and 1909. Yet, curiously, Calgary was being promoted as "The Denver of Canada" and was recommended by doctors from as far away as Hamilton, Ontario. Ruby's friends from Hamilton, the Whittemores, were also sent to Calgary for their health (W6188).

Ruby does not mention much about her medical treatment. She takes her own temperature and weighs herself regularly. She does not mention a doctor or a nurse in all of her time in Calgary. There may have been some medical advice connected with the YWCA but Ruby gives no indication of this. The Calgary Public Library supplies some further details about Calgary as a tuberculosis treatment centre in 1908 and 1909 that conform to Ruby's experience there:

> Although the climate of the city was touted as restorative for people suffering from TB, there doesn't appear to have been a san in the city until . . . 1913. . . .

---

[18] Calgary Central Library e-mail States: "From the 1908 Henderson's Directory: Motter, Jesse h 316 15th Avenue West. There is no entry in the 1908 directory for the YWCA, but it does appear in the 1909 Henderson's Directory: YWCA, Elizabeth Bradshaw, secretary, 222 15th Ave W. Phone 1425." This is very close to where Ruby was living. This Y may have been in existence in 1908 but was not counted in the Directory, OR there may have been a temporary building that was being used as the Y until the new one was built at 223 12th Avenue S.W. in 1910 to 1911, but this was *after* Ruby left Calgary. "In 1915 construction began on the Central Alberta Sanatorium. It was also known as the Keith Sanatorium and the Baker Memorial Sanatorium." (Calgary Public Library)

In Calgary in 1908 it looks like a patient suffering from tuberculosis who was severely debilitated, may have been in the isolation Hospital which was part of the Calgary General Hospital. In many cases, however, TB sufferers may have been left to their own devices. . . . The result was that many people came to Calgary for the restorative climate, but there were no facilities to care for them. It appears that many people believed that the dry mountain air would, itself provide a cure. (E-Mail from Calgary Public Library archives, July 2008)

Neither the doctors nor the McQuesten family had yet admitted that Ruby had developed the dreaded "Con," and the family hoped that she just needed a rest, fresh air and feeding. Ruby's uncle, Dr. Calvin Brooks McQuesten appeared to know the situation, though, since he told her that she should expect to stay for two years.

Ruby took pleasure in tramping the Calgary hills and enjoying the scenery, doing her sketching and even horseback riding (W-MCP3-5.003). She visited Lake Louise and Banff, although her mother initially begrudged the expense since finances were still tight. Mary became satisfied when she found that a trip to the Rockies was involved. Ruby was feeling much better, her spirits were high and they continued high through July, August and into September.

TO REV. CALVIN MCQUESTEN from his sister Ruby (W6229)
Glenhurst, Saskatchewan   Lake Louise Chalet,
                                                 Banff, Alberta
                                                 Jul 22 & Jul 28 1908

My dear old Cal,

Have been having the time of my life here to-day, tremendous excitement. It is really this stiff new pen that causes the wriggles, not the excitement.

When I look at this disreputable sheet it seems a shame to send it however if I hadn't started this before it mightn't be going on now. I'm feeling better I'm sure only at present after drinking my three glasses of milk with cream in back and having finished my third meal. I feel as Tom says or is it your wicked expression swollen like a p. p. if you can't translate I refuse anything more.

Now you see I've returned to ordinary life yet it doesn't seem ordinary either— This morning I started out from a real walk around the hills that surround Calgary. I started at twenty minutes to nine, a beautiful cool breezy morning with plenty of clouds that cast fine shadows here & there and made the scene a perfect picture. I often wished you were there with me.

Calgary has really a most picturesque situation and to see the city below & the rolling hills & hollows the mountains beyond so faint in color & yet so distinct in outline, it was all just charming. I suppose I encircled a quarter of the city & it was eleven o'clock when I reached home. The flowers are very pretty. I heard squeaks which might come from a bird or a cricket & which I suppose the gophers make—there was nothing alive in sight & plenty of gopher holes. I just longed to take you away from your nasty 'mosquitoey' country where you could enjoy life. It is wonderfully free from such things here.

Well as you have been in Laggan, I'll not have to describe it. It is certainly a gem of a place, I couldn't imagine anything more beautiful than that lake and in the midst of those mountains such a green lake & the snow on the mountains & the lawn in front of the chalet had rows of fairy poppies, orange and yellow & white. The whole coloring was wonderful. I think I did pretty well for one day.

Mrs. Whittemore was not able to attempt anything & quite satisfied to sit on the veranda, so about ten o'clock I started up the mountain very slowly. I took the path to the right all the way up which is longer but more interesting I think & I broke the ascent by gathering flowers,—such lovely mauve daises & rose colored 'painters' brush & pale yellow columbine & something that looks like heather. A nice fat man gathered me the red flowers & he had been very warm before & it didn't cool him any.

And so I saw Mirror Lake and went right up around Lake Agnes & rested & took a lovely drink & then trotted merrily down the other way, hippity-hopping & any old way as I was by my lonesome & enjoying myself immensely. The fragrance of the pines was wonderful after the scentless Calgary air. By the time I reached the bottom I realized that I felt somewhat shaken up & perhaps it would have been better to have come down soberly—but who cares!

Then in the afternoon—there is nothing like being reckless you know—I was induced by two fat Americans who nevertheless did not offer to treat tho' my lady wore diamonds in her ears & fingers & toes?—to go for a pony ride around saddleback Mountain a trip of from two to three hours. I'll have to tell you some other time about those funny people—how the little fat man had to be boosted over the saddle & how when he reached the summit he positively & I'm afraid rudely refused to mount again—his wife whispered in my ear he was scared—how he trotted all the way down ahead of us. Well it was most interesting & I really wasn't nervous but I was most dreadfully weary when I reached the chalet. However the beautiful bath with its steaming water came to the rescue. How we did enjoy the luxury of a bathroom, snow white & spotless, just to ourselves!

Then it was dinner time & then a rush to pay our bill & pack the grip & take the stage down to Banff. We spent the night at the Sanatorium there & in the morning I had just time to see the Cave & Basin when it was train time & one o 'clock found us in Calgary, the roughly wearied & yet well satisfied. And ever since I've been getting the stiffness out of me & I think it has just gone to-day.

Did I tell you we have a couple of good singers in the house here, very comical chaps too & it makes things quite cheerful. I've been here three weeks yesterday & with my trip to Laggan included in that time it seems a long time.

But my spirits have gone up considerably & I just try not to think or plan about anything for I think someway things will work out as they should. It is cool to-night & I'm sitting out buttoned up to the neck.

Well good-bye Sonny—I wish you were enjoying good things such as I have but your time is half over.

With much love
Your affectionate sister, Ruby

Ruby continues to have a pleasant time; she is feeling well, putting on weight and generally "loafing" around Calgary during August and into September:

For I really am getting on well now. Yesterday morning I went to see a procession—it was labour day and though I stood around all morning & felt pretty tired my temperature was normal at noon and again at night. . . . So really I'm doing well and I'm going to keep my temperature now every day since it is so good & I'll let you know next week the result. I'll try & remember to get weighed again to-morrow.

Really I hadn't wanted to stay longer than Sept. but in Tom's last letter he
was so insistent that I was more than prepared for it. It is a nuisance to have
to send out my big coat. . . .

(Wednesday) Was weighed this morning & have gained 4 1/2 lbs more &
now weigh 123 1/2 lbs—no fairy. If I put on 4 more it will be as much as I ever
weighed in my life. Just see me put on those lbs and come prancing home. I
had no temperature to-day—that is three days running.

This morning was out on the hills & never saw the mountains so beautiful
before—white & shining with the snow on them. I just wish you could see them.
These hills will be worn away with my pacing. (W6266, Sep 8 1908)

In September, the doctors decided that Ruby would benefit from staying longer
and then declared that she should stay all winter. Ruby was concerned about the cold,
yet fresh cold dry air was the recommended medical treatment for tuberculosis, and
patients were frequently bundled up outdoors on verandas in fur coats and hats.

It's all finally off between David and myself

Did Ruby and David meet while they were both out west? Possibly they did since
he was already out west, although some distance away from Calgary. As mentioned
earlier, David had taken a homestead north of Regina with his mother and sisters. In
July 1907, Mary had received a letter from Mrs. Ross describing her life with David
out west *in glowing colours,* but it is obvious from Mary's negative comments that
she is not impressed, and is still not prepared to consider David Ross as a possible
partner for Ruby:

Mrs. Ross writes of her Western home in glowing colours, but I understand
why she enlarges on the beauty of David's homestead as well as her own. In
the meantime they and their belongings are crowded into D's small house,
theirs will not be built till next year. Poor David has to build it, it will be
of logs plastered over. Of course I can understand Mrs. R's satisfaction in
having a spot she can call her own and being with David, but when the
winter comes it will not be so delightful. Eleanor had received letter from
Jean [Ross] telling of her trials, she had bought some hens and put 12 doz.
eggs (Plymouth Rock) under them but they ate and broke the eggs and two
chickens were the result. (W5908)

David and Ruby may have met at Banff, but there is no written record of it.
Ruby's high spirits might have been an indication of some contact between them.
They did, at the very least, correspond with one another. Eventually Mary found
them out and was extremely angry; she blamed them for bringing on her nervous
heart.

In September 1908, Ruby wrote to Calvin from Calgary in response to his
suggestion that she visit the Rosses:

I couldn't do it . . . without Mama's knowledge—she would certainly hear.
And I wouldn't mention the name to her again. It would spoil any good she
may have rec'd and I'm afraid from the last letter she is really very poorly
again. (W6281)

About a month later, Ruby informs Calvin that the relationship with David Ross is *finally off*:

TO REV. CALVIN MCQUESTEN from his sister Ruby McQuesten (W6302)
Glenhurst, Saskatchewan   1510 Fourth St. West,
                                                      Calgary, Alberta
                                                      Oct 1 1908

My dearest Cal,
I suppose there is not much time left for this to reach you but it should be plenty if you don't leave [for home] till the 8th. Poor old fellow you'll be glad to get back to civilization again. It is a good thing to have variety in life even of a mosquitoey [sic] variety. No more humming except in your dreams. And no more dainty bachelor drinks? Do you feel entirely glad Cal or a little sad? Mostly glad I expect.
I suppose I may as well tell you, if it will make you happier, that it's all finally off between David & myself. It was his decision and everything is now over and done for. So you can burn this letter & we'll not mention the subject again.
Last week it was winter from Wed. till Sunday. I wonder if you suffered from the cold. However it is warm again now.
The last time I was weighed I had gained another five pounds. So I'm 128 now or 1/2 lb. more than my heaviest weight in Ottawa. I have just written to Dr. Caven. Tom is to phone & find out his decision as to whether I stay till the end of Oct. or Nov.
They say now that it is to be beautiful weather since the snow is over but people romance a good deal I find. Harry Whittemore said one day how I was sitting on their verandah & it was a lovely cool day but not cold—"you should stay all winter Ruby— it is weather just like this."
A lady told me she found the winters bitterly cold here another that the dust storms were constant every day last winter. Then another lady said for the first year she was cold all the time winter & summer. And so it goes. Between them all & in spite of them all the weather takes its course & [is?] finishing out its [whines?] & into smiles. However it is not a bad climate by any means & I'd be an ungrateful fatty if I didn't like it.
With much love old boy, (I don't mean the "old boy").
                                                      Your affec'ate sister
                                                      Ruby

It is obvious that Ruby trusted Calvin and confided in him about her continuing relationship with David. She also requested that he burn the letter, which he obviously did not to do. Unfortunately, a calamity struck when one of her confidential letters to Calvin went astray and was sent to the dead letter office and then to Whitehern, so her mother found it. This would have reflected poorly on both Ruby and Calvin since their mother now knew that he was complicit. Ruby reveals this unfortunate incident to Calvin in November 1908:

> *Did Mama tell you that a letter I had sent to you in Aug. had been returned to me from the dead letter office [?]. It had your address on in full & <u>I would rather that any other letter had gone astray. You must have wondered at not receiving it until the enclosed. However, I'll finish the process & cremate the whole business</u>* [emphasis added]. *Thank you for answering my last letter so completely. It eased my mind as after receiving this one from the dead letter office I would have been wondering about the fate of the other.* (W6310)

Several photographs offer a good indication that a relationship continued between Ruby and David even after her promise to her mother. In one photo Ruby had let down her hair and bared her shoulders. In the Victorian age a woman would never have let her hair down except in private, and a photo of this type would have been taken for an intimate friend, lover or fiancé.

Was Mary responsible for the break-up of the romance between Ruby and David? Was she so financially desperate that she really <u>needed</u> Ruby to work for another two years so that Tom could finish University? Did David break off the relationship because he could see that Ruby was not recovering? He carried the memory of having already lost his sister, Margaret, to the dreaded *inflammation of the lungs*, and now Ruby was displaying similar symptoms and was being treated for the *Con*. Was the winter in Calgary too severe for Ruby's condition? She complained that it *checked her energy* and made her lazy (W6334). Or was the failed romance the psychological trigger that precipitated Ruby's decline? I leave it to the reader to judge on these many questions, but it can be argued that the answer to all of the above queries is, Yes. A further question: would Ruby's health have allowed her to withstand the rigours of a homesteading life in the Canadian northwest?

In attempting to form a conclusion, one must take into account the historical determinants of the Victorian age which governed the tragic set of circumstances that worked against the two young people, and especially against a woman.

Ruby stayed in Calgary for nine months, from early July 1908 to the end of March 1909. She felt quite well during the fall and into November 1908; she had gained weight and was in good humour. Then began Ruby's decline, which coincided with both the break-up of her relationship with David and the onset of winter.

Even though Tom was working in December 1908, the McQuesten Christmas again was lean. Mary was under expense for some painful dental work and regretted that she had to spend Tom's $2.00 on that, and she *was so disappointed that [she] cried*. The dentist gave her tooth a *severe treatment with iodine*. Tom had been sending some money to Ruby, but Mary instructed him:

> As to the money for Ruby if you are so short you need not send it at all . . .
> and we can send it in January. I have none to spare now and am not sending

any. But just thought you might be thinking of sending something for Xmas
and it would be better to send money. (W-MCP3-5.080, Dec 10 1908)

Before returning home in April 1909, Ruby wrote to Calvin to meet her in
Winnipeg as they crossed paths; she on her way home and he on his way farther west
to his preaching post in Saskatchewan (W6369, W6377). After seeing Ruby, Calvin
gave a report of her poor condition, not to his family, but to their friend Marion
Robinson, who replied:

I was grieved to hear of her condition when you saw her in Winnipeg. I . . .
was disappointed that she was not better for her long stay in Calgary. I fancy
she got too homesick out there and that now she will gain and perhaps feel
the good of her months in the West. (W7798, May 29 1909)

* * * * *

Nearly a century after these events transpired, the dramatic monologue which
follows drew its inspiration from Ruby's story and the Whitehern letters:

In Confidence *(Calgary, November 1908)*

Thank you, gentle lady, for your kindness these afternoons.
Our luncheons are a solace and a boon, you're the only one
with whom I can unburden my aching heart. Quiet attention
and the wisdom of your years are balm to my wounds. I know
my secrets are safe here with you; no confidence will go
beyond this room. Strange I've had to journey so far to be free
to speak of these things.
                    It's all over between David and me.
He broke it off, seeing me here and it's clear they're treating me
for the "Con," and I can't say I blame him. Mother still doesn't
know, she thinks this dreadful cough is bronchitis and every day
that I can spare her the truth is a day made easier in a life
that's been too hard.
                    My Mitherkins isn't hardy, you see,
her iron will's just façade. We took such a fright when father
died and left poor Mither with no money, and six of us to raise
by herself in that big house. She said we every one had to be
strong for her, she'd never bear it if we weren't. So I had to help
in every way I could, she'd never manage it all on her own.
That's why when David proposed to me two years ago
and she said *NO*—oh not in so many words, just *Wait two years*
but what she meant was *No*—I dared not cross her. Had to bide
my time and hope for the best but all that's gone now. Why,
this past spring she even blamed her heart trouble on my
corresponding with David and seeing him!

Afternoon Tea with Biscuits,
painted by Ruby in 1903
(Also reproduced as
Colourplate 19)

Did she really think
"waiting two years" meant we'd no longer see one another?
Oh, how different things might have been if only she'd embraced
David's proposal, seen how happy we would be. But she could
only conceive of material prospects. David's homesteading
was too modest for her grander vision. *Ruby was fitted
for a fine place*, is what she said to Cal. So I went back
to teaching, had to help her, you see, and help Tom to finish
school for he will be a great man one day, I know it. But
I kept getting sick in Ottawa, and now it's come to this. . .
        Thank you, yes, a cup of tea would be lovely. Yes,
please, cream. You see, I've never felt my mother's need
of material comforts. A humble home with the man I love,
a simple life in service of God and community, would suit me
just fine. But there's no chance of that now;
                        my poor health will never allow it.
I feel as though some part of me died when we were denied; and
her lack of faith broke something in David's spirit, too. Strange,
that a wee frightened bird should wield such power over others' lives!

        So, my service has been to family, and that's as it should be.
We all of us, after all, are leaves blowing in the wind, it's not for us
to pick and choose. Now it's for me to pick myself up and put on
a cheery face, write thank-you notes to people back home who send
me little books and other fine things. But oh! I'd trade these trinkets
in a snap for one more day with my David, we two alone and him
brushing out my long hair as he'd do. His gentle stroke: that's what
I long for. That's the place where this broken heart belongs.

by **Eleanore Kosydar** (Box 14-112, 2006)

Chapter 20

RUBY COMES HOME AND
THEN TO THE GRAVENHURST SANITARIUM

It is really disappointing to have her come home in such poor shape
after [Calgary]. (W6387)

Muskoka Cottage Sanitarium *[sic]* **at Gravenhurst,**
Canada's first sanitarium, officially opened in 1897 *(courtesy of Muskoka Hospitals)*

When Ruby came home from Calgary in early April 1909, it was obvious that she was not well. Mary laments her condition to Calvin:

> *Ruby reached us only last night. When she got to Toronto on Monday, she*
> *thought she would see Dr. Caven . . . as she had such a miserable cold. . . . She*
> *is naturally tired out. At the same time it is really disappointing to have her*
> *come home in such poor shape after nine months absence. Do not think she*
> *has been well since journey.* (W6387, Apr 8 1909)

Ruby required two weeks' rest at home and then was sent to a sanitarium[19] in

---

[19] **A note on the spelling**: As previously noted in the Introduction, the reader's attention is drawn to the various spellings for **"sanatorium"** throughout. In Canada the first anti-tuberculosis association was formed in 1895. The first institution was built on Muskoka Lake near Gravenhurst in 1897 as "The Cottage Sanitarium," followed by the "Gravenhurst Free Sanitarium" in 1898. The name **"sanitarium"** was in their charter, so it is still being used. In 1904, it was felt that a distinction should be made between the health resort type of **"sanitarium"** and the new tuberculosis hospitals, so a switch was made to the Latin root *sano*, to heal. The Hamilton Health Association received its charter in 1905 and opened the **"Mountain Sanatorium"** in 1906; this convention was followed by most tuberculosis hospitals (www.lung.ca/tb/tbhistory/sanatoriums). If any alternative spelling is used in a direct quotation, we have transcribed it as written.

Gravenhurst. Later she was moved to the "Minnewaska," another Gravenhurst sanitarium, which was surrounded by tents and cottages so that patients could benefit from the "fresh air cure." By this time, Calvin was at his homestead in Saskatchewan and his mother delayed for nearly four months before telling him that Ruby had to be sent away again. Possibly she feared alarming him further. Or she may have been waiting so that she could report some improvement in Ruby's condition.

The Minnewaska Sanitarium at Gravenhurst, Ontario, c.1909 *(Ontario Archives)*

Finally, at the end of August 1909, Mary gave Calvin a full report. It must have been a very difficult letter to write—and to receive, especially as she had to admit that the Calgary treatment had been a failure. She quoted Dr. Parfitt as saying that *"Calgary was too windy, not a place for R. at all."*

TO REV. CALVIN MCQUESTEN from his mother, Mary Baker McQuesten (W6509)
Glenhurst, Saskatchewan,   Whitehern
                                                     Hamilton, Ontario
                                                     Aug 30 1909

My dear Calvin,
*   After I wrote you on Saturday, it occurred to me, supposing you had a chance to sell your homestead when you were ready to leave there would be the $500 mortgage on it. If you once put it on, then you would almost have to keep it till you paid that off and what would your taxes be? Your belated letter came this morning and you question me as to my summer outing and I had been expecting it and I feel that I owe it to you to spend the money you sent me in that way and yet I need it so much for other purposes that I did not like to spend it on a trip.*
*   So I think I must just at last tell that we have been under extra expense for Ruby. Before going further I want to tell you so that you will not be alarmed, that she is now we believe out of danger and getting on rapidly.*
*   Well, when Ruby reached Toronto from Winnipeg she went to Dr. Caven and he advised her to go to a Sanitarium at Gravenhurst under a Dr. Parfitt in whom he had the greatest confidence. This was a new place started in March. Dr. C. said for her just to go for two or three months, and there she could learn how to take care of herself. I suppose he did not wish to discourage her, but he must have known that it takes at least a year to make a cure.*

Of course this gave us all a terrible shock and we decided as you were so far from home, it was useless to tell you, and we would wait till you came home and by that time she would be better. After she had rested here for two weeks and Heurner [Dr. Mullin] attended to her, her fever was lower and Mrs. Mullin and Hilda were up with her, they were delighted with the doctor, the nurses and everything about the place, and Ruby was quite happy too.

The present system is to keep the patient perfectly quiet and feed them well. By the blessing of God Ruby never went back. And when Tom went to see her in June on his way from Elk Lake, the doctor said the disease had been checked, at first he was afraid it was in her throat but it was not.

Then two weeks later Hilda went to see her. About the first of July she was moved into a tent a fine large one with floor and comfortably furnished, R. said she felt better immediately; the nurse says she is getting fat and she enjoys her food thoroughly and eats well. Her card on Friday says "I must touch wood, have been feeling especially well these last few days and my temperature is 'out of sight'" so we feel she is getting on finely.

The doctor also uses the new treatment of injecting tuberculin into the back to destroy the germ, the effect of this is to increase the temperature, but evidently now since it was "out of sight," it has had a fine effect upon her. Dr. Parfitt himself nearly died of it and was given up but fought it out and is now a strong fine looking man; he is a very fine man too and takes the greatest care of his patients. His wife also is a fine woman and so is Mrs. Fournier the head of the house.

It is called "The Minnewaska" and was an Hotel which was bought with 14 acres of land, it is fitted up with steam heating &c and very comfortable, they have excellent food, and we can but feel grateful to God that such a place was ready when we needed it. Crawford Pawis is up there and though he seemed very ill, the doctor thinks he will be moving round by the spring, it is quite wonderful the cures we hear of.

Gordon Gates was there but there was no hope of him from the first, it had gone on too long, so he was brought home. Whilst there he was very kind sending Ruby papers and magazines and made his sister come to see her, and Miss Gates came to see me after she returned and sent garden roses while we had them. The poor sister said he was her child companion. They always went every place together for they did not go into society.

Dr. P. [Parfitt] said Calgary was too windy, not a place for R. at all.

I must tell you that Jean Black McKerracher is in the Manse at Gravenhurst and she wrote inviting any of the family that wanted to go up and stay with her, so H. [Hilda] did and found Mr. McK. so kind & nice and most hospitable, so I am sure if you could stop off on your way home, you could just stay overnight with him and you could get meals at the sanitarium for 25cts. Jean will probably be here in October, but you could introduce yourself and get your meals at the san. Mr. McK. & all the Blacks have been so nice and kind in visiting Ruby.

"The Minnewaska" is not far from the Manse, within the limits of Gravenhurst. I cannot tell you how thankful we are for the good hope we have, for it was a disappointment when she came home from Calgary and had to be sent right off again. Now I think the very hot weather is over, really cold *to-day. You see I could hardly go to a place by myself and it takes the two girls to keep the house going.*

Maggie [MacKay] asked me to Toronto, but think I will wait till you are back here before I go, it would be nicer to go out for little walks with you. Tom helps all he can

and he wants to get your answers to his questions before deciding. Of course if one
risks nothing one wins nothing. We pray that you may be guided.
     R. [Ruby] will be writing you now as I have told the tale.
                                                  With much love,
                                                  Your mother [M. B. McQuesten]

It is a curious example of family intrigue that Mary had been keeping Ruby's
condition secret from Calvin throughout the summer of 1909, and Calvin had also
been keeping his own knowledge of Ruby's condition secret from his mother. Calvin
already knew that Ruby was failing since he had seen her in Winnipeg at the end
of March or early April, and he revealed this when he wrote to Marion Robinson
and stated his alarm at Ruby's condition—but he did not tell his mother (W7798).
Perhaps they did not wish to alarm one another or others in the family, particularly
Edna. Ruby is complicit in the ruse, since she sent two letters to Calvin during this
time but enclosed them in letters from Whitehern so that she appeared to be writing
from home (W6402, W6472).

Mary acknowledges that Ruby's illness has created *extra expense* for the family;
Ruby was receiving the homeopathic treatment developed by Dr. Koch in which the
tuberculin is injected into the back of the patient in order *to destroy the germ.* It brought
good results if the fever was not too high, and it seemed to be working for Ruby and
her fever. It may have been the same treatment that Margaret Ross received, but her
dreaded inflammation of the lungs was too far advanced and she died.

Ruby received one final letter from David Ross in September 1909, but she tore
it up and refused to discuss it with her mother. Did Ruby bear a grudge against her
mother for delaying the relationship and for forcing her to work the extra two years,
during which time she became seriously ill? That is the last note from David Ross
and, as Ruby noted previously, she had *cremated* all of their correspondence, so there
is no personal written record of their romance—sadly, no love letters—although the
relationship lasted from 1906 to 1909.

TO REV. CALVIN MCQUESTEN, B.A. from his mother, Mary B. McQuesten (Box 12-471)
Glenhurst, Saskatchewan   Gravenhurst, Ontario
                                           Sep 16 1909 [approximate date]

My dearest Cal,
     Your letter of the 9ᵗʰ seemed to come very quickly it reached us on the 14ᵗʰ. I forgot
in very last letter to mention, that R. [Ruby] received David Ross's letter with yours.
Shortly after I gave it to her, I found her tearing it to bits, did not know if she was
pleased or displeased, <u>looked</u> the latter, said she had not heard from him, since she
was in Calgary. I said, I wondered he had not written long ago, but she would say
nothing; to-day I asked her if we would acknowledge it or tell you to do so, but could
get no satisfaction, she said, he knew she was not able to write & "there was no use in
your butting in."
     I was relieved to hear, that you quite agreed with us about not going to Arizona,
had an idea you were building greatly on R.'s going there. I am thankful to have
come to a decision, for the indecision was wearing me out. R. has been having some
very good days and I feel we are just in the hands of God, and He will do right; these

months have taught me resignation for which I am very thankful, as it keeps me from being so painfully nervous as I was.

I get a warm stone and wrap myself up thoroughly so I can sit out and read to Ruby with the lamp on the shelf, which she enjoys very much. . . . Last week's British Weekly with Whyte's address on James Fraser was very uplifting to me, the Christian Life is a constant struggle and it is comforting to hear how others found it and how they finally overcame.

[Your loving mother, M. B. McQuesten]

Ruby was not able to write many letters while at the sanitaria because she was compelled to rest. She was bedridden and reclining on the veranda of the tent most of the time and, consequently, had to write in pencil. Writing was not encouraged as it was considered to be exhausting; nevertheless, several key letters in Ruby's hand are extant from her time at Gravenhurst.

TO MARY BAKER MCQUESTEN from her daughter, Ruby (W6532)
Whitehern   [Gravenhurst, Ontario]
Hamilton, Ontario   Sep 20 1909

My darling Mother,

Am writing by candle light for the evenings are closing in so early now and dinner is so late that it is dark before I put in my last mouthfuls. To-night I had ice-cream sent by one of the bed patients, a Mr. Grant, before I had eaten, besides the soup & meat course, bread pudding & peach tart. I can hear you crying out that you want peach tarts too! Poor little thing!

I can't say that my fever is quite extinct yet but if it keeps coming down it will be sure enough. I'll send Mrs. Fournier's receipt. The doctor was away, so he didn't get his money so soon and he hasn't given me his receipts yet.

The last few inches of the pencil Tom gave me never came back and I have a new one and it is not as nice and never will be.

Mr. McKeracher came in this morning with a beautiful bunch of asters of all colors. Hilda's letter had just come and I was laughing over it when he appeared around the corner of my tent. She's a bad girl, Tousie [Hilda].

This is only to take the place of a card. My real letter is coming next. Just change about this time. It has been a soft mild day to-day. It seems to me I've made that remark every time I've written. Next time I'll say sharp biting weather even if it is warm.

Look at this wretched bill from Dr. Caven, you redirected it a little while ago.

Those Globe Nos. about [Admiral Robert E.] Peary were most thrilling. I'm so glad you sent them. You're a fine little mother, I wouldn't have seen them otherwise tho' I do see an [?] no. of the Globe and the Mail, Night Eds. as some of the papers go around. My purple jacket is much admired. Dr. Lyle calls me the 'Lady of the Decorations.'

Well, it is bed time now so Good-night dearest with much love to your little self, and love to Mary and the fat girl & boy [Hilda & Tom].

Your affectionate child, Ruby

Although Ruby mentions Mrs. Fournier and the doctor's *receipts* and a *wretched bill* from Dr. Caven, there is little indication of the actual cost of the treatment at Gravenhurst, except Ruby's mention that her fees were *wretched*. Several reports indicate that there was a "Muskoka Free Hospital for Consumptives" established in 1902 at Gravenhurst, but this is not where Ruby stayed (Williamson, *Chedoke*, 15).

It is probable that Tom helped with the costs, as he was now the wage earner in the family. No doubt he felt a responsibility to help with Ruby's care, since she had been so generous to him.

The accepted treatment for Tuberculosis in 1909 was the "fresh air cure," which involved living in a tent or on a veranda in the fresh air and being almost totally bed-ridden. This "fresh air treatment" was the basis of tuberculosis treatment for many years until after World War II, when vaccinations came to be widely used. Then the sanatoria were gradually closed and used for other purposes. Later in the letter Ruby indicates that the cold air was thought to be the best treatment for *this trouble*. Yet, Ruby did not fare well in the cold in Calgary, and she improved only so long as the weather was warm and dry. She describes the arrangement of tents and other patients at the Minnewaska in Gravenhurst, and continues with her characteristic good humour:

TO MARY BAKER MCQUESTEN from her daughter Ruby (W6537)
Whitehern   [Gravenhurst, Ontario]
Hamilton, Ontario   Sep 23 1909

My darling Mitherkins,

Here it is Thursday again and actually I was washed and be-pigtailed before the rising bell rang. If such things occur after they won't be able to hold me in bed long. It has been very sultry the last few days and this morning I didn't need a dressing jacket at all but donned my green robe for my light one.

There are two more patients in a tent in a line with mine on the other side of Miss Roberts, my neighbour; young Robertson & a Mr. Myers in the old tents. Young Robertson got very gay and went in swimming and so had to retire to bed. Mr. Myers only passes my tent once in the day on his way to wash & back before breakfast. They look comical these chaps in their gay coloured bathrobes.

Various people are going off. There were a Mrs. Kay and her daughter from Winnipeg. They attend Charles Gordon's church. She is a widow and the daughter is a teacher. The daughter is such a nice girl and I'll miss her very much. The mother is not so very ill but not likely at her time to recover and not able to stand the strenuous life of the fresh air cure, so the doctor said to take her home and make her comfortable. The daughter is just at the beginning of it but the doctor thinks she will be able to teach by Xmas.

Then Mr. Rugg-Dugg-Bugg. I gave him Hilda's message & told him she was calling him names & he said he'd get after her. He is going to-morrow.

The McArthurs, tho' it isn't known yet, so don't mention it to Jean if Hilda happens to write—are expecting to go within a month too. And some are preparing to go to Denver but none of these I know. Most are staying on as the winter is said to be the best time for this trouble.

Well I think that is all the news. There are quite a few more birds here now on their way south. A couple of little wild canaries stayed several days. I wonder what that sweet little note was. It was interesting to hear of those people in the West keeping track of the birds. It would really be something to find and know the names of the birds. More should go in for it.

Well here comes my breakfast. 6 a.m., but I'm an early bird. I beat you this morning I'm sure. I do hope you're feeling stronger.

With very much love & love to all,
Your affec'nate child, Ruby

Five weeks later Ruby remains cheerful and upbeat, and would even like to get up and dress and go for a walk, but that is not yet permitted. She provides a clearer description of her location, on a river with a scenic view. She also identifies some of the medications that she has been given:

TO MARY BAKER MCQUESTEN from her daughter Ruby McQuesten (W6551)
Whitehern   [Gravenhurst, Ontario]
Hamilton, Ontario   Nov 1 1909, Monday

My darling Mitherkins,
    Such a glorious morning! My calendar says "The wild Nov. comes at last"—but he's all out this time for it's like summer and the air is beautiful blowing in. I'm perched up looking out on the shining river and the firs along the bank. Across the river I can see a train pass occasionally—they're interesting, not like the horrid unromantic T.H. & B. trains [in Hamilton]. Also there is a lumber mill and the sounds in the distance are cheerful.
    My bed has been moved & I've turned head to feet and I really enjoy my view more than any I've had. The leaves are thick and brown under the trees and there is a delicious fragrance from them that makes me think of the days we went nutting. That makes me think—I'm always eating you know—I believe I'd like some hickory nuts when you come up. I'd amuse myself picking them out. Really I wish you could smell this air. I don't believe there's any time of the year so perfect if the leaves are down. I think it might inspire Tom to go nutting. He might get Mr. Chisholm to go with him over the mountain. Only I'm afraid it's late for nuts.
    I sent word to the doctor that I was going to get dressed and go for a long walk. But I'm afraid he's evading as usual for there's no sign of answer or person. Mrs. Minns and a friend came to see me yesterday. It wasn't a very long call but she is a very nice kind person.
    On Hallow E'en night the patients dressed up—the girls, some powdered their hair and wore old fashioned gowns—Mr. Chipman had a long nightgown and represented a baby with a bonnet on and a bottle. Now they say he refuses to drink his milk out of anything else. Dr. Lyle was dressed as a nurse. He had shaved his moustache and made a wonderful flaxen wig out of unravelled rope & really with his mask on I had no idea who it could be.
    My room is gay with flowers—various patients sent me them, yellow & mauve & my white chrysanthemums & geraniums and my fern.
    The doctor read the prescriptions and said the pellets were calomel—a mild dose—(I can't get away from calomel!) and I think he had no objection to the salts though it wasn't a kind he used. I'll send back the prescriptions.
    Well my dearest Mother there is nothing more to jabber about. . . . I hope you're taking good care of yourself—with much love and love to all.   Ruby
    Turn over [P.S.] Here is Mrs. F.'s [Fournier] bill. She added the last to this not that she is in any hurry she said but simply it was her custom the first of each month. . . . I'm getting so that really I can't scrape up any nausea and I shouldn't be surprised if I'd have you bring me a pot of marmalade or preserves of some kind. I'll let you know later. The quinces made me think of it—quince & apple used to be a special weakness.
                                             [Ruby]

Ruby includes the bill from Mrs. Fournier and it is obviously in arrears for her accommodation and treatment. She notes bills and arrears in many of her letters.

Ruby's comment about the calomel treatment suggests that calomel was a standard medication for tuberculosis at this time; she received it regularly and dreaded it. Calomel is a mercury-based compound used as a purgative. Ruby also suffered from indigestion and calomel was a common cathartic or laxative given for dyspepsia which accomplished a severe purging. Unfortunately, even the doctors appeared to be unaware of calomel's toxic qualities. Yet there were known warnings about calomel. Calomel, or chloride of mercury, was a colorless, white or brown tasteless compound, injested as a purgative to bring a fever down. It could have other drastic side effects: salivation, soreness and/or inflammation of the gums, and sometimes even loss of teeth. It was harmful if swallowed, inhaled, or absorbed through the skin; it caused irritation to skin, eyes, and respiratory tract, allergic reaction, kidney damage, and damage to the central nervous system. In time, when the dangers were widely known, castor oil became a substitute as a purgative.[20]

Yet knowledge of mercury's harmful effects was available, and the "Mad Hatter's Disease" and "Hatter's Shakes" were known to be caused by the mercury used in the felting process for hats. Many nineteenth and early twentieth-century medications included calomel, but doctors did not often connect it with dementia or insanity. It is probable that the McQuesten family took it regularly. In fact it may have been their use of calomel that accounted for what they considered to be an inherited mental illness. Years earlier, in 1828, Dr. Calvin McQuesten, Ruby's grandfather, prescribed calomel in his medical paper on "Dyspepsia":

> *There are some cases of simple dyspepsia that after having resisted the usual remedies readily yield to mercurial alternatives. The particular circumstances under which this remedy should be used must be left to the judgement of the practitioner. The compound calomel Pill or the Blue Pill may be given at night from 5 to 10 grains of the former or 3 or 4 of the latter followed the next morning with a small dose of rhubarb.* (W0410 & n5, W2469) [Rhubarb is also a purgative]

Dr. Calvin McQuesten had developed an extreme case of senility as he aged, but it is not known how much calomel he took. By comparison of dosage, Mary sent a prescription to her son, Calvin, for his indigestion and it was *1/2 gr. of calomel, so to be of much use you could take two* (W6374, Mar 24 1909). It is not know what dosage of calomel Ruby took, was it one grain or ten? Nevertheless, Ruby *dreaded* its effect.

In December, Ruby is still living in the tent and without an electric heater. Many of the patients stayed in their tents all winter. She and the family are alarmed about the unsuccessful surgery on Harvey Gunn's lungs, and his sudden death after surgery. As winter descends and Ruby's condition does not improve, they all have the memory that she did not fare well in the winter in Calgary. Discussion is again taken up about sending Ruby to a warmer climate, perhaps Arizona, but the cost would be prohibitively great. Ruby acknowledges that they are already *spending everything* on her.

---

[20] Calomel. "Various Treatments and Frequencies of Use." From the notebooks of: Dr. Samuel Overton (1821-97) MSDS Material Safety Data Sheet. Dec 10, 2003. (www.jtbaker.com/msds/english.html) (www.rootsweb.com/~txsmith/Pioneers/Childress/treatment.html)

TO MARY BAKER MCQUESTEN from her daughter Ruby McQuesten (W6576)
Whitehern   Gravenhurst, Ontario
Hamilton, Ontario   Dec 13 1909

My darling Mother,

Your letter came to-day and you needn't have worried about the amount of fresh air I get. There is about ten times more than I can use at present & I dare only open it a crack with the present gale. On Sat. my window was fixed. Mrs. Fournier thought of the idea & won't let me pay for it at all. A man did it in half-a-day, but it is very decent of Mrs. Fournier all the same. The two sashes of the window were fixed into one and it just opens with hinges like a door and it lets in a great amount of air & then I can partly shut it or just open it a little as at present. I wouldn't take Mr. Powis' room as a present even with an electric heater. And a view doesn't count compared with comfort. I'll get the [heated] stone if I want it—I haven't wanted anything these nights. Yes, Mrs. Motter's address is 316—15th Ave W., Calgary.

Poor Tousie [Hilda] I can thoroughly sympathize with her about her nose and I hope by next letter it will be better.

I haven't the slightest idea who Mrs. Dr. Ross would be. If I knew her maiden name I might remember her.

Yes my temperature still goes to 99 or 99 2/5 in the afternoon & evening. It is generally normal in morning. It will probably continue that way for a couple of mos. I can't expect it any better. It is good for it.

Yes, I saw what it said about Harvey Gunn in the Times. I never heard that version. I knew what you heard about the kind of operation and I just heard that his death had been caused not by haemorrhage of the lungs or pneumonia as is often the case after such operations but that the stitches had given way. Everybody felt very badly about it but they said if he had not had the operation it would have meant a great deal of acute suffering. Harvey Gunn & his cousin left here about three weeks ago—they left suddenly at the last I think it was on a Wed. & the last time I had seen Mrs. Gunn was on the Sat. before & she just told me very much what you knew that they were waiting for the doctor's brother & trying to decide where to go for the operation. Then when the brother came from the West they hurried off & I expect poor Mrs. Gunn was too [?] to come and see me. I feel so sorry for them all. I've less chance of hearing about him for the nurses & Mrs. Fournier don't encourage you in asking about such things. I know he rested at the Gunns in Toronto for some days before the operation & then it was quickly over.

Am sure the bows will be enough for the nurses. I don't want the girls bothering.

I haven't asked Dr. Parfitt about climates. I know he wouldn't let me go any place this winter or spring & I don't think it would be the thing in summer. We might consider it for next fall. When Cal asked Dr. Parfitt about places he said [?] California, or the Okanagan Valley is simply an experiment—they know nothing about it, and from what I've heard definitely about California, I've quite dropped from considering it.

I fancy from hearing "lungers" talk & there is more information that way than from the doctors—the best places are Arizona & New Mexico & Texas.

It would be nice to know about that Sanatorium she speaks of. So many "lungers" go wandering about because they are able just to go to boarding houses & take care of themselves. By next fall I'll probably be at that stage but it would do no harm to find out about the Sanatorium.

I can't help feeling that when I gained so much in Calgary as long as it was warm & dry & it was only the cold that knocked me out, that some climate with the dryness

& heat & without the cold would be the place. But at present if we go by the doctor I
stay here for six mos. anyway.

I'm sorry to hear Mrs. Whittemore is so poorly that she has to be sent on such a
long trip.[21] I only wish you could be sent for a trip too instead of spending everything
on me. However, you can rest contented about me for the present. I've everything I
need & there's time enough for the future though it's good to keep one's ears open.

With much love to all,

Your affec'ate daughter, Ruby

Ruby refers to herself and some of the other patients as *lungers*. This appears
to be the term used for tuberculosis patients at this time; also Ruby speaks of being
treated for *the Con* meaning consumption. The more advanced cases were referred to
as *bleeders*. Ruby sometimes speaks of her illness as *it* as in *it is good for it*. The term
"tuberculosis" is rarely mentioned in the family letters. No doubt it was a dreaded
term carrying the fear and stigma of contagion and death, and they avoided its use.
Certainly the term was well known in medical circles ever since Dr. Koch isolated
the *tuberculosis bacillus* in 1882. As we have seen, Ruby knew the term even when
she was in Calgary, remarking that a certain young boy was a *hopeless tubercular*
invalid (W6355).

At Christmas 1909, Ruby received so many presents that she could not possibly
write to thank even a fraction of them, so she asked her family to send out her thank-
you notes. She would be "breaking rules" if she were to write herself. In her letter to
her mother, which she compiled over several days, she lists at least sixty gifts. The
letter has been excerpted here to include only some of the text and a few examples of
the items on the lists. The names were "crossed out" when the notes had been sent.

TO MARY BAKER MCQUESTEN from her daughter Ruby McQuesten (W6583)

Whitehern   Gravenhurst, Ontario
Hamilton, Ontario   Dec 30 1909, Thursday night

My darling Mother,

Here I've had Tom and another Xmas, when will wonders cease! 6 full surprises
to see Tom walk in! Then he began to unload like Santa Claus—A delicious Charlotte
Russe and lady fingers, now extinct, beautiful nut cake also nearly extinct. I'm
certainly a total and entire pig, head, hoofs, tail & all. But still I keep on eating. And
my family provide. You're all just too good and you'll just get a hit in the eye each
separate individual one of you, if you send me another thing for mos. to come—I was
going to say years *[emphasis added].*

And then I had lovely letters to-night from little Teddy [Edna] & I can hardly
refrain from writing to her. And 'Aunt Annie' is a hardened criminal and little Laura
is nearly as bad. I do want to break rules & write to them.

1. Mrs. Fletcher [crossed out] *a very pretty book, "Lavender and Old Lace."*

2. Mr. Murray—a comical Xmas card & poem.

3. Mrs. Ketchen [crossed out]—*a dainty little purple leather book "A Wallet of Wit."*

4. Mrs. Bogue [crossed out]—*a box with a lovely pair of pink and white striped*
bed room slippers with pink bows, a big bunch of green grapes, a package of

---

[21] This may be the same Mrs. Whittemore who was being treated in Calgary with Ruby, see
W-MCP2-4.070.

delicious home made cookies and another package of short cakes. The eatables were exceedingly good and have nearly all departed this life. It was certainly exceedingly kind of Mrs. Bogue.

Mr. Bogue [crossed out]—*a card of their street [?] with their place marked. Thank him too.*

5. Miss Grantham [crossed out]—a very pretty box which is nice for my table and [?] to write a little round piece of glass to cover my tumbler with a beautifully worked little white [?] covering it & tied with white ribbon. It is very pretty & useful.

6. Annie Woods [?]

7. Mrs. Arnott [crossed out]—*a pretty little red blotter and calendar—it looks quite gay on my table* [crossed out]—*a most beautiful fancy leather edition of Whittier's poems. I've never had Whittier & will be [?] to read it. Also a pretty little Xmas card.*

8. Mr. & Mrs. Geo. Hay [crossed out]—*The Bank Ottawa—that dainty little edition of "The Dawn by Galilee" by Ralph Connor [Charles Gordon].*

[list of gifts continues, at least forty more items]

Well I've been toddling away at this list & now it is my last night. Many thanks for the two beautiful rose calendars. I'm sending the enclosed if Tom thinks it should be answered. It has been stormy unsettled weather but only one day very cold. I'm very comfortable. Mrs. Young called in to-night & Margery Black & a Miss Parker on Sunday afternoon. Your letter has just come.

Will just send this off with Tom's. I'm just overwhelmed with presents. People are very kind & I was thinking Cal might thank all the "Toronto people," or some of them. I'm afraid you'll be sick to death of my lists of people & there are still a few more. Well it is bed time.

> *With much love to all*
> *Your affec'ate child, Ruby*

The most poignant part of the letter is Ruby's correction of terms: *if you send me another thing for mos. to come—I was going to say years.* Ruby obviously is afraid to hope for her future beyond *months to come.* The profusion of gifts attests to the fact that Ruby was much-loved. The circumstances also suggest that she *and* her friends felt that her chances of seeing another Christmas were not good.

Ruby in 1909

Chapter 21

Ruby needs to have her own people *[at Gravenhurst]*

She was compelled to take calomel which upsets her dreadfully.
(W-MCP6-1.411)

By February 1910, Ruby had been moved indoors to a private room on an upper floor of the Minnewaska at Gravenhurst. This suggests that she was isolated and confined to her bed. While examining her, Dr. Parfitt recommended a change in accommodation so that she could have a veranda. This would give her the fresh air she needed, in a protected and secluded environment. She describes the meeting with the doctor, and praises her mother for her devotion to the family:

> *The doctor examined me yesterday and when I asked him if he really could say that I'd be up by summer he said he certainly expected to see me sitting out on the verandah by then. He is planning if he can arrange it to get me down to a lower room off a verandah. You know last summer . . . the doctor never said I'd be up and he's very [?] about saying things so I feel quite satisfied. I think if we can get this room it will be a good thing though I'm sorry to leave this comfortable little room. However we'll not talk about it till it is settled. I left it to the doctor whatever would be best. . . . Your letter has just come. Darling Mitherkins I don't think you're impatient but you've had many things to try you. And it's much harder having others ill than being ill yourself. Time seems much longer. Mrs. McQuesten, you'll just get a black eye from me if you ever say you're perfectly useless. What a **L.I.E.** pronounced fib. It is the most nonsensical thing when you're the indispensable hub of the whole family wheel & your family would be utterly wretched & lost without you.* (W6646, Feb 17, 1910)

Ruby's condition continued to worsen; her letters and postcards become increasingly illegible and brief, and she is now *in the habit of doing nothing.* She is delighted that Tom is beginning to advance in law: *And Hurrah for Tom! Think of him as legal examiner!* (W6665, **Mar 21 1910**). Tom's success justifies her faith in him and the future that she envisioned for him (W-MCP2-4.053, May 8 1905).

Thomas visited Ruby regularly and was very attentive, sending flowers and bringing treats. He usually conferred with the doctors while he was there. On March 28, 1910 (W6673), he waited for the doctor's examination and report, and the doctor told him then that Ruby needed to have her family with her. Mary informs Calvin about Dr. Parfitt's visit and the recommended change in Ruby's accommodation and treatment. She does not mention that it is an indication that Ruby's health is deteriorating, but she cautions Calvin not to reveal this news to Edna or Mary yet:

> *When Tom was up at Gravenhurst, he spoke with the doctor and found a cottage close to the Minnewaska and when he told me I decided to take it at*

A Patient's Cottage at the Minnewaska, Gravenhurst
(photo courtesy of Gravenhurst Public Library)

once. The Dr. thought R. [Ruby] needed a change and to have her own people.
So Hilda is to take charge and I am to be there as much as possible. It is $15
a month and we have to take it for eight mos. Say nothing if you write, as we
have not told Edna or Mary yet. (W6676, Mar 30 1910)

THE COTTAGE AT GRAVENHURST: *The What shall I call it*

Ruby was at the Gravenhurst sanitaria for approximately eighteen months, from April 1909 until early October 1910, including the winter months. In May 1910, at her doctor's suggestion, she had been moved from the main building at the Minnewaska into a cottage on the same grounds so that she could have her family with her. Her sister, Hilda, became the primary caregiver, and others in the family came to live with and look after her. Dr. Parfitt continued as Ruby's doctor.

Before Ruby could be moved into the cottage, it had to be prepared for her. It had already been fumigated, but her family still washed everything including the mattresses with carbolic acid, and aired them as a safety measure. The cottage required additional furnishings and the necessary equipment for cooking and washing, and arrangements were made for shopping. This must have created a serious added financial burden for the family. Hilda explains the arrangements to her mother:

The coal will come in to-day it was $7.25 it seems a lot. Mr. S. was not
quite sure of the wood. I had to get a number of things from the hardware,
kettle, pail (milk) frying pan etc. etc. which came to a little over $3.00 (paid
for). Am going to try and find out about a wash woman next week and see
if we can get it done out for I don't want to get tubs & wringer they are so
dear. The stove is small & it would be very awkward. At Homer's the grocer
& departmental store I got a white bedroom set for $1.50 which I thought
reasonable. Ruby would need it, there is no article belonging to the set here,
so if when the family come up they could bring one it would be very useful.
The granite ones here are very dear. The things Calvin saw in the stable

are all leaky. The dairy butter here is 32 cts a lb., very good. Mrs. Minis is
going to try and get butter from her woman for us but I did not think it very
extra, however it was cheaper & would do as for cooking any way. Bruce
M.'s eggs are lovely 25 cts. a doz. He had not saved any but I am going to try
and get all I can from him. About the curtains for verandah I thought dark
green glace lining would do quite well. It would take about 8 yds. of 27 in.
material. Denim is rather dear [and] not necessary. Can pay milk man by
month also the grocer.

Mrs. Fournier said her bill could go till June 1ˢᵗ unless she should have to
pay down some money for a cesspool she is having made. However, she will
let us know in that case. I think I have mentioned every thing. Don't do too
much at those meetings. Save yourself as much as possible. With heaps of love.
Your loving daughter, H.B. McQuesten [Box 04-077, Apr 29, 1910]

This recording of costs gives some indication of the expenses that were incurred in Ruby's move to the cottage at the Minnewaska. However, some bills had to be deferred, and Hilda's letter does not mention the cost of Ruby's medical care and treatment. Since Tom was working as a lawyer with James Chisholm at $1000 per year, he was able to help with expenses. It is impossible to calculate the cost of travel to and from Gravenhurst for the family, and almost every letter during this time recounts expenses and supplies needed.

In making this move it is apparent that Ruby was either incapable of walking or was not allowed to walk to her new home, even though it was not such a long distance away since two men were able to carry her in a makeshift "soudan" chair or litter. Ruby made the trip on her birthday, May 3, and she describes the move in her letter. This is the last extant letter in Ruby's handwriting. She was growing weaker, and writing was increasingly difficult. Nevertheless, her letter conveys her characteristic good humour.

TO MRS. MARY B. MCQUESTEN & FAMILY from Ruby McQuesten (Box 04-088)
Whitehern   Cottage at Gravenhurst
Hamilton, Ontario   Gravenhurst, Ontario
                                                           May 4 1910 [estimated date]

[written at top of letter] *"The What shall I call it"*

My dear darling mother and family,
Here I am in my happy home and really it is delightful. My birthday will extend
over to-morrow as well for I have still some letters to read. But the excitement of coming
yesterday and my presents & family letters kept me busy. My parasol is simply beautiful,
the most perfect thing of its kind you could have planned. It's just a delight. (I just
had to put it down & look at the outside again for I have it up & am enjoying the nice
light through the green). I put it up when I first came yesterday and it is just the thing.
For this month anyway I like the sun shining into my verandah but the little
parasol just protects my head & eyes and leaves the sun to warm all around. You are
just a darling child to plan it all for it is such a comfortable thing and then you know
I can't help liking awfully pretty things too.
I came over here in a chair on long sticks carried by Mr. Graham & Mr. Harris &
felt like an Indian princess & the parasol made me proud as the queen herself. Poor
old Mr. Graham, I made him put me down on the way for it was really too heavy for

him and he was just puffed out when he reached here. But he never let on and he was so anxious to get me over that he fixed the poles for the chair & stayed to carry me. He's really been very kind about things for one of his best men had a stroke & he's been worried about his work but he's fixed this verandah so nicely—the glass sliding panes work so nicely & fit so well & tarpaulin is snug as anything & my two little shelves. And all done in time tho' I'm sure he had other jobs ahead of this. He's a dear old man I think.

Did you hear why it was yesterday noon that I came? Well first on Monday a sick boy from Toronto train-then rain-then stay at home. Then Tuesday, all ready—no rig—no rig- 11 o'clock- 11—12—horses all off indulging in a funeral to Bracebridge, no horses—long faced me—most inconsiderate stiff said I!—put me in a wheel barrow I'll go any way. So Mrs. Fournier thought of the chair I had & four people carrying it & the doctor said he had for a long time wanted an arrangement for carrying patients so hence the two poles tied on to the arms of another chair.

The air was just beautiful when I got out & it's all along seemed much warmer than in the house. Last night I was just perspiring because I had on my long bathrobe instead of my short jacket & I took the whole thing off & slept blissfully till morning. I wonder if it is because I'm stronger or if it is that in summer after a warm day one notices the cold of the night air about 2 a.m. But now there seems no great difference & the morning air didn't seem very chilly at all—always perfectly comfortable anyway & lovely to awaken & see the sun over everything. . . . Well, my darling mother & family, many, many thanks for everything, for letters & presents and all the planning that has given me a perfectly lovely place.

Much love
Ruby

Ruby says she feels better already (Box 04-066, May 3, 1910)

Fortunately, during Ruby's critical time, Edna was feeling quite well and was at home with their sister Mary, so Hilda also writes home to her. We notice that when Edna is mentioned in the letters, it is usually with some deference to her sensibilities or her eccentricities; her nicknames "Oddy," "Teddy," "Mikey" or "Mickey" are often used. The family is careful not to upset Edna, because she is prone to hysteria and mental breakdowns.

Hilda adopts a light-hearted tone in this excerpt as she describes Ruby's diet and the routine of care, to their youngest sister:

Edna "Oddy" McQuesten

> *By the time you get this your little mother will have arrived home in all probability an utter wreck after all her meetings. However I hope she kept the people in Toronto in their places and did not let them have their way too much! We have had lovely weather since Tuesday and Ruby is most comfortable outside, the evenings are so calm. This morning there was ice on the door step and it was decidedly*

cool but the sun soon warmed things up. Ruby is much better to night the 'jim jams' have departed and she is looking forward to good course meals to-morrow.

To-day she had a large bowl of arrowroot gruel at 7:45 a.m., another bowl at 10:15 a.m., a bowl of onion soup made with milk, 1 p.m., whites of 2 eggs at 3 p.m., a large bowl of strong beef tea with three pieces of toast at 6 p.m., and at 9 p.m., she will get 2 whites of eggs again. Not so bad for a person just recovering, eh!! She is a pretty tough character though does not like being washed. As soon as she arrived over here she decided that she would breakfast when she first woke, then have a snooze and then be washed 'slightly' if she could not escape. However I <u>see</u> that she performs her ablution properly!! . . . Ruby got 30 cards & letters combined for her birthday as well as a handkerchief and some daffodils from an old pupil. . . . She is very popular, eh Mickie doo [Edna]? I feel very guilty up here having such a lazy time. . . . (Box 04-070, May 5 1910)

Ruby's room is on the verandah of the cottage to gain the full benefit of the "fresh air cure" as a mainstay of her treatment. When the whole family is at the cottage it is exceedingly crowded, with a bed or cot in every available space. Also, many supplies are needed, as Hilda indicates to her mother:

I have large bed in sitting room, another in bedroom a cot in room off kitchen . . . a cot in dining room and another cot not in use can go in sitting room or where we prefer it. Do not worry about where beds will go. . . . I have kept all bills for groceries, meat, milk and fancy they will be about the following: Homer (grocer) $13.00, Passmore (butcher) $7.00, white (milk) $3.50, Total $23.50. I have four dollars and a little more left. (Box 12-618, May 30 1910)

The reference to Ruby's diet suggests that these foods constitute the prescribed diet for a tuberculosis patient. Many of these letters from Hilda or Mary at Gravenhurst describe Ruby's condition, care, diet, and the family financial matters. Most of the reports of Ruby's condition are somewhat favourable, such as that she is *feeling better today,* and rarely is a bleak assessment reported to the family. It is likely that Edna is reading these letters, and any deterioration is being kept from her. Mary reports in a postcard to Tom:

Just a few lines to say that Ruby is feeling much better. Did not know it, but after she came to cottage had one of her attacks of chills and fever, but now her stomach seems to be recovering itself and she enjoyed her meals yesterday, is free from nausea, and last night said she felt better than she had done for many weeks. Cough better too; enjoys the heat. Very warm yesterday, but night cool. . . . The netting round verandah great comfort. Elsewhere mosquitoes terrible, that is outside. (W-MCP6-1.405, Jun 10 1910)

Ruby's care and her medications create a considerable financial drain for the family, and Hilda is careful to manage the finances. Hilda thanks her mother:

Have just rec'd your letter with [money] order enclosed, many thanks, I will settle <u>all</u> bills. It has been pretty cool but Ruby is not suffering and is feeling pretty well to-day, only of course she has to remain under cover. The medicine seems to be helping her & it is warmer to-night. (Box 12-624, Jun 1 1910)

Mary's letters from Gravenhurst to Tom at Whitehern are full of requests for supplies and errands, and we can imagine Tom searching out and packing up all of these items, although he never complains, at least not in writing.

> *Suppose you are coming Thursday and Reding could fix the basket for you of the various things, chicken, vegetables, especially the vegetables, strawberries, he has a basket larger than ordinary fruit, and it would not be impeding. When you are coming to Muskoka he could send it down to Station for you. There is a pink muslin runner in Mary's wardrobe, bring it if you can. I do not know if you manage to bring me some honey it is all in a big jam jar. Never mind if you can not. If Miss Gansby does not bring in the rent on Wednesday as I have asked her to do, I would need to bring up my balance. . . . Edna very well indeed, much improved. I'm writing Mr. Wade to send up something to the house. I am wanting just a little thing. [I] Am sending the label for the darning cotton, get two or three of each, the black and the white. Think they are 3 for 10 cents, but not sure. [P.S.] Cannot get cracked wheat. Please get 2 or 3 pounds of fine cracked wheat from Dunlops.* (W-MCP6-1.388, Jun 27 1910)

The financial concerns are easing a little at this time and Mary finally has a bank balance *in her favour,* which has not been the case for many years. However, she continues to keep a keen eye on the bills and bank balances. Undoubtedly, Tom's salary is assisting. She remarks:

> *Glad my statement is in my favour, <u>a new thing</u>, perhaps it would be a good idea to reserve a hundred out of Bush and [money?] that added to Sept. Montreal Dividend would go a way to taxes. When you call let me know what is to my credit at Ham. Prov. Received the last $10 as well as the $25.* (W-MCP6-1.409, Jul 9 1910)

This letter indicates that Tom is sending small amounts regularly since the family is undergoing large expenses for Ruby's care at the Minnewaska cottage, as well as for the upkeep of the house in Hamilton.

Tom was now home at Whitehern, and no doubt feeling clearly responsible for his mother and sisters. He was twenty-eight years of age, whereas his mother was sixty-one and had no hope in sight of an easy life in her aging years.

Calvin was thirty-four years of age and was not yet established, so he could not offer any financial help to the family. He was at his homestead in Saskatchewan and had high hopes for a good profit from his crops and the rising value of the land. In June he was highly optimistic at the prospect. Unfortunately, Calvin's optimism was shattered by a hail storm in September which ruined his crops and garden and damaged his shack. He never recovered from this disaster; he sold his possessions and his horse, and left his homestead in the care of neighbours in Saskatchewan while he took a preaching post in Bracebridge, Ontario. At least now he would not be too far from Ruby (W-MCP6-1.408, Jun 16 1910; W-MCP6-1.410, Sep 13 1910).

Mary and all of the girls—Hilda, Mary and Edna—spent the summer with Ruby in the cottage at the Minnewaska Sanitarium. Even though they were crowded, it was an ideal place for some summer relief from the city, and they wished to be near

Ruby. Ruby continued to have sick turns and she was failing. She *was compelled to take calomel, which upsets her dreadfully* (W-MCP6-1.411, Jul 14 1910).

In the meantime, Tom became the beast of burden for the whole family. He repeatedly accepted lists of instructions for supplies and delivered whatever was requested. Some letters are almost totally devoted to instructions for Tom, some of which are convoluted or personal and might have been quite difficult for him to fulfill:

> *I hope not to burden you with things, but would be much obliged if you could bring up a piece of brown and white striped gingham which is in the sitting room sideboard, then will you please look in the first drawer of my ward-robe, for a new pair of woollen soles, they will be in a paste-board case if I have them at all, look if they are no. 5, if so, do not bring them, but get Jeanie to get you a pair of no. 4 soles for bedroom slippers. They [look?] about [?] getting some wool, if you would please pay her and when Miss Gansby brings rent, please bring it with you, do not deposit.*
>
> *There is nothing else I would like, but a spring chicken, we get all the vegetables fresh from the garden. We get berries too and peaches which R. specially likes for her breakfast. It will be lovely to have you here. . . . If you get time take another look in my little top drawer for that list of mortgages and telephone Mack if [ink blot?]. Is there a food called [Sarratogus?], if so tell him to send you it, and charge to me. . . .*
>
> *[P.S.] Isa Black came on Saturday. She came by CPR to Bala. It leaves Toronto at 12.15 & gets to Bala at 3.30. The boat left at once but at Beaumaris you wait an hour for another boat reaching here by about 7.30, bus meets the boat.* (W-MCP6-1.398, Jul 26 1910)

Mary states that she hopes *not to burden Tom with things,* but judging by her directions in the *P.S.* it is not an easy trip. Tom would need to carry his load by horse cab from Whitehern down to the harbour, then to Toronto by boat on the *Turbinia* or the *Modjeska*. At Toronto, he would get the train to Bala, and then travel by boat to Beaumaris, and then take another boat and a cab to *here* [Gravenhurst]. All this time Tom would be lugging supplies on and off the vehicles as he makes his way to the cottage. Fortunately, the load this time is not so heavy, but the mission is more complicated because Tom is also bringing his own luggage since he will be staying for a summer vacation of his own.

With Tom at the cottage, they enjoy some boating and outings when the weather is good. But the cold windy days bring foreboding as they begin to think of winter and Ruby's care. Ruby's fever is often high and never below the 99 mark. Mary prays: *If that fever only would not return! I have been praying specially that God would glorify Himself by healing her by His miraculous power* (Box 12-405, Aug 5 1910). They begin again to consider sending Ruby to a warm climate but the reports about Arizona are not good:

> *Willie Ambrose wrote me, that the climate [in Arizona] was beneficial, but they were a race of blood-suckers (this is the universal report) Ethel stayed on a ranch, poor food and cooking and they robbed you whenever possible, a wretched desert and a wearisome journey, but Mr. Cook, who has just come from there does not seem to think so much of the journey. I am waiting to*

see how Ruby keeps this month and will then talk to the doctor. Tom thinks if R. wants to go, there is nothing else to be done and I must say; I dread the misery for her of another winter in Canada.[22]

A few days later Ruby's temperature is down, after being as high as 102 and 103 for four or five days, and Mary again mentions Arizona: *Yesterday [I] showed her the [famous?] letter about Arizona and in the evening she said she felt like passing up Arizona and going to our own [Hamilton] Mountain* (W-MCP6-1.386, Aug 10 1910). Ruby felt that the time would be too short before the really hot weather became unbearable and then she would have to come home again.

Since it is nearing the end of August, Mary juggles the finances again to pay the taxes. She confides her concerns to Tom and asks for his help.

> *As to the taxes, I can easily make up the $20.82, there is an interest due in Sept. besides the stable rent; if you cannot find that mortgage list when you look again in my drawer, (it was in an old envelope). . . . The Sept. tax payment is a large one, if you pay balance of $147.76, I'm afraid it will leave you very short.* (W-MCP6-1.395, Aug 18, 1910)

As the weather grows colder with heavy rains and wind, Ruby's veranda begins to leak and it is not quite as cosy and convenient. Her condition worsens; the high fevers return and she is subjected to the calomel ordeal regularly. Mary commiserates: *Poor Ruby had finally to go through the calomel ordeal yesterday before she could finally get her fever [down] and is feeling better today* (W-MCP6-1.395, Aug 18 1910).

The decision about Arizona is a constant refrain in late August. The debate involves consideration about finances, the cost of sending Ruby and the added cost of sending another family member to be her caregiver, since that would not be supplied by the facilities there (W-MCP6-1.415, Aug 22, 1910). Mrs. Stafford, owner of the Desert Inn in Arizona, describes the facilities and the cost:

> *We are posting you a booklet descriptive of our place, Desert Inn six miles from Phoenix, Arizona. As you will see from the prospectus, we have sixteen rooms in the Inn and eighteen tent houses in the desert. I think the tent houses are usually considered more desirable than the rooms—though the rate is the same for both. There are no nurses provided by the Inn, and we do not take fever cases such as you describe your daughter's to be unless the patient has a relative—such as you suggest—to take care of her. Under those conditions we are glad to take such cases. The rate for both your daughter and her sister (or nurse) would be $30.00 a week for board and two connecting rooms, or a double tent house.* (W-MCP6-1.415, Aug 22 1910)

The cost of the Inn at $30 a week for eight months would amount to $960, nearly Tom's full year's salary of $1,000. This does not include the cost of transportation for two, medications and any extras. There is little doubt that this would have been prohibitive for the McQuestens. Compare this with the cost of the Gravenhurst cottage at $15 a month, for a total of $120 for the same eight months. They continue to debate the issue until finally, Dr. Parfitt frankly declares against it as being *useless.*

---

[22] The McQuesten family considered sending Ruby to Arizona, and several letters discuss this subject, see W-MCP6-1.386, W-MCP6-1.415, W-MCP6-1.416, W-MCP6-1.417, W-MCP6-1.418, W-MCP6-1.419.

Mary and the rest of the family are worn out with care, worry, and hopelessness. Mary also considers bringing Ruby home and into the dining room but she fears for Edna's health if Edna becomes depressed and unstable. They decide that they might bring Ruby home and find her a small house in the southern part of Hamilton or on Hamilton Mountain. Mary weighs all the pros and cons and pours out her heart to Calvin in a particularly poignant letter:

TO REV. CALVIN MCQUESTEN, from his mother, Mary B. McQuesten (Box 12-323)
[Bracebridge, Ontario]   Whitehern
                                                        Hamilton, Ontario
                                                        Aug 27 1910

My dearest Calvin,

This week I received a letter from the wife of Dr. Stafford of whom Mrs. Miller wrote me some time ago. Dr. Stafford's wife was a friend of Edith Coleman's and they have been for years in Arizona near Phoenix, where he went for his health. They now keep "the Desert Sun" six miles from Phoenix and from many I hear it is good in every way. Dr. P. had a patient there who said food &c. was good. They only take 16 in the Inn but they have tent houses nearby. Ruby and Hilda could have two rooms connected to the Inn or a two roomed tent house for the same price, $15 a week each. This seemed so remarkable that R. was quite excited about going and I am very sorry I told her about it, for certainly the booklet sent by Mrs. S. is most tempting. (I wrote her to send you one) and R. had made up her mind just to go to our mountain.

Dr. Parfitt is much opposed to her going [to Arizona], told me we <u>might</u> get her there, but we would certainly never bring her back. I cannot repeat all he said, I believe he told you; if her fever had gone down, he would say go, but as it is he says it is useless.

If we had not Edna to consider, I think I would make the effort, by taking Hilda with me, but I am so worn out, I could not undertake it alone and H. feels it to be such a terrible thing to take her there to die; and both of us cannot leave Edna, tho' well enough, when carefully cared for, she could not be left depressed, and tired. Mary is getting very tired too.

Sometimes I think of taking her home and letting her room be our dining-room, she could have the grate-fire and be beside us. Then again fear the strain for all, the coughing at times is so distressing, and the fever affects the stomach but all of us would stand it for R's sake, if we had not to consider Edna, tho' I do not sleep half the night; now that Dr. P. has taken away all hope from me.

Then again, I remember God's power to heal and I think if it is his will to restore her He will do it without our going so far from home. R. did say one day she would be satisfied whatever I decided but other times she speaks of having a chance if [she] could go to Arizona. Was so glad of your letter, thought Bruce's thought [sic] very helpful.

If I do not take R. <u>home</u>, will try for a small house in quiet part of city where she can have a South-room and H. will go with her alone perhaps for awhile or else with some one to help her. Just hoping every day for some special guidance. Tho' certainly I do not see how we are to get R. so far away, the fever is so continuous, and for that reason you see the doctor says change of climate would be no help, but if we could get her there and the whole family with her, she could enjoy the climate. . . . Think you will enjoy Mrs. Mullin's letter. It seems so hard to think of others going about enjoying themselves and darling Ruby always so cheerful and patient lying in her bed month *after month. God's ways are very mysterious; her illness not only makes her useless but all of us.*

Tom can find no suitable place on mountain. R. says it was very good of you to write so soon again and sends love as all do. H. says it is disgraceful, she has not written, but really she has scarcely a minute, E.'s [Edna] plans for use of five dollars are countless. You will be very cold sometimes, we had a terrible rain, windstorm Thursday night very cold afterwards but to-day in bed till house warms up.

> *Your loving mother*
> *M. B. McQuesten*

That note of hopelessness coming from Dr. Parfitt must have been shocking news to the family, as their worst fears would finally have been conveyed to them by a medical authority. It was an agonizing time for all. Two days earlier, Mary had expressed her despair to Tom:

> *Since I wrote you Hilda and I have been talking it over; this taking a house on the Mountain is no joke, there will be the rental, a certain amount for furnishing, and I doubt if H. could stay there alone with Ruby, tho' she thinks she might. Then we would keep going backwards and forwards daily, which will be a great strain, and Edna will see and hear far too much of it. It would be easier for H. to be just where she had only to attend on R. and have a rest from cooking. She is getting so tired of it.*
>
> *It would be a pretty dreary winter for Ruby and we would be worried looking at her. At home, I think, we must go out for our dinners, that would be a great relief for Mary, and she must get it, for she is very tired too. This hot close weather has been very tiring. If we got a servant she might not cook and that would be no help....*
>
> *There is an enormous cavity on the top of the right lung and left one much affected. I am so sorry I let her see the booklet [about Arizona], it is so attractive, and I cannot tell her it is all so hopeless, and yet it seems to me it would be wrong to let her go away out there only to grow worse and worse away from her mother and all [on] her own. I think too sometimes, that if God intends to heal her, it would make no difference what climate she is in.*
>
> *Well, dearie, we must pray earnestly that God will guide us at this time for sometimes it*

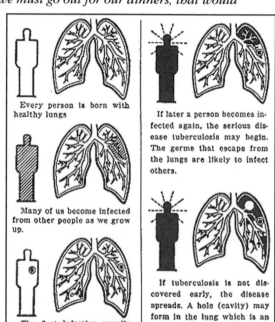

Every person is born with healthy lungs

If later a person becomes infected again, the serious disease tuberculosis may begin. The germs that escape from the lungs are likely to infect others.

Many of us become infected from other people as we grow up.

The first infection usually heals. The person is well and no germs escape from his lungs. It is important to find this first infection in children.

If tuberculosis is not discovered early, the disease spreads. A hole (cavity) may form in the lung which is an incubator of germs that escape and menace everybody who comes in contact with the sick person.

Stages of Tuberculosis
(www.lung.ca/tb/)

*seems more than I can bear. So hard to look at this darling child and believe
she must go. Take care of yourself.* (W-MCP6-1.417, Aug 25 1910)

With a cavity in her lung Ruby would have become highly infectious. Amazingly,
none of the other members of the family became infected, not even Hilda, Ruby's
constant companion and caregiver, who was exhausted and exceptionally vulnerable.
It is fortunate that they were aware of the "germ theory" and were particularly careful
about antiseptic conditions and used disinfectants such as carbolic acid.

The family focus then shifts to Hamilton Mountain. It is obvious that Mary
had come to realize that Ruby is dying and, while she wants Ruby to be at home
or nearby, she does not want to put Edna under the strain of having to watch her
sister weaken and die. If Edna had another breakdown, the cost of medical care
would escalate beyond their financial capabilities. Understandably, Mary is deeply
distraught and concerned about the cost.

Mary's acceptance enters the dialogue in response to a comment of Tom's, who
was brave enough to confront the inevitable. Mary responds:

*Noted all you said dearie, and have thought the same, but feel my strongest
prayer has to be for faith to believe always in God's love and wisdom.
So many things are contrary to our idea of what is best for every one.*
(W-MCP6-1.393, Aug 22 1910)

This exchange suggests that Mary and Tom have resigned themselves to Ruby's
eventual death, and that Mary is struggling with her faith in God and His *mysterious
ways.* When she received the conclusive diagnosis that Ruby was dying, Mary
informed Tom without stating the name of the doctor, and closed by saying, *So hard
to look at this darling child and believe she must go* (W-MCP6-1.417, Aug 25 1910).

So many conflicting diagnoses of Ruby's condition were made; just a few days
later, Dr. H. Arnott in Hamilton assured Mary that he had seen many patients
recover who had enormous cavities in the lungs. He again suggested Arizona and a
tent. However, he diagnosed without seeing Ruby, and was more concerned about
her digestion, which no doubt involved more calomel (W-MCP6-1.418, Aug 28 1910).
Consequently, Mary and the family were almost daily shunted back and forth
between hope and despair.

But Mary had already determined her course: *Then again, I remember God's
power to heal and I think if it is his will to restore her He will do it without our going so
far from home* (Box 12-323, Aug 27 1910). Thus, the family began the search for a final
residence for Ruby on Hamilton Mountain and close to home.

Chapter 22

HOME TO *COSY COTTAGE* ON HAMILTON MOUNTAIN

It would be useless to go to Arizona. (W-MCP6-1.399)

TO THOMAS B. MCQUESTEN from his mother Mary B. McQuesten (W-MCP6-1.399)
Whitehern   Gravenhurst, Ontario
Hamilton, Ontario   Aug 29 1910, Monday

Dearest Tom,

I have just had a long talk with the doctor. He says R. is so ill, that it would be useless to go to Arizona. Since Ruby has heard that owing to the heat she could only stay there so few months, she has given up the idea of going, and should like to go to our own mountain. The doctor says just to make her as comfortable as we can, need not sleep outside, and not to put off going too long, as she might grow worse.

I really do not know how you are to go about looking for a house on the mountain. Telephone Hattie Hope and ask her if the Doolittles' is rented for the winter. Still I do not like it is too near the Incline [railway] I think for summer time and would probably be unnecessarily expensive. Willie Ambrose ought to know the Mountain well; he is in the Spectator Bldg.

If our rooms were differently situated and Edna was different would take her home [to Whitehern]. We might be obliged to go to East End, but would not like that, fancy you get more of the damp lake air there.

I wonder if there could possibly be any place near Mr. Chisholm's it would be a great point not to be far away. Then I want you to telephone Dr. Arnott and ask him, if that person who kept the boarding house and he thought would do to go to Arizona, could go to the Mountain and what are her terms. I would require to see her before doing anything. You could ask him too if he knew any place on the mountain.

As to my watch, Lee must see what it requires; it has not been cleaned for a long time. Of course, I would come down to see house, if you could find out about any.

> *With fondest love,*
> *Your mother, M. B. McQuesten*

In the midst of the deep distress over Ruby's failing health and the need to find a cottage for her in Hamilton, Mary continues to supervise work at both the cottage and the house at Whitehern. Fall is approaching and it is essential that food supplies be preserved for the winter, so Hilda must go home to do the preserving, leaving Mary to care for Ruby.

After extended searching and several letters back and forth, Tom wrote with the encouraging news that Chisholm, his law partner, had secured a cottage near his house and near the Mountain View Hotel at the top of James Street near the Incline Railway. The tenants had to be moved out but that did not present a problem and it was done without rancour. It was a house that Chisholm either owned or managed for a client. The Incline Railway was just a few blocks from Whitehern and it made

**The Mountain View Hotel and the Incline Railway Station, at the top
of Hamilton Mountain. Ruby's *Cosy Cottage* was located just beyond the hotel.**
(Courtesy Hamilton Public Library)

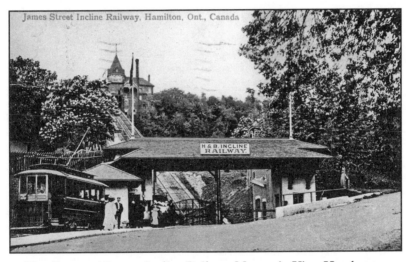

Hamilton and Barton Incline Railway, Mountain View Hotel at top
(Courtesy Hamilton Public Library)

daily visiting and delivery of supplies very easy. It was ideal, combining all of the
characteristics necessary for Ruby's comfort: fresh air, good breezes, scenery and
easy access for the family.

The costs continue to mount up relentlessly and, in September Tom *disgorges* to
pay for the taxes on Whitehern:

> *The taxes are payable to-morrow. I disgorged to the extent of $147.77 to make
> up the amount of the 2nd instalment which is $252.77. That is off our hands
> anyway. It's a good thing that we have a little extra income.* (W8709, Sep 13 1910)

The *extra income* is, of course, Tom's salary in the legal office with Chisholm. It is both appropriate and generous now of Tom to assume the responsibility for their home, which must have been a great relief to his mother.

During the time that the family was away in Gravenhurst and Ruby was ill, Tom could have continued his affair with Isabel Elliot, or with another woman. If he did so he was most discreet and made no commitment. He did not shirk his responsibility but was devoted to his family. Tom had become the man of the house—that is, as much as his mother, the matriarch, would allow. He never married.

WHY WAS RUBY NOT SENT TO THE HAMILTON MOUNTAIN SANATORIUM BUILT IN 1906?

Before continuing with Ruby's tragic story, it is important to note that Hamilton Mountain, where they were planning to send Ruby, was also the location of the Hamilton Mountain Sanatorium which opened in May of 1906. This facility included several cottages, shacks, and tents in the apple orchard, for the accommodation of smaller groups of patients, both male and female. During 1907, a total of 78 patients were admitted . . . . Of the 78, only three died (*Chedoke* p. 27).

**Official opening of the Hamilton Mountain Sanatorium on May 28, 1906
with Governor General Earl Grey in attendance.**
(Photo, courtesy Hamilton Public Library)

This begs a question: Why then was Ruby not sent to the Hamilton Sanatorium in 1908, since it was so much closer to home? One answer might be that it was very small. Yet when Ruby was sent to Calgary, there was no Sanatorium at all, for it had not yet been built, and she actually had to fend for herself for nine months, staying in boarding houses and taking her meals at a temporary YWCA.

There is absolutely no discussion of this Hamilton Sanatorium in the McQuesten letters. A possible reason is that the family preferred to keep Ruby and her illness as

Hamilton Mountain Sanatorium Cottage, 1906 - Why was Ruby not sent here?
(Photo, courtesy Hamilton Public Library)

private as possible since tuberculosis carried a stigma at the time. This is why the word "tuberculosis" was never used. It is difficult for us to appreciate how strong the stigma was in the early part of the twentieth century. The concept of the "Germ Theory" was relatively new, and the spread of infections was becoming known; therefore, many in the general public came to view tuberculosis as a disease connected with germs and unsanitary conditions; in short, as being *dirty*. Consumptives were treated as *unclean*. Tuberculosis became known as the "White Plague," and the social stigma continued long after the disease was well under control. Out of ignorance, fear and panic, patients and their families were shunned (*Chedoke*, p13-35).

Perhaps another and more compelling answer lies in the fact that their friend Miss Grantham, the "lady superintendent" of nurses for the Hamilton hospital system, had objected to housekeeping and staffing conditions and, when she received no co-operation from the Board, had resigned. These "troubles" had become public knowledge, and she may have influenced many people against the hospitals. The *Hamilton Spectator*, June 1, 1905, provides a statement from Miss Grantham with the headline: *Her Version of the Trouble.* It states that there was friction between the women and men executives, and she resigned under a cloud of controversy. "The troubles . . . have now become so public that they have been broadcasted all over the country."

Alternatively, why was Ruby not initially sent to the sanatorium at Gravenhurst rather than to Calgary, since it was so much closer to home and promised some of the same qualities of clean air and sunshine? The Muskoka Cottage Sanitarium, as we have seen, was built at Gravenhurst in 1897.[23] Was this alternative also rejected at the time because of the stigma attached to tuberculosis? Many Hamilton families had summer homes in Gravenhurst, and it would have been difficult to keep Ruby's condition a private matter. Ruby had lived away from home in Ottawa for so long that there would have been little social comment on her absence if she was in Calgary.

[23] An History of the Fight against Tuberculosis (www.lung.ca/tb/tbhistory/sanatoriums/first.html)

We can only speculate on the outcome of Ruby's illness if she had been sent immediately to either Hamilton or Gravenhurst, closer to home. The family had accepted the guidance of the doctors, and Dr. Arnott's stated opinion was that *they do not think so much of Muskoka now* (W-MCP3-5.004, May 16 1908).

To return to Ruby's story, Mary's letters of September 1910 indicate that finances are becoming desperate—a constant concern. The cost of caring for Ruby, renting a cottage and paying her medical bills, had become a large financial burden. Tom had been able to assist with the taxes, for which Mary is duly grateful. Fortunately, Calvin had finally been able to earn or accumulate some extra money, and Mary indicates to him that the family would need some of it. Calvin had been selling his belongings at his *shack* in Saskatchewan.[24] Mary then writes to Calvin from Gravenhurst, to bring him up to date about Ruby and the cottage and to thank him for the money he is to *hand over:*

> We are so thankful to have got the cottage. I feel it was just a special Providence that got it for us, as it would simply be impossible for me to go up every day if she were far away on the mountain. Did I tell you that it is next the Mountain View Hotel, but that will not trouble us in winter and in the Spring, we will see how things are and the cottage is only $19.00 a month. Of course we shall have to get a certain amount of furniture, stoves, &c.
>
> It seems hard for you to hand over your savings to me and yet I know it will be a great help if you can let me have some, I hope not to take all you have. If you are settled someplace, you will need some money, probably to start you. But I am very thankful you and Tom are both started. . . . We have just been washing R.'s [Ruby's] hair and she is sitting in her reclining chair out on back stoop to get it dry. She stood it very well and says she is not tired. . . . It seemed such a special Providence that Mr. C. [Chisholm] should be part owner of house and tenants lease expire just the day ours expires here. Wonderful how God helps us! (Box 12-482, Oct 1 1910)

It is not known how the family managed to move Ruby from Gravenhurst to the cottage in Hamilton. Presumably it would have been by the identical series of boats and trains that the family took to visit her at Gravenhurst (W-MCP6-1.398, Jul 26 1910). Then she would need to transfer to a horse and buggy ambulance to travel through Hamilton and up the Incline Railway to the cottage on the brow. Ruby stood it well and there can be little doubt that she was happy to be back home in Hamilton with her family again.

Ruby was delighted with the cottage and Hilda was *quite charmed* (Box 12-478, Oct 15 1910). Hilda wrote to Calvin about the *"Cosy Cottage"* on an unusually windy day in December: *I hope we won't be swepted [sic] over the mountain, but we are very cosy inside* (W9050).

Mary was exhausted: *it is quite a business arranging for two households. . . . All morning have been running after various things and must now out again to see a washwoman and go up to the mountain. . . . I am very tired of houses.*

After the move, Mary attempted to reassure Calvin that *Ruby was feeling finely.* Unfortunately, Ruby's health did not improve after her move to Hamilton. About a

---

24 Calvin sold his "shack" but had left his homestead in the hands of a local farmer, a Mr. Glendinning, to plant and harvest, which eventually had a poor outcome (W8944, Jan 15 1912).

month later, Tom wrote frankly to Calvin to inform him of the state of Ruby's health and the outlook for the future, which was bleak.

TO REV. CALVIN MCQUESTEN, ESQ. B.A. from his brother, Thomas B. McQuesten
(W8705)
Edmonton, Alberta

Chisholm, Logie & McQuesten,
Barristers, &c.
James Chisholm, W.A. Logie, T.B. McQuesten
Office, Victoria Chambers
69 James St. South, Hamilton, Canada

Nov 14 1910

My dear Cal,
Your letter of Nov. 8th has just come and I will reply to it as well as I can.
First in regard to Ruby's health. Just now she is not at all well and since she has come home so far as I can see her condition is just the same as it was in Gravenhurst, a few days well and a number of days ill. If your observation is that a great many of these cases drop off suddenly, you know what [Dr.] Parfitt said and I cannot give you any definite information. Dr. Arnott here holds out hopes and in her present condition it would be a great surprise and shock to me if she died but I know in two or three cases around here the end has come very unexpectedly in a case of such long standing with the system so undermined as it is I doubt if anybody could speak with any certainty at all for as long a time ahead as two months.
I ought to tell you however that Ruby herself seemed a little disappointed when we got your last letter as we were all expecting you home the end of last week. You know just about as much about the case as I do and I certainly couldn't advise you that she will last until spring, you'll have to take chances yourself.
I have read your letter over again and I think I have answered everything you ask as well as I can.   *Yours in haste*
T. B. McQuesten

Calvin did not come home immediately, because he had accepted a position as assistant to the minister of a church in Edmonton, Alberta. He sent a telegram home and his mother encouraged him to take the position even if just for a few months, as this would provide some much-needed income. It is fortunate for the archives that Calvin was away during these months, since letters continued to go out from Whitehern with reports of Ruby's care and condition.

Tom's handwriting,
from letter to Calvin
(W8705)

TO REV. CALVIN MCQUESTEN from his mother Mary Baker McQuesten (Box 12-504)
[716 Twenty-first St., Edmonton, Alberta]   Whitehern
                                                    Hamilton, Ontario
                                                    Nov 22, 1910

My dearest Calvin,

Tom has just brought in your telegram and I feel glad you have the opportunity to try it till January. For if you see, the work is going to be too heavy for you, you can just leave it. What we all feel about it is, that you would have no friends of your own age or tastes here, and every thing seems to attract you so much there. As you have the opportunity you could try life in a Western City and come East later.

Then just now R. [Ruby] is as well as she has been for some time, or may be, and if she grows worse there would be the time for you to come. I was up at the cottage this morning and R. said not to come home for her and they both (H. & she) thought it was a fine opening and congregation, here [it is] so unattractive. I just had time to read Ruby one sermon, so I will keep them till after Sabbath before returning. Am sending Mary right up to tell Mr. Ketchen.

It is disappointing about Christmas, but with Ruby and Hilda up at the Cottage it cannot be the day it used to be; in fact I try not to think about it, for life is made up of change. Edna has just been out and got weighed and came in jubilant because she has reached 140 1/2 lbs., of course with winter coat on.

Old Dr. Arnott never saw R. before and is much struck, thinks her such a beautiful girl. So many send her things and come to see her. Grace Rioch had the florist send her a dozen beautiful roses. Mrs. Geo. Lynch-Stanton sent her chrysanthemums; Mrs. Walker sends her roses quite often, Mrs. McDonald and Hattie Hope too. Ernest Bruce sent her a beautiful plant of yellow and Mrs. Lyle pink chrysanthemums. The cottage is really perfect I feel disappointed you cannot see the arrangements such pretty papers on the walls, matting on floors and Electric light to make it bright.

As I was saying to Tom, I cannot be thankful enough that God has so wonderfully provided the means for me to do every thing possible for my sick children. If I had millions, I could not do more for R. than I am doing.

Aleck English you know drove the ambulance; and Mary and he were up afterwards and saw [that] R. could not see the view of the city without sitting up in bed, so he made arrangements of wood and brought them to raise the bed, so each foot sits on a block and she can see to the Beach. So many people walk up there, it is never dull. Mr. Chisholm had a pair of partridges sent him, and sent her one, supplies them with apples, comes in to see her too; and Lizzie C. is great company for them.

Well, I must send the British Weekly out to you and such of back numbers as interesting. It seems to me your best suit is here, but I will wait till I hear from you. I am so glad to think you have fallen among friends; it makes such a difference to have even a few really feminine friends like Lorna. Be sure and spare yourself.

                                        May God bless you
                                        [M. B. McQuesten]

[P.S.] *Love to Lorna & her husband.*

Now that Calvin was working as an assistant minister, he was at last able to earn a little extra money to send home to his mother. Mary is very grateful, and details numerous expenses for Ruby's care and her debts. She is also frank about the possibility of *giving Ruby up*:

> *I cannot tell you how rich your cheque made me feel, it seemed such a large*
> *sum for you to give out, but it enables me to pay off $100 on a $350 note*
> *due on the 3rd of this month; the year R. [Ruby] came from Calgary I had to*
> *borrow from the bank at different times $500 and I have never been able to*
> *catch up. Indeed if it had not been for you and Tom I could not have paid*
> *my taxes this year. As it was I did not have to borrow any more; and now I*
> *am paying a hundred off, and if nothing unforeseen occurs I shall manage*
> *very nicely. . . . But we feel wonderfully rich. Ruby was talking about it too,*
> *how wonderful it seemed and how thankful we should be, that the two sons*
> *were both earning their own incomes and such fine ones too. God has been*
> *wonderfully good to us; and hard as it sometimes seems to look forward to*
> *giving Ruby up, still I just feel, it is part of God's plan for us, she is His child*
> *and He will carry us all through to the end of life, and then there will be one*
> *long glorious eternity.* (Box 12-540, Dec 1 1910)

Mary's final remark illustrates the family's deep Christian faith in God and their belief in His plan for each individual. Mary felt that she had a personal relationship with God, and believed that her decisions were directly guided by Him, although she also came to admit that His ways were *mysterious*. She eventually came to some introspection into her motives: *Well, when I come to think it over, there has been much of self-seeking in my service, I am afraid, and most certainly, we do not know what is really best for us* (W5654, Sep 17 1906).

Christmas was approaching and Mary wrote to Calvin to tell him of the family's plans to have Christmas dinner at the cottage, even though Ruby's diet was especially limited.

> *Have just heard from John Baker, the turkey is coming. As the time draws on I*
> *feel more and more sorry you are not to be with us. We are planning to have*
> *our dinner up at the Cottage. Ruby is enjoying so much seeing our various*
> *purchases, we take everything up to show her, even to the smallest card,*
> *before we send them. . . . You know I get utterly bewildered at this season of*
> *the year; there is just so much to plan for and the constant running up to the*
> *Cottage and thinking what Ruby can eat is very wearing. Tho' I think I have*
> *got wonderfully strengthened to bear things without fretting. . . . [P.S.] Edna*
> *remarkably well, a great comfort.* (W9058, Dec 19 1910)

It was a relief that Edna was well at this time. If she, as well as Ruby, had been ill, the emotional and financial burden might have been unbearable for Mary. This in turn would have been a great strain on Ruby. The current success of Mary's two boys was a great consolation to her, and helped to buoy up her spirits. Christmas was held at the cottage, but it was an arduous undertaking, as Mary explains:

> *Well Christmas is over and I am somewhat thankful. The dread of what*
> *may happen before the next, which always oppresses me, hung over me more*
> *than ever. Perhaps this is due somewhat to the fact that I am so very tired.*
> *Of course, getting everything necessary for the Christmas dinner besides all*
> *the presents up to the cottage entailed a great deal of labour mental and*
> *physical. . . .*
> *I do wish you could have seen R.'s room. The things poured in, as Mrs.*
> *Colquhoun said, it looked like a conservatory. Her mantel is long and high*

just like the one in our sitting-room. It was covered from end to one [sic] with
cut flowers cards and china and the top of your little book case too and
another table in the corner (a packing box) besides plants all round the room. . . .

  Altogether the poor child was tired out with the number of things and the
excitement. Things arriving for days. We had the table set in her room and
the uncle came, (late as usual) escorted by Tom. We had a very nice dinner,
grapefruit first, which we all enjoyed, particularly it being a very mild day
and the little cottage roasting, then tomato soup, then turkey &c. plum
pudding, Charlotte Russe and nuts & raisins, coffee.

  Ruby ate some of most things and said she had enjoyed the day very
much. I stayed on till bed-time and the rest of the family left. . . . Fortunately,
Mr. Allan, the city missionary brought us an awfully nice Scotch girl just a
week ago, she was trained in the old country, wears her cap and apron and
knows how to work, and is quick and willing to learn. It was just a special
Providence sent her; she went up with us to the cottage and was so nice and
helpful, and seems very pleased with every thing & sleeps in the room off
kitchen and likes it. (Box 12-240, Dec 28 1910)

Having the *Scotch girl* as a servant would have cheered everyone up, since they
were finally able to afford a servant after so many years without one. Ruby did have
many visitors and it is a testament to her character that she was so well-loved, and
that her infectious condition did not deter well-wishers.

  In fact, Mary is concerned and continues to complain that *Ruby is having far too*
many visitors and it is exhausting for her (Box 12-381, Jan 3 1911); *[she is] almost afflicted*
with visitors (Box 12-388, Jan 12 1911). Finally, Hilda is forced to curtail the activity:

  Ruby's Xmas was almost too much for her, though she did enjoy it all
thoroughly. Then she had a lot of visitors, . . . numerous other people all
through, till finally last Thursday I simply would not let her talk to anyone,
so she is getting rested. (Box 12-258, Jan 16 1911)

This ordeal of so many visitors wore Ruby down and she suffered for it. Mary
explains to Calvin that Ruby is weakening and her diet is very limited:

  Ruby is more comfortable now than before and [at] Christmas, but it is by
taking the simplest nourishment, lime-water and milk bread and butter and
rice. Last Sunday she lost her voice, but it had been very damp weather and
we are hoping it will return, but of course she is not gaining in strength. (Box
  12-459, Jan 20 1911)

In late January of 1911, Calvin lost his position as assistant minister at Edmonton
rather abruptly and he came home. Since all the children were at home in Ruby's
last months, there were no more letters going out from Whitehern. The following
is quoted from the final letter in the archive that mentions Ruby before her death.
Mary tells Calvin: *We trust that God is still leading us, we cannot look ahead as He*
does, but He will make it alright with us. . . . So glad to think you are coming and Ruby
will be too (Box 12-449, Jan 27 1911).

  It is clear that Ruby was weakening and it is not known if she recovered her
voice. Calvin's arrival would have pleased Ruby as she would have had her beloved
brother at home for her remaining months.

Chapter 23

RUBY'S DEATH: THE TRAGIC VICTORIAN HEROINE

And dear old Tom comes up every day if it is only for a few minutes. (W6680)

Ruby died at *Cosy Cottage* on April 9, 1911 at thirty-one years of age. There was a brief notice in the *Globe & Mail* on April 10. The *Hamilton Spectator*, Ruby's home newspaper, printed a death notice one day after her funeral, April 12, 1911:

> *All that was mortal of Miss Ruby B. McQuesten was laid at rest in Hamilton cemetery yesterday afternoon [April 11]. The funeral took place from the home of her mother, Jackson Street West, where an impressive service was conducted by Rev. Dr. Fletcher, Rev. H. B. Ketchen and Rev. Dr. Lyle. The pallbearers were: Jas Chisholm, J. C. Thompson, William James, Alexander Davidson, S. B. McDonald and W. A. Logie.*

According to the notice, Ruby's burial took place on April 11, two days after her death on the 9th, and the notice appeared in her home newspaper the day *after* her funeral. This suggests that Ruby had a private funeral, since the public was not notified until after the funeral and had not been invited for visitation or viewing.

Thomas received a letter of condolence from an old friend, William Mactaggart, who compliments him on his success as a lawyer, and suggests that Tom will now accept his responsibilities as a man and will take his father's place in the family.

TO THOMAS MCQUESTEN from W. A. Mactaggart (W8233)
Whitehern   Colbourne, Ontario
Hamilton, Ontario   Apr 10 1911

Dear Tim [Tom],
> *I am here for a day or so helping Thornton out. Am picking up the Globe and this morning I noticed the announcement of your sister's death. Having passed through an experience something similar in the loss of my father recently I am in a position to appreciate your loss.*
> *I do not see you often Tim [sic], but I hear great and promising reports of your work in your profession and, in the name of our old associations in Varsity I felt constrained to write you a line, extending to you and your mother my sincerest sympathy.*
> *Your mother will feel this loss keenly but she is very fortunate in having such a son to take your father's place in such a time as this. It is just such responsibilities as have fallen upon you Tim that make us men. I wish you success in your work and God's own comfort in your troubles.*   *Yours sincerely*
>   *W. A. Mactaggart*
>   *538 St. Clair Ave., Toronto, Ontario*

Helen Locke, another friend of Tom's, writes a poignant note of condolence expressing her love for Ruby, and her grief at her death:

> *I heard from Mother this evening—and of your loss. I knew it must come soon and yet I cannot realize it. I did not know how much I loved her till that*

day last Fall when I said good bye and felt it really was good bye. I cannot tell you and I am sure I need not try for you must know how I sympathize with you. There is only One we can go to and He understands it all without our even telling Him—and she is at rest and free from all pain. And what a comfort it must be to know how happy she was being at home and seeing all so often. She spoke of it to me and said, "And Dear Old Tom comes up every day if it is only for a few minutes." You don't mind me repeating that now? And still I can't believe I am writing about Ruby. I can't write these letters, Tom. I can't put it into words what I feel. But I want to send you the very deepest sympathy. From your sincere friend, Helen E. R. Locke. (W6680, Apr 12 1911)

RUBY IS FORGOTTEN

The family would have been exhausted after Ruby's death. Her care and the daily vigil as she weakened and died, would have been exceedingly difficult, especially as she was such a beautiful person and much loved.

Curiously, there is little mention of Ruby in the numerous extant letters following her death. The silence suggests that the family may have felt a kind of collective guilt at the circumstances of Ruby's prolonged financial and physical sacrifice for the family. This sacrifice was also the direct cause of her thwarted relationship with David Ross. It is difficult to know if the collective silence in the letters is a result of their Presbyterian stoicism, or the consequence of a deep regret bordering on guilt.

It is apparent that except for a few scant, enigmatic comments, <u>Ruby's name disappears from the family letters</u>. Ruby appears to have been forgotten. Mary's concerns thereafter are usually about her own health and suffering as she ages, and they may appear to the reader as somewhat self-centred. It bears repeating that Mary believed that she had a personal relationship with God and that every decision she made had first been sanctioned by God. However, she previously admitted to her service having had *much of self-seeking* (W5654), and she may now have had the leisure to assess whether there had been some of this in her advice as well.

While on vacation in Bayfield just a few months after Ruby's death, Mary comments on her own lack of *cheer.* She may be alluding to Ruby's death and to what might have been done differently:

TO REV. CALVIN MCQUESTEN from his mother, Mary Baker McQuesten (W6736)
Staney Brae,   Bayfield, Ontario
Muskoka, Ontario   Jul 25 1911

My dearest Calvin,

Just inclosing [sic] these letters for your entertainment. We are having a very windy time which set in yesterday morning, not so very cold but a high wind, so that we can go out very little, so thankful to be going home on Thursday.

You are really most enterprising at Staney Brae glad to hear of your doing something to amuse yourself. It really is so tiresome if one cannot get up something. Edna is very well indeed and endeavours to <u>cheer me up</u>. <u>All she can</u> (emphasis added). *It does not do for me to have nothing to do, I have*

*decided this is the trouble, at home there is always something to occupy my mind.
Hope you have bed clothes enough; I had to send home for blankets. Glad to know
you are feeling so well.*

> *With much love,*
> *Your affectionate mother*
> *M. B. McQuesten*

Henceforward, Ruby's actual name is mentioned only twice in the letters, one
year after her death; it then disappears from the (numerous) extant letters. Mary
comments on Ruby's death on the one-year anniversary, April 9, 1912, and again on
Ruby's birthday, May 3, 1912. She observes that Calvin's loss is the greatest, and she
pays tribute to Ruby's loveliness. The letters and the envelopes are edged in black, as
was the custom for at least one year after a death in the family:

> *This is a dull heavy morning, and I seem equally dull; we have been on
> the continual go this week, and I am just tired. Altho' the 9th was the date
> when darling Ruby left us, it was more present to me on Sunday; I seemed to
> go over it all again. It was indeed a loss to us all never to be repaired, but I
> do not grieve about it now, she just seems to have gone a little before. I think
> the greatest loss was really to yourself, she would have been such a help to
> you, and I always planned that she would be with you at first; I used to fancy
> her charming the people. But God plans for the best.* (W8867, Apr 12 1912)

> *This is poor Ruby's birthday. How often I think of her, taken out of all this
> hurry and bustle! And yet how lovely it would be to have her here. It was such
> a delight to look at her. I see her always before me.* (Box 12-296, May 3 1912)

The tone of Mary's comments to Calvin suggest that she has some regrets
regarding Ruby, as she *seemed to go over it all again,* possibly implying that some
things might have been done differently. Unfortunately, Calvin's replies to these
letters are not extant. Calvin may have suffered a deep depression after Ruby's death,
and he experienced a breakdown in 1912.

It is never stated openly in the letters, but Calvin appears to hold some resentment
against his mother for two reasons regarding Ruby's illness and death. First, he
supported Ruby and David Ross in their engagement and in their defiance of Mary's
edict that they wait two years. In fact, he acted as a go-between for them. They were
thwarted by Ruby's mother and, eventually, by Ruby's illness. Second, Calvin likely
felt that Ruby was kept working far too long in order to pay for Tom's education, to
the extent that it endangered her health and shortened her life. Mary's closing resort
to a religious platitude, *But God plans for the best,* may have had a hollow ring in
Calvin's ears.

Calvin eventually found some redemption in his semi-volunteer work as the
well-loved chaplain of the Hamilton Mountain Sanatorium from 1920 to 1950. *(In
the photograph opposite, Calvin is with a nurse at the San during that period.)* There is
no indication in the letters of how Thomas managed his grief; however, his devotion
to Ruby in her illness was exemplary. He went on to fulfill Ruby's prophecy for his
future and, to a large extent, his many accomplishments can be seen as the tokens of
his profound sense of gratitude for Ruby's sacrifice.

Chapter 24

A TRAGIC POSTSCRIPT TO RUBY'S DEATH

"If their uncle had been considerate and generous,
Ruby's story could have been very different." (M.J.A.)

To add to the tragedy of Ruby's sacrifice and her untimely death, their uncle, Dr. Calvin Brooks McQuesten, died on February 19, 1912, just ten months after

Dr. Calvin Brooks McQuesten
(1837-1912)

Ruby's death. In his will he left Mary *about $35,000* and made her sole executor, although succession duties would take ten percent of that amount (Box 12-712, Feb 24 1912). This revealed clearly that in all those difficult years of poverty, when Ruby toiled to exhaustion and worse, to pay for Tom's education, the uncle had not offered to help his nephews (Calvin or Tom) with the cost of their education. Also, he did not offer to contribute toward Ruby's medical care, yet he was a doctor.

This is doubly tragic. If their uncle had been considerate and generous, Ruby's story could have been very different. She would have been able to pursue her artistic talent in painting, and she might have become an important woman artist in Canada. She would have been able to keep most of her salary and she could have travelled. She would not have had to continue working to pay for Tom's education long after her illness became chronic. She might also have found a suitable marriage partner and she might have had children. The whole family must have felt a deep sorrow and regret at this discovery, but there is no statement of this in the letters.

Their Uncle Calvin never married and he had no other heirs, so the revelation in his will created a compound tragedy. One might expect that some reaction would have been displayed at the uncle's lack of sympathy and miserly neglect of the family. A certain resentment is indicated in a brief letter fragment from Mary to Calvin. When cleaning out the uncle's flat after his death, Mary declares that his framed portrait presented a *great difficulty* and she did not want it hanging prominently in the house. Tom did not hesitate to voice his bitterness and suggested they *have it crated and out of sight*; however, Mary was even more forthright in her reply that she *did not want any useless things put there in the cellar*

THE CANADA BUSINESS COLLEGE.
Arcade Building, Hamilton, Ont.

Alexandra Arcade, Hamilton, Ontario

(Box 12-730, Mar 30 1912). Consequently, there is no framed portrait of the uncle at Whitehern today.

Is it possible that Dr. Calvin Brooks did not know of their plight? This seems unlikely since he owned property in Hamilton that he received in the settlement of Isaac's estate. He was granted the Alexandra Arcade, a large rental property from which he agreed to pay the annuity owing to his step-mother. Dr. Calvin Brooks came to live in an apartment in Hamilton in 1908 and he visited Whitehern on holidays. His funeral was held at Whitehern and he was buried in the family plot at Hamilton Cemetery.

One likely explanation might be that Dr. Calvin Brooks continued to carry a grudge against Mary after Isaac died in 1888. In the settlement of Isaac's estate and bankruptcy, he felt that Mary had been unduly favoured and he had been cheated. He penned his objection to Chisholm:

All the money Mary paid out to cancel debts was in reality making investments and no loss to her. . . . All that I have done . . . by settling with the creditors of Isaac is clean mine, out of pocket, and put into her pocket. . . .

The six to eight thousand a year they were spending was half mine & was not a very honest way of treating the poor fool of a brother. (W1652, Jun 21 1888)

Calvin Brooks was eccentric, but to carry that grudge into the next generation, in light of the family's desperate financial woes, was unconscionable.

Thus, Ruby's death is a double tragedy—in fact it takes on the elements of a Greek tragedy, with the family letters acting as the chorus, commenting on events and occasionally delivering invocations to God.

Dr. Calvin Brooks McQuesten visits Whitehern. (L. to R.) Ruby, Uncle Calvin Brooks, Tom, Hilda, Edna, mother. (Centre) Miss Mewburn, Mary c.1903

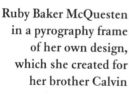

Ruby Baker McQuesten
in a pyrography frame
of her own design,
which she created for
her brother Calvin

FOR RUBY

When will we see another such
As Ruby, polished jewel of
A brood that forged its wealth from love
And mined its future through her touch?

The grace of self-denial set
Its gem in her slight gentle frame,
And all her income homeward came
For siblings' needs and household debt.

If not for her would there have grown
The gardens brother Thomas brought?
The harvests which his vision wrought
From sparkling Ruby's seeds were sown.

For her no change of name, nor ring,
For her there was no life with Ross;
Yet she did not complain of loss,
Betrayed no sign of suffering.

While cheerful in adversity
She shed her light too short a time;
A nagging cough sliced through her prime
And cast her tragic history.

But keep alive her memory:
Her paintings brush and warm the heart,
Her sense of duty adds its part;
Take courage from her legacy.

by **G. W. Down** (2007, Box 14-116)

PAINTINGS & PYROGRAPHY
by Ruby Baker McQuesten
(Research and captions by Julie Nash)

Colourplate 1. **Music (After J.R. Seavey), by Ruby B. McQuesten, undated** [968.961]
Ruby completed this painting at the Hamilton Art School under the tutelage of
Julian Ruggles Seavey.

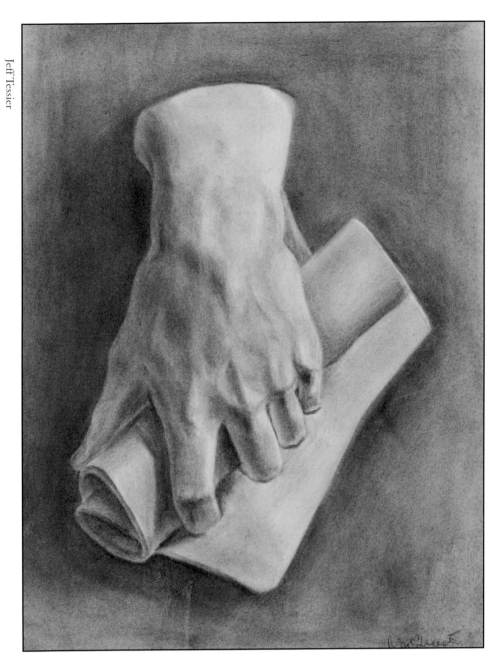

Jeff Tessier

Colourplate 2. **Hand Holding a Scroll, by Ruby B. McQuesten, undated** [974.619.125]

This is an early example of Ruby's art work. While a student at the Hamilton Art School she completed many studies from cast objects, including fruit, flowers and more challenging subjects such as this one from the human figure.

Jeff Tessier

Colourplate 3. **Sepia Castor Plant Leaf, by Ruby B. McQuesten, 1896** [2009.30.001]

In 1896 Ruby received praise at the Hamilton Art School for this drawing and was awarded a prize for it as well. In addition to acclaim from her teachers, an undated newspaper clipping at Whitehern mentions: "in sepia work the best thing shown for years is a castor plant leaf by Ruby McQuesten" (News clipping, n.d., Box 8).

Jeff Tessier

Colourplate 4. **Charcoal Landscape with Ducks, by Ruby B. McQuesten, 1894** [968.1279]

Ruby was similarly praised for this charcoal drawing as a new student of the Hamilton Art School. A newspaper clipping of September 15, 1894 praises Ruby and many others for achieving original compositions in lieu of copying the work of their teachers. The columnist writes: "Rubie *[sic]* McQuesten and Mary Lyle have excellent charcoal landscapes." This is the only known charcoal landscape completed by Ruby. It also bears an identifying label from the Hamilton Art School.

Colourplate 5. **White Stem Rose, by Ruby B. McQuesten, undated** [968.1066]
The rose with thorns symbolizes sacrifice or martyrdom,
while a white petal is a symbol of death.

Colourplate 6. **Pink Stem Rose, by Ruby B. McQuesten, undated** [2009.13.001]
The rose without thorns symbolizes a virtuous woman,
while the pink colour denotes innocent, romantic love. (www.columbia.edu/)

Jeff Tessier

Colourplate 7. **Summer Strawberries, by Ruby B. McQuesten, undated** [2009.03.001]

This photograph shows the test brushstrokes made by Ruby as she completed the painting. At the upper right corner she also made pencil notations of the colours she was using in the image.

Jeff Tessier

Colourplate 8. **Pottery and Green Grapes, by Ruby B. McQuesten, undated** [2009.02.001]

Colourplate 9. **Autumn Maple, by Ruby B. McQuesten, undated** [968.929]

Jeff Tessier

Colourplate 10. **Afternoon Tea with Biscuits, by Ruby B. McQuesten, 1903** [968.926]

Ruby mentioned this painting in a letter to her brother Calvin, stating: "I'm doing one of those studies I know you admire-- biscuits & cheese & teapot & cream jug (I suppose you think a mug of beer would be more appropriate) well I'll do one with that one of these days when the cheese has a stronger look--as long as it will stand steady long enough to be painted" (W4753). This letter shows both the camaraderie between Ruby and Calvin, and her joking demeanour as she teases that the cheese may be eaten before it can be painted.

Colourplate 11. Sailboat and Seagull Returning to Harbour, by Ruby B. McQuesten, undated [968.934]

Jeff Tessier

Colourplate 12. **Sailboats and Five Windmills, by Ruby B. McQuesten, 1907** [968.1276]

Ruby completed two versions of this painting, a study and a polished final copy. In 1907, she challenged Calvin to search the painting for hidden symbols: "And as for the windmills——they suggest a breeze that blows away the clouds. I've done pretty well for you my boy for I think I've put in five windmills. You may possibly only be able to see three. The other two form the poetic touch and are understood. They're in there though someplace to the left of the big boat. When you look at the arms of the windmills you're to see them waving good luck to you. And with twenty arms of Zeus himself will be moved." (W5828)

Jeff Tessier

Colourplate 13. **Daffodils in a Ginger Pot, by Ruby B. McQuesten, 1903** [526-2]

A 1903 letter from Mary Baker McQuesten to her son Calvin mentions that Ruby "has brought home some lovely pictures [from Ottawa]. One of a tea pot, sugar bowl and tea cup with biscuits and cheese on a fringed napkin. They are really lovely, and some daffodils in a ginger pot, but my table is wonderful" (W5002). In this note Mary mentions the daffodils as well as Afternoon Tea with Biscuits, which appears to be her favourite.

Jeff Tessier

Colourplate 14. **Early Winter, by Ruby B. McQuesten, c. 1899-1907** [1991.4]

The reverse of this painting has 'Ruby B. McQuesten, Ottawa Ladies College' inscribed in Ruby's hand. This note establishes a rough time frame for the date of completion, in this case while Ruby was teaching at the Ottawa Ladies College from 1899-1907.

Jeff Tessier

Colourplate 15. **Poet's Daffodil** (*narcissus poeticus*)**, by Ruby B. McQuesten, undated** [968.924]

Jeff Tessier

Colourplate 16. **Pyrography box with Yellow Tulips, by Ruby B. McQuesten, undated** [2009.23.001]

Jeff Tessier

Colourplate 17. **Pyrography tie rack with Irises, by Ruby B. McQuesten, undated** [2009.18.001]

In a letter from 1903 Mary Baker refers to a gift of pyrography given to her by her daughter. Despite the fact that the term 'pyrography' was in common use at the time, Mary refers to the object as 'poker work.' (W5002)

Colourplate 18. **Grey Vase with Virginia Creeper, by Ruby B. McQuesten,
undated** [2009.27.001]

Jeff Tessier

Colourplate 19. **Bridging the River, by Ruby B. McQuesten, 1904** [2009.32.001]

This painting was a gift to Calvin from Ruby on the occasion of his birthday. On the reverse of the frame she inscribed a note reading "wishing my dear Cal a very happy New Year - Ruby." A letter from 1904 between Ruby and Calvin reveals her brother's reaction to the gift. Ruby responds: "I'm so glad you like your picture—I wondered whether it was as refreshing as the brown & yellow scene, but the people here all thought you'd approve of it." (W5191)

Part Three

TRIUMPH:
THOMAS BAKER MCQUESTEN
(1882-1948)

The Honourable Thomas Baker McQuesten, BA, MA, KC, LLD

Thomas Baker McQuesten
ELECTIONS AND APPOINTMENTS

HAMILTON

Alderman, Ward Two 1913-20
Hamilton Town Planning Commission 1916-47
Hamilton Board of Parks Management
and Chairman of the Works Committee 1922-47
Honorary LLD from McMaster University 1944
Man of the Year Jan. 5, 1948

LIBERAL PARTY

President of the Hamilton Liberal Association 1921-23
Management Committee of the Liberal Party in Ottawa 1925
Vice-President of the Ontario Liberal Association 1931
President of the Ontario Liberal Association 1932-43

King's Counsel January 1934

ONTARIO

Commissioner of the Hydro Electric Power Commission 1934-37
MPP for Hamilton-Wentworth 1934-43
Minister of Highways (Bridges) 1934-43
Minister of Public Works, 1934-37 & 1942-43
Chairman of the Niagara Parks Commission, 1934-44
Minister of Northern Development 1936-43
Second Vice-President of the Canadian Good Roads Association 1936-38
President of the Canadian Good Roads Association 1938-39
Canadian Chairman of the Niagara Falls Bridge Commission 1938-1947
Minister of Mines, September to October 1940
Minister of Municipal Affairs, November 1940-43

Chapter 25

THE "FORGOTTEN BUILDER"

We have to do good by stealth in this world. (Thomas B. McQuesten)

Do good by stealth and blush to find it fame. (Alexander Pope)

Thomas B. McQuesten (1882-1948)

Thomas Baker McQuesten was a visionary and a master builder. As his vast accomplishments come to be known and appreciated, he is becoming a legend, a veritable Renaissance man. Yet, for many years he was relatively unknown, in part because people are loath to believe that one man could have accomplished so much. Also relevant was McQuesten's preferred method of operation, confided in a letter to his close associate, Matt Broman: *I have often said that we have to do good by stealth in this world and of course it is a fact of life which is evident in many activities that a man who is striving to occupy himself with what are undoubtedly higher things is called upon to meet never ending difficulties in the way of performing them* (W9864t, Dec 23 1943). It is evident that here was a man of action and moral conviction, but also a man of caution and humility. He had a clear plan of life in which he anticipated difficulties and found ways to manoeuvre around them.

T.B. McQuesten is gaining recognition for his prolific works as a master builder of roads, bridges, parks, gardens and historical restorations. Yet little is known about his personality, character and methods, or his relationships with associates and family. Tom often appeared reserved and somewhat remote; he had an aristocratic bearing and may have appeared formidable to many who met him. But to his friends and associates, even those in lesser positions, he was considerate and kindly, even somewhat deferential. All shared the same goals, and Tom was highly respected by those who worked with him. His objective was always to get the job done in the best, quickest, and most economical manner, sometimes growing frustrated and even vindictive when impeded by political posturing.

Thomas had a Classical education and had a keen interest in history and political science. As a Renaissance man, he had the "imagination of the lawyer-engineer-artist" (Best 125). He also had a deep appreciation of the arts, and commissioned many artists to add decorative and historical details to his architectural and garden projects. Many details are typically Canadian in theme and articulation. Some of the artists were women, which is not surprising since his sister Ruby, who influenced him in so many ways, was an artist. Just as Tom is the "Forgotten Builder," Ruby is the "Forgotten Artist"—and it is hoped that this writing will serve to counter both oversights.

Tom's family circumstances played a role in his choice of methods and his success. The family was in the habit of guarding its secrets, and was considered somewhat eccentric and mysterious in Hamilton. Tom must have known when growing up that he was being groomed to be the "saviour" of the McQuesten name. In spite of suffering social stigma and prolonged poverty, the McQuestens retained their dignity. A great deal of emphasis was placed in the family and home on art and culture, and Tom was raised to be every inch a gentleman and an aristocrat. His mother was a beacon of duty and purpose for him, and his sister Ruby's advice and sacrifice for him provided a major source of inspiration. The only way that he could justify their faith in him was to restore the honour and prestige of the family name.

Tom took care to surround himself with like-minded associates. In many cases he envisioned the project, organized his associates, achieved his purpose, and then stepped aside to let others accept credit while he was quietly busy with the next undertaking. In this way many of his works were well under way before any politician could raise an objection or interfere on purely partisan grounds. Dr. Leslie Laking provides the example that McQuesten and the Hamilton Parks Board had worked on the possibility of establishing a botanical park in the city for some twenty years, during which time various tracts of land were secured, "so a great deal had been accomplished towards the founding of a botanical garden before any public revelation of the fact" (Laking 11). Tom likewise planned and quietly built small sections of divided highway in various locations, with boulevards of greenery, so that motorists would become accustomed to the benefits of a safer and more attractive motor trip, and would come to expect the same throughout.

His approach was effective, and McQuesten completed more development in his short career than any other politician before or since. Yet the habit of stealth prevented his leadership being acknowledged for many of his projects. Perhaps their sheer volume also kept him so occupied that he was unable to attend some of the ceremonials connected with them. Partly for these reasons, he became known as "Ontario's Forgotten Builder" (Barnsley 63). Later in his career, partisan politics interfered with recognition for his accomplishments as well.

Tom's method of stealth also arose from a fundamental modesty; his devout Presbyterianism would have prevented him from any public boasting. Pride is one of the seven deadly sins, and Tom would have followed the Biblical edict in Matthew 6: "when you do a charitable deed do not sound a trumpet." In a related vein, and in view of Tom's very productive career, he certainly never indulged in the sin of Sloth.

The *Hamilton Spectator* paid tribute to Tom's quiet method: "It is not the Hon. T.B. McQuesten's way to make a loud noise about what he is doing. He goes ahead with it, and when the job is done, lets it speak for itself" (Jan 14 1935).

HAMILTON'S HIGH LEVEL BRIDGE—Majesty and Mystery

*High Level Bridge, Hamilton, 1932
(City of Hamilton Engineer's Dept.)*

Hamilton's High Level Bridge, now Thomas B. McQuesten High Level Bridge

Unlike many politicians, Thomas McQuesten never sought to have his name perpetuated on any of his works, not even in his own city. For instance, his name did not appear on Hamilton's High Level Bridge until 1988. The High Level Bridge, built in 1931-32, was a key feature of McQuesten's vision for a grand entrance to Hamilton. Yet, the original plaque did not mention his name, although several other Hamilton dignitaries were named, including the mayor and the Board of Control, the engineers, consulting engineers, and John Lyle, the architect. In point of fact, McQuesten as Chairman of the Works Committee of the Hamilton Board of Parks Management would have granted the commission to Lyle and the engineers; yet McQuesten's role and name were excluded.

On July 11, 1988, more than fifty years later, and forty years after McQuesten's death, the bridge was formally renamed the Thomas B. McQuesten High Level Bridge. At this time it was also recognized as a historical landmark under the Ontario Heritage Act. HRH Princess Margaret officiated at the re-dedication of the bridge, and unveiled a plaque in McQuesten's honour which stands today just north of the bridge on a grassy berm with an impressive concrete staircase:

Thomas Baker McQuesten, 1882-1948

An influential proponent of landscape improvement pro-grams, McQuesten was raised here and educated at the University of Toronto and Osgoode Hall. He joined a Hamilton law practice in 1909 and eleven years later was appointed to the city's Board of Parks Management. In this capacity and as Minister of Highways (1934-43) and Chairman of the Niagara Parks Commission (1934-44), McQuesten devoted himself to the development of parks and scenic parkways. He effectively combined attention to aesthetics with engineering requirements in the design of bridges and roads, including the Queen Elizabeth Way, that were constructed under his charge. McQuesten also actively promoted numerous beautification projects, the park lands along the Niagara River and RBG nearby remaining today as the greatest legacies of his efforts.

Erected by the Ontario Heritage Foundation, Ministry of Culture and Communication

Princess Margaret

A second, smaller plaque marks the occasion and honours HRH Princess Margaret:

THIS PLAQUE WAS UNVEILED
BY
HER ROYAL HIGHNESS THE PRINCESS MARGARET
COUNTESS OF SNOWDEN
C.I., G.C.V.O.
11TH JULY, 1988
ON THE OCCASION OF THE DEDICATION
OF THE
THOMAS B. MCQUESTEN HIGH LEVEL BRIDGE

The Thomas B. McQuesten High Level Bridge is notable for its four monumental pylons, two at each end of the bridge. Faced in Queenston limestone, each pylon is forty feet high (12.2m), and bears the City of Hamilton Coat of Arms; each contains a life-size sculpture niche that remains empty to this day—seventy-eight years after the bridge was built, and twenty-two years after it received its rightful name. When driving over the bridge one is struck by the majesty of those four pylons. They are magnificent in themselves, but remain vacant and compelling.

Several attempts have been made to reach an agreement on which worthy citizens might be immortalized in the niches. Hamilton lawyer Adam C. Zimmerman related a story, perhaps an urban legend, to Roland Barnsley, that T.B. McQuesten had named four prominent Hamilton citizens for the niches. The four cited were

Pylon, niche vacant

Adam Zimmerman (1852-1919) Liberal Member of Parliament, 1904-08; Sir John M. Gibson (1842-1929) a Lieutenant-Governor of Ontario; Colonel William Hendrie (1831-1906) military leader; and Major-General S.C. Mewburn (1863-1956) Minister of Defence during the First World War. The families of these men presumably were approached to have bronze likenesses made for placement in the niches when the bridge opened. But the four men to be honoured "all represented the influential Presbyterian Church," and other churches objected on the basis of "Family Compact." Barnsley continues the tale: "Then the whole idea collapsed, and those pylons have been empty to this day" (35-6).

Other attempts were made, notably in 1949 and in 1952, when the Hamilton Spectator suggested that T.B. McQuesten ought to be celebrated with a sculpture in one of the niches and the bridge re-named for McQuesten. The re-naming was finally accomplished in 1988, but McQuesten's niche is still waiting for its rightful and logical occupant.

The present writer respectfully suggests four meritorious sculpture subjects to fill the niches: (1) Hon. T.B. McQuesten; (2) John Macintosh Lyle, architect, a Hamiltonian and one of Canada's foremost architects; (3) Adelaide Hoodless, the founder of the Women's Institute in 1897, a group that Tom and his family promoted; and (4) Chief Joseph Brant, whom Tom admired for his contribution to the British during the War of Independence and for his success in fostering peace between communities and nations. These sculptures could then form the basis of a walking tour that would be invaluable for the teaching of history.

A sculpture to T.B. McQuesten would be most appropriate and timely to celebrate Tom's foresight in planning and building a bridge to accommodate and serve the transportation needs of a future city of 500,000—a milestone that Hamilton has now reached some seventy-eight years later.

Thomas McQuesten is gradually taking his rightful place in Hamilton and Ontario history. In the late 1970s, RBG named its amphitheatre the "McQuesten Theatre." The City of Hamilton named a park for T.B. McQuesten on Upper Wentworth Street and began planning a multicultural peace garden there in 1989. The park serves a heavily populated area of the city's East Mountain, and Thomas would wholeheartedly approve of the gardens (many yet to be landscaped), sports facilities, paths for strolling and roller-skating, benches and ample parking. A district in northeast Hamilton in Ward Four also bears the McQuesten family name, although Thomas acted as Alderman for Ward Two, in which the McQuesten home,

Dedication of the Hon. T.B. McQuesten Rose
Rev. Dr. John Johnston & group at
MacNab Street Presbyterian Church (1990)

Whitehern, is located. And in 1990, the MacNab Street Presbyterian Church, the McQuesten's home church, dedicated a rose to the family.

As he emerges from relative obscurity, Tom is being recognized as a visionary and a master builder. However, as a man, he remains a mystery. When you look around you in Hamilton, Niagara and other parts of Ontario, you are surrounded by McQuesten's accomplishments. The question arises, how could one man achieve so much of such beauty and grace? Several factors in Tom's life shed light on his personality and purpose.

Foremost is the fact that Tom was groomed almost from birth to achieve greatness. He was the second of two sons, and the only one who was robust and healthy. The McQuesten family fell from aristocracy to impoverishment when he was six years of age; he alone of the six children could possibly redeem the family name.

Tom's sister, Ruby, sacrificed herself for him and for his success; no doubt he felt that he owed it to her to make a success of his life—and hers. Together they formed a team: Tom was the only one in the family capable of achieving success, and Ruby, his older sister, was the only one capable of earning a wage to pay for his education toward that success. Ruby became his mentor and played a large part in his education and formative years, but she died at a young age, becoming the "Forgotten Sister."

The McQuesten Theatre at RBG

Chapter 26

THE HONEST LAWYER AND HAMILTON POLITICIAN

My Dear Mother. . . . If I am going to achieve anything
and come to you for commendation, I must come with clean hands.
T.B. McQuesten, Mar 6 1906 (W5440)

Chisholm, Logie & McQuesten, Barristers at Law,
69 James Street North, Hamilton, Ontario

In June 1909, Thomas Baker McQuesten became established as a lawyer in James Chisholm's law office, Chisholm & Logie. It was the very office where Tom's father, Isaac, prior to his death in 1888, had partnered with Chisholm. Tom had already done his articling at Toronto and Elk Lake. He began with Chisholm at a salary of $1,000 per year, the same salary he had earned with Masten, Starr and Spence when articling at Elk Lake (W5912, Jul 20 1907).

Tom had not been certain about where he wanted to settle for his law practice and this gave rise to some family discussion. He agreed with his brother, Calvin, and with his mother, that his political chances would be better in Hamilton. But Tom was not enthusiastic about settling back home in Hamilton. While still at the University, and three years before he would graduate in law, he conveyed his reluctance to Calvin:

> *I note what you say re politics. . . I will think it over. If I did have the idea of*
> *eventually going into politics I would have to consider where to settle down.*
> *It would be almost hopeless for a Liberal to try and get elected in Toronto.*
> *I think I would stand a far better chance in Hamilton, <u>but then I could not*
> *afford to be a stranger there</u>.* (emphasis added, W8176, Jul 17 1904)

Was it Hamilton in general, or being back home under the matriarch's thumb that Tom resisted? At the time when Tom's articling work was finishing up and business was no longer brisk, his mother was urging him to come home. Ruby was ill and no longer working; her income had stopped at the end of Spring term in June 1907, just before Tom's graduation. Mary wanted Tom home and wrote to Calvin several times, hoping, no doubt, to influence Tom through Calvin:

> *It is a difficult matter to decide as to Tom's final start, but he thinks, and I think, perhaps it is as good a place as anywhere else here in Hamilton where Mr. C. would give him a chance, and he has a certain standing and <u>could enjoy the home</u>. It takes time to get a practice and we are not sure there is any special advantage in Toronto. I had always thought perhaps some special opening would come, but at the same time on the other hand hope that <u>here I may get him interested in some good work besides his business</u>. In Toronto he will be old before he begins anything and in a smaller place too one's influence tells more. It is a matter for earnest prayer by us all, for it is a critical time.* (emphasis added, W6318, Dec 1 1908)

It is not surprising that Mary prayed to have Tom at home with her; he was her favourite son, she was very proud of him, and his success would reflect favourably on the family. As she stated, Mary had another motive for wanting Tom at home and that was to influence his career, which she certainly did, as Tom's future accomplishments will demonstrate. Mary was jubilant when her prayers were answered and Tom took the position with Chisholm, and moved back home. She exulted: *Tom just started to his office a week ago Saturday that was on the 19th. It really seems scarcely possible that he can be there, but it is certainly going to mean a great difference to us* (W6460, Jun 28 1909).

What did Mary mean by that final statement that it would *mean a great difference to us?* Is it that Tom's salary would be coming into the household to help defray the bills? Is it that he would become the titular head of the household and thus relieve some of her cares? Is it that the family would immediately rise in prestige by virtue of having a lawyer in the household? Is it that Mary would now be able to exert some influence over Tom's career to encourage him into *some good work besides his business?* The answer to all of the above is a resounding, Yes! This was a milestone. With Tom educated in law, and living and working at home, the family was well on the way to restoring their former status, shattered more than twenty years ago with the bankruptcy and sudden death of their father, Isaac.

Another important question: Could this outcome have been achieved without Ruby's help and sacrifice? The evidence in the letters demonstrates that it could not. When we take all things into consideration, Tom would not have been able to get the education that he needed to reach this point; he might have become a bank clerk or some other such career, but he could not have graduated in law without the money that Ruby provided, and continued to provide, even after she became ill. Her sacrifice was great; she had to give up a marriage prospect and she also endangered any hope of her own recovery. So Tom was launched and Ruby was gravely ill—but the family had a new starting point.

Shortly after Tom came home and began working in the law office with Chisholm, he and his mother made a trip together by train to the Fonthill Nurseries.

One wonders if some of the seeds of Tom's success with parks and gardens were gathered here. Was this early trip a part of Mary's plan to get Tom *interested in some work besides his business*? If so, Tom was certainly not a reluctant participant. Mary describes the botanical wonders to Calvin:

T.B. McQuesten and his mother, Mary Baker McQuesten (c.1925)

Tom and I started off on the long-talked-of-trip to see the Fonthill Nurseries. . . . We saw a great variety of evergreens most interesting and beautiful. I never saw anything like them; some had been there for twenty years and showed what they could become. Beautiful golden tipped ones and then the Kastor and Colorado spruce were a bright light blue, it is when they grow larger you see how blue they can be and very fine Irish junipers. Then there was an immense hydrangea covered from the top to the ground with flowers. Then we saw most beautiful varieties of grasses making a very effective bed. Then we were much taken with a Chinese rose, it flowers the whole season, pink ones and white ones very sweet scented and grows in a very fine network which is not pruned and the leaves very stiff and glossy. (W6521, Sep 10 1909)

During Tom's advancement in career between 1908 and 1911, Ruby's health continued to decline. She was sent first to Calgary in 1907 for treatment, then to Gravenhurst and finally to the cottage on Hamilton Mountain. Her travel and medical expenses were high and Tom was called upon to begin to contribute to *her* care. He did not hesitate to do so, but it was too late and her illness was too far gone; she did not recover and died of tuberculosis in April 1911. Tom certainly felt a responsibility to Ruby and contributed to her travel and medical expenses to the extent that he was able, but he was still earning just $1,000 per year. Ruby's expenses were high, and the family was not yet solvent.

As a lawyer with Chisholm & Logie in Hamilton, Tom informed Calvin in the summer of 1909 of his good fortune:

I think this office will be all right. They have an immense number of small clients and quite a good sprinkling of good ones. I am quite sure the firm's receipts are a good size . . . and after I get some connections up, Chisholm said he would discuss the question of sharing the profits. (W8212, Jul 15 1909)

Although Tom had been trying to reassure Calvin about his salary and future prospects, he was prematurely optimistic. He did not receive a salary increase for two more years, until the summer of 1911, three months after Ruby's death. The family by then had endured a great many hardships for the past twenty-three years.

In July 1911, Tom again wrote to reassure Calvin at Muskoka: *Don't worry about the money, there's plenty of it* (W8237, Jul 10 1911). In August 1911, Mary reports to

Calvin that Tom is to have a wage increase to $1,200 per year, and she comments on Tom's generosity to the family:

> *Tom came home with good news last night; his salary is raised from July 1st to $100 a month. Mr. C. [Chisholm] said they cleared last year $12,000, of this Mr. C. gets 3/5, Mr. L. [Logie] 2/5; next year they expect to make more and then Tom is to have a very substantial increase. This is very encouraging and Tom certainly deserves it from the way he treats us.* (W6746, Aug 11 1911)

When Tom wrote to Calvin to tell him the good news about his salary increase, he added a rather droll note about his mother's snobbish disapproval of his small office: *I am getting a larger office, which I suppose will be a gratification to Mrs. McQ. She sniffed every time she came into the present office* (W8239, Aug 17 1911). Logie became a judge in 1918, and the annual statement for 1920 shows that by that time the formula was 2/3 to Chisholm: $9,532.67; and 1/3 to McQuesten: $4,766.33 (W-MCP7-1.209).

In August 1911, just four months after Ruby's death, the family had a scare and the memory of her illness and death came flooding back to haunt them. Daughter Mary developed an ulcerated throat and symptoms similar to Ruby's chronic cough. Naturally, the family became alarmed, knowing the contagious nature of the disease. Fortunately, Mary's throat cleared up without any long-term effects, and she lived to the age of ninety. Had it been otherwise, and had she followed Ruby's fate, there would have been many more years of heartache and hardship for the family. In fact, none of the other members of the family ever contracted tuberculosis despite being continuously exposed to Ruby during her illness.

Mary wrote to Calvin of her relief that daughter Mary's throat condition was not serious. She also relates the many circumstances adding to her feeling of relief so that finally she felt quite *care-free, not for many years have I felt so and must try to build myself up and thank God with all my heart* (W6752, Aug 17 1911). It had been twenty-three years since Mary Baker McQuesten had known any financial relief; Calvin and Edna had suffered mental breakdowns, and Ruby suffered a long incurable illness and tragic death. It is strange that in that care-free letter, just four months after Ruby's death, Mary does not mention feeling any grief at the tragedy of losing Ruby.

One year later, Mary again comments on their eased circumstances but does not mention Ruby:

> *It is certainly wonderful to look back over the years and realize that they are past and that we are in such easy circumstances. Sometimes one is tempted to think that the sorest trials might have been averted if there had not been such a scarcity of money, but then we feel that is not for us to say. God was managing our affairs for us, and He surely knew the best way.* (Box 12-720, Mar 7 1912)

Mary frequently invokes the name of God as the manager of their affairs. One wonders: was this Mary's way of rationalizing any feelings of guilt that she might have had? When Ruby was in Gravenhurst ten months before her death, Mary remarks on what she terms Ruby's *exile: it is terrible for poor Ruby to be thus exiled for years, indeed it does not do for me to think of it and I have to pray for grace to submit and leave it in God's hands* (Box 12-626). There is both regret and guilt in Mary's use of the phrase, *exiled for years*, and the Biblical connotation of banishment and homelessness lends an even greater pathos to Ruby's plight. Although Ruby was often homesick, she never complained, but her brief and lonely refrain, *I, who Love in letters*, is a cry of abject despair in her years of isolation from her beloved home and family (W6555, Dec 2 1909).

The family letters continued back and forth for many years after Ruby's death, but her name is not mentioned; it is as if Ruby had been too easily forgotten. Of course, we cannot know how, or if, Ruby was spoken of at home after her death. On the back of one of Ruby's paintings, her mother had written, *one of dear Ruby's first paintings*. It is conceivable that the family managed their grief with Presbyterian stoicism—that is, in relative silence, their grief sublimated into good works that might serve to ameliorate the guilt of Ruby's sacrifice.

The mystery deepens: most of the family letters written *to Ruby* are missing. In fact, with the exception of a single letter from Calvin, <u>all</u> of the letters that the family wrote to her while she was *exiled* are no longer extant. There would have been many letters from Tom to Ruby thanking her for the postal money orders that she regularly sent from the College. Ruby's letters often thank Tom for *his* letters, which, in turn, would have thanked Ruby for her money orders, but *his* have not been preserved—could this be the reason that they were destroyed? Or, were some of the letters destroyed by Ruby when she *cremated* David Ross's letters?

Were the letters destroyed by the family for fear of the TB germs they might carry? This hardly seems likely since most of Ruby's letters *to the family* are extant, and their germ content would have been much greater. Was it because Tom's dignity and honour might be tarnished if it became known that his sister sacrificed her salary and her health for his education? It is certainly true that the matriarch Mary and others in the family always sought to protect Tom's honour. It is possible that Mary might have destroyed the letters while she was grooming Tom and preserving his image. Was it done to erase any sense of guilt or blame? Did Tom destroy the letters?

Further, in light of the family's habit of preserving *all* letters, sending them to one another and demanding they be returned to Whitehern after reading, it is surprising that all but one of the letters from Tom and the family *to Ruby* have been expunged from the archive. Why did the family preserve several thousand letters, but the letters to Ruby are not among them? Calvin sorted many of the letters when he was arranging to leave Whitehern and all of its contents to the City of Hamilton. Did Calvin destroy them to protect Tom's honour? Did Ruby destroy them in a fit of pique against the family?

Another possibility concerns the preservation of the Whitehern artefacts. After Calvin died in 1968, boxes of letters and documents were removed from the house and languished in the basement of City Hall for a few years while Whitehern was being prepared as a museum. Were the letters to Ruby separated and destroyed then? It is a great mystery. One thing is clear: they must have been sorted and separated from the other family letters. That this was not the usual practice can be seen by the numbering of the letters, for many are neither in order by date nor by writer.

When Mary Farmer retrieved the letters from the basement of City Hall and made her *Calendar of McQuesten Papers at Whitehern*, she sorted, separated, numbered and catalogued them as best she could, but many were left to be microfilmed later, and these are definitely not in order of date or writer. This poses questions for those who analyze literary estates: What has been preserved? what might have been destroyed? what might have been deliberately distorted or destroyed—and why? Or, finally, what is yet to be found?

After Whitehern became a museum in 1971 and public tours began, Ruby was introduced briefly as the beautiful daughter who had died young of tuberculosis—a sad, but not unusual occurrence in the Victorian age. In fact, during conducted tours at Whitehern, Thomas receives a great deal of credit for his accomplishments as the successful lawyer, Member of Provincial Parliament, and master builder; but very little is said of Ruby's vital contribution to Tom's success. Much of this is changing now that Ruby's letters have been researched and the extent of her contribution and sacrifice are becoming known.

Another mystery: why did Tom never marry? He was one of Ontario's most eligible bachelors: handsome, robust, educated, charming and successful. No doubt the family circumstances of Ruby's illness and death and the fright of daughter Mary's possible illness prevented Tom from considering taking a wife when he was young. The finances would not have allowed it. He could not abandon his family, and he could not afford to keep a wife *and* his family in separate dwellings. Also, it would have been unthinkable to have a wife move into Whitehern to live with a dominating matriarch and three spinsters in their thirties, one of whom suffered frequent

Mary Baker McQuesten, seated
Daughters, L to R., Edna, Hilda and Ruby, c.1900
INSET: daughter Mary

mental breakdowns, as well as a brother who was mentally fragile and physically disabled.

Obviously, Tom accepted his duty and his role. He became the man of the house, took on its financial support, and the telephone directory reverted to his name. He had already given up a marital prospect in Isabel Elliot, just as Ruby had been forced to give up her fiancé,

David Ross. It was not unusual in a Victorian household for the children to make sacrifices for the family. It is clear that their mother was particularly dominant— perhaps for fear that they might be led astray with no guiding hand of a father to lead them.

Tom might have considered marriage after his mother inherited $36,000 from his uncle, Dr. Calvin Brooks McQuesten in 1912. However, Tom would have felt deeply indebted to Ruby following her death in 1911, and he had already dedicated his future to politics and good works for the people. For him to wrench himself away from his mother and family at that point would have been a great struggle, especially since his mother was already well past the age of sixty. The family had made many sacrifices for him and he may have felt that it would be dishonourable for him to abandon them. Nevertheless, at thirty years of age Tom was a most eligible bachelor to whom many women were attracted.

THOMAS THE CIVIC POLITICIAN—Alderman for Ward 2 (1913-1920)

The McQuestens were dedicated Liberals. They were also Presbyterians with a strong missionary leaning and a profound compulsion to improve their world. Harvey McCulloch stated that Tom McQuesten had no real interest in law as a career and always seemed driven by a desire to "do things for people" (Best 207n12). Tom had a keen interest in history and politics which he turned to municipal affairs and public service.

In 1912 he campaigned for city alderman and ran on a platform of defeating the TH&B railroad plan to build a track through the elite southwest of Hamilton that would separate Whitehern and the Presbyterian Church. He organized local women with the help of his mother and sisters, but he was narrowly defeated and the railroad was built. He ran again in 1913 and won the seat on Council to become Alderman of Ward 2, his home ward. He held this position until he resigned in 1920.

Tom might have run for mayor; he was encouraged to do so, and from time to time he served as acting mayor. His mother refers to a note she received from their friend, William Murray, a Hamilton poet and raconteur, affectionately known as the *Bard of Athol Banks*. Mary reports: *Tom acting mayor yesterday, received this morning a card with*:

> *Joy from the acting Athol Bankers*
> *to acting mayor McQ.*
> *Who where so'er he sails or anchors.*
> *With flying flags gets through.*
> *We'll by & bye expect with glee.*
> *Him mayor-elect elect to see.*
> (Box 12-112, Mar 6 1913)

Hamilton's Old City Hall
James St. N. (1889-1961)

Thomas had his sights set on the provincial government, and in his dealings on the Hamilton Board of Parks Management and in council, he gained a reputation for both honesty and honour. There was a strong streak of the Presbyterian work ethic in Thomas and he implemented his agenda with a sense of mission. The Parks Board under his guidance became known as a strong ethical, even incorruptible, body. Tom made it a policy never to accept graft or gifts in any form, however innocent it might appear.

Years later, while Tom, as Chairman of the Works Committee on the Hamilton Board of Parks Management, was arguing for the acquisition of the Rosedale-Albion lands in the east end, an article appeared in a Hamilton newspaper praising the Board for being "singularly free" from graft. The lands were purchased in 1929 against opposition. An undated newspaper clipping in the Whitehern Archives states:

> *It appears that this arrangement was all open and above board and that no graft was involved or possible. The Parks Board has been singularly free from even the suggestion of such a thing. It remained for some aldermen to circulate rumours that there had been 'graft' in connection with the Rosedale-Albion lands purchase. One statement was that a land-owner had expected to sell his property which he held at $15,000 for $25,000. Graft insinuated the whisperers. But the property in question is held under option by the Parks Board for $15,000. What have the whisperers to say about that? And what have they to say about anything in the matter, if they will speak out openly and above board, instead of whispering behind doors.* (W-MCP3-5.014, 1927, date estimated)

Tom and his associate, C.V. Langs, were very far-sighted in their planning. They often placed options on properties long before they were needed and thus secured good properties at non-inflated prices.

It is apparent that Ruby's influence continued to motivate Tom, and there can be little doubt that as a politician he remembered her aspirations, her generosity and her sacrifice for him. Perhaps a deep sense of remorse spurred him on in his determination to excel as a lawyer and a moral politician. Although there is no extant record that Tom

ever noted Ruby's name in his writings, her guidance and vision for him became the model for his life as a businessman, a politician, and a humanitarian. His memory would echo back to Ruby's letter, reproduced in full in Part Two, in which she addressed him in the first person as his mentor and spiritual guide:

> *You know Tom I have often wondered what you were going to make of your life, I have wondered if in the course of time you mightn't become a Member of Parliament, and I have no doubt that you would do well. I can't help thinking of you and praying that God, in mercy to a country that has so many sin-blind leaders, may in His time raise up a saviour. God will*

Ruby Baker McQuesten

give His spirit to enable you as a lawyer to distinguish that faint line between right and wrong. (W-MCP2-4.053, May 8 1905)

The quality of Tom's character and the quantity of his remarkable deeds are indications that this vision echoed in his consciousness throughout his life and his career. He followed the Biblical edict: "By their deeds shall ye know them."

Rev. Calvin McQuesten

Calvin's life also parallels the spiritual vision that Ruby outlined for him. He became a minister, and from 1920 to 1950 was the semi-volunteer chaplain at the Hamilton Mountain Sanatorium, possibly in a determination to help others who suffered from tuberculosis, even though he had been unable to help his beloved sister. Calvin also supported Tom in every way that he was capable. Calvin gave a "Social Gospel" address to the Temperance and Moral Reform League and, in the spirited speech, notes candidly the prevalence of municipal and provincial politicians who are *lacking . . . in common honesty.* The Social Gospel was a shared vision with his family and with his church, and the family read this speech aloud and passed it on to their friends:

The Christian's Place in Politics

It is not the superior numbers of the crooks and grafters in the country that enables them to dominate political life. It is simply the culpable indifference and abject cowardice of the so-called respectable proportion of the community. There are altogether too many of us who do nothing but wring our hands and make loud lamentation about the corruptness of the public life without doing one single thing to cleanse the corruption that we howl about. . . .
The two-party system is the only system we know of that provides us with both a responsible government and an organized opposition to watch the government. . . . But I do hold that the only effective way in which either you or I can contribute to the purification of politics is by first contributing our part to the purification of either one party or the other. . . . It is a shame to us that we find time to devote to all kinds of lodges and societies whose excuse for existing at all is very difficult for me to discover--And to leave the affairs of our country to be controlled by selfish grafters and corporation plunderers. . . . Let us stop running up and down the touch line wringing our hands because politics are such a dirty game, and let us get into the game ourselves and do our part to make the play clean. (Excerpt, Box 03-164, Jan 1 1911)

This is the very path that Thomas followed in his political and legal careers. For Tom, political life was not an end in itself; it was an obligation and a duty. Following the Presbyterian missionary tradition in his family, it became the equivalent of a religious calling for him.

Tom also gave his mother credit for her moral guidance. Several years earlier, on the eighteenth anniversary of his father's death, he praised his mother in a letter:

TO MARY BAKER MCQUESTEN from her son, Thomas Baker McQuesten (W5440)
Whitehern,   22 Grosvenor St., Toronto, Ontario
Hamilton, Ontario   Mar 6 1906

My dear Mother,

Am writing this letter from my house instead of the office as usual.

To-morrow is the seventh of March and I was just thinking the other day that surely a man was never blessed with a better mother in every way. I don't know what it is about you but you seem to demand the best of a man. It is not that you talk much, your discourses are what constitutes the legitimate end of high ambitions, have been few and brief, thank Heavens. There are some worthy mothers whom I have heard devote hours telling their children what they ought to do. [?] are not much the better for it. Whatever we may do be assured of this at least that we know distinctly the difference between right and wrong, and I don't know that any mother can obtain a very much higher result. It all goes to show that it is example which people want in this world and not precept.

You were always thoroughly consistent, and a youngster, mind you, is mighty sharp to notice inconsistency. He does not recognize it by that term but if it is lacking he notices at least that there is a want of sincerity in his parent. If you have taught us to be unselfish with each other, I don't know whether you did or not, but I do know that I have seen you actually stinting yourself in the matter of food and clothing so that we could have more. And I also know that you have given away a pretty large proportion of your income, which serves to inculcate a much more forceful lesson of benevolence than if you were to devote hours in enlarging upon its principles.

Be that as it may, I do know my dear mother that if I am going to achieve anything and come to you for commendation, I must come with clean hands.

I haven't got much more to say I just thought that a word of appreciation on the anniversary of my father's death might not be ungrateful.

Your loving son, T.B. McQuesten

Tom kept his solemn promise, made at the close of this letter, throughout his life. A poignant comment appears on the envelope in Mary's handwriting: *A very precious letter.* Following is an example of one of Mary's replies to Tom. In this case it was just before his graduation, and also on the anniversary of his father's death. The deep bond of love and respect between mother and son is apparent in both letters:

TO THOMAS B. MCQUESTEN from his mother, Mary Baker McQuesten (W-MCP2-4.037a)
(c/o) Messrs Royce & Henderson Barristers,   Whitehern, Hamilton, Ontario
Molson Buildings, Toronto, Ontario   Mar 7 1907

My own darling boy,

This is just a little letter to yourself, you know you are the only one who remembers to write me on this day and to me your letter is just the sweetest gift and always cheers me up so much that instead of feeling sad I always feel particularly cheerful. Last night my mind was so full of plans that I did not get to sleep till this morning, so I was having my breakfast in bed and feeling very stupid when your dear letter came. You do not know just what a help and strength you have been to your mother. I am so very nervous and anxious minded that if you had been anything else but what you are I would certainly have broken down. If you had been a lazy idle good for nothing, selfish and unsympathetic, it seems to me I would have died, for people do die of broken hearts. And it is really terrible the number of selfish men, sons who are positively cruel to their mothers and sisters through self indulgence without apparently any thought of it.

To one of my disposition and views it would seem to me life would have been impossible. As it is you were strong and vigorous and unlike son Cal, physically fit to go into any kind of a rollicking life and so have been led into many things altogether

Mary Baker McQuesten

ruinous but thank God, you did hear His voice, I am sure, speaking to you, and you have been enabled to live a pure life and thus have been an unspeakable strength to me.

Many times, I have had grave anxiety as to whether my standard of right has been too puritanical and has shut out the girls from any opportunities, but yet I could not forget that 'We are not to do evil that good may come,' and I believed that it is only when obeying God, that we receive His help, and I always felt far too weak to go into anything without His approval. And as I look back and read my Bible, it still seems to me the only Safe Course. The only anxious thought I have for you dearie is, lest you should by mixing continually with those who have really scarcely a thought of God, you should grow formal in serving Him and not be spiritually minded. Sometimes you seem a little hard and unsympathetic with people and you know we ought to have 'the mind that was in Christ.' For this we both need to strive and pray earnestly if we are really to attain to what our Saviour expects of us. With fondest love, my dear son Tom, and earnest prayers.

Ever your loving Mother,
M.B. McQuesten

There is no doubt that Tom's mother and his sister Ruby influenced him profoundly in his career. Nevertheless, Tom was also a leader and a man of vision in his own right and was capable of forming and fulfilling his own aspirations. Mary was right: Tom could be *hard and unsympathetic with people* if they did not agree with his methods. He could be stubborn and vindictive, but he was also generous and grateful to his many associates who shared his vision.

The McQuestens were devout evangelical Presbyterians; Tom never missed a service at the MacNab Street Presbyterian Church when he was at home, and he was a member of the church management board. In spite of their fundamentalism, the McQuestens demonstrated the enlightened Victorian belief in a kind of social

Darwinism: an optimistic and scientific approach that enlisted humans in God's evolutionary plan to improve the human race. They held the belief that humans are shaped by their environments as well as by their wills. A wholesome environment was seen as an essential part of the evolutionary plan, which assumed a trust in human progress through the natural sciences, eugenics and social reform.

The Whitehern library contains 3,500 books. Several are written by Charles Darwin or about his theories. One might expect that Mary's fundamentalist convictions may have caused her to restrict her children's reading and education, but she encouraged an enlightened outlook. Mary insisted on a Classical education for her children and promoted an interest in the broader world of literature, art, science, music and travel, all in the interest of preserving a high intellectual and cultural standard. Mary comments to Calvin on their sense of superiority:

> *Tom has been about a little, went up to the Golf grounds, says the young men are just a dreadful set, 'such muffs,' not one he can make a friend. I was always afraid of that and felt rather sorry for that reason to have him come to Hamilton. It was the same in your father's day, and we got into a way of living by ourselves, which is a bad thing.* (Box 12-405)

This upper-class attitude gave the McQuestens an air of snobbishness that set them apart from many of their friends and neighbours in Hamilton. Although they no longer enjoyed the superiority of wealth, Mary insisted that they conform to the Presbyterian family tradition, and conduct themselves with aristocratic manners and breeding. Her insistence on quality in education is one of the factors that led to a search for a university for Hamilton, and in time one would be found.

Chapter 27

T.B. McQUESTEN AND THE HAMILTON BOARD
OF PARKS MANAGEMENT
(The "City Beautiful" and the "Social Gospel")

*Hamilton is a modest-sized city
with breathtaking natural potential.* (Laking 13)

In 1912, Tom was made a law partner and the office was renamed Chisholm, Logie and McQuesten. Tom enjoyed politics more than law, and entered the political arena in 1913 as Alderman for Ward 2. He was appointed to the Hamilton Town Planning Commission in 1916, and to the Hamilton Board of Parks Management in 1922 where he was made Chairman of the Works Committee. Tom's family had always been staunchly Liberal, and he served as President of the Hamilton Liberal Association from 1921-23. His role in the party would later include terms on the executive branch at both the provincial and federal levels. For Tom, these were all pathways to purpose.

THE "CITY BEAUTIFUL" AND "SOCIAL GOSPEL" MOVEMENTS

Tom was an enthusiastic advocate of the values of the "City Beautiful" and "Social Gospel" movements, which grew out of awareness of the squalor of crowded tenements and the rapid and random urban growth in the nineteenth century. The City Beautiful adapted *Beaux-Arts* Classicism to city planning and architecture. Tom also favoured the Arts and Crafts movement (1880-1910) which held that labour and art could be a means for radical social change.

The City Beautiful in America was launched at the Chicago World's Fair of 1893 by architect Daniel H. Burnham and landscape designer Frederick Law Olmsted. They were spurred on by a broader movement for urban reform which sought to create healthier, more equitable living conditions. Pioneering social reform settlements such as Toynbee Hall in London (1884) and Hull House in Chicago (1889), had been built by then. In Canada, the City Beautiful and its corollary, the Social Gospel grew out of England's Garden City movement which originated in 1898 as an approach to urban planning. The library at Whitehern contains many books on these numerous related subjects, including thirty-two books by John Ruskin (1819-1900) on art and morality.

In all of McQuesten's efforts, he and his associates were guided by these closely aligned philosophical visions. In simplest terms, beauty and aesthetics in urban design were viewed as a necessary prerequisite to morality. That is, nature and parks and beautiful surroundings would naturally aid in the development of a law-abiding and moral citizenry.

These enthusiasts were following the Classical interpretation of Beauty. In the Socratic sense, Beauty is a powerful force in its capacity to generate and regenerate human thought, behaviour, morality and productivity. Beauty is never static but engenders a "longing for the conception and generation that the beautiful effects" (Plato, Symp. 206e). This was also its link to the Social Gospel, an optimistic and progressive movement that believed that the ills and ugliness of the city and its people could be overcome by a program of civic beautification achieved through good design, effective planning and regulation, and a healthy environment. This environment would naturally be productive of social good.

The National Council of Women carried on one of the biggest lobbies for city parks in Canada, and worked with the Ontario Government to create municipal parks commissions. Many churches took up the challenge. The Rev. Dr. Charles W. Gordon, a friend of the McQuestens, was a dedicated and vocal advocate. As a Presbyterian minister and moderator of the church, he preached from the pulpit and wrote treatises and newspaper articles on the subject. Under his pen name, Ralph Connor, he became the most popular and best-selling novelist of the early twentieth century. His second novel, *Sky Pilot* (1899) sold more than a million copies internationally. The work of this literary giant demonstrates that the emphasis on beauty and social reform was a shared focus in keeping with the belief that human nature could align itself with God's benevolent and progressive plan for humanity and the world.

Thomas and his associates were visionaries who would design and build according to *Beaux-Arts* principles to create a Renaissance for Hamilton and for Canada that has never been equalled before or since. Their vision has been proclaimed a "cult of beauty" and a "pursuit of excellence." When they praised the power of beauty, they were stating their belief in its capacity to shape human thought and behaviour.

Such a shared aesthetic vision cannot be duplicated today in the current Modernist and Post-modernist environment; politicians and population no longer share a common philosophical ideal that would make it possible. In fact, the opposite is true today, although there is some indication of a renewed interest in beauty. A recent article about architecture by Richard Rogers argues for Beauty: "Beauty is not a dirty word . . . a building without beauty is not architecture: it is a construction. . . . Beauty makes our public servants nervous. . . . I was strongly advised not to use words like 'beauty,' 'harmony,' 'aesthetic' . . . if I wanted the report to be taken seriously by those who counted" (*Resurgence* 207, July 2001).

The City Beautiful movement influenced many architects, landscapers and urban planners throughout North America. Among them were a number of Tom's associates: Cecil V. Langs, chairman of the Parks Board from 1923 to 1949; W.A. Logie, Tom's partner in law; Noulan Cauchon, a railway engineer and town planning pioneer; John M. Lyle and William Lyon Somerville, *Beaux-Arts* architects; Lorrie and Howard Dunington-Grubb, Carl Borgstrom and Matt Broman, landscape architects; Dr. H.P. Whidden, McMaster University Chancellor; Dr. Leslie Laking and others. Many of these became Tom's friends. Tom also courted numerous artists and sculptors for his work, including Frances Loring and Florence Wyle, Elizabeth

Wynn Wood, and Emanuel Hahn. These individuals shared Tom's aesthetic and social vision, which he implemented with a missionary zeal almost in the sense of a calling. They admired him and accepted his leadership in urban and regional planning, making them leaders in the City Beautiful movement. But all this still lay ahead.

WORLD WAR ONE: 1914-1918

In 1915 Thomas was determined to enlist in the war effort but his mother was equally determined that he must not go. Tom was robust and a sportsman. He

played football for the Hamilton Tigers in 1897; during High School he played football on the Hamilton Collegiate team that won the Ontario Championship in 1900; he had been on the winning rugby team in university where he played half-back and his team won the Mulock Cup in 1903; he was a junior fencing champion; he rowed with the Argonauts while at university; he became an expert swimmer when he worked at log-rolling on the Ottawa River. Tom

Tom's high school basketball team (Tom, far right)

had also served as a Corporal under Major John S. Hendrie, Commanding 4th Field Battery, C.A; he had spent a summer in the Royal Canadian Artillery (1903) and became an expert marksman. Thomas felt trained and prepared to go to war.

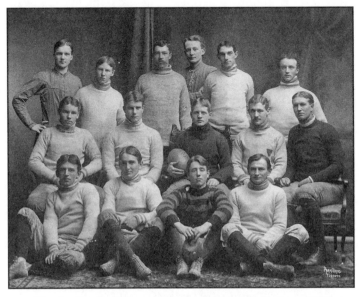

Varsity Rugby Team, winners of the Mulock Cup, 1903
(Tom, back row, far left, played snap back)

Tom's friends, Chisholm, Logie and Dr. Norman Leslie, were enlisting, and Tom insisted that he wanted to go, too. There were fierce battles at home, as his mother refused to allow it. The mother/matriarch was adamant. She did not favour the war and said so, repeatedly:

> *The war news seems terrible just now, it hangs over one, and we feel as if we didn't know what would happen next. It seems so fearful to think of the awful slaughter, thousands of men handed over to death. Such fine fellows too! It makes one ill to think of it, and no one can stop it, we are just helpless. . . . and all of these young Canadians cut off in the prime of life and their mothers left to mourn them all their days.* (W6820, Apr 22 1915; W6828, Apr 30 1915)

Mary was often critical of men in general, whether they were of the military or the ministry: *We are getting quite tired of the way men do things* (W6975, Mar 17 1916).

Calvin favoured Tom's enlistment and recorded in his diary: *Pray that Tom may go. That Mother . . . may tell him so* (Box 14-002). But Mary continued unwavering in her resolve to keep Tom at home and keep him safe. Tom was her favourite son and she was determined not to lose him.

Calvin had applied to enlist to become a chaplain and Mary did not object, although he was not selected. The family had a great deal invested in Tom. Ruby had already been sacrificed for the family cause and Mary was not about to sacrifice Tom just as he was becoming successful and on the verge of becoming their redeemer. Tom was taking his father's place in the family and he was their only hope for the restoration of the family. Mary ultimately won and Tom stayed home, but he did not remain idle and was to accomplish much beautification work in Hamilton and the Niagara peninsula.

Tom began receiving letters from Dr. Norman Leslie (1883-1947) from the War Front in France, and the graphic descriptions of the trenches, the dead bodies, the rats and the stench, might have made Tom glad that he had not enlisted:

> *After the last big affair we were certainly busy getting very serious cases and lashings of them. Poor devils. Such hellish injuries, bones smashed to splinters, great chunks of flesh and muscle torn away, and on top of that pus running from them: nearly all, and very frequently gas-gangrene and infections which develops with great rapidity and eats up and destroys good healthy tissue. The buglers of the camp were busy calling the last post for a time. This is the hideous part.* (W-MCP6-1.458, Oct 17 1915; W-MCP6-1.448)

Dr. Norman Leslie was a good friend of Tom's, and after the war they used to spend time together on a Saturday afternoon at the Hamilton Club or at the Thistle Club. Likely through Tom's recommendation, Leslie later became a Niagara Falls Bridge Commissioner, serving from July 22, 1941 until January 9, 1947 (Seibel, 231). He also accepted a position on the Hydro Commission. A Spectator article dated July 13, 1938 states: "Dr. N.V. Leslie fills in vacancy in Hydro body. Prominent Hamilton physician and war veteran to succeed John Newlands." Mel Smith, in a letter dated March 26, 1947, mentions Leslie in failing health: *I have heard nothing further since I left Toronto as to the health of our friend Dr. Leslie, and I trust he is quite himself again. This also applies to many others of his type that we know in Hamilton* (W-MCP7-1.129).

The phrase "of his type" suggests injuries or shell shock suffered by Leslie and many others as a result of the war.

It is sobering to contemplate that if Tom had succeeded in convincing his mother to let him go to war in 1915, and if he had been killed or severely injured, or if he had returned shell-shocked, none of his wonderful work with parks, highways, bridges, gardens and forts, would have been accomplished; for he was the man with the vision and the master-mind behind all of his projects. Consequently, we owe a debt of gratitude to Mary Baker McQuesten, the Victorian Matriarch, for preventing Tom from enlisting in the war, and for encouraging him to continue in his beautification work for Hamilton and Ontario.

ON THE BOARD OF PARKS MANAGEMENT

Tom had no doubts about what needed to be done for Hamilton, and immediately upon election in 1913, had begun to implement his parks and beautification agenda. He served as alderman for the City of Hamilton from 1913 to 1920, and as previously mentioned, was appointed to the Hamilton Town Planning Commission in January 1916. He was appointed to the Board of Parks Management (BPM) in 1922, serving as Chairman of the Works Committee until 1947. Consequently, he had a grasp of all local improvements. When McQuesten accepted the provincial Highways portfolio in 1934, he retired from Council but continued to serve concurrently for the Hamilton Parks Board and the province.

Cecil Vanroy Langs

C.V. LANGS was Chairman of the Parks Board from 1923 to 1949, and he and Tom collaborated frequently. The acquisition of land was primary, and the two had already become a "dynamic duo" when as aldermen they embarked on some frenzied activity to accumulate land for parks. They even resorted to conniving when necessary, usually by presenting a deal as complete when it was still in the works. This strategy, as well as some shrewd negotiating, prevented leaks that would inflate real estate prices.

The Parks Board with T.B. McQuesten at the head of the Works Committee was so successful that Barnsley conveys Tom's sense of achievement after only ten years: "Tom McQuesten had now reached a kind of heaven. Within ten years, Hamilton would have the largest acreage of developed park land in any Canadian City. Not only would it be the largest, but it would include the most scenic, the best-planned and executed, and the best variety in form and theme" (Barnsley 26; Best 205). And yet, this was just the *beginning* of Tom's creative achievements.

While all of T.B. McQuesten's achievements in Hamilton parks are important, they are too numerous for everything to be covered in detail in this text. The box on page 171 lists many of the parks that were developed under his aegis. Several of the major developments will be addressed at length presently.

Noulan Cauchon

T.B. McQuesten surrounded himself with the best professionals available in architecture, landscape design and town planning.

NOULAN CAUCHON (1872-1935) first came on the scene around 1917, and he and Tom worked closely together on many major projects. Cauchon was one of the pioneers of town planning in Canada, and a noted railway engineer. He was from Quebec but was working at the time in Ottawa. His father, Joseph-Edouard Cauchon (1816-85) had been a lawyer, a journalist, and a colourful and controversial Quebec politician. Mayor of Quebec City from 1865 to 1867, he later became lieutenant governor of Manitoba (1877-82).

Noulan Cauchon was a founder of the Ottawa Town Planning Commission and played a significant role in the planning of Ottawa in the early twentieth century. He was also a close ally and founder with Thomas Adams (1871-1940), of the Town Planning Institute of Canada. Thomas Adams is considered to be the "godfather of Town Planning in Canada," and Cauchon and Adams collaborated during 1914-26 to extend town planning across Canada. Adams' ideas about the "wasteful use of natural resources, the follies of premature subdivision and the need to plan roads concordant with the topography are as true today as they were then" (David Lewis Stein, ThomasAdams, www.cip-icu.ca).

Cauchon and Adams were advocates of England's Garden City movement, and they proclaimed many of the City Beautiful ideals in Canada. As an engineer, Cauchon was also an advocate of the City Scientific approach to planning, which he integrated with City Beautiful goals. He and Tom managed to form a practical symbiosis of these ideals for their projects in Hamilton and throughout Ontario.

In 1917, Tom and the Parks Board hired Noulan Cauchon as a consulting railroad engineer for the railway relocation that was planned for Hamilton. In July of that year McQuesten, in collaboration with William Francis Tye (chief engineer of the C.P.R., 1904-6) and Cauchon, presented their first report in the relatively new field of Town Planning: *The Railway Situation in Hamilton, Ontario.*

Their report gives a good topographical description of the city in 1917:

> The City occupies a comparatively narrow strip of land, from one and one-half to two and one-half miles in width, between Burlington Bay and the Mountain. This narrow strip is further restricted by broken ground and deep marshes on the west. A certain amount of settlement has developed on the mountain which has not been included in the City Limits. This section is

difficult of access, and is not likely to grow rapidly until better facilities are provided. (Cauchon 7)

Cauchon recommended depressing the railroads to make roadway accesses possible. Although their report was well received, it was defeated in council; nevertheless, Tom learned a great deal from the experience. He was left bitter by the defeat, especially since the railroad cut a path that separated his home, Whitehern, from his church, the MacNab Street Presbyterian Church, and the noise of the trains was a constant annoyance to his family and other residents in their upper-class neighbourhood (Best 42-45). Cauchon alluded to this when he noted "the many afflictions that evolve from the strenuous activities of railways in the wrong place— injuriously affecting well-being" (9). It may have been partly in retaliation that Tom spent the rest of his career building highways. More to the point, he felt correctly that the heyday of the railroad was ending and that the automobile was in the ascendance.

Cauchon worked on a consultant basis and he and Tom became good friends. He presented Tom with *A Book of Bridges* (1915) with the inscription, *To my friend T.B. McQuesten 'Enthusiast,' Hoping that the spans of Hamilton may rank with the noblest of these, September 1918.* Cauchon often stayed at Whitehern for extended visits while he was working in Hamilton. Tom's mother enjoyed these visits and planning sessions and, no doubt, gave them the benefit of her matriarchal guidance. Cauchon, a visionary like Tom, would have been inspired by Mary's passion for beauty (W-MCP1-3b.015, Aug 19 1918; W-MCP2-3b.058, Aug 19 1918).

Cauchon collaborated with McQuesten for many years on the latter's public works and City Beautiful projects in Hamilton and throughout Ontario. Theirs was

---

SOME OF THE HAMILTON PARKS developed by T.B. McQuesten as Chairman of the Hamilton Parks Board Works Committee

Gage Park	Hendrie Park	Dundurn Park
La Salle Park	Donohue Park	Victoria Park
Bruce Park	Inch Park	King's Forest Park

Northwest Entrance Project and park lands
Rock Garden and Royal Botanical Gardens
Cootes Paradise and lands
McMaster University grounds & Sunken Garden

Stewart Park on the eastern waterfront	Red Hill Valley
Mahony Park (originally Crerar Park)	Mountain Park
Rosedale-Albion Falls lands & Park	Scott Park
Hamilton Civic Golf Course	Chedoke Park
H.A.A.A. Sports Park	Mountain Facelands

Playgrounds and athletic centres throughout the city
(new and refurbished)

(Best 51-68, 113-18; Barnsley 26; Minnes 2; Yorston, Box 14-129, Box 14-131; W-MCP7-1.204)

a Renaissance movement, influenced partly by Cauchon's *Beaux-Arts* education and his experience in Classical design and reconstruction in Greece. Their Hamilton projects came to include the northwest entrance to Hamilton, the High Level Bridge (now named for McQuesten) and many parks: the Rock Garden and Royal Botanical Gardens (RBG), Cootes Paradise and the Desjardins Canal, McMaster University and grounds, Gage Park, and many more. In all their work, they always planned for the scenic and recreational characteristics that the topography of mountain, bay and lake provided. They also built roadways along Hamilton Mountain for access purposes.

MOUNTAIN FACE PARK

In 1919 McQuesten hired Cauchon again to do a report on the road system, and specifically the mountain roads. Cauchon advocated the need to plan roads according to existing topography, and it is in this regard that we see him converge with McQuesten and the City of Hamilton. In his Report on Mountain Highways of Hamilton, Ontario, 1919, Cauchon signs himself: "Consulting Engineer and Town Planner." In the report, he comments on Hamilton's unique problem of access between the city and the mountain top and recommends roads of no more than three percent grade as compared with the very steep and tortuous route through the Jolly Cut that was one of only two mountain roads in existence. He declared the "Magnificent Mountain Face Park" to be of major importance, along with:

A road system that will enable access for the enjoyment and for the further development of the Park. . . . The Mountain Face Park of Hamilton is a rare natural health resource of exhaustless value to its citizens. It is the City's great playground—its training camp of potential energy and efficiency. Town Planners and Sociologists, all those concerned in the welfare of the public, no longer look on parks as mainly ornamental features to a city, but as being of essential economic necessity in fostering and sustaining the development of human energy and efficiency in the rising generations, who are the citizens and the workers of to-morrow. Your mountain face park stretches for five miles along a populous area, but is separated from it in large measure by a railway barrier which denies to much of this population the free enjoyment, the recuperation, and enhancement that is within its gift, and theirs by right. (Cauchon 5)

The *Spectator* said of Cauchon that "he was hypnotized by Hamilton's natural beauty," and that his "artistic temperament had got the better of him" (Best 60). This was hardly a criticism from Tom's point of view, but Cauchon's plan was rejected for being <u>too</u> beautiful.

In his 1919 report, Cauchon acknowledged that "auto power to date is largely light traffic, yet it points to the growing power on our highways and to the future doubling, trebling, and quadrupling, within measureable grasp, of motor traction and the economic advantage." Cauchon was very optimistic about the potential of this unique city that "has but broadened my understanding and deepened my insight into the wonderful possibilities of making Hamilton not only one of the most productive, but also one of the most attractive cities on this continent" (13).

Within the next ten years many of Noulan Cauchon's recommendations were implemented, both in mountain access roads and in parks. A newspaper clipping, for example, indicates that McQuesten and Cauchon "built a mountain roadway with a grant of $50,000 to start in 1922" (*Hamilton Spectator*, Jun 25 1934).

Cauchon proposed one particular grand plan that never materialized. It was a very ambitious plan to develop Ferguson Ave into a kind of *Champs-Élysées* from the bay to the top of the mountain. The design included a Greek amphitheatre carved into the mountain side, with arches and colonnades and statuary. Unfortunately it was too lofty and aesthetic a concept for Hamilton Council to approve and was voted down. As often happens with architects and builders, T.B. and Cauchon's aesthetic vision exceeded Council's ability to grasp its benefits and Tom and Cauchon were required to compromise their plans.

View of East End Section of Mountain Face Before Reforestration

The Free Press (**Hamilton**),
February 6, 1930 *(HPL photo)*

By 1930, the mountain face had been denuded by people scavenging the mountainside for firewood and gravel. Thomas and the Parks Board decided to restore it as the Mountain Face Park. Typically, Tom gave credit for his vision for the mountain face lands to another associate, Thomas S. Morris, a member of Council. In fact, Thomas credited Morris as the "father of the mountain" as they proceeded to beautify the denuded mountain face lands by replanting thousands of trees, creating parks, and improving mountain roads. In this way Thomas often gave credit to others for projects that he had been planning for many years.

An article in *The Free Press*, February 6, 1930 describes the results of the beautification project, roads and recreational facilities that resulted:

HAMILTON MOUNTAIN FACE

There have been fifty thousand (50,000) young trees planted on the East End face of the mountain. These trees were presented by the Forestry Department of the Ontario Government, in answer to the request of the Parks Board. It is gratifying to report that apart from those destroyed through boys lighting fires, many thousands have taken hold and will present a wonderful array of beauty in a few years.

A picturesque scenic driveway is now under way, for which plans are being laid, which will extend from Niagara Falls all along the mountain brow to connect up with the new mountain road and Horning road, which leads onto the Hamilton and Brantford highway on the west side.

The beautiful lands which the Parks Board has under its jurisdiction are divided into 27 parks, comprising 1706 acres of park lands, including the recently acquired Albion Falls property of 645 acres.

That the following figures may give an idea of the work which is being carried on by the Parks Board of this beautiful city, we append the following for winter sports:

SKATING & HOCKEY & TOBOGGAN SLIDES

Skating: Eight rinks. Average daily attendance 2500; Saturdays and holidays 4,000; during season, 100,000.

Hockey: Twelve rinks. 1,600 registered players; 6 leagues; 106 teams; average daily attendance; 500; during season, 20,000. Toboggan slides provide pleasure for over 25,000 children and adults, each year.

The foregoing indicates what an enormous total must attend all sports which are played in the various parks. Many games of Tennis, Golf, Bowls, Cricket, Hard Baseball, Soft Baseball, Ladies' Softball, Soccer, Running, Jumping and Rugby.

McQuesten, Cauchon and the Parks Board felt that Hamilton had some of the finest topography in the world for recreation in all seasons and decided to focus their efforts on developing and beautifying Hamilton for the health of all citizens. McQuesten arranged for the purchase of Albion Falls to be included in the new King's Forest Park. He had to argue for this park in the east end of the city: "Surely it is unreasonable, for . . . the young people resident [in the east end] to be required to go from five to eight miles . . . for golf or for tobogganing rather than to have facilities for these sports at their door" (Minnes 3, Best 67). He also acquired the old Hamilton Golf Links and made of it a self-supporting public recreation site as the Chedoke Civic Golf Course, including ski and toboggan runs. McQuesten took the same care in developing other, numerous parks.

Albion Falls, King's Forest Park
Some stones were used for the Rock Garden (public domain)

Chapter 28

PARKS, GARDENS, AND "DIET KITCHEN" ASSOCIATES

"Hamilton has become too much a factory town."
T.B.McQuesten (Best 58)

Gage Park was built at the foot of the mountain in the south east end of Hamilton; it opened in 1922. Nine years earlier John E. Brown had attempted to acquire the Gage lands for a park but they were still outside the city limits and Council voted the concept down. When Tom became Alderman, he revived the plan. The *Hamilton Spectator* reported an amusing story about the Gage Park issue when it came before Council: "The motion was in danger of being defeated when Mr. McQuesten, leaning over the desk of a green member, whispered loudly in the latter's ears: 'Stand up you darned fool!' The flustered but obliging neophyte rose hesitatingly and the issue was won" (Jun 22 1934). Tom negotiated with the Gage family of Hamilton for the acquisition of land for a large east end park covering thirty hectares (75 acres) at the foot of the escarpment.

McQuesten hired the finest landscape architects he could find among the few to be had in this young profession. He chose **H.B. & L.A. DUNINGTON-GRUBB, Landscape Architects** to design the overall concept of the park. Tom and the Dunington-Grubbs shared a similar aesthetic vision for Hamilton. They were to work together on many projects both in Hamilton and throughout Niagara. Gage Park as seen today still contains much of their early vision, consisting of gardens, fountain, forested sections, large lawns, playing fields and courts, bowls and rinks. A greenhouse and band shell are later additions. It has become the favoured venue for citywide festival events.

HOWARD BERLINGHAM GRUBB (1881-1965) met LORRIE ALFREDA DUNINGTON (1877-1945) in England when he attended one of her lectures on landscape design.

Lorrie Dunington-Grubb

Portrait of
Howard Dunington-Grubb
Courtesy Ontario Association
of Landscape Architects

Their horticultural interests soon blossomed into marriage and they formed the Dunington-Grubb team of landscape designers. In 1911 they immigrated to Canada and became two of the first landscape architects in this country. Lorrie Alfreda Dunington was in business professionally and giving lectures even before she met Howard Grubb, and she continued in her profession throughout her life. As well as her work with garden design, she lectured and published frequently for magazines, such as *Canadian Homes and Gardens*.

Disappointed with the lack of a garden industry in Canada, the couple opened a plant nursery. Located in a small town named Sheridan just west of Toronto, it became the Sheridan Nurseries. The Dunington-Grubbs insisted on quality so they advertised in Europe for a nursery manager for Sheridan. Sven Herman Stensson, a gardener at Kew Gardens in England, and formerly chief gardener for the Crown Prince of Denmark at Knuthenborg Castle, answered the ad and in 1913 he and his family immigrated to Canada. His son Jesse Vilhelm Stensson (Wilhelm) and his wife Janina became active members of the Dunington-Grubb and McQuesten team. Lorrie Dunington-Grubb died of tuberculosis in 1945. Rev. Calvin McQuesten would likely have visited her at the Hamilton Mountain Sanatorium since he was chaplain of the *San* from 1920 to 1950. We can speculate just how her illness and death might have affected Tom in view of the memory of his sister, Ruby, who died in 1911 of the same illness.

Tom McQuesten had a passion for history, and the Gage property park was to be named after the hero of the war of 1812, Sir Isaac Brock. But the Gage family intervened and donated $20,000 toward the erection of a fountain dedicated to Gage's mother and the preservation of the Gage name. The dedication is carved into the stone in large letters encircling the base of the fountain:

THIS FOUNTAIN ERECTED BY EUGENIE HELEN GAGE IN LOVING MEMORY OF HER FATHER ROBERT RUSSELL GAGE AND HER MOTHER HANNAH JANE GAGE (1927).

Gage Park Fountain, 1929

Architect John Lyle's prize-winning design for Gage Park fountain

Architect **JOHN MACINTOSH LYLE** (1872-1945) was commissioned by McQuesten to design and build the fountain and its series of seven cascading dams, which won a first prize in memorial classification in 1929. John Lyle was raised in Hamilton. He had been a student at the Hamilton Art School, which his father Rev. Samuel Lyle had started (Hamilton 2). He trained as an architect at Yale University and *École des Beaux-Arts* in Paris. After working in New York City for fourteen years he returned to Canada to practice and to teach his *Beaux-Arts* ideals to others in the architectural profession, eventually becoming one of Canada's leading architects.

Lyle incorporated aesthetic touches in his work wherever possible. He included four brass/bronze turtles around the basin of the Gage Park fountain, four swans protruding from the central pillar, and a low relief sculpture of children dancing around the fountain's drum. All were executed by Florence Wyle. The fountain was obviously designed as a children's playground, and Hamilton children have since enjoyed many hot summer days as they splash in the wading pools and ride the turtles. Gage Park as seen today maintains much of that early vision of excellence in spite of the passage of time, largely due to careful maintenance and conservation. The fountain is undergoing a complete restoration to be completed in 2011; and the gardens are being restored to "something of the historic glory of the original Dunington-Grubb design" (*Bay Observer*, Aug 2010 p. 21).

By the time of the Gage Park project, Lyle had established himself as a prominent architect in Hamilton, Toronto, and throughout Canada. His works include the Royal Alexandra Theatre (1906) and Union Station (1913-27) in Toronto, many banks, civic and private buildings throughout Canada, and the Central Presbyterian Church

**Central Presbyterian Church,
Charlton Avenue, Hamilton
(Architect: John Lyle)**

(1908) in Hamilton. Rev. Samuel Lyle of the Central Presbyterian Church was John Lyle's father. When the church was destroyed by fire in 1906, John Lyle became the architect for the new church.

 John Lyle died in 1945 at the age of 63. Lyle was ten years older than Tom, and he and his family were good friends of the McQuestens in Hamilton's Presbyterian community. Mrs. Lyle and Mary Baker McQuesten were very active in the Women's Foreign Missionary Society, the National Council of Woman, the Public Library, the YWCA, and in many cultural and social efforts for the city. John Lyle was President of the Art Gallery of Toronto in the years just prior to his death, from 1941-44.

 Lyle sought to blend modernism with the traditional, and he created a uniquely Canadian style in theme and in motif. For instance his design for the Central Presbyterian Church blends Colonial and Georgian lines with strong geometrics in brick (Hunt, *Toward* 71). In his later work, Lyle hired Canadian artists to integrate symbolic Canadian touches within the modern style, such as aboriginal scenes, farming, hunting and fishing. He employed what became his trademark Art Deco style, which is reflected in the sculptural decoration of many of his works.

 Lyle's buildings integrated art with the bricks and mortar, but he insisted that the ornamentation needed to be symbolic: "There was a rich field of inspiration lying dormant in the fauna, flora and marine life in Canada. . . . and Indian decorative forms" (Lyle, *Canadian* 36-37). In 1936 Lyle's designs influenced the adoption of animal and leaf motifs used in contemporary Canadian coinage. Lyle's unique artistic development for Canada paralleled the radicalism in the art of the Group of seven (Hamilton 7).

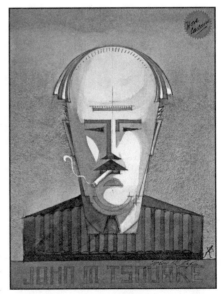

**John Macintosh Lyle (1872-1945)
Self-portrait**

Frances Loring and Florence Wyle

Elizabeth Wyn Wood

For many of the Canadian designs, McQuesten and Lyle commissioned the sculptors Frances Loring and Florence Wyle, or "The Girls," as they came to be known. This helped to promote the work of these Canadian women artists and assisted them in becoming prominent in their field. Elizabeth Wyn Wood and Emanuel Hahn were also employed; they had worked with the Group of Seven and provided some of the fountains and panels in the Rainbow Bridge Gardens (1940-41).

McQuesten and Lyle did not shy away from employing women artists for many projects. Lyle had encountered many excellent women artists at the Hamilton Art School, and Tom had the precedent set by the art of his sister Ruby to inspire him, as well as the general emphasis on art in the McQuesten family.

HERITAGE GARDEN

Welcome as an oasis to the eyes
Of travelers in climes of desert heat,
Between oppressive towers of stone, here lies
A garden granting respite from concrete
And asphalt in the city's bustling core.
Shaded by broad-crowned trees, the terraced ground
Surrounds a heart-shaped drive before the door
Of this mansion.
Take time to look around.
Perceive the scent of herbs in the still air.
Admire the fruit trees and the flowerbeds
Shaped by a woman's hands, a mother's care,
Who fiercely wished her private love could spread:
And, impelled by her dream, her son would grow
The parks and gardens of Ontario.

by **Jeff Seffinga**, 2005 (Box 14-112)

Landscape architecture for the garden at Whitehern was provided by the Dunington-Grubbs. To this day the garden is kept in heritage condition. In a *Globe & Mail* article of July 21, 2004, Barbara Ramsay Orr declares it to be one of the five outstanding heritage gardens in Canada. She states that "Whitehern has been lovingly restored to the design created in the early 1930s" and is one of the gardens founded for the "health and cheerfulness" of all citizens, thereby acknowledging the City Beautiful inspiration for the garden (Box 14-110).

Heart-shaped garden at Whitehern

The Spectator of July 14, 1934 comments on the unique iron flowers that grace the stone wall in the garden at Whitehern. They are life-size iron replicas of calla lilies, sunflowers and hollyhocks painted in natural colours:

> The wrought iron flowers set into the stone wall continued to decorate the gardens all year round. Fred Flatman, a local craftsman, had continued the garden's ornamental theme when he fashioned these unique objects objects of folk art without the use of a mould; instead he worked the metal with anvil and hammer, creating each leaf in a unique and totally distinct way. (Box 14-126)

The iron flowers are particularly appropriate to Whitehern; they are a fitting tribute to Dr. Calvin McQuesten (1801-85) who opened the first foundry in Hamilton in 1835, from which Hamilton's famous iron and steel industry got its start. There is beauty in iron, indeed.

GARDENS OF WHITEHERN

Ghosts walk the grounds of this garden—island
of tranquil beauty, oasis within
bustling urban core. Mother Mary's hand
is everywhere: in flowers, trees, and in
the very air. We breathe the scents of rose
and lilac, sit in tall catalpa's shade;
admire gold lilies and hollyhock shows,
stroll by the heart-shaped planting bed she made.
Honourable Thomas B. McQuesten
transported this spirit elsewhere. Gardens,
parks beautified city of steel; upon
Niagara's rocky verge blossomed Edens.
Mother, son, visionaries of their time;
these gardens still a living paradigm.

by **Eleanore Kosydar**, 2005 (Box 14-112)

'The Diet Kitchen Group' Feb/fév. 1927, standing l. to r./au debout à g. à dr.,
John M. Lyle, MacKenzie Waters, C. Barry Cleveland; seated/assis William Somerville, Martin Baldwin,
A.H. Gregg and A.S. Mathers.

The seven "Diet Kitchen" Architects *(photo courtesy of Geoffrey Hunt)*

ARCHITECTURAL GROUP AT THE DIET KITCHEN

In 1926, a group of Ontario architects under the unofficial leadership of John Lyle began to meet daily at the Diet Kitchen restaurant in Toronto. Other members of the group were William Lyon Somerville (notable for his long association with T.B. McQuesten), Mackenzie Waters, C. Barry Cleveland, Martin Baldwin, A.H. Gregg and A.S. Matthews.

WILLIAM LYON SOMERVILLE (1896-1965), a native Hamiltonian with an architectural office in Toronto, assisted Tom in his efforts to bring McMaster to

Hamilton, and was the architect for the original complex of six buildings that made up the University in the early 1930s. He later worked with Tom on the restoration of forts; he designed the Henley Bridge at St. Catharines; and he was a consultant and architect for much of McQuesten's future work at Niagara. T.B. McQuesten and James Chisholm engaged Somerville personally to do the major alterations and renovations of the MacNab Street Presbyterian Church in 1934-35.

William Lyon Somerville

Somerville was also architect for several Canadian hospitals, schools, housing developments and industrial buildings. He designed the wartime workers' or veterans' houses that are still ubiquitous throughout Canada—modest clapboard single-family dwellings on small lots, mostly one and one-half storey. They were built to last about ten years, and it was expected they would be demolished after the war so they were built with no basements, to make removal easier. Nevertheless, many have survived, and the design is so practical that whole neighbourhoods of these houses remain viable. They have been renovated, basements have been excavated, and they are attractive and affordable houses even today. An estimated one million wartime houses are still standing in Canada. Somerville wrote several articles on the subject for *Canadian Homes and Gardens* magazine.

Wartime houses, architect William Lyon Somerville

Although we have no evidence that T.B. McQuesten was directly involved in this housing plan, he was closely associated with Somerville in town planning and the Social Gospel philosophy. The plan would have garnered his approval since he was always concerned with providing jobs and housing for veterans and their families during and after World War II.

In February of 1927, the seven Diet Kitchen architects organized an all-inclusive architectural exhibition at the Art Gallery of Toronto to claim for architecture an affiliation with all of the related arts and crafts:

The Diet Kitchen School and Its Propaganda for the Arts

An Exhibition, unique in the annals of Canadian art history, held captive the imaginations and interest of many visitors to the Art Gallery of Toronto during February. Never before were so many of the arts gathered together at one time in these halls of beauty. The connecting link was the architectural one. It is claimed by the architects . . . that an isolated art does not exist, but that all the artistic products of civilization fit into the architectural scheme of things. Who can gainsay the truth of this? Take furniture, fabrics, silverware, metal, glass work—to name only a few of the 101 allied arts—and each of these stands in relation to some kind of architectural setting. . . . Many Canadians may not be aware of it, but a new school has come into existence within the last year. This school designates itself, 'The Diet Kitchen School of Architecture,' and the name arose in this wise: About a year ago, a little group of leading architects, members of the Toronto Chapter of the Ontario Association of Architects, met every day at the Diet Kitchen on Bloor St., Toronto. (*Saturday Night*, Mar 12 1927)

This all-encompassing art exhibition recalls the Arts and Crafts Movement which had its origins in Britain with William Morris in the late nineteenth century, and which was practised in America by Frank Lloyd Wright with his "organic architecture." Toward the end of the Industrial Revolution when many workers were being replaced by machines that mass-produced goods of inferior quality, architects and others combined complementary aesthetic designs and furnishings of fine craftsmanship. The Diet Kitchen School can be seen as an extension of the City Beautiful and Social Gospel movements inspired by social reform thinkers who were attempting to preserve high-quality craftsmen and craftsmanship. As a result, artists' collectives flourished during the Depression.

For instance, in the fall of 1928, Elizabeth Wynn Wood and her husband Emanuel Hahn founded the Sculptors Society of Canada (SSC) with fellow artists Frances Loring, Florence Wyle, Henri Hébert, and Alfred Howell. Wood became president of the SSC in 1935, serving as national spokesperson and advancing the appreciation of sculpture in Canada through exhibitions and competitions for public monuments. Tom and his associates commissioned members of this group for many of their art projects.

MCMASTER UNIVERSITY

In close association with so many architects and artists, it is not surprising that Thomas was caught up in the beautification of all things. While he was on the Parks Board, Thomas was directly responsible for winning the competition that brought McMaster University to Hamilton from Toronto.

One of the deciding factors was that Tom could promise acres of landscaped and wooded campus and ravine property. He planned that the university would be indistinguishable from the neighbouring Royal Botanical Garden parkland, of which he said, "Not only is the [RBG] site favourable to botanical purposes, but it is also historical. Burlington Heights is associated with the War of 1812, to cite just one historical point of interest" (Laking 43, 50). William Lyon Somerville was appointed architect for the six new university buildings, and later for Mills Memorial Library and some of the student residences.

Mills Memorial Library, McMaster University, under construction (1937)

McMaster University opened in Hamilton in 1931. Chancellor Howard P. Whidden, who collaborated with Thomas, stated that McQuesten was *one of the great big factors which has made the whole thing possible* (W7095n). Whidden later wrote to Tom: *Do not forget that from the beginning I have*

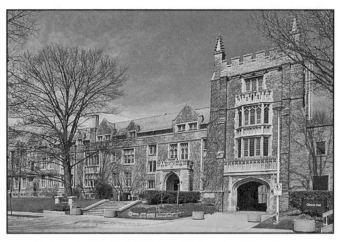

University Hall, McMaster University, Hamilton

been under indebtedness to you for constant support and inspiration in connection with the bringing of McMaster to Hamilton, and the making possible of its beautiful surroundings and setting (Box 08-138a, Mar 21 1941).

Tom saw the acquisition of McMaster for Hamilton as a great coup and a collective achievement:

> We've never landed such a fish as this. . . . In Hamilton, our whole development has been along mechanics lines. And the result has been, the owners don't live here. . . . and Hamilton has become too much a factory town. This is the first break toward a broader culture and higher educational development. It was sorely needed. Did you ever think what a great word 'university' is?—It has never been let down, never become stale or commonplace, always dignified and lofty. (Best 58)

In May 1944, the University conferred on T.B. McQuesten an honorary degree of LLD. In May 1954 William Lyon Somerville received the same honour.

The need for a university was consistent with the McQuesten family's shared vision for Hamilton. It had been noted as sorely lacking by Tom's mother as early as 1910: *You see, Hamilton is altogether commercial, having no seats of learning* (Box 12-405, Aug 5 1910). Tom as Chairman of the Works Committee, and C.V. Langs as Chairman of the Parks Board, offered McMaster 50 acres of property. They committed to develop a park setting free of charge and to provide the campus; and *a citizens committee pledged to raise $500,000*. When donations came pouring in, Mary was jubilant: *Very large individual contributions coming in for McMaster; nearly the $500,000* (W7010, Jun 18 1928). Whidden gratefully acknowledged the university's indebtedness to Thomas and the Parks Board for their generosity in offering what he called "exceedingly reasonable terms." Whidden describes the setting of the university in a kind of prose poem:

> The new university starts with a plenitude of groves of Academe . . . right on the brink of a sylvan paradise. Its scholars will at their back door have cool

ravines and marsh meadows in which to meditate the theological and other muses. . . . And they will have red-winged blackbirds and whistling swans and canorous Canada Geese to keep them company. Hamilton is proving itself a generous host to higher learning. . . . A broad tree-lined avenue . . . a sunken garden . . . lily ponds and grottoes containing fountains and flower beds suggesting the work of La Notre, the famous architect of Louis Quatorze. (*The Hamilton Spectator*, Oct 5 1929)

Unfortunately the spectacular Sunken Garden designed by the Dunington-Grubbs was razed to make way for the McMaster Medical Building that opened in 1972. The medical complex was built in a quadrangle around a centre of public open space and, in retrospect, it would have been more beautiful *and more therapeutic*, if that open space had contained the Sunken Garden, or at least some part of it. Thomas had attempted to include an *in perpetuity* clause to protect the Sunken Garden but was unable to make it binding. The City Beautiful impulse had expired in the modernity of the 1970s, and the Sunken Garden was bulldozed in spite of protest from the citizens. Rev. Calvin McQuesten, the last remaining member of the family, died in 1968, so there was no protest from that source—although there may have been several McQuestens turning in their graves in the nearby Hamilton Cemetery as a result of the wanton destruction of so much beauty.

Sunken Garden, McMaster University

SCOTT PARK—BRITISH EMPIRE GAMES, 1930

At the same time that McQuesten and the Board of Parks Management were building McMaster University and the northwest entrance to the city *(see Chapter 29)*, they were also negotiating with sports promoters who were proposing Hamilton as the site of the first British Empire Games. The promoters approached McQuesten and Langs, who helped secure the finances and the clearances to build high quality facilities that were required to bring the games to Hamilton. The 1930 games proved to be a huge success, with eleven countries participating.

A concrete stadium and a swimming pool built for the games are still in use today. The stadium (now Ivor Wynne Stadium) is in Scott Park, east of downtown Hamilton. After the first British Empire Games it became the home of the Hamilton Tiger Cats Football Club. Prior to the construction of this stadium, football was played on the Hamilton Amateur Athletic Association grounds just west of the city centre. Built in the 1890s, these grounds were under the aegis of the H.A.A.A, a private sports body, but in 1943 arrangements were made for transfer to the Hamilton Parks Board, under McQuesten's direction (W-MCP7-1.204). These facilities have been a great asset to Hamilton for many years: *Perhaps there is no single park in Hamilton which is so bound up with the childhood, youth, and adult life of so many of its citizens as the H.A.A.A. grounds* (Box 14-131).

The new Municipal Pool became Hamilton's first indoor pool. A recent *Spectator* article by Paul Wilson applauds the foresight of the builders of the pool which opened eighty years ago: "The wonderful thing is that, in these times of disposable buildings, they're still splashing about in this handsome pool today. . . . It was one of the finest in the Western Hemisphere . . . the largest in the Dominion. And it had a skylight that during the day would make the pool as light as if it were out of doors" (Jan 29 2010). It is a credit to T.B. McQuesten, C.V. Langs and the Hamilton Parks Board that the pool was built to last and is still a viable swimming pool to this day.

The Hamilton Spectator (Jul 4 1935) carried an article with the headline, *Learn to Swim Campaign Found Most Popular. Hon. T.B. McQuesten Lauds Efforts Made.* The campaign was carried throughout the entire province of Ontario. There was a special impetus for children in Hamilton, who often ventured into the dangers of the Lake and the Bay before they were able to swim. Parents enthusiastically enrolled their children, who learned to swim under the stern and dedicated eye of Jimmy Thompson. Thompson with his relay team had won gold at the first Empire Games, and he was the first coach of the Hamilton Aquatic Club in 1932. Jimmy Thompson devoted more than thirty years teaching 60,000 Hamilton children to swim, and the pool was eventually granted his name, the Jimmy Thompson Memorial Pool.

Jimmy Thompson, 1906-1966

LANDSCAPE DESIGNERS AND THE DIET KITCHEN

In 1934 a veritable artistic flowering was taking place in the Diet Kitchen Restaurant garden. A group of landscape architects, many of whom were McQuesten associates, formed in a fashion similar to that of the architects eight years earlier. John Danahy states that nine enthusiasts—six men and three women—used to meet in the Diet Kitchen garden: Howard Dunington-Grubb, Lorrie Alfreda Dunington-Grubb, J. Vilhelm Stensson, Carl Borgstrom, Gordon Culham, Helen Kippax, Edwin Kay, Frances Steinhoff and Humphrey Carver.

Humphrey Carver recalls that he was part of "a small group of landscape architects who came to know one another and enjoy one another's company very much. The Grubbs were the centre of this circle.... Together we founded the Canadian Society of Landscape Architects and Town Planners."[25] Gordon Culham was elected president and H.B. Dunington-Grubb was vice-president. Lorrie Dunington-Grubb became president of the Society in 1944, and after she died in 1945 her husband assumed the position. The association continues to thrive today.

We are given an indication of the convivial nature of the group's meetings in Carver's description of Howard Dunington-Grubb: "He was a witty Englishman and as tall as a Lombardy poplar. He was also known for his love of parties and theatricals, which was a key to both his character and his sense of design" *(The Canadian Encyclopedia)*. He was fondly nicknamed "Grubby" by his friends.

The Dunington-Grubbs produced such major landscape design projects as University Avenue, Toronto; Victoria College and Government House, Toronto; Shakespeare Garden, Stratford; and landscaping at Expo 67. Their work included landscaping for many industries, hospitals, schools, churches and private estates. Working with T.B. McQuesten they produced the landscape designs for Gage Park, McMaster University, RBG and Dundurn Castle, Hamilton; Oakes Garden Theatre, Rainbow Bridge Park and many other locations at Niagara Falls; Ontario Department of Highways from Toronto to Niagara; Battlefield Park, Stoney Creek; and the Garden House and garden at Whitehern.

Helen Kippax has been honoured at RBG for the development of a garden of natural plants on a one-acre parcel bounded on three sides by the natural lands of Grindstone Creek and Hendrie Valley. This garden commemorates her life as one of nine founding members of the Canadian Society of Landscape Architects. The garden features native plants and native plant cultivars, shrubs, perennials and grasses. It showcases sustainable gardening for RBG visitors.

The various architects, landscape designers, craftsmen and artists who met at the Diet Kitchen constituted a large group of like-minded men and women, and the cross-pollination provided by their meetings would have been inspirational for all. The Arts and Crafts movement in Canada represents a virtual renaissance of the arts in the country. It is not surprising that Tom, his associates and his family were caught up in the enthusiasm of these visionaries.

It is not known if T.B. McQuesten and Noulan Cauchon were actually members of the Diet Kitchen groups, but it would be difficult to imagine that they did not attend some of those convivial meetings with their associates. Thomas certainly agreed with their philosophy and hired many of the members for his projects.

Later in his career, there were cries of *patronage* but T.B. always conducted the bidding and contracts as legally as required by law. He had learned by experience that his associates were professionals to whom he could entrust a job and find it both bid and completed to his standards.

---

[25] http://www.oala.on.ca/articles

Chapter 29

CREATING A GRAND ENTRANCE FOR HAMILTON

"One of Hamilton's demonstrations of superior virtue is
the art of planning noble entrances and gateways,
putting its scenic assets into communal circulation."
(*Toronto Star Weekly*, Nov 16 1929)

**John Lyle's concept for the new High Level Bridge
for the Northwest Entrance to Hamilton**

In 1928 the city offered a competition for the best design for the beautification of the northwest entrance to Hamilton. It would include a new High Level Bridge and a botanical garden. The judging was blind. The winner was Carl Borgstrom of Wilson, Bunnell & Borgstrom, for the design prepared by Knut Mattias (Matt) Broman, a Swedish designer who drew up a comprehensive plan on a massive scale. Broman's strong points were design and development, and Barnsley describes the plan as enormous in scope:

> [Broman's design] reached from the present Royal Botanical Gardens Headquarters, past the grounds of Dundurn Castle, to the Harbour front at Wellington Street. The future Rock Garden and a host of other features, from small hidden gardens, raised lookout points, boulevards, and avenues of trees, to waterfront developments, all were detailed meticulously. It was truly a master plan! So attractive was its concept that implementation was almost immediate and most of the principal elements were completed within a few short years. (Barnsley 34)

Borgstrom and Broman won the competition for overall design. The Dunington-Grubbs won second prize with elaborate details of architecture and garden design; and John Lyle was third with a grand architectural concrete bridge complete with majestic pylons and statuary. The Parks Board wisely decided to employ the best characteristics of all three winners, but used the Broman design as the model from which they worked (Best 59-64).

Hamilton Council balked at several of the costs for what they considered to be unnecessary adornment, and some concessions had to be made for the northwest entrance. Tom had been successful in approaching the provincial government to share the cost of the road and bridge. Now he had to devise a means of combating Council's resistance.

Tom knew the value of the media. He invited *Toronto Star Weekly* columnist R.C. Reade to view the plans and visit the lands. Reade applauded the vision and was quite enthralled by the concept of a great Canadian botanical garden and a grand entrance to the city. He praised Hamilton for its "cult of beauty" and its "superior virtue." Tom took Reade on a scenic tour of the city and up to Hamilton Mountain for a view of the panoramic scene below, which they both declared was "the most striking view to be had from any city in North America." Reade published an article and some sketches. He was especially impressed with the non-commercial nature of the project, compared with Toronto's "glorified midway":

HAMILTON SHOWS TORONTO HOW

Hamiltonians have been long conspiring secretly to show Toronto how to construct stately portals and thresholds that will compel the speeding tourist to jam on his brakes and pause and look about him in awe and wonder.... One of Hamilton's demonstrations of superior virtue is the art of planning noble entrances and gateways, putting its scenic assets into communal circulation. (*Toronto Star Weekly*, Nov 16 1929)

The grand plans had to be modified to suit City Council's more modest tastes (and finances), but Tom, John Lyle and Noulan Cauchon argued successfully to retain the four majestic pylons on the bridge. The Parks Board was able to proceed immediately because they had previously been guaranteed one mill on the tax levy, giving them some autonomy over budget matters. They also had first call on the interest payments and a portion of the principal of the city's long term debentures (Laking 7).

It is a credit to McQuesten and the city that the three plans were integrated, compromises made, and concessions granted quickly so the job could proceed. After an engineer's report disclosed that the existing bridge would last only two years, some urgency developed to replace it. Hamiltonians still remembered the collapse of the railroad bridge at the Desjardins Canal on March 12, 1857, when seventy people died.

Because of the financial costs and the Depression, Tom and many others thought that completion of the bridge might take twenty years but it was completed in five. The collapse of the Stock Market in 1929 provided an abundance of labour, skilled and otherwise. Construction began in 1929, and the bridge was dedicated in 1932 with great fanfare. Many who previously balked now claimed and accepted credit.

That is, all except Tom who avoided the accolades and left the speaking job to Langs. This was characteristic of Tom who was already *stealthily* planning the next move; or perhaps he felt that this project was not yet complete as, indeed, it was not. He had managed to lure McMaster University to Hamilton and had promised acres of landscaped gardens and vistas. Now he needed to focus on the creation of a botanical garden. But before plans could proceed, some unsightly aspects of the balance of the land around the High Level Bridge and Cootes Paradise would require attention.

Inspiration for the garden, however, was clear: in the summer of 1924, Tom, his mother, Mary and sister, Hilda, had toured England with a Canadian Bar Association delegation, and were able to visit the botanic gardens at Kew, southwest London and at Edinburgh. No doubt Thomas gained many insights into parks and gardens while there, especially as the Garden City Movement was flourishing in England at the time.

Newspapers were quick to notice the increased activities of T.B. McQuesten and the Parks Board, which became noteworthy news. Barnsley informs us that:

> In reading the city page of either the Hamilton *Herald* or *Spectator*, a visitor would note that, column for column, the affairs of the Board of Parks Management outnumbered all other city activities by at least two to one. A steady stream of development and beautification plans was conceived, adopted, and developed, within the span of the late twenties. (33)

Barnsley also comments that from 1934 to 1939, "[McQuesten] truly created a century of beauty in a mere five years" (47).

THE SQUATTERS' LANDS

McQuesten's plans for the northwest entrance included a university and a botanic garden. Before the vast raw lands for these projects could be developed and beautified, they had to be cleared. One of the Parks Board's reform goals was the acquisition and clearing of the squatters' lands and the boathouse colony that had grown up in the area below the High Level Bridge at Cootes Paradise, and along the shores of the bay. This collection of boathouses and tar-paper and tin-roofed shacks caused some controversy in Hamilton. There were those who viewed the community in its "rustic charm on the water," and those who saw it as an eyesore and an affront to any City Beautiful ideals for Hamilton.

Ultimately those who recognized the natural beauty of the area organized to transform it into a public garden and nature preserve. Dr. Leslie Laking is one who saw potential beneath the ugliness imposed by humans, and saw the natural beauty of the landscape itself as a "catalyst" that "propelled" the founders of RBG to expose the beauty beneath. Laking remembers well the pre-1928 view of Hamilton, particularly its approaches from Toronto and Guelph: "Billboards, gas stations and run-down dwellings

Squatters' shacks and boathouses dotting the shore near the High Level Bridge *(HPL)*

line the High Level entrance—and the gravel pits! Below to the west, the tar-paper shacks, boathouses and sheds blotted the eastern shore of Cootes Paradise" (Laking 2, 3).

These lands and their rustic occupants have been variously documented in photographs, in a brass plaque at the head of the Hamilton Waterfront Trail, and in several accounts of social and political analyses that continue to be debated into this century (Bouchier and Kruikshank). The newspapers carried reports of "moves made to eject squatters at the Marsh," and Tom suggested more game wardens to protect marsh wildlife. He also deplored the damage to parks and properties by boys lighting grass fires (*Spectator*, Oct 2 1934).

The lands were gradually cleared by the Parks Board, and work on the vision of a grand city entrance proceeded. Dr. Laking notes that "a policy decision was forced at the April 7, 1925 meeting of the Parks Board. The record carries a terse statement: 'Keep private and corporate interests out of Cootes Paradise'" (Laking 10). Tom had seen the condition of Niagara Falls with its hucksters and racketeers and was determined that such should not be allowed to happen in Hamilton.

Because much of the work took place during the Great Depression, McQuesten and the Parks Board sought wherever possible to hire the unemployed and the indigent, some of whom would have been squatters and residents of the boathouse colony. Tom even arranged a three-day week so that more men could be employed. The *Herald* reported that "Ontario was to pay two-thirds of the cost of the relief projects." Tom had formed the deputation, obtaining assurances to that effect from the Ontario Government (Sept 20 1934).

Humphrey Carver worked with Borgstrom on the project and paints a less rosy and benevolent picture of the employees and their work; but he also comes to admit the worth for the workers. He first describes it as Depression "work-relief in which every able-bodied unemployed citizen of Hamilton had to earn his dole." He describes "men handling their spades like

Demolishing a boathouse on RBG property
(Photo courtesy of RBG, Burlington, Ont.)

convicts, undernourished and forlorn." Nevertheless, even Carver admits that there was some merit in the system for the men who had been able to earn an income and could boast that they had a part in building something extraordinary for Hamilton. They had transformed a scar on the environment and made it "bloom like a garden, so that it became one of the principal tourist attractions of the city and an enormous pleasure to generations of children exploring its alpine paths" (Carver 45).

T.J. Newlands, in a 1964 address about the parks of Hamilton, applauds the resulting effect: "From a landscaping point of view, the Western Entrance to Hamilton has often been mentioned as one of the finest approaches to any city in Canada. Hills were moved, gullies filled in, trees and shrubs planted, and bridges were built. Out of it there emerged today's beautiful entrance" (Box 14-131).

Drawing for the proposed Northwest Entrance
with trees, gardens and pathways to replace the squatters' shacks and boathouses

As part of the northwest entrance to Hamilton, the garden complex designed by Tom's associates, Matt Broman, Carl Borgstrom and the Dunington-Grubbs would incorporate Cootes Paradise, which is the section of water and marshy land off Burlington Bay at the westerly tip of Lake Ontario.

First, the unsightly gravel pit was gradually transformed into an alpine rock garden. The landscape architects carved out paths, ponds and natural areas, and planted flower beds and trees. They transported stones from Albion Falls and the Niagara escarpment, and the stones were as carefully selected and placed as the plantings. Mary Baker McQuesten had remarked beforehand on *Tom's mania for old stone* (W7064, Aug 14 1928). Broman selected the stones and their placement as if they had landed there naturally during the last receding ice age.

Construction of the Rock Garden began in November 1929 and was completed two years later. Parkland gradually expanded outward from the Rock Garden and under the High Level Bridge, stretching from Burlington around Cootes Paradise and into Hamilton along York Blvd. past the Hamilton Cemetery. On the east side of York Blvd. it joined with Dundurn Park and Castle, the former home of Sir Allan Napier MacNab; it also included the McMaster University lands which were maintained by

Dundurn Castle (former home of Sir Allan MacNab)

the Parks Board. All these areas were landscaped by the Dunington-Grubbs. Dundurn castle is now a museum and has been designated a National Historic Site.

Tom continued to live at Whitehern while working on the Hamilton projects. He escorted his mother, Mary, on many excursions to inspect his projects, which she enjoyed immensely and recounted with great pride: *Last evening Tom took us all to see the Rock Garden and also approach to McMaster. It is all beyond description simply amazing. At Gage Park, 120,000 seedlings were grown and used, the rock work is marvellous* (W7085, Jul 8 1930). On July 3 1930 Mary exulted, *We are having beautiful weather and on Tuesday morning Tom took me to Gage Park and as it was rainy and a holiday at noon he drove over the grass. The ramblers over the bed and roses in the bed in front of greenhouse are beyond description; and long rows of scarlet geraniums etc.* (W7080). On May 15 1931, *Rock Garden brilliant* (W7124); on May 19 1931: *Had been down to Gage Park the day before (Sunday). The honesty is a sight to behold in that bed against the fence. The whole place beautiful* (W7128, see also W7136).

Mary's letters provide seasonal descriptions of the Whitehern garden and she was proud of her botanical knowledge. In her many comments about the plants, she invariably uses the Latin name. Ruby also uses the Latin in describing one of her paintings as *a little study of phlox drummondii, pink, dark red & white*; this picture hangs at Whitehern today (W4657, Sep 26 1902).

In early 1930, T.B. McQuesten sought support from the Parks Board for his projected botanical garden in Westdale Park, made up of an exceptional 400 acres of Westdale ravinelands and adjacent waterlots in Cootes Paradise. He proposed to rename the 162-hectare (400-acre) park, "Royal Botanical Gardens." He obtained Royal assent on May 13, 1930, and the next day the *Spectator* applauded his triumph: "The gardens are to occupy the fine site covering about 400 acres in Westdale, . . . and as this property connects with. . . Cootes Paradise and the beautiful expanse of water to be seen from the highway western entrance, there is no reason why in time it should not become one of the finest gardens in the world" (Laking 13). It was also "next door to a 50 acre university site" which in 1931 became McMaster University (Laking 13, 34).

The *Royal* designation has served as an *in perpetuity* clause to protect the gardens with its greatly expanded lands from commercial development. This last was always a vital consideration for McQuesten. "The Parks Board records show a terse statement: Keep private and corporate interests out of Cootes Paradise" (Laking 10). Any change at RBG would require a dispensation from the Crown to remove the *Royal* designation, and that would be difficult to justify. RBG remains the largest botanical garden in Canada by land base, and the only one in North America with the right to use the *Royal* appellation. RBG is further acknowledged and protected under the Ontario Heritage Act.

Royal Botanical Gardens, which began as an Alpine Rock Garden in a gravel pit, gradually grew to 971 hectares (2,400 acres) by the addition of various lands. In 1931, George M. Hendrie, son of William Hendrie (1831-1906), donated 122 acres (49.3h) of his historic horse-breeding farm to RBG to celebrate the centenary of his father's birth. At the same time, the Hendrie family commissioned Frederick John Flatman to design and build a magnificent set of wrought iron gates as an entrance marker to the Hendrie lands. It was Flatman who made the life-size flowers in the Whitehern

Hendrie Gates designed by Fred Flatman

garden. He also made many railings and gates and various pieces of functional and decorative ironwork at Niagara.

Flatman was the master craftsman blacksmith to the Hendrie Cartage Company (Laking 32, 33, 106). He had apprenticed in England, and his design was adapted from the gates at Trinity College, Cambridge. Flatman embellished the Hendrie Gates design with symbols appropriate to their Canadian setting: a sheaf of Durham wheat, a cluster of Ontario grapes, and a horseshoe to commemorate the Hendrie's love of horse breeding and racing. Flatman's craftsmanship is distinguished and so exacting that he took eighteen months to make the gates. He supervised the proper hanging of the gates "so that a child may easily open and shut them with one hand." The Gates were erected in June 1953 and designated under the Ontario Heritage Act in 1991.

Conservation was an important aspect of beauty to the McQuestens. When Calvin, as president of the Bird Protection Association, enlisted the aid of his friend Jack Miner for the Cootes Paradise preserve, this helped to promote Hamilton's northwest entrance project and to lure McMaster University to Hamilton (W-MCP2-4.048, Feb 25 1907; W8084, Jan 10 1932). The McQuestens, being intent on the education of children, would have been pleased that the Junior Audubon Club of the Bird Protection Society has continued to develop from its beginning in the 1920s. In 1983, RBG initiated a young naturalists' club in partnership with the Hamilton Naturalists' Club, forming the current Hamilton Junior Naturalists' Club.

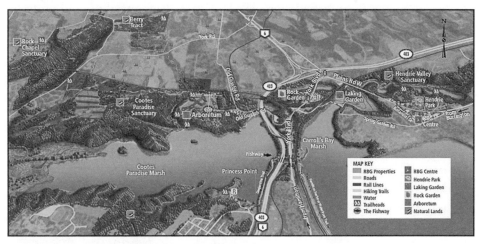

RBG Sanctuaries, area 971h (2,400 acres)   *(photo courtesy of RBG)*

Thomas always sought to add an educational component to everything that he did. He and Broman worked together to add a Children's Garden to RBG in 1947 (Laking 61). It is obvious that Tom cared very much for the health and well-being of the children of Hamilton and Ontario. He understood that the training of the younger generation establishes values for the future. To this end he developed many parks and playgrounds for their education, exercise, and enjoyment. He also improved the City's existing playground system and expanded their programmes and supervision (Barnsley 28).

Although Tom never married and had no issue, C.V. Langs, his friend and associate on the Parks Board, expressed McQuesten's dedication with an analogy: "Tom is a bachelor . . . whose bride is the City Parks System" (Best 68). No bride was ever more beautifully appointed or better dressed, and no children were ever more thoroughly encouraged to develop robust bodies and healthy minds. It is likely that Tom provided for the children of Hamilton partly in compensation for the fact that he and his siblings would never have children of their own, and the branch would die out. This would have compounded his regret concerning Ruby's death, since she had prospects for marriage and children, but was forced to delay her marriage to David Ross until Tom graduated, and then it was too late.

Rumours of liaisons after Tom's broken engagement to Miss Isabel Elliot are not verifiable. However, we have seen that for many years, his secretary, Miss Yorston did the shopping every Chrismas for gifts that he gave to several women friends (Minnes 5). Miss Yorston, who lived near Whitehern, became Tom's secretary at a young age; he also appointed her as his secretary at Queen's Park. Those who knew Yorston suspected that she was in love with Tom. There is ample evidence that he knew how to charm women. Dr. Whidden of McMaster wrote in a letter to Tom, *but then you are a ladies' man and, of course, that is natural* (Box 08-138a, Mar 1941). In a similar vein, Mitchell Hepburn recommended Tom McQuesten highly to the young ladies in the audience when introducing him (Jul 20 1934).

Barnsley describes Tom as quite exceptional in appearance and bearing:

> He was extremely personable, above average height with a rugged physique and athletic build. His grooming and clothing usually brought admiring comments from women. Many fashionable ladies were quite prepared to drop other interests if they chanced to encounter Thomas on a stroll. His male friends were equally impressed, and friendships once made were long standing. His intimates preferred to call him "Tim." (Barnsley 38)

Is Appointed

MISS JESSIE YORSTON
Who has been chosen by Hon. T. B. McQuesten to act as his secretary, in connection with his duties as minister of highways and Hydro commissioner.

Jessie Yorston,
T.B. McQuesten's secretary

Rev. Calvin, as the last remaining member of the family, was the champion and protector of the McQuesten legacy in the years prior to his death in 1968. When Calvin was making plans to deed the house to the City of Hamilton, he commented that its garden is: *An Oasis in a Downtown Desert* (Box 09-233a, Jan 30 1954). At the actual dedication to the Hamilton Parks Board, Calvin employed his typical Social Gospel oratory and granted Whitehern to all the people and particularly to the poor in the slums of Hamilton:

Public picnic in Whitehern garden with music in the gazebo (c.2000)

And I hope that many of the people who in earlier years knew the bitterness of the squalor of such slums and the children who were born in them may enjoy, whenever they please, the beautiful rooms of Whitehern and eat their lunches in its pleasant garden. (Box 08-140, Nov 3 1959)

The garden at Whitehern Historic House and Garden is a testament to the McQuesten's love of beauty, conservation and horticulture. It is presently slated for restoration to the original Dunington-Grubb design.

Chapter 30

ONTARIO MINISTER OF HIGHWAYS
AND CHAIRMAN, NIAGARA PARKS COMMISSION

"Mary had lived long enough to see Thomas become a lawyer
and King's Counsel, a prominent Hamilton and Liberal Party politician,
and a Member of Parliament. He had restored the McQuesten name
in dignity and prestige, if not in wealth." (M.J.A.)

Tom's family had always been staunchly Liberal, and Tom served in the executive branch at both the provincial and federal levels of the Liberal party during the 1920s to the 1940s. He was a tireless worker for the party in Hamilton and for the Ontario Liberal Association where he rose to President from 1932 to 1943 (Minnes 2). During his tenure he was instrumental in rebuilding the Liberal Party in Canada. Also, he usually managed to organize women voters with the help of his powerful female contingent at Whitehern and in the church. Tom fulfilled his public duties admirably, and through his work he developed a reputation as a master-worker, a unifying force and negotiator.

Tom was elected to the Provincial legislature in 1934. It was largely through Tom's efforts that Mitchell Hepburn was elected as Liberal Premier of Ontario on July 10, 1934; he would remain Premier until 1942. This was the first Liberal Party victory in Ontario in thirty years. The Liberal party also won a political victory in the 1935 federal election, with Prime Minister Mackenzie King at the head of a majority government.

When the 1934 provincial election fell to Hepburn and the Liberals, Tom could expand his horizons, and the broader Ontario work began in earnest. Immediately after the election, Premier Hepburn presented Tom with the portfolio of Minister of Highways. Tom's appointments quickly accelerated, and he accepted several offices and portfolios: Minister of Highways 1934-43; Minister of Public Works 1934-37 & 1942-43; Commissioner of the Hydro Electric Power Commission 1934-37; and Chairman of the Niagara Parks Commission 1934-44.

(L-R.) Sir James Dunn, Mitchell Hepburn, T.B. McQuesten

R. E. Knowles Jr. in *Saturday Night* predicted that Tom would likely succeed to the Provincial Liberal leadership, and gave McQuesten credit for the Liberal victory:

Hon. T.B. McQuesten would be the most likely person to succeed to the Provincial Liberal leadership. . . . [his] executive ability, level-headedness, keen insight and the many desirable qualities implied by the word "wisdom" are the factors that determine the standing of a man around the council board. None will deny that T.B. McQuesten possesses these qualities.

Ontario Parliament Buildings

Five years ago he was elected V.P. and three years ago President of the Ontario Liberal Association. He addressed more than a hundred political gatherings during the election campaign last summer, so that he must be given no small measure of the credit for the sweeping Liberal victory that ensued. (Apr 30 1935)

While holding his various provincial positions, Tom arranged with Chisholm that he would retire from the firm and would no longer share in the profits, but his name would remain on the letterhead (W-MCP7-1.211). He continued his work with the Hamilton Parks Board and remained Chairman of the Works Committee—work that ultimately spanned twenty-five years, from 1922 to 1947.

With so many offices to fill it is remarkable that Tom was able to stay in touch with all of his associates. He had established good relations with many who were honoured to call him a friend, such as his deputy minister, Robert Melville Smith; Chief Engineer, A.A. Smith; and Matt Broman, with whom he had worked during the development of Hamilton's northwest entrance. C. Ellison Kaumeyer of Chippewa was appointed as Superintendent of the Niagara Parks Commission. He and McQuesten often worked with architect William Lyon Somerville, the Dunington-Grubb garden designers, sculptors Frances Loring, Florence Wyle, Elizabeth Wynn Wood and others. These associates all subscribed to the City Beautiful philosophy.

McQuesten's numerous provincial projects include the Queen Elizabeth Highway, many highways in Southern and Northern Ontario, the Niagara Parks system and School for Apprentice Gardeners, and three international bridges—the Ivy Lea, Blue Water and Rainbow bridges, as well as many other bridges and historical restorations. It is difficult to imagine that one person could have his hand in so many enterprises and achieve so much. T.B. McQuesten's prolific accomplishments during this time are truly astounding. No one before or since has equalled his record.

Tom's scrupulous honesty is apparent in even the smallest of matters. For instance, in a memo to Matt Broman, Tom requests that Broman:

Please send someone up to my garden, 41 Jackson Street West, to trim the trees and bushes. I have a number of fruit trees against the walls which were not trimmed last year and I am afraid to let them go another year. Please see that this is charged to my account and forward it to me here [at Queen's Park].

A hand-written notation at bottom states: *A. Pain, J. Waters, April 11, $1.50* (W9861l, Apr 8 1938). In another letter Tom requests that Broman give some dahlia roots to his friend Mr. Norman, but he clearly stipulates that the charge should be made to him:

Dear Matt, I have given a letter of introduction to Mr. Norman who is a friend of mine in Hamilton. He may be calling on you some day and I would be obliged if you would show him every attention. I should also like to make him a present of a number of dahlia roots when they are available. I should like you to charge these to me. He may indicate when he calls on you the varieties that he specially admires. With kind personal regards, Faithfully yours, T.B. (W9861s, Jul 15 1940)

An anecdote is told of Tom that when a construction company sent him a gift one Christmas he instructed Hilda to *send it right back!* However she refused to return it, complaining that he had never received anything for all his hard work. The Hon. Thomas B. McQuesten refused to be party to that kind of political pressure, and was never accused of graft.

Tom's associates had the highest respect for him, and he for them, as evident in another letter to Broman:

On the whole permit me to congratulate you on a very successful year's work. . . . I meant to say that irrespective of anything that has been done in the way of plans, I would like you to feel that you are in entire control to plan and execute, as means permit, the development of the garden in and around your nursery and including the area around the Glen, Restaurant, and in fact any distance which you wish. . . . I want you to feel that this area is your job and you will have no interference in any way whatsoever. (W9865q, Dec 20 1939)

Having been successful with Hamilton's northwest entrance, RBG and High Level Bridge, Tom made plans for similar undertakings in the Niagara Parks. But a new highway and bridges would be needed to unite the gardens and beauty spots across Ontario from one border to the other. As Minister of Highways, McQuesten launched a province-wide highway improvement programme that involved spending more than $200,000,000 over his nine-year tenure (Minnes 3).

In the same year that he was elected as MPP, Tom was also appointed King's Counsel. His mother must have been very proud of him; her faith in him had been fully justified. A year later he received an honorary LL.D. degree from McMaster University. Tom's family rejoiced in his successes; he had fulfilled the family's dream. They all felt that the family name had been redeemed through his political success, his fine character, and his many good works. He had risen on his reputation as a leader, a builder, a visionary, and an honest politician.

Although he had become a Member of Provincial Parliament and Minister of several key portfolios—political positions with power—these were never ends for Tom. Like his mother, he had an impregnable sense of duty and there was much more work to be done.

Tom continued to live at Whitehern while working at Parliament. His mother was now 85 years of age and in failing health, so he devoted as much time to her as possible. He visited her often and reported on the progress of his many projects. Mrs. McQuesten suffered a stroke during the summer of 1934, and as she neared the end her condition was regarded as so grave that Tom remained at her bedside all day. The *Hamilton Spectator* notes Tom's devotion to his mother on the occasion of his appointment to Cabinet, less than four months before her death:

> Mr. McQuesten has a 'chum.' Sometimes long miles from home and fighting his earliest battles of life he could only be with her in his thoughts. . . . A venerable lady who sits in the beautiful garden at the rear of the historic old McQuesten mansion . . . [She] followed the campaign battles of her son with intense interest. . . . He found time an hour a day to take his mother for a motor ride. Time also to spend an hour or so sitting with her reading to her and answering the questions of a still keen mind about public affairs. . . . Today Mrs. McQuesten is sharing her son's honour and he is enjoying the success in life that attends respect of parenthood. (June 30, 1934)

After his mother's death, R.E. Knowles, Jr. in *Saturday Night* continues in the same vein:

> Alone among the members of the present Liberal Cabinet, Mr. McQuesten is a bachelor. Until her recent death, his mother Mrs. Mary Baker McQuesten was always his 'best chum.' . . . Her death makes a gap in his life that is hard to fill, though he takes what consolation he can from the fact that during the few months before she passed away, he shared with her the honour and distinction that comes to a Cabinet Minister. (Apr 30 1935)

MARY BAKER MCQUESTEN DIES, DECEMBER 7, 1934

Large areas of Hamilton are, in the last analysis,
a reflection of her love for beauty. (Eulogy)

Mary Baker McQuesten died on December 7, 1934; her mind remained sharp and focused to the last. Tom was her favourite child and she was very proud of him. Two years before she died, she sent him a card on his fiftieth birthday, addressed:

> *My Darling Tomsy,*
> *on your fiftieth birthday,*
> *Your Mother*
> *June 30th, 1932.*
> (W-MCP3-5.071, Jun 18 1932)

Mary lived long enough to see Thomas become a lawyer, a King's Counsel, a prominent Hamilton and Liberal Party politician, an MPP and a Cabinet Minister with several portfolios. He had restored the McQuesten name in dignity and prestige, if not in wealth. She, as the Victorian Matriarch of the family, had finally seen the fruition of her efforts.

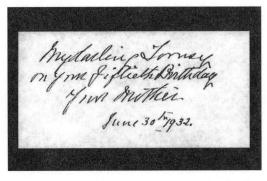

In Mary's obituary for the *Hamilton Herald*, Tom gave his mother credit for his dedication to beauty:

SHE LOVED BEAUTY

When beauty is created, its author is entitled to gratitude and so is a person who inspired it. The late Mrs. M. B. McQuesten, who died this morning, was the inspiration behind many of Hamilton's most treasured beauty spots—spots that are the basis for a large part of our civic pride.

True, it was her son, Hon. T. B. McQuesten, who played a leading part in bringing those places of beauty into being. But Mr. McQuesten himself has told of the large part his mother played in moulding his tastes, his standards and his plan of life. Not the least of her contributions to him was to give him a love for beauty that was large enough to spread out and influence the appearance of a great city.

Mrs. McQuesten was well-loved within her immediate circle of friend *[sic]*. She loved flowers. About her she gathered possessions that were rich in charm and character. And so even those who did not know her very well have reason for regret at her passing. Large areas of Hamilton are, in the last analysis, a reflection of her love for beauty. (Box 08-140a, Dec 7 1934; see also W0144a, *A Fitting Eulogy for a Christian Life*)

It is indicative of Tom's regard for his mother that he sent an order to the *Canadian Clipping Service* requesting copies of all of his mother's death notices the Service could find; thirty-nine notices are carefully combined in a packet in the Whitehern archives. It is a testament to her that notices appeared in so many papers throughout Canada, even from some of the small towns where she made speeches to recruit members for the WFMS. Several of these speeches now appear on the Whitehern website. Four excerpts from the clippings illustrate Mary Baker McQuesten's legacy and her influence on family and community (W-MCP1-3a.049):

MISSION CAUSE LOSES FRIEND
Mrs. M. McQuesten Wielded Powerful Influence in Presbyterian Councils

In the passing of Mrs. McQuesten, the Presbyterian Church has lost a devout and faithful daughter, and the mission field one who was ever on the alert to help the cause. Mrs. McQuesten's advice, always considered and wise, was much sought on many matters, and in the organizations in which she was such a power her loss will be keenly felt. No woman in Canada probably has filled high offices with such dignity, ability and tact; and her gentle personality and wide sympathies made her beloved far beyond the confines of her own city. A pattern of Victorian womanhood, her home and family and her church constituted her world, and in all that pertained to them she upheld by her life and works, her own high and impregnable sense of duty. Many friends will mourn her.

Mrs. McQuesten . . . was one of the founders of the Women's Foreign Missionary Society of the Presbyterian Church in Canada, and later served as Vice-President [and President] of the Hamilton Presbyterian Society. She was deeply interested in and active in public affairs, particularly in matters that concerned the city of Hamilton. She was well known for her support of the Lord's Day Alliance . . . Her minister, Rev. H.B. Ketchen, D.D., of MacNab St. Church, at the funeral service, paid her very high tribute, but wholly in keeping with her character and career. Dr. Ketchen said, "For nearly three-score-years-and-ten she has been one of the most conspicuous Christian workers and spiritual forces, not only in this congregation and community, but in the Church at large. She came to the church as a young and strikingly beautiful bride, and although her life had been unusually trying, that singular loveliness was in her face to the last. As the spirited daughter of a Commander in the Royal Navy, she knew how to weather stormy seas and to fight a good fight. Her rare and steadfast courage was doubtless more deeply rooted in her unshakeable faith in God from whom by daily communion she gathered strength and guidance as needed through the years. Blended in her were

inflexible integrity and the kindliness and graciousness of the true lady. Known to many only in her public life, it was in her home that she was at her best where her wit sparkled most, and where her sweet gentleness overshadowed her cleverness. Her memory will ever be cherished with reverence and affection.

Like her distinguished son, she was a lover of nature and in her declining years her garden was one of her greatest delights. To her Hon. Mr. McQuesten has frequently attributed much of the credit for his success in life and for the civic beautification plans he has from time to time put into effect.

The Hon. Thomas Baker McQuesten and his mother, Mary Baker McQuesten, c.1934

In eulogizing her, Dr. Ketchen said, in part: Mrs. McQuesten had a real puritanical sense of right and wrong. Her uncompromising conscience would not countenance anything that was not utterly honourable. She was an aristocrat by birth and breeding and an aristocrat intellectually and spiritually too. . . . To see her in the home or about the garden she loved was to think inevitably of "Lavender and Old Lace."

Two McQuesten Ladies in Lavender and Old Lace:

Mary Baker McQuesten (1849-1934)

Ruby Baker McQuesten (1879-1911)

Mary Baker McQuesten was highly respected throughout Ontario, and almost the entire Cabinet attended her funeral (*Globe & Mail*, Dec 10 1934). Tom was clearly devoted to his mother in a chivalrous manner, and was quick to give her credit for his success. Nowhere, however, does he mention Ruby, who slips more and more into obscurity as Tom champions on. No doubt, his praise of his mother and his gratitude toward her is inclusive of Ruby, as it was his mother who planned and executed the financial arrangement that resulted in Ruby's sacrifice for Tom's education.

One may criticize Mary for her overbearing control of her children, thwarting their marriage prospects and controlling their lives. From the vantage point of the twenty-first century, she can be seen as the enigma of the "good mother/bad mother." She is certainly a complex personality. Whatever else can be said of Mary Baker McQuesten, when we take into account her full history and what she accomplished against all odds, we must celebrate her determination to restore her family to its former place as one of the first families of Hamilton. Did she make some errors in judgement along the way? Did she have God's guiding hand at every turn, as she believed? Or, were some of her decisions self-serving as even she came to realize? When we view the outcome, that is, Tom's Triumph, does the end justify the means? I leave it to readers to debate this issue.

Mary accomplished what she set out to do. As the matriarch, she can be seen as a Victorian Moses who guided her family through more than twenty years in the wilderness of impoverishment and stigma, and then made of them a great family. In fact, there is no other family in Hamilton that has done so much for the built heritage and the beautification of the city and the province. Tom's greatest tribute to his mother and to his sister is, undoubtedly, that after they died, he continued the momentum of his City Beautiful and Social Gospel agendas, just as they would have wished.

Chapter 31

HON. T.B. McQUESTEN AND HIGHWAY SAFETY

**"Tom, being of a rational and moral nature, found it difficult that
drivers did not share his common-sense attitude to driving and safety."** (M.J.A.)

Tom did not rest after his mother's death, but began an even more feverish agenda of construction and beautification. Several very large journals at Whitehern are full of newspaper clippings dated in the 1930s and 1940s with articles, announcements, and Calls for Bids and Tenders on road and bridge building. For instance, "Hon. T.B. McQuesten announced reinforced concrete bridges over Etobicoke Creek on Highway 2 near Long Branch." These clippings demonstrate that McQuesten embarked on a very ambitious plan to build new roads and bridges throughout Ontario—roads that he felt were needed for the increasing automobile traffic, and to encourage commerce and tourism.

A series of news clippings in the archive note much activity. "T.B. McQuesten is in favour of widening the Oshawa to Toronto highway" [32m, 51km] (December, 1934). "[The] Pembroke to Hawkesbury highway is to be started with a new bridge over Bonnechere to be included" [138m, 223km]; the Dominion Government was to contribute 50% and the highway was to be part of the Trans-Canada Highway that was not under the Department of Northern Development. "It also proposed to improve the Ottawa to Morrisburg highway [37m, 60km] giving the Capitol better conditions. . . to points south" (*Renfrew Mercury*, June, 1935). The *Daily Commercial News* announced an intention to construct a 40ft (wide) road from Kingston through Toronto and Hamilton to London with initial work planned for 1936 (Feb 19 1936). In July, 1936 McQuesten called for bids on a three-lane highway via Browns Line through Kleinberg and Schomberg [10m, 16km] (*Mail & Empire*).

As Minister of Highways, Tom soon became aware that traffic fatalities on highways were increasing, and he sought ways to prevent them. Speed limits seemed to him the most logical and practical measure by which to reduce fatalities. For the next several years, newspapers carried many reports of Tom's attempts to enforce limits. The results speak much about human nature, especially when provided with power and speed. Tom, being of a rational and moral nature, found it difficult that drivers did not share his common-sense attitude to driving and safety.

MCQUESTEN'S SAFETY AGENDA ON ONTARIO'S NEW HIGHWAYS
"McQuesten Threatens to Impound Vehicles if Safety Measures Not Followed."

Safety became a major moral issue for Tom as traffic and fatalities increased. He struggled in Parliament, making many speeches in an attempt to establish and enforce speed limits. Many members were lobbying for removal on the grounds that the speed limit, which in 1935 was 35 miles per hour, was being ignored and was not being enforced. Tom countered in an address at the Motor Show dinner that year, "So I propose to retain the speed limit at present. . . . even though it is disregarded, [it] has a certain psychological effect on a large majority of drivers." Tom appealed to automobile manufacturers for built-in controls: "Speed is the efficient cause of 99 percent of accidents. If all cars were geared to run not faster than 25 miles per hour there would be practically no accidents" (*Herald*, Jan 16 1935).

No doubt this was hyperbole on Tom's part, to impress the fact that speed is the major cause of fatalities. But if he was serious, he clearly did not share the imperatives of most drivers or automobile manufacturers.

Tom appealed to drivers for the sake of children: "The lives of children of the Province are more valuable ever than the men's are. It is imperative that we educate and act for safety. So act that the advantages of modern machinery can be used in our Province without bringing harm or sorrow to anyone" (*Globe & Mail*, Jun 24 1935). Tom felt that safety was a moral imperative and he appealed to drivers' finer natures, to no avail: "After deep study, the [Highway] department experts are forced to the

Middlle Road (QEW) Divided Highway near Port Credit
August 1937
(Photo courtesy Ontario Ministry of Transportation)

conclusion that highway safety in Ontario today is largely a question of good manners and unselfishness" (*Globe & Mail*, Jun 30 1936).

These appeals had little effect. Finally, Tom resorted to threats:

I wish to specifically warn all drivers that, in future, in all cases of conviction for wilful, careless and negligent driving, consideration will be given by the Department, not only to the suspension of the operating license, but also to the revocation of the vehicle permit. In other words we will, in those cases which justify such action, impound the car—by removing the markers therefrom—of every driver convicted of a major traffic offence. In Ontario during the first five months of this year the number of fatalities resulting from motor traffic was thirty percent greater than in the same months in 1934. . . far out of proportion to the increase in the registration of vehicles or vehicle traffic. In other words reckless driving has increased. (*Ottawa Journal*, Jul 15 1935)

Tom may have made some enemies during his campaign for safety. Drivers in the early years of the automobile obviously were much like the drivers of today; reckless driving, speeding, accidents and fatalities were, and are, a fact of life. Tom's appeal at the Motor Show Dinner, although rational, evidently had no influence on the very people who were determined to build and to drive cars that would operate at increasing speeds and power ratios. Many of those at the Motor Show constituted an automobile lobby that would have enjoyed Tom's highways and bridges, but not his restrictions. Tom made many appeals to *Please be Courteous!* especially during holidays such as Labour Day and during the Canadian National Exhibition, but they fell on deaf ears.

"ONTARIO TO TEST FOOL-PROOF ROAD"

Tom McQuesten sought to build roads for the purpose of efficiency and safety, and he added boulevards for safety and beauty to encourage tourism between Canada and the U.S. He also widened and beautified smaller sections of highways in Ontario

to familiarize drivers with the convenience and safety of better roads, and in some cases he built four-lane roads with centre boulevards and pedestrian walkways.

In 1936, determined to build safer highways, Tom's Department released an announcement: "Ontario to Test Fool-Proof Road." Tenders were called for two highways, the Toronto to

QEW with grassy median, 1939

Barrie road, and the Toronto to Niagara Falls Highway: "The first section of the Niagara Falls road will be a six and one-half mile stretch between St. Catharines and Stamford. It will be a test of a fool-proof highway. It will consist of two strips, each 20 feet wide, with a third strip with shrubs and trees in the centre. Each paved strip will be a one-way route of two lanes" (*Ottawa Evening Citizen*, Jul 7 1936). In other early "fool-

proof" projects, McQuesten built wider and more modern bridges such as the Etobicoke and Bronte Creek Bridges, including pedestrian walkways whenever possible (Best 115).

As another safety measure, McQuesten and his associates decided that taking out the curves in highways would provide more "fool-proof" driving conditions. A.A. Smith,

Etobicoke Creek Bridge

Bronte Creek Bridge

Chief Engineer of Provincial Highways, announced at a conference that, "elimination of curves will cut seven miles off the present shortest route from Toronto to Niagara Falls. The saving in pavement alone will pay for the wider right-of-way." Smith presented it as a safety measure and predicted that without curves the highways would be more accident-free and drivers would eventually be able to drive at greater speeds safely (*Toronto Star*, Feb 22 1937). It is doubtful if Tom would have agreed with the last part of that statement. In May of the same year McQuesten announced that he would "take out curves on the Kingston Road with a new highway" (*Toronto Star*, May 8 1937).

There were many who agreed with Tom, and in 1936 he was elected second Vice-President of the Canadian Good Roads Association; in 1938 he was elected President of the same group for a term (*Daily Commercial News*, Sept 4 1936 & Sept 9 1938).

RAISING SPEED LIMITS

Although Tom's objections were clearly known, a measure was introduced in Parliament in 1937 to raise the speed limit from 35 to 50 miles per hour. Tom fought this vociferously, but failed to influence the outcome. He could build fine roads and bridges but he could not control how they would be used.

The newspapers carried reports almost daily. *Evening Telegram*, Mar 22 1937: "Over the protests of Hon. T.B. McQuesten the legislature apparently favours increasing the legal speed limit to 50 miles an hour on the open highways and 30 miles an hour in congested areas." *Toronto Star*: "Speed limit change opposed by Minister (again). Bill in third reading and approved by Hepburn." *Globe & Mail*, Mar 25 1937: "T.B. very definitely opposes increasing the speed limit to 50 miles per hour it is known." Hepburn was the consummate political opportunist, whereas McQuesten was first a rational moralist and, following his sister's edict, he was not a "sin-blind" politician who didn't know the difference between right and wrong (W-MCP2-4.053).

In March of 1937 some members proposed bringing in a law to *end speed limits of any kind*. The pragmatic McQuesten was firm, stating that skilled drivers would be able to control their speeds but many are not skilled. The police also urged against the "no limit" law. McQuesten pleaded, "it's not the best or even satisfactory but under all circumstances I feel there is a need for a limit" (*Spectator*, Mar 16 1937).

A law was finally passed to increase the speed limit to 50 miles per hour on the open highway. McQuesten managed to delay the third reading but was absent for the final approval, and the speed limit was changed. Tom had to be gracious in defeat and in the *Globe & Mail*, "T.B. McQuesten gave credit to the press for the horror campaign to reduce recklessness" (Oct 27 and Nov 7). Hepburn supported the new law, and he also pandered to the auto lobby by announcing a reduction in car licence fees (Best 122).

A rift between Tom and Hepburn was already present over an earlier Hydro crisis in which Tom had favoured the cancellation of Quebec Hydro contracts. He made a strong moral statement as to his reasons: "Here was an evidence of fraud which warranted the cancellation of any contract and we did it" (Best 121-22). The *Hamilton Herald* noted that:

> McQuesten approved the cancellation of Hydro contracts with four Quebec Hydro companies for 40 years. He empowered Ontario Hydro to undertake financing by issuance of Hydro bonds guaranteed by the province. This will wipe off 187 million of provincial debt. . . . Tom received a strong endorsement of the cancellation of Quebec power contracts voiced in parliament. (Apr 5 1935)

In June and July of 1937, after the defeat on speed limits, Tom spent several weeks at home amid rumours that he was ill, and that there was a rift between himself and Hepburn. There was speculation that Tom was refusing to return. Hepburn visited him at home, a clear sign that there was trouble between them, and then commented that Tom was expected to be away from Queen's Park for two or three weeks. The *Evening Telegram* carried a headline: "McQuesten Is Ill Asserts Premier"; he "is really ill at his home in Hamilton. . . . The story of a pending resignation is misleading" (Jun 26 1937). Did the moral defeat on speeding make Tom ill? Was he disenchanted with Hepburn and with politics? Did he consider resigning? Did he make a deal with Hepburn? Yes, probably.

While at home, Tom would have discussed his future with his brother Calvin, his law partner Chisholm, his minister, Rev. Ketchen, and his associates in Hamilton. It appears that he decided on a change of direction and a clearer political agenda.

From time to time Tom had been considered for the position of Premier if Hepburn were to resign. In 1935, there had been some talk of Tom as Premier, but Harry C. Nixon and Arthur Roebuck were also linked with the position (*Spectator*, Nov 5 1935). In March of 1936:

> [Hepburn was] unwell and was expected to resign or retire from the legislature at the end of the current session. . . . It is more likely that Hon. T.B. McQuesten,

Hamilton, Minister of Highways will have the first call to fill his chair. . . .
Mr. McQuesten is in a strong contending position, due to the fact that he
is now handling and with great efficiency, the government's biggest revenue
producing department outside of the Treasury itself, which collects the bulk
of the taxes. (*Hamilton Herald*, Mar 14 1936)

Earlier that month, McQuesten's honesty had been called into question and
suspicions were raised when it was discovered that he had not tabled his travelling
expense accounts when requested to do so. Thomas was vindicated when the
headline appeared:

HON. T.B. MCQUESTEN PAYS OWN TRAVELLING EXPENSES

Considerable talk has been heard in Queen's Park corridors on the non-
inclusion of the name of T.B. McQuesten, Minister of Highways, in the
list of cabinet ministers' travelling expenses tabled last week in answer
to a question by an opposition member. The reason has just leaked out—
Hamilton's Minister of Highways pays his own expenses wherever he goes.
The automobile expenses of other ministers ranged from $2000 to $6000, but
the Minister of Highways uses his own car, buys his own gas and pays all other
expenses. Since he has become Minister of Highways, Hon. T.B. McQuesten
has travelled thousands of miles from one end of the province to the other on
official business, but has yet to submit his first travelling expense account.
(Toronto Bureau of the *Hamilton Herald*, Mar 13 1936)

McQuesten also personally paid for all his overnight stays in the Niagara Parks
Commission administrative building (Best 178). Because of quiet gestures like this,
and in keeping with his family's tradition, Tom's commitment to government as a
Minister takes on the aura of a calling or a mission.

When Mitchell Hepburn was ill in January 1937, Harry C. Nixon became acting
Premier until February when Hepburn returned from Arizona, where he had gone
for treatment of a bronchial ailment (*Spectator*, Feb 10 1937). Possibly Tom by then had
given up all consideration of becoming Premier; he might have realized that the job
required much deal-making and too many ethical compromises, which he was not
prepared to entertain.

GOVERNMENT MONEY FOR THE UNEMPLOYED

At the height of the depression in 1936, the Ontario Government and the
Dominion of Canada entered into an agreement for a relief program. This provided
Tom with the money to advance his highways and bridges program on a larger scale.
An announcement read, "Ontario and the Dominion to spend $6,000,000. They
approved a relief public works agreement . . . in which the administration and the cost
is shared equally by the two governments" (*Toronto Star*, Aug 12 1936).

This injection of funds allowed McQuesten and William Lyon Somerville to
expand and build new bridges and highways. They now entered into a feverish
campaign to finally build the Toronto to Niagara Highway, including an international
bridge to the U.S. which became the Rainbow Bridge. They also continued their

plans for two other international bridges: the Ivy Lea Bridge over the Thousand Islands, and the Blue Water Bridge at Sarnia.

However, many objections were voiced about this money being spent on employing immigrants and indigents on relief. Tom came to their defence and praised the relief workers: "Many employers of labour, and to a general extent the general public as well have the mistaken impression that men who are on relief are

Depression Unemployed 1935
(collectionscanada)

either incapable of performing skilled work or are unwilling to give a fair day's work for a fair day's pay. The conditions under which the Oakville Bridge has been constructed prove conclusively that neither impression is correct" (*Toronto Star*, Dec 31 1936). In 1937, a minimum wage act was proposed because of the exploitation of workers. Many abuses were cited: 70-99 hrs for $10.50 to $12.00 per week; 60 hrs for $10.87 per week; 99 hrs over 2 weeks $19.06; 80 hrs over 2 weeks for $11.08. Response to this proposal was favourable throughout the Dominion (*Toronto Star*, Mar 12 1937).

In the midst of Tom's defeat on the speed limit issue, he welcomed headlines about aid to the unemployed. This was a social issue that, if handled properly, would not compromise his morals: "Dominion To Spend Seven Million on Roads. Huge Program Planned as Aid to Unemployed. . . . The increased allowance will be made for men who go to work on municipal or public works. A man getting $40 a month would

Labourers, River Road Stone Wall Construction 1936

probably get $45 if he accepted employment" (*Globe & Mail*, Apr 27 1937). McQuesten determined to create work projects for as many of the unemployed as possible and he even instituted a split week system so that more people could be employed. When World War II broke out on September 10, 1939, work had to be curtailed somewhat because metal and concrete supplies were needed for the war effort and men were needed at the front, but the work did not cease altogether. Bridges and roads were considered to be strategic in war time.

1937 ELECTION A LIBERAL SWEEP

During the 1937 election campaign, the *Spectator* supported Tom strongly and he was able to make several announcements that pleased him and his public—they were the Social Gospel type of announcements: new buildings for the Hamilton Mountain Sanatorium (Tuberculosis), a new three million dollar mental hospital for Hamilton, and money for conversion to buses and electric trolleys (Best 122). These were projects dear to Tom's heart and conscience. Ruby had died of tuberculosis and his brother, Calvin, was the chaplain at the San; the family had recurring mental problems and his sister, Edna, had died in the Homewood Sanatorium at Guelph (Mental Hospital) in 1935. The much-needed St. Thomas mental hospital was already under way with Somerville as the architect and was to be completed in 1939.

The election of 1937 was a Liberal sweep, and Tom was returned with 500 votes more than he had in the 1934 victory. He promptly declined the Attorney General position, relinquished Public Works and resigned as Hydro Commissioner. He retained only Highways, bolstered by the 1936 addition of the scandal-ridden Northern Development, which he was in process of reorganizing. Tom had prevailed as one of the most respected members of the Cabinet, devoid of any "personal egotism," and his fellow politicians and constituents were impressed by his "scrupulous honesty" (Best 123-24). Tom could now get on with what interested him most: highways, bridges, parks, restorations, and developing the North.

After the election, Tom made a final plea for safe driving. He publicized a list of eight safe-driving rules—the same basic rules that eventually became enforced as laws: safe speed, keep right, passing rules, safe parking, signals, road signs, auto maintenance, "and most emphatically, if you drink don't drive" (*Toronto Star*, May 16 1938). Seat belts and their requirements had not yet been introduced. In September, when Tom was elected by the Canadian Good Roads Association as its president for 1938-39, he arranged for large safety posters with photos to be circulated in the newspapers. Tom advocated the Golden Rule of road courtesy, featured on some of these posters: "Show to that motorist the same courtesy that you would like to have him show to you."

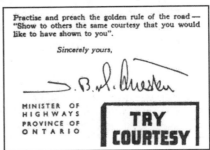

Practise and preach the golden rule of the road — "Show to others the same courtesy that you would like to have shown to you".

Sincerely yours,

MINISTER OF HIGHWAYS PROVINCE OF ONTARIO

TRY COURTESY

I appeal to you.........
on behalf of the car ahead

It carries a happy little family—treat them as though they were your friends—they are nice people . . .

WHEN YOU AND I talk about other motorists we usually mean the car ahead but I wonder if we ever stop to realize who is in that car.

Probably people just like ourselves who are deserving of every Courtesy which we can extend to them. People who will appreciate our Courtesy and consideration and act the same way towards us.

So when motoring on the holiday, I appeal to you to think kindly of the people in the car ahead.

- If you wish to pass them, give your horn a cheerful toot and give them a wide berth as well.
- If *they* wish to slow down or turn off the road, give them a "break".

- If they have just overtaken you, because they prefer to drive more quickly, refrain from racing or otherwise inconveniencing them.
- If there is a car following you, remember that to him *you* are the "car ahead" so be sure to drive and signal and otherwise show to that motorist the same courtesy that you would like to have him show to you.

In other words, "Try Courtesy" on the holiday, in all your driving and thus do your part to help yourself and other motorists enjoy a holiday free of accidents—"A holiday free of accidents"—what a grand heading that would be for Tuesday's newspapers. Do *your* bit and "Try Courtesy". It is the new spirit of the road.

Sincerely yours,

TRY COURTESY

IT WORKS BOTH WAYS

MINISTER OF HIGHWAYS
PROVINCE OF ONTARIO

Safety poster signed by Hon. T.B. McQuesten, Minister of Highways

Chapter 32

INTERNATIONAL BRIDGES

"No agency can compare with the highway and the tourist business
in bringing harmony and peace between two great nations."
T.B.McQuesten (Best 134)

T.B. McQuesten's work with the highways and bridges of Ontario is so extensive that it would be impossible to recount them all, and certainly impossible to provide a chronological assessment since much of the work was in progress simultaneously. Tom had a vision for Ontario and kept a close watch on all work on highways and bridges during his tenure as Minister of Highways from 1934 to 1943, and thereafter on the Niagara Bridge Commission until 1947.

Between 1937 and 1941, McQuesten was involved with building the new Toronto to Niagara highway which became the Queen Elizabeth Way. The famous Rainbow Bridge at Niagara Falls, the third of his international bridges, will be addressed presently in connection with the QEW. Less well known is that during the late 1930s, T.B. McQuesten was responsible for building two other international bridges to unite the United States and Canada: the Ivy Lea Bridge crossing the St. Lawrence River from Ontario to New York, and the Blue Water Bridge crossing the St. Clair River from Ontario to Michigan. He additionally planned and constructed the various highway links, approaches and garden accesses to the bridges. The dual highway link from Gananoque to Brockville along the St. Lawrence River is one of the most beautiful sections of road in Ontario (Minnes 4).

When we view the breadth of Tom's provincial accomplishments we see that a significant number of his construction projects were designed to unite Canada and the United States in peace, power, politics, travel, tourism and industry. The Ivy Lea and Blue Water bridges carry a large amount of commercial traffic, while the Rainbow Bridge carries more tourist traffic. Thomas planned well. He obviously had a major plan in mind and wished to concentrate his efforts to ensure peace and an easy and lasting dialogue between Canada and the United States.

Tom was an avid student of history and political science, with a particular interest in the War of 1812 and the Rebellion of 1837, both of which involved his grandparents—the maternal being British and the paternal, American. With relatives on both sides of

**Rev. Thomas Baker
(1796-1887)**

these conflicts, he had a familial motivation for building these international bridges.

THREE INTERNATIONAL BRIDGES

The Ivy Lea Bridge, or **Thousand Islands Bridge System** crosses the St. Lawrence River from Collins Landing near Alexandria Bay, New York to Ivy Lea near Gananoque, Ontario. The American span from abutment to abutment is 4,500 ft. (1371m). The Canadian span from abutment to abutment is 3,330 ft. (1015m). The bridge system covers a distance of 8.5 miles (13.6km) and provides a direct connection between the USA and Canada. Groundbreaking ceremonies were held on April 30, 1937; the bridge was opened officially on August 18, 1938.

The Blue Water Bridge crosses the St. Clair River, connecting Point Edward, Sarnia, Ontario, with Port Huron, Michigan. The initial 3-lane Blue Water Bridge construction is a steel camelback and has a main span across the St. Clair River of 875 ft. (266m). The total length of the bridge including approach spans is 1.9 km (1.19 miles). The Blue Water Bridge Authority and the Michigan Department of Transportation held groundbreaking ceremonies on June 23, 1937 and the bridge was officially opened on October 10, 1938. It carried two lanes of traffic and a sidewalk. Construction of a second span was completed in 1997, and retrofit of the first bridge for a complete strengthening and deck widening was completed in 1999. When it re-opened, the Blue Water Bridge was the largest infrastructure-crossing project in North America (http://www.bwba.org).

The Rainbow Bridge crosses the Niagara River, uniting Niagara Falls, Ontario, with Niagara Falls, New York. Groundbreaking took place on May 16, 1940, and the bridge was dedicated by King George VI and Queen Elizabeth on June 7, 1939. It opened to traffic on Nov 1, 1941. The Rainbow Bridge rises 202 ft. (61.5m) above the water and is 950 ft. (289.5m) in length. It provides access over some of the most treacherous water in the world, with water depth in excess of 175 ft. (53m). It is estimated that six billion (6,000,000,000) pounds of water flow under the Rainbow Bridge in one minute; the current averages 26-30 miles per hour (42-48km).

Tom's maternal grandfather, Thomas Baker R.N., was in the Royal Navy during the War of 1812, and fought for the British on Lake Ontario. Baker was a first lieutenant under Captain Yeo on the *H.M.S. St. Lawrence*, the largest ship to date. With 112 guns it was the ship that eventually determined the victory on the Great Lakes; the very sight of its size and complement gave the British uncontested control of the lake during the final months of the war. Baker was later given a pension and a commission as Commander in H.M. Fleet. After the war, Baker

H.M.S. St. Lawrence

returned to England to study for the ministry and came back to Canada as a missionary minister of the first Congregational Church in Canada, at Kingston. The missionary spirit was a primary family tradition embraced by Baker's daughter, Mary Jane Baker, who became Mary Baker McQuesten, Tom's mother. She was a founding member of the Women's Foreign Missionary Society, became its president, and was one of the most ardent recruiters for the WFMS auxiliaries throughout Ontario. Tom would have absorbed his family's social conscience from birth.

Tom had relatives living in the U.S. during the War of 1812 and during the Upper Canada Rebellion of 1837. His grandfather, Dr. Calvin McQuesten, came to Hamilton from New Hampshire to open Hamilton's first foundry, McQuesten and Co., in 1835. He did not take up residence at that time because his wife, Margarette Barker Lerned was in delicate health. Instead, he left his cousin John Fisher in charge of the foundry while he travelled back and forth and exchanged letters. His wife became pregnant in 1837, and gave birth to their son Calvin Brooks McQuesten (later Dr.) approximately five weeks before the Rebellion. After the Rebellion was quelled, Dr. Calvin McQuesten finally deemed it safe to move his family to Hamilton, which he did in 1839.

The Rebellion of Upper Canada perpetrated by William Lyon Mackenzie and his rebels was an extension of the War of 1812, with some of the same goals and hostilities. It was another attempt to overthrow the British Colonial elite and form a Republican Government. Some of the family letters describe the fear, tensions and hostility that led up to and continued during the Rebellion because of the McQuestens' affiliation with the United States (W-MCP4-6.193).

The enormity of the danger is described in one of John Fisher's letters from the McQuesten foundry in Hamilton to Dr. Calvin McQuesten in Brockport, New York—a letter that he doubted would ever get through. John Fisher was living in Hamilton with his family, guarding the foundry, and reporting to Dr. McQuesten. The date of the letter is significant, being the precise date of the beginning of the Rebellion. The Fishers' fear for themselves and their children is palpable:

TO DR. CALVIN AND MARGARETTE MCQUESTEN from their cousins John and Catherine Fisher (W-MCP4-6.193)

Brockport, New York,	Hamilton, Upper Canada
Monroe County, U.S.A	Dec 7 1837

Dear Cousin,
　　We are in the beginning of a civil war. We shall probably deeply regret that we came to this province—& this morning sent the Children to Warsaw [NY] to Mother—Catherine remains at present—We have no mail from the east side of the Lake—Quebec Montreal Toronto &co they have robbed it once and now there is no one sent.—This was done by Mackenzie on the night of the 6th—It is now reported

that not a letter which has the least appearance of any importance is permitted to pass without being opened.

Our business is at an end—We have a Cavalry force under arms day and night to guard us—[Rev] Parker—he lays in irons and there is the determination to execute him—he was my best friend—There was a hot engagement last night in which 30 riflemen were killed and 40 made prisoners. All is consternation—The Country is ruined for years and ages—each man is suspicious of his neighbour.

[signed] John Fisher.

[The page continues with a note from Catherine Fisher to Margarette McQuesten]

These are troublesome times—I write with an aching head and heart. My little children are on the road to Warsaw and you must know that I shall not spend many happy hours untill [sic] I get news of their safe arrival at Warsaw. We live in constant fear that our lives and property are in danger. I cannot consent to leave without Mr. Fisher and he is determined to stay untill he is obliged to flee for his life. My poor little children riding over these bad roads in an open carriage my heart almost breaks at the thought. In haste,

Catherine Fisher.

P.S. It is very doubtful when [if] you receive this—the direct mail is cut off—some expect Martial Law in a few days.

Before, during, and after the rebellion, there was much bitterness toward Americans living in Upper Canada. Dr. Calvin McQuesten even had trouble borrowing money from the banks because he was an American. In another letter John Fisher describes the dire financial situation for Americans in Upper Canada:

Confidence is destroyed—and but very few feel under obligation to pay—To sue is more than useless—The destruction of the Sir R. Peel has exasperated the people beyond measure—It was well that the American Boats did not venture to this port directly after the loss of the Peel—It would have been destroyed—What next I know not—Hope they will not burn the property of Americans. (W-MCP4-6.161, Jun 16 1838)

It is appropriate that Thomas built his first international bridge over the scene of the sinking of the *Sir Robert Peel*. The Canadian steamer was sunk at Alexandria Bay, New York, on May 30, 1838 by American patriots during the Rebellion. They were disguised as savages and armed with muskets and bayonets and boarded shouting, "Remember the *Caroline*!" The passengers and crew were ordered ashore as the ship was set afire and pushed into the river. The sunken hull remains there today as a reminder of the conflict. The American ship *Caroline* had been sunk by the British five months earlier after setting it afire and sending it crashing over Niagara Falls. The American patriots named their conflict "The Patriots War" while Canadian history knows it as "The Rebellion of 1837-38." Alexandria Bay is the site of the American footing of the Ivy Lea Bridge; the bridge became a concrete symbol of unity and peace between the nations.

Thomas was only three years old when his grandfather McQuesten died in 1885, and he was five years old when his grandfather Baker died in 1887. Tom would have grown up hearing their tales from a very early and impressionable age. Their stories would have become a part of the family history. As Tom was growing up, Rev. Baker's entire library was kept in a massive bookcase in his room at Whitehern; this later became Tom's room. The library stands there today, and contains many books and several first-hand accounts on the subject of the War of 1812—for example, *History of the Late War between the United States & Great Britain comprising a Minute Account of the Various Military and Naval Operations*, by H.M. Brackenridge (Hayes & Zell, Philadelphia 1854). Tom specifically notes having read two of these: *Recollections of the War of 1812* and *Narrative of the Affair at Queenston in the War of 1812* (Best 52). There are also many writings about Mackenzie's Rebellion of 1837-38. More cogently, throughout his life Tom had access to the library and to the family letters that had become the literature and lore of the family.

Thus we see that Tom had loyalties on both sides of the border, and was personally motivated to steer his work toward ensuring peace between the two countries. Beauty and peace are noble goals. One obvious means to encourage dialogue is to provide easy, safe and pleasant access between the two nations. As a historian, Thomas was ever mindful of the reasons for the previous conflicts, so one hundred years later, with international rumblings of war in 1937, he sought ways of uniting and binding the two countries in peace through commerce and tourism.

McQuesten had prepared himself well for this ambitious role. Few politicians could have been entrusted with such responsibility on both sides of the border, or would have been capable of doing so. He had proven himself to be a scrupulously honest politician. In the 1937 election he enjoyed an overwhelming victory, largely because of his honesty and integrity. He entered now into what was to be his most productive and creative phase as an Ontario Cabinet Minister (Best 124). From this time forward, peace and commerce between nations was to be his objective in everything that he did.

THE IVY LEA OR THOUSAND ISLANDS BRIDGE

T.B. McQuesten's first international bridge consists of five spans extending across the Thousand Islands in the St. Lawrence River from Ivy Lea, Ontario near Gananoque, to New York State at Collins Landing near Alexandria Bay. John Best applauds Tom's efficiency in pursuing goals after others had failed. Although the

Ivy Lea Bridge was "under discussion prior to the 1934 election, it became a reality only when McQuesten assumed the Highways' portfolio." The complex interrelated financing was quickly put into place as a four-way deal involving Ottawa, Ontario, New York and a bond issue (Best 115).

The Ivy Lea Bridge

The bridge was completed in less than sixteen months (two and a half months under deadline) after the groundbreaking on April 30, 1937 at Collins Landing, New York. The Ivy Lea bridge was officially opened on August 18, 1938. Several thousand American and Canadian citizens were on hand for this eventful occasion.

The completed bridge hops from island to island. The five spans are of four different types: one is a two-span continuous truss, one a steel arch, one a stone-faced concrete rigid frame, and two are suspensions. The Ivy Lea Bridge forms a very important highway link between Canada and the United States.

The only truly international span of the five is the Rift Span between Wellesley Island, N.Y. and Hill Island, Ontario. Its length of a mere 90 feet (27m) was reportedly the shortest of any international bridge in the world at the time of its construction. The tiny Rift Span is an attractive concrete rigid frame structure clad in decorative stone to complement the peaceful, natural surroundings of the Thousand Islands region. The decorative stone facade greatly enhances the

**The tiny International Rift Span,
Ivy Lea Bridge c.1938**
(courtesy Thousand Islands Bridge Authority)

aesthetics of this small but important highway bridge (http://www.tibridge.com/facts. htm). Symbolically, this little decorated bridge represents the beauty of unity, remindful of Tom's priorities. When the bridge was twinned in 1959, this tiny span was preserved and trusses added at the sides to widen it.

The opening festivities for the Ivy Lea Bridge proceeded on August 18, 1938. Unfortunately, the temperamental Premier Mitchell Hepburn had revived a dispute

with Prime Minister Mackenzie King over federal plans for navigation and power plants on the St. Lawrence River. Consequently, "Hepburn refused to welcome President Roosevelt to Ontario and, at the same time, he refused to

U.S. President Roosevelt and Prime Minister Mackenzie King at the Ivy Lea Bridge opening
(Photo courtesy of Thousand Islands Bridge Archives)

play second fiddle to the two national leaders at Ivy Lea." Hepburn was erratic; he considered his grievance to be a critical political matter and he boycotted the opening of the bridge, thus preventing McQuesten from attending. Newspapers criticized both of them for their absence and their snub of the President of the United States and the Prime Minister (Stamp, *Bridging* 118).

At the opening, President Roosevelt and Prime Minister Mackenzie King arrived in the same automobile. They "drove to the midpoint of the bridge, and the two dignitaries, holding the same pair of scissors, cut the ceremonial ribbon and dedicated the bridge to peace and lasting friendship between the two nations. . . . And both men rocked, laughing, on the rear cushion of the back seat" (Stamp, *Bridging* 113). It is a pity that McQuesten was not present to hear these words and the accompanying laughter, since they would have reflected his sentiments exactly.

THE BLUE WATER BRIDGE—SARNIA

The international Blue Water Bridge crosses the St. Clair River, connecting the communities of Point Edward in Sarnia, Ontario, with Port Huron, Michigan. The St. Clair was the only large river in Ontario that had not been bridged. The new bridge would provide a short route between Toronto and Chicago for tourist and commercial traffic. Again, T.B. McQuesten achieved success where others had failed. A bridge spanning the St. Clair River had been conceived in the late 1920s and early 30s, but attempts to have it built ended in failure.

After many frustrations, Murray Van Wagoner of Michigan found sympathetic listeners in Highways Minister Thomas McQuesten and Deputy Minister Melville Smith, who were "true believers in the gospel of superhighways and high level bridges." They were already building Canada's first superhighway—the Queen Elizabeth Way, "and, yes, they were most interested in linking Ontario with Michigan across the St. Clair River. Modjeski and Masters were the engineers for the design of the entire structure and for supervision of construction of the main bridge, with Monsarrat and Pratley as Canadian Associates" (Stamp, *Bridging* 114, 116).

The Canadian Associates completed a technical review of the U.S. engineer's plans to ensure that they conformed to Canadian standards. Because of the job's international nature, officials treated the bridge's main span as a joint venture. Work for the approach spans fell to each respective country under separate contracts.

This sharing of responsibilities might have created many delays, overruns, and opportunities for budget manipulation in the form of graft; however, once the engineering preliminaries were completed the work proceeded quickly, and the bridge was completed in fifteen months. The first bids (American and Canadian approach and main piers)

Blue Water Bridge construction
(Photo courtesy of www.BWBC.gc.ca)

**Blue Water Bridge construction
with self-supporting trusses (1938)**

were taken May 15, 1937. Construction work started on June 24, 1937 and on October 8, 1938 the bridge was formally opened (Stamp, *Bridging* 116).

The groundbreaking took place separately at both ends: Port Huron on June 24, 1937 and Point Edward on July 14, 1937. Two massive concrete-and-steel piers as supports for the bridge were constructed simultaneously. These sit atop two huge caissons sunk one hundred feet down to bedrock Robert Stamp describes the construction process:

> Concrete abutments were laid, derricks lifted the first steel girders into place on December 14, and the superstructure moved out from each side of the river toward the centre. On May 24, 1938, crowds gathered to watch placement of the first piece of steel connecting the two halves of the bridge. Once the girder was in place, construction worker 'Buck' Buchanan walked along the length of the narrow skeleton and became the first person to cross the St. Clair River on a bridge. (Stamp, *Bridging* 116)

Because the Blue Water vista was spectacular, McQuesten provided for pedestrian tourists as well as automobiles. The bridge originally had sidewalks along with two lanes for vehicles. Unfortunately, the sidewalks were removed in the 1980s to make room for a third lane for automobiles.

Pedestrians used the bridge easily and frequently, and the ease of tourist access is illustrated by a story told to me by my cousin Eloise—a story that would have pleased Tom. Eloise, who is now 94, remembers vividly that she and her sister Blanche had been deported back to Canada across the Blue Water Bridge. She recounts the story soberly. In the early 1940s they had gone by train to Sarnia, where Blanche applied for a teaching position. After the interview they took in the sights around the city and strolled onto the bridge to view the remarkable blue water and the scenery. Eloise and Blanche continued sauntering, until they were apprehended by a guard who insisted on knowing their purpose in the USA!

They were astounded to learn that they had just strolled into another country. They looked back across the bridge and saw no barrier or impediment, so explained that they had just been viewing the river and the sights. They promptly apologized and immediately turned to start back. But the guard prevented them, barking sternly, "you are now in the United States of America illegally and you will have to be deported." He ushered them into his office and took their names and all particulars, which they provided, nervously glancing at one another. They grew even more alarmed when the guard officiously escorted them out again toward some parked vehicles.

Then the severity of the sentence took on a humorous tone as he, smilingly, handed them each a dime and helped them onto a bus to "deport" them back over the bridge to Canada. Tom McQuesten would have been delighted at Eloise's story since it was just that kind of seamless tourism that he had planned for.

Officiating at the dedication of the Bridge on October 8, 1938, were Mitchell F. Hepburn, Premier of the Province of Ontario and Frank Murphy, Governor of the State of Michigan. T.B. McQuesten was also on hand for the opening and he and Hepburn gave speeches. Best describes the event:

First Blue Water Bridge, completed 1938
The original span built in 1938 was redecked, refurbished and reopened in 1999

> Standing on the American side of the bridge in front of a crowd estimated at 50,000, they spoke briefly on a North American radio hookup. McQuesten declared: "no agency can compare with the highway and the tourist business in bringing harmony and peace between two great nations." He was firmly convinced that tourism alone would cure Ontario's economic ills and assigned responsibility for promotion of tourism to the Highways Department. In fulfillment of Tom's aesthetic belief that cities and nations should have artistically imposing entrances, the Sarnia and Kingston bridges presented American tourists with two impressive gateways to Canada. (Best 134)

The Blue Water Bridge was doubled in 1997-99. The twin was kept harmonious with the original. Together, the two bridges constitute one of the busiest transportation arteries between the United States and Canada, and receive heavy commercial and private traffic use daily. The Blue Water Bridges are jointly owned and maintained by Canada and the United States. (Blue Water Bridge Canada: www.BWBC.gc.ca).

Blue Water Bridge Canada, twinned in 1997
(www.BWBC.gc.ca)

Completed within a few years of one another, the three international bridges *(the Rainbow Bridge is dealt with in Chapter 34)* served to open up Canada and the United States for tourism and commerce. They provide complete access across Ontario into New York State and Michigan.

Chapter 33

THE QUEEN ELIZABETH WAY

Pontifex Maximus: Chief Bridge and Road Builder
"The finest of the titles of the Caesars, and high among the most constructive
of the public works . . . was the building of roads."
(Best 193)

Following Tom's re-election to the Provincial Parliament in 1937, he pressed
forward more energetically than ever. Having received funding for the relief program,
he was now able to complete the highway linking Toronto to Niagara and Fort Erie,
via Hamilton. The scope and speed of construction correspondingly increased. The
resulting highway became the Queen Elizabeth Way (QEW), and stands as one of
T.B. McQuesten's major accomplishments.

By the early 1930s,
intercity traffic between
Hamilton and Toronto had
outstripped the capacity of
Lakeshore Road and Highway
5; traffic was slowed further
by numerous small towns
along the way. A small rural
road between these roadways,
aptly named the Middle Road,
had been chosen for widening
into a four-lane highway
with a grassy median; work
on widening had begun, and
by 1937 a few short segments
were already built.

Middle Rd (QEW) at Bronte 1937
(Photo courtesy of Ontario Ministry of Transportation)

The *Hamilton Spectator* in 1935 had applauded McQuesten for his work and his
methods in building the highway thus far:

The Middle Road to Toronto which Hon. T.B. McQuesten, Minister of
Highways has been pushing forward quietly and unobtrusively . . . It is
not the Hon. Mr. McQuesten's way to make a loud noise about what he is
doing. He just goes ahead with it and when the job is done, lets it speak for
itself. We know how much energy he has put into such local developments
as Gage Park, the Botanic Gardens and the King's Forest. . . . The width of
the new highway between this city and Toronto is an illustration of Hon. Mr.

McQuesten's vision and confidence. He believes in the future of Ontario's highways becoming more and more travelled. . . . four lanes and a path for pedestrians. (January 14, 1935)

McQuesten realized that the new highway should incorporate, as much as possible, the technology of the future: multiple lanes, median strips for safety, limited access, and cloverleaf interchanges to handle intersections with other roads—in short, the modern freeway with its ability to move traffic quickly and safely. The highway would follow the general contour of the shore around Lake Ontario from Toronto to Hamilton (at the head of the Lake), and then on to Niagara. This area from Toronto to Niagara has come to be known as the "Golden Horseshoe" because of its shape and the commercial prosperity made possible, first by shipping on the lake, and later by the QEW.

The highway was to link with the existing Peace Bridge at Fort Erie, and with a new international bridge being planned for Niagara Falls. Initially McQuesten would complete the section of highway between Toronto and Hamilton; then he would extend it to Niagara and Fort Erie, for a total length of 86 1/2 miles (144 km).

Once again McQuesten collaborated with his preferred associates to achieve his

Dual highway and bridge with fruit trees in blossom, QEW near Grimsby, 1949

(Photo courtesy of Ontario Ministry of Transportation)

objectives. The thoroughfare was intended not just to move goods and people as quickly, effortlessly and safely as possible. It was also to be a parkway—a roadway that seemed to pass through an endless park bordered by trees and farm fields. Driving on this roadway was to be pleasant and relaxing, and a satisfying aesthetic experience.

William Lyon Somerville was the architect for the new highway. McQuesten and Somerville determined to beautify it along its entire length, as they intended the highway to encourage tourism and commerce by providing easy access to and from the United States. Their vision was to unite two renowned Ontario beauty spots: RBG and Niagara Falls. The latter would be enhanced by garden beautification and by a new international bridge across the Niagara River at the falls. They also planned for monuments to be built at both ends of the highway—at Toronto and at Niagara Falls, and designed a sculptural bridge to be built *en route* at St. Catharines.

Borgstrom and Carver were engaged to lay out a planting scheme for the Middle Road. They introduced a number of pine and spruce plantations as evocations of a more natural landscape: "[the] planting was to restore the impression that here one was passing through orchard land, now through a strand of mixed woodlot. . .

hedges and tall elms. . . . to disguise and conceal the rigidity of engineering and to simulate the Ontario landscape." Similar plantings were likewise provided along the

Divided highway and roadside park near Jordan
(Photo courtesy of Ontario Department of Highways)

extension of the highway from Hamilton to Niagara. A series of roadside parks were also developed, such as Jordan Park at Vineland which provided access to a beach on Lake Ontario.

Some resistance and hostility to the new highway were encountered from farmers along portions of the route, reflected in a dramatic headline in the *Evening Telegram*: "Road Through Fruit Belt Compared to Invasion of Belgium by Kaiser" (Jul 7 1937). As traffic increased over the years, a certain amount of additional farmland was subsequently lost to highway widening.

To mark the Toronto entrance to the highway, Somerville designed a forty-foot high column of Classical *Beaux-Arts* design. The column is guarded by an Imperial British lion, eight feet tall, executed by Frances Loring. The lion had to be carved on site since the stone from which it was to emerge was part of the vertical column; the actual cutting did not get underway until August 1940. Loring was not pleased with the tradesman who was hired to do the carving; he attempted to alter the design without her consent and she fired him on the spot. She finished the lion herself in the November cold under a tarpaulin and suffered some permanent physical arthritic debility as a result (Stamp, *QEW* 45).

QEW Lion Monument costruction 1939

**Lion sculpture on monument,
by Frances Loring**

The column is embellished with a medallion of a double-profile portrait of the King and Queen and topped with the British Crown, executed by Florence

QEW Lion Monument, completed 1940

Wyle (Boyanoski 30-32). Since art was considered a frivolous expense during war time, much of the expense for the art work was folded into the construction budget.

Several highway interchanges were built along the new highway. These were the first traffic interchanges ever built in Canada, and included a full cloverleaf at Highway 10 in Port Credit and a partial (trumpet) cloverleaf in Burlington. Most of the route was lined with lamp standards, each featuring a stylized *ER* (Elizabeth Regina). This was reported to be the longest continuous lighting system in the world.

Cloverleaf at Highway 10 in 1940

Longest continuous lighting in the world, 1939-40

The highway was named the Queen Elizabeth Way to commemorate the 1939 Royal Visit to Canada of King George VI and Queen Elizabeth—the first time a reigning sovereign had entered a Dominion of the British Empire. Although the highway was not yet complete, Tom took advantage of the Royal visit to name and symbolically open the QEW at both Toronto and St. Catharines. On June 7, 1939, the King and Queen attended a dedication ceremony for the new Henley Bridge in St. Catharines. An inscription on the bridge reads:

**Their Majesties, King George VI & Queen Elizabeth, in the Royal Motorcade
at the Queen Elizabeth Way Dedication Ceremonies in St. Catharines, June 7, 1939**

**HENLEY BRIDGE
WAS OPENED BY
THEIR MAJESTIES
KING GEORGE VI AND QUEEN ELIZABETH
ON THE
SEVENTH DAY OF JUNE 1939
AND COMMEMORATES THE FIRST TIME
A REIGNING SOVEREIGN HAS ENTERED
ONE OF THE SISTER DOMINIONS
OF THE BRITISH EMPIRE**

**The Royal Signatures
1939**

The Henley Bridge was designed by W.L. Somerville, who shared McQuesten's Classical aesthetics and who became known as the country's leading "sculptural architect" (Stamp, *Bridging* 128). His massive sculpture of a stylized ship at the centre of the bridge is decorated with the coats-of-arms of Canada's then nine provinces (1939), automatically aligning the QEW with a Trans-Canada Highway which was partially built and still in the planning stages. The sculpture is a stylized Egyptian barge or a Neo-Classical design similar to a Greek or Roman trireme, suggestive of two great historical roadways: the Appian Way and the Pharaoh's Way.

**Sculpture of ship on Henley Bridge,
St. Catharines, Ontario**

**Official Opening
of QEW
by T.B. McQuesten
at St. Catharines**

The Appian Way may have been the inspiration for designating the new Ontario highway named after the reigning queen, as a "Way"; for the *Via Appia*, the most important ancient Roman road, was referred to in its time as the "Queen of the Long Roads." Leading to the south of Italy, the Appian Way was a road of strategic importance, vital in Rome's conquest of southern Italy.

To extend the Roman reference, the Henley Bridge with its Classical accoutrements lends further weight to designating T.B. McQuesten as the Canadian equivalent of *Pontifex Maximus*—Chief Bridge and Road Builder. This appellation was considered to be "the finest of the titles of the Caesar. . . . And the most constructive of public works was the building of roads" (Best 193).

Following the Royal visit, the QEW was quickly completed to Niagara Falls by late 1939. An extension was also constructed to provide access to the Rainbow

QEW Paving operations, 1940

Bridge, which opened to traffic in 1941. But because World War II had broken out in Europe by September of 1939, some construction had to be curtailed. The highway was extended to Fort Erie in 1941, but wasn't paved for the duration of World War II.

It would take another 40 years before all of the grade level intersections with their traffic lights, lift bridges such as the one over the Burlington Canal, and traffic circles like the one at Stoney Creek were replaced, and the QEW would be a true freeway in the complete sense of the word.

In the mid 1970s, Somerville and Loring's Lion Monument was in danger of demolition for highway widening in Toronto. Public pressure prevailed and the monument was re-located to nearby Sir Casimir Gzowski Park on the east side of the Humber River. A plaque was added, indicating that for more than thirty years the monument stood at the original eastern entrance to the QEW, officially opened by the Queen and King in 1939. In 1989 the Lion Monument was re-dedicated by Queen Elizabeth, who was by then the Queen Mother.

The QEW or the "Queen-E" as it came to be known, was the first inter-city divided highway in Canada and has been one of the most influential highway developments in Ontario's history. Unique in its day as a divided two-lane highway, it was planned for safety and for future growth, but also for aesthetics. The ambiance and beauty that McQuesten sought to create can still be experienced today along the Niagara Parkway, in some areas of the Niagara Peninsula, and when crossing over the High Level Bridge in Hamilton.

American Tourists arriving from the Peace Bridge approach onto the QEW, 1945

Modern traffic on the QEW

In economic terms McQuesten's vision of the QEW has been a great success. It is the key artery of the Golden Horseshoe—a major industrial engine in Canada—and continues to be essential to Ontario's economic growth almost seventy years after it was completed. In fact just six years after T.B. McQuesten's death, his work was already being appreciated for contributing to the economic development of Hamilton and of Ontario. The phrase "Golden Horseshoe" was first used in a speech to the Hamilton Chamber of Commerce on 12 January 1954 by Westinghouse President Herbert H. Rogge: "Hamilton in 50 years will be the forward cleat in a 'golden horseshoe' of industrial development from Oshawa to the Niagara River."

Chapter 34

THE RAINBOW BRIDGE

"The final symbol of the eternal friendship between the two nations:
a means of easier access, instead of a fortified barricade,
a utility of convenience rather than a monument to hate . . .
an international bond and pledge, a tangible, durable expression
of the great friendliness which exists between our two great nations."

T.B.McQuesten at the groudbreaking for the Rainbow Bridge (Stamp, *Bridging* 126)

The Rainbow Bridge was built in the early 1940s to replace the Falls View Bridge (originally Honeymoon Bridge, built in 1897). On January 23, 1938, the Falls View Bridge (Honeymoon Bridge) was struck by an ice jam. The bridge was severely damaged but remained intact for several days while thousands of people gathered to watch and wait for the final collapse.

The end of the Upper Steel Arch Bridge (Honeymoon Bridge) came at 4:20 p.m. on January 27th 1938, when the span broke free and fell into the gorge onto the ice on the river below. The ice had pushed the bridge away from its abutment on the American side causing the bridge to be pulled off its abutment on the Canadian shore. (http://www.niagarafrontier.com/bridges.html)

Falls View Bridge Collapsed by an ice jam, Jan 27 1938

McQuesten was one of the observers and when the bridge collapsed, he is reported as stating: *We will build a beautiful stone Bridge with a Carillon and Tower— the finest in the world* (Box 14-122). This statement proved to be true, and Robert Stamp reflects a general appreciation of the Rainbow Bridge: "The American Institute

The new Rainbow Bridge

of Steel Construction awarded the structure first place in its 1941 competition for the most beautiful bridge in the United States. With its magnificent setting and clean, graceful design, it remains beautiful half a century later" (Stamp, *Bridging*, 128). The beauty would extend to its surroundings. The bridge's approaches and facilities were designed to be both efficient and aesthetic, and included magnificent gardens, neo-classical structures and Canadiana artwork.

The day following the collapse, McQuesten announced plans for a joint Ontario/New York public bridge to replace the collapsed bridge (Stamp, Bridging, 123). The *Globe & Mail* later confirmed the announcement: "While the famous Falls View Bridge lay a heap of twisted steel across the bottom of the ice-choked gorge, Hon. T.B. McQuesten said another bridge was planned by Ontario and New York State about 1,000 feet downstream from the Falls View Bridge" (Feb 22 1938).

McQuesten already had a new bridge in the planning stage, but after the collapse of the Honeymoon Bridge, the need became urgent. Much discussion ensued in Canada regarding the location of the new bridge and who should build it. Thomas did not favour a private profit-making bridge, preferring a joint effort with the United States in keeping with his priorities about peace, co-operation and tourism. While some favoured a private company, he introduced a bill in the Provincial Legislature to prevent this: "Ontario's move is to bar a private bridge company" (*Hamilton Spectator*, Mar 19 1938). President Roosevelt similarly blocked the possibility of a privately owned bridge (Lewis 89).

On August 12, 1938, the first meeting of the newly formed Niagara Falls Bridge Commission took place in Niagara Falls, New York. New York State Governor, Herbert Lehman appointed four Commissioners to represent the State of New York, with Samuel S. Johnson as Chairman. Canadian Commissioners appointed to the board were current serving members of the Niagara Parks Commission: T.B. McQuesten, Chairman; Archie Haines; Ross Hartstone; and C. Ellison Kaumeyer as secretary-treasurer and general manager. With the approval of both governments, the Niagara Falls Bridge Commission became responsible for the administration and maintenance of all international bridges crossing the Niagara River. A bond issue for four million dollars signed by the commission was subscribed entirely in the U.S.

The new Commission decided to place the bridge 550 feet (168m) north of the original Honeymoon Bridge and 1,000 feet (305m) north of the American Falls. The abutments and approach spans would then rest on solid rock on the sides of the gorge and would be high enough to avoid a catastrophe similar to that caused by the ice jam.

The Niagara Falls Bridge Commission was responsible for selecting a design for the new bridge and its approaches. The design was drawn up by Shortridge Hardesty of Buffalo, in conjunction with consulting engineer Edward Lupfer and architect Aymar Embury. It was decided to name it the Rainbow Bridge because, "The rainbow at Niagara Falls denotes peace and happiness and is a symbol of friendship between the two lands whose borders extend along the Niagara River" (Seibel 16, 8). McQuesten may have named the bridge himself, gaining his inspiration from the fact that an act of God had destroyed the old bridge; and in the story of the flood in Genesis, a rainbow is a token of God's covenant never to destroy by flood again. Niagara Falls is appropriately famous for its rainbows, produced by sunlight on the mist.

McQuesten, armed with his triple responsibilities—Department of Highways, the Niagara Parks Commission, and the Niagara Falls Bridge Commission—had very definite ideas regarding the design of the bridge and his aesthetic vision for the entire Niagara area. Paul Lewis informs us that T.B. McQuesten was "primarily

Niagara Falls, N.Y., May 16, 1940
Two-handled spade for Rainbow Bridge sod-turning

L. Samuel S. Johnson, U.S. Chairman of the joint
Niagara Bridge Commission. **Rt.** T.B. McQuesten,
Canadian Chairman. Note the two flags.

responsible for the selection of the design for the bridge and its approaches" (90). Marjorie Campbell describes the bridge in superlatives: "The 288m, 1450ft bridge is the longest single fixed or hingeless steel arch in the world. Its landscaped approaches are of unparalleled beauty" (252).

The groundbreaking ceremony took place on May 10, 1940 with a symbolic two-handled spade wielded by T.B. McQuesten for Canada and Samuel S. Johnson for the American side. Stamp describes the celebration:

T.B. McQuesten digging,
Samuel S. Johnson at his side

A toast with Niagara grape juice
T.B. McQuesten at centre,
holding black hat

Dignitaries toasted each other with Niagara Grape Juice—deemed the "final symbol of the eternal friendship between the two nations." McQuesten stressed the theme of international friendship: . . . "Much more than a bridge, the steel which will soon be moving across the border line will be an added bond between the two great and friendly nations, a means of easier access, instead of a fortified barricade, a utility of convenience rather than a monument to hate . . . an international bond and pledge, a tangible, durable expression of the great friendliness which exists between our two great nations." (Stamp, *Bridging* 126)

McQuesten, through his lineage and heritage, considered himself to be a part of both of these great nations.

In 1939, with his usual foresight, Tom seized the opportunity of the Royal Visit to dedicate the bridge. Some exceptional planning and logistics must have been required, as the Depression was raging and wartime loomed. The bridge site was dedicated and the bridge named by King George VI and Queen Elizabeth eleven months <u>before</u> the first ground was broken on May 4 and May 16, 1940 on the Canadian and American sides respectively. The stone monument to the Royal Visit

**1939 Royal Tour. Presentation of flowers to Queen Elizabeth
by David Hanniwell and Eleanor Donald, NPC Administration Building.**

Carl Hanniwell, mayor of Niagara Falls, is bending over, forcing the bouquet of flowers
from David's hands. David refused to present the flowers because, "They are not wearing
their king's hats." Hon. Mackenzie King, Prime Minister of Canada stands smiling
behind Dr. Hanniwell. T.B. McQuesten, top hat on his arm, is at the far left.

reads—accurately—that, "Their Majesties, King George VI and Queen Elizabeth
viewed [emphasis added] the site of this bridge on June 7, 1939 and laid this stone."
The bridge was actually opened to traffic sixteen months later, on November 1, 1941
(Lewis 90, 91, 102).

With his family and friends present at the 1939 ceremony, Tom officiated for the
Royal introductions. The two ornate oak chairs used by the King and Queen have
been preserved and are on display in Tom's lounge at the Whitehern Museum.

Once the Rainbow Bridge had been named and dedicated, its site viewed and the
Royals had departed, work began in earnest. "The first steel grillage weighing sixty tons,

arrived in February 1941, and McQuesten
took it as a photo opportunity and a kind
of benediction. The Commissioners all
climbed down the 494 steps to the site
where Chairman McQuesten christened
the occasion with a bottle of Niagara River
Water" (Lewis 94).

**A toast with river water celebrating
the setting of the grillage and the workers**

Angus Beauvais on Rainbow Bridge

INDIAN RAINBOW BRIDGE WORKER GAZES AT FALLS.

Angus Beauvais, Canawaughna Indian, looks at the mighty falls known to his forefathers from his perch on a narrow beam of the Rainbow Bridge at Niagara Falls which is more than twenty stories above the roaring river. More than fifty per cent of the workers on this bridge, and practically every other bridge that is built on this continent, are Canawaughnas whose ability has made them excellent in this precarious work. The steamboat Maid-of-the-Mist, familiar to many thousands of tourists (and honeymooners) looks like a dimunuitive toy far below.

FROM HERB FOSTER
Daily News Building
220 E. 42nd St., NYC
VAnderbilt 6-4030   GRATIS-IMMEDIATE RELEASE

Paul E. Lewis celebrates the high steel workers: "The unsung heroes of the Rainbow Bridge construction were certainly the 'high steel' workers. More than half of the bridge crew (of about sixty members in total) were Kahnawake Indians. Their fearlessness and unique ability made them invaluable in this precarious work. . . . No lives were lost to accidents during construction, although five workers did fall into the safety netting" (100).

Inspection of Rainbow Bridge construction.
Front row: Ross Harstone; Fred H. Krull; Hon. T.B. McQuesten, Canadian Chairman; Ralph Hochstetter, C. Ellison Kaumeyer, General Manager.
Back row: Archie J. Haines; Will Alban Cannon; Samuel M. Johnson, U.S. Chairman.

Construction of the new Rainbow Bridge
Final steel spans being placed across the border line, 1941
(American and Horseshoe Falls in background, Niagara Falls)

During the war, it proved impossible to arrange an official opening for the Rainbow Bridge. However, an informal ceremony with no national leaders present was held on November 3, 1941, and was the occasion for some rejoicing. At the international boundary line on the middle of the bridge, T.B. McQuesten raised the Canadian flag on the Canadian side and Samuel Johnson raised the American flag on the American side; they reached across the border and shook hands. The celebrants then proceeded to the General Brock Hotel (Canadian side) for lunch and something stronger than grape juice, although Tom "could be described as perilously close to being a teetotaller" (Barnsley 63).

The Rainbow Bridge was McQuesten's third international

Samuel Johnson raising American flag & T.B. McQuesten raising the Canadian shake hands on the Rainbow Bridge on the international boundary line

Kaumeyer (right foreground) is the Bridge Commission's General Manager.
Rev. Calvin McQuesten (left rear) wears clerical collar.

First cars on the Rainbow Bridge, 1941

bridge, located midway between the Ivy Lea Bridge at the eastern end of Lake Ontario and the Blue Water Bridge in the southwest corner of the province. He could rejoice in having united the two countries across the province at three points—two from Ontario to New York State, and one to Michigan. Robert Stamp relates a portion of McQuesten's speech that afternoon which might appear to be somewhat out of character, but reveals Tom's deeper political sentiments and ideals:

> For once, the luncheon speakers seem to have forsaken Niagara frontier grape juice for stronger liquid refreshment. The usually staid McQuesten was particularly outrageous. "The border between the two countries is now just a matter of brass buttons," he declared. "It is a ridiculous thing, this border, and it is becoming more obnoxious to us every day. The bridge is a highway and in the time to come it will help to make the border cease to extend between us."
> (*Niagara Falls N.Y. Gazette*, Nov 3 1941; Stamp, *Bridging* 127)

In Vino Veritas. Tom was uncharacteristically frank in this speech and probably betrayed his true feelings: his ultimate wish for a unification of Canada and the United States—the two countries that featured in his own family background. He could reach back in time to see the bloodshed and strife that had taken place before the two came to accept peaceful relations. This international sentiment had come to lie behind everything that Tom built or restored. The bridges and highways were both practical and political. They were transportation arteries, but also acted as political treaties that ensured peace, co-operation, tourism, trade and communication between the two countries. In the late 1930s and early 1940s, using their three new international bridges—the Ivy Lea, Blue Water and Rainbow—Canada and the United States were moving closer to an intercontinental highway network.

Marjorie Freeman Campbell closes her book, *Niagara: Hinge of the Golden Arc*, with a prose poem describing the evolution of the bridge in human history—a little story that Tom McQuesten would have fully endorsed:

> **At first there was no bridge.**
>
> **On either side of the wide river people lived. But those on the far side and those on the near didn't know each other. They had no way to trade happiness or help or friendship. Each was the poorer because no highway lay between them.**
>
> **But a bridge builder came.**

Oakville Bridge

Across the river, reaching to the far shore, he made his bridge—a thing
of substance, solid and lasting. And at once the people on the far side
and those on the near became one people. Across the bridge flowed an
exchange of all the good things that each possessed. Over the bridge moved
friendship, understanding, affection and mutual regard.

And the name of the bridge shall be PEACE.

OTHER SOUTHERN ONTARIO BRIDGES

John Best reports that by 1936, although Prime Minister Mackenzie King was
impressed with the work to date by the Ontario Government, he granted "miniscule
federal aid" for continuation of the work. Did King fear that McQuesten was
becoming too successful and too popular and might eventually unseat him as Prime
Minister? Tom was already President of the Ontario Liberal Association.

Nevertheless, Tom was determined to continue building. "Two graceful concrete
bridges were speedily built over the Oakville and Bronte creeks. The two spans were
more than 600 feet long and crossed the creeks on 100-foot arches. The style revealed
a continuing debt to John Lyle's earlier work on Hamilton High Level Bridge."
Underpasses were also constructed (Best 115).

A *Globe and Mail* headline read: "Hundreds attended the Oakville Bridge Formal
Ceremony . . . of the new $150,000 bridge on the Middle Road west of the 6th line. It
represented the last word in modern design. It is 615 feet long, 40 feet wide and has a
6 foot sidewalk on either side" (*Globe & Mail* Dec 31 1936). On the same date a photo
appeared in the *Evening Telegram* of McQuesten and Thomas A. Blakelock, mayor
of Oakville, as they opened the new Bridge. McQuesten and Mayor Blakelock also
opened the new bridge at Bronte.

SOME OTHER SOUTHERN ONTARIO HIGHWAYS & BRIDGES

HIGHWAYS:
-The QEW easterly extension to Oshawa which became Hwy 401
-The QEW Westerly extension to Windsor
-Highway entrance to Ivy Lea Bridge
-Highway entrance to Blue Water Bridge

BRIDGES:
-Bridge at Credit River
-Bridge at Bronte (Best 115)
-Bridge at Oakville (Best 115)
-Bridge at Highland Creeks
-Bridge at Scarborough
-Bridge at Etobicoke Creek, Hwy 2, near Long Branch and Mississauga
-Bridges and under-passes and over-passes all along the QEW
-Bridge at Port Stanley

-McQuesten also planned a high level bridge over the Burlington Beach and canal area. The Skyway Bridge was not completed until the 1950s.

As Chairman of the Highways Commission, Tom was responsible for many, or most, of the bridges in Ontario that were built during his tenure. These were all part of his vision of the bridge as a unifying principle that would bring peace, prosperity and tourism to often remote areas. Over the years, many of Tom's bridges have been widened but retain their original graceful lines.

Credit River Bridge

Chapter 35

THE GORGEOUS GARDENS AT NIAGARA FALLS, ONTARIO

"From Fort Erie to Niagara-on-the-Lake, the successive floral displays
of Ontario's Niagara Parks are, to lovers of beauty,
attractions that rival the cataracts." (Way 173)

As Ontario's Minister of Highways, Thomas B. McQuesten exercised great influence in the design and construction of the Queen's Highway from Toronto to Niagara. As Chairman of the Niagara Parks Commission he was a powerful voice for the beautification of the entire area along the Niagara River from Lake Erie to Lake Ontario. He played a pivotal role in developing informal parklands along the riverbank as well as numerous formal gardens, and restoring sites of great Canadian historical significance, all of which still retain his characteristic aesthetic imprint.

By the late 1800s, thanks in part to the growth of railways, Niagara Falls was a major attraction, and the adjacent area had turned into an unsightly, unregulated tourist trap. A Niagara Parks Commission report describes the situation: *Before the establishment of the Niagara Parks, the Falls had been the lair of rapacious cab-men and unscrupulous concessionaires located on both the Canadian and American shores for the ruthless exploitation of visitors* (W-MCP7-1.154, Dec 31 1941).

In 1878, Canada's Governor General Lord Dufferin was the first individual to articulate the need for public parkland around the Falls. Seven years later the Ontario legislature passed the Niagara Falls Park Act of 1885. The Niagara Parks Commission (NPC) was formed to carry out its objectives, and land along the Canadian river front was expropriated for park purposes.

On the American side, industrial development and lack of public access likewise led to a movement to restore the natural beauty of the Falls and surrounding area. Frederick Law Olmsted, the country's highly influential landscape architect, played a key role in the preservation effort that led to the creation in 1885 of America's first state park, the Niagara Reservation. Olmsted, who with his partner, Calvert Vaux, had been granted the commission to

Frederick Law Olmsted, Sr.
by John Singer Sargent (1895)

The name Olmsted translates into Place of the Elms. Some say his planting of these trees could be considered similar to the signature of an artist.

develop the Reservation as parkland, was also the force behind the preservation of Goat Island, which separates the Canadian and U.S. Falls. He and Vaux were also authorized by New York Governor Grover Cleveland to purchase Goat Island and neighbouring Bath Island. They returned the islands to a state of natural beauty, and added pedestrian foot paths.

THE NIAGARA PARKWAY—*From Battlefields to Beauty*

In Canada, the newly formed Niagara Parks Commission initially focused its attention on the area around the Falls, transforming the expropriated properties into Queen Victoria Park. With the creation of this park in 1887, the NPC established the blend of natural scenery and landscape architecture that still characterizes the lands under its jurisdiction. Oakes Garden Theatre (1937) and the Rainbow Gardens (1941) implemented by T.B. McQuesten half a century later are prime examples of this blending of architecture and horticulture.

The Parks Commission was also the beneficiary of an earlier governmental decision. In 1786, the British Colonial Government had commissioned surveyor Augustus Jones to create a military reserve one chain wide along the entire length of the Niagara gorge and river. A chain, equal to 66 feet (20m), was the standard measurement of the day. The military chain reserve along the river's west bank kept ownership of this land in government hands. In 1852, ownership and jurisdiction were turned over to the Government of Upper Canada (eventually Ontario). When this land came under the Commission's control, beautification schemes along the river were greatly facilitated. Tom McQuesten, passionate about celebrating peace between Canada and the U.S., and imbued with City Beautiful ideals, would have been particularly pleased with the opportunity to transform land where battles once were fought, into a beautiful garden for all citizens to enjoy.

Under McQuesten's leadership, the NPC built the Niagara Parkway along the full length of the river, with the section through the city of Niagara Falls named the River Road. Completed in 1936, this scenic drive extends from Fort Erie to Niagara-on-the-Lake, and features a walking and bicycle trail for its entire 56 km (35 miles). Picnic areas are interspersed along the way. The Parkway is spectacular at any time of year. In spring, summer and fall it is full of colour; in winter when the trees are bare, the view of the powerful fast-flowing river with its build-up of snow and ice is awe-inspiring. Sir Winston Churchill in August 1943 declared it "the prettiest Sunday drive in the world." McQuesten restored the forts along the route and they are excellent tourist and student destinations for the teaching of history and for family enjoyment.

OAKES GARDEN THEATRE

After the Clifton Hotel burned down in December of 1932, Harry Oakes (1874-1943), a wealthy mining magnate, purchased the Clifton Hill hotel property along with the adjacent Lafayette Hotel, which was then demolished. He became a Niagara Parks Commissioner in 1934, the same year in which Tom became the Commission's Chairman. Oakes, who was eight years older than Tom, had been educated in

Harry and Eunice Oakes in Toronto in the 1930s
(Niagara Falls Public Library)

medicine at Bowdoin College, the same college that Tom's grandfather attended many years earlier. Just as Dr. Calvin McQuesten had left medicine to establish a foundry, Harry Oakes gave up medicine for the mining industry.

In 1935 Oakes turned the Clifton Hill properties over to the Niagara Parks Commission. "Oakes took a small nursery acreage in exchange. The announcement was made by C. Ellison Kaumeyer, general manager of the Niagara Parks Commission" (*Hamilton Spectator*, Jul 6 1935). In 1939, Harry Oakes was granted the title of baronet by King George VI as a reward for his many philanthropic efforts. He became known as Sir Harry Oakes.

Tom immediately began the work of developing the newly acquired properties. The job of designing and laying out the site was awarded to Howard Dunington-Grubb, landscape architect, and William Lyon Somerville, sculptural

Beginning of construction at Oakes Garden Theatre

architect, who had similar ideas about how it should be developed and landscaped. Both Somerville and Dunington-Grubb favoured a formal garden fashioned on a French style. Somerville designed an attractive curving walkway with columns; Howard Dunington-Grubb, assisted by his wife Lorrie and Janina Stensson, did the landscape design.

The land slopes toward the river, forming a natural amphitheatre from which both the Canadian and the American Falls can be viewed. The designers took full advantage of this slope, utilizing architecture and sculpture to provide striking

Oakes Garden Theatre,
 aerial view

views and vistas. The theatre is fan-shaped, with the stage so placed that the panorama of the Falls forms a natural backdrop. Shrub borders were created around formalized gardens, with attractive ornamental iron gates and Queenston limestone around the perimeter.

Florence Wyle, Frances Loring and Elizabeth Wyn Wood, three significant Canadian sculptors from Toronto, were commissioned to design the fountains and bas-relief sculptures within the garden. Their works are neo-classical, featuring uniquely Canadian indigenous plants and animals. In the words of the Niagara Parks website, "this surprising garden surrounded by an ornamental stone wall provides visitors with a feeling of fantasy and escape."

Rainbow Gardens,
Canadiana bas-relief

Johnny Canuck meets Uncle Sam,
Rainbow Gardens

The curved pergola at the rear connects two open pavilions—one oriented on the axis of the Horseshoe Falls, the other on that of the American Falls—and overlooks the central amphitheatre. Behind the pergola, a beautiful and serene Japanese-style garden with a lily pond and wishing bridge *(right)* is often the setting for wedding and other photographs.

The curved Pergola at Oakes Garden Theatre

The Oakes Garden Theatre forms a spectacular entranceway to Queen Victoria Park, the key central area of the Niagara Parks systems which showcases the Falls. Its location at the foot of Clifton Hill offers a superb panoramic view of the American and Horseshoe Falls.

> Oakes Garden Theatre is a highly decorative *Beaux-Arts* landscape, including classical and picturesque elements, with the central point a grass Greco-Roman amphitheatre surrounded by a limestone staircase, and features fountains, urns, statuary and sculptured bas-relief panels and medallions. It is historically significant, as very few examples of landscape architectural design of this age or complexity exist in Ontario or Canada. (P. Berketo, NPC Study, 2000)

Formally opened in September 1937 with the Honourable T.B. McQuesten officiating, it has been preserved in essentially the same style as conceived by the Dunington-Grubbs and Somerville. Unfortunately it was never successful as an actual theatre because of the roar of the Falls, but music events continue to be held there regularly (Seibel 293-94).

The Oakes gardens were developed at the height of the Great Depression, just a few years before the beginning of the Second World War, at a time when the world needed the beauty and order of formal gardens, as well as fantasy and escape. Considering the time and circumstances, it is surprising that these gorgeous gardens could have been achieved at all, let alone so magnificently. Considerable will must have been required, and there can be little doubt that Thomas McQuesten was the driving force. These were the years just after Tom's mother died; he knew that he had been charged with the task of bringing beauty into the world, just as his mother and Ruby had done. Tom determined to include the arts and culture in his work even if he personally had to absorb some of the costs. He was sometimes criticized for his extravagance, but mostly by the opposition Conservative Party.

Following construction of the Rainbow Bridge in 1941, the Niagara Falls Bridge Commission partnered with The Niagara Parks Commission to create the Rainbow Gardens as a link between the bridge and Oakes Garden Theatre, and an entrance to Canada and Queen Victoria Park. The Rainbow Gardens were designed by Dunington-Grubb and Somerville, the same team who designed the *Beaux-Arts* style Oakes Garden Theatre. The Rainbow Gardens "are equally as formal but have details typical of the Art Deco and Moderne period" (P. Berketo, NPC Study, 2000). The two gardens complement one another almost like a conversation between periods. Both showcase early twentieth-century Canadian art, architecture and landscape architecture. Together with the RBG gardens at the Hamilton end of the QEW, they form bookends of beauty for citizens and visitors alike.

BOTANICAL GARDEN AND
TRAINING SCHOOL FOR APPRENTICE GARDENERS

Soon after assuming chairmanship of the Niagara Parks Commission, Tom realized that a horticultural school would be necessary to train workers in the skills necessary to keep the Niagara gardens in optimum condition. The School for Apprentice Gardeners was founded on July 26, 1936; it was the only residential horticultural school in Canada (Way 178). The botanical garden on site is an outdoor classroom of one hundred acres. Located on the Niagara Parkway, it became known as the "Kew Gardens of the North." It was later renamed the School of Horticulture; its mission was to supply workers for many of Canada's parks.

Apprentice Gardeners, 1938

Niagara Parks School of Horticulture
(Niagara Parks Archives)

A three-year course for young men was organized upon British lines. The students were in charge of all aspects of running the school and botanical gardens. Some of the students were sent to England to take a course at Kew Gardens (W9861m, Apr 19 1939).

McQuesten selected Matt Broman, who had worked with him at RBG, to be the Principal of the Training School for Apprentice Gardeners, which Broman combined with his other duties at the Niagara Parks. Tom's confidence in Broman was not misplaced, as evidenced in the following excerpt from a letter Tom sent to Broman:

*On the whole permit me to congratulate you on a very successful year's
work. I do not know if you appreciate the extent to which you are giving
some direction and purpose to quite a number of boys who would otherwise
be without a job or a calling. The habits of industry and simplicity in which
these boys are brought up, to my mind is a priceless advantage to them and
this feature of the school is worth more than any expert training.*

*I meant also to say to you that irrespective of anything that has been
done in the way of plans, I would like you to feel that you are in entire
control to plan and execute, as means permit, the development of the garden
in and around your nursery and including the area around the Glen,
Restaurant and in fact any distance which you wish. For a number of reasons
I have had to occasionally bring in outsiders and I may say I always do it
with hesitation and regret, but I want you to feel that this area is your job
and you will have no interference in any way whatsoever.*

With kind personal regards,
Believe me, Faithfully yours,
T.B. McQuesten. (W9865q, Dec 20 1939)

One of Tom's priorities was always the education of youth, and Broman obviously
agreed with him. Matt Broman was given a free hand at the school and he often
brought forward ideas of his own for the school and for the gardens. In the following
letter he makes a suggestion to open the school to girls:

TO T.B. MCQUESTEN from his associate, Matt Broman (W9865a)
Whitehern, Hamilton, Ontario   Niagara Parks Commission
                                                 Training School for Apprentice Gardeners
                                                 April 14, 1944

Dear Sir,
*I have a little idea of my own here, and I think it will work out all right, if we
obtain your permission to carry out the idea. There are many young girls, in our
collegiates around here, who would like to know something about gardening. The*

*boys from the High
Schools seek a job
where they can get high
pay and that is the
reason we are thinking
about the girls. It is
our intention to give
them a few lectures
and general practical
work in gardening. It
will be very helpful and
educational to them,
and in return they
will assist in keeping
the School in good
condition.*

The original Boys' Residence,   *Yours respectfully,*
School for Apprentice Gardeners, 1938   *Matt Broman*

The reply from McQuesten to Broman's request is a simple: *I am quite content to leave the matter with you* (W9865b). However, it appears that the time was not favourable to implement Broman's idea, since the first female students were not admitted to the School of Horticulture until 1973, graduating in 1976.[26] If there was some resistance to women as horticulturalists, a precedent had already been set by Lorrie Dunington, Janina Stensson and others. However, if we consider that Broman made his proposal in 1944, it is possible that those apprentice positions were being reserved for returning servicemen, and a public protest might have ensued had women been invited to apply

Broman's Rose Garden, established in the 1940s, is just one of the many exceptional features of the Horticultural School. "The Victorian Rose Garden reflects the Broman style of a grand landscape vista, similar to the classical landscape design of the 18th century and reminiscent of English estate gardens. It encompasses over 2 acres (.85 hectares) and includes 54 rose beds and 31 annual display beds. It boasts 2400 colourful and fragrant hybrid tea, floribunda, grandiflora and climbing roses."[27] Plans are being made to include the T.B. McQuesten rose in 2011.

The Rose Garden designed by Matt Broman in the 1940s (above)

The Niagara Parks Botanical Garden

Broman also developed the complete Botanical Garden that serves the school. The Showhouse or Greenhouse opened in 1946; the Floral Clock, which was in the planning under Tom's aegis, opened in 1950, two years after his death.

Niagara Falls is one of the natural wonders of North America, and the city of Niagara Falls, Ontario has become the "Honeymoon Capital" of the world. The Rainbow Bridge has been a huge success, and the Niagara gardens, parkway, and Horticultural School have been the crowning glory for tourism in Ontario for many years. Unfortunately a Midway, amusement park and casino eventually came into existence and a general carnival atmosphere prevails in the city—except, that is, in the protected park areas along the parkway and around the Falls: *i.e.*, along the military chain reserve. These gardens are protected *in perpetuity*; they remain as horticultural masterpieces and continue to draw thousands to the Falls daily.

---

[26] Ruth Stoner, Librarian, Niagara Parks Botanical Gardens, School of Horticulture.

[27] http://www.niagaraparks.com/garden/BotanicalGardensFacts.php

Hon. T.B. McQuesten, K.C. officiating at opening of Mather Park, Fort Erie, Aug. 31, 1940

MATHER PARK AT THE PEACE BRIDGE

The Peace Bridge at the southern end of the QEW was built in 1927, before Tom became Minister of Highways for Ontario. Bridging Fort Erie, Ontario and Buffalo, New York, it afforded an occasion in 1936 for McQuesten to express his views on the peace between Canada and the U.S. At a dedication ceremony honouring women's federations[28] (much favoured by the McQuesten family), the Hon. T.B. McQuesten spoke in his capacity as Minister of Highways for Ontario: "May I say this Peace which exists between the United States and Canada was based on a just treaty. Neither party gave up nor acquired any territory. There were no harsh penalties. The efficacy of such a just agreement is demonstrated by a century and a quarter of peace" (*Niagara Falls Evening Review*, Jun 17 1936). The "just treaty" refers to the Jay Treaty of 1794, which formed the basis of all future treaties; the time span refers to the peace that followed the war of 1812.

The approach from the QEW to the Peace Bridge was widely acknowledged to be unattractive; and beautification of the entrance to the bridge was necessary for completion of the Niagara Parkway. In the early 1940s, assisted by a bequest from Alonzo Mather, McQuesten was able to accomplish this. The 1943 Annual Report for the Niagara Parks Commission provides a short history of Mather Park:

> *Alonzo C. Mather was a wealthy inventor and manufacturer of Chicago. . . .*
> *Almost half a century ago, Mather had hoped to finance the cost of a bridge*
> *on a site close to the location of the present Peace Bridge. He secured the land*
> *for a terminus on the Canadian side but he failed to secure the land for a*
> *terminus on the American side. Several years before his death, this visionary,*
> *who was also a philanthropist, gave to the Niagara Parks Commission*
> *seventy-five acres of land fronting on the Niagara River immediately south of*
> *the Canadian approach to the Peace Bridge, together with a sum of $35,000*

[28] *viz.*, the Federated Women's Institutes of Ontario (FWIO) and the Federated Women's Institutes of Canada (FWIC)

Mather Arch

towards the development of a park and the erection of a memorial gateway
on the site. The project was undertaken without delay and an outstanding
event of 1940 was the official opening of Mather Park on August 31st when
a service of dedication was carried out within the completed Memorial
Gateway, which is an impressive arch in modern monumental design,
located at the important junction of the Peace Bridge outlet from Buffalo, the
Niagara River Boulevard, the Garrison Road, and the provincial highway [the
QEW] leading to points in Western Ontario. (W-MCP7-1.154)

The words carved in stone on the front of the monument reflect both Mather's
and McQuesten's sentiments: "Let the peaceful surroundings of this Park be enjoyed
by the People on both sides of the water to signify the blessings of lasting peace and
that only friendship and goodwill shall bridge the frontier between these two nations."
Carved on the south side of the Arch are the names of all of the Niagara Parks
Commissioners and the bridge design team in 1939.[29]

In 1941, Alonzo Mather died at the age of ninety-two. Mather's will reflects his
affection for Canada and his regard for T.B. McQuesten's work:

A sum of $250,000 jointly [bequeathed] to the Peace Bridge Authority
and to the Niagara Parks Commission, to be spent for the erection of
suitable memorials to the memory of Canadians and Americans who have
contributed to the building up of friendly relations between their two
countries and in maintaining and beautifying Mather Park. (W-MCP7-1.154)

The Whitehern archive contains a list of expenditures for Mather Park, addressed
to T.B. McQuesten prior to Mather's death (Box 08-203, Jan 1, 1940, estimated date). The
total of expenditures on Mather Park, including the expenses on the Memorial Arch,
came very close to the $250,000 that Mather left in his will.

---

[29] Commissioners: Hon. T. B. McQuesten, KC, Chairman, Hamilton; Dr. Geo S. Snyder,
Vice Chairman, Niagara Falls; Hon. Wm. L. Houck, BS, Niagara Falls; Archie J Haines, MPP,
Jordan; John C. M. German, KC, Toronto; Ross Harstone, Hamilton; A.T. Whitaker, Brantford;
Donald McGillivray, Port Colborne; C. Ellison Kaumeyer, General Manager; Designed by Carl
Borgstrom, Associates; H.S.M. Carver; E.L. Sheppard.

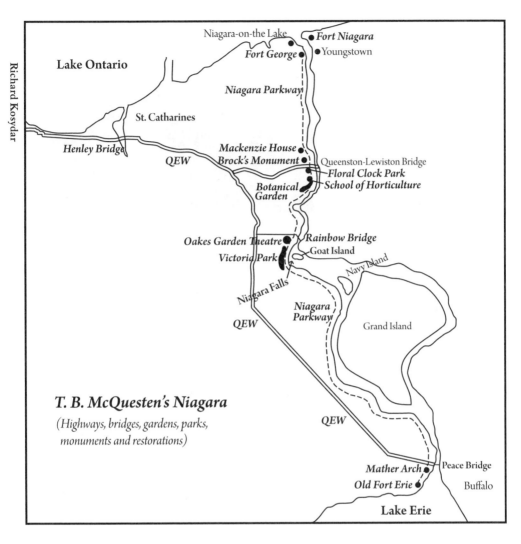

Richard Kosydar

T. B. McQuesten's Niagara

(Highways, bridges, gardens, parks, monuments and restorations)

The NPC report of 1943 continues:

By means of a recently completed sea wall, lands have been reclaimed from Lake and the Park now extends from the Peace Bridge to the grounds of the Old Fort—a distance of half a mile. With its beautiful arch; attractive gardens, bold sweep of traffic circles and promise of arboricultural developments, Mather Park is destined to be a place of rare beauty and a fitting entrance to the Niagara Parks.

A concise statement that reflects McQuesten's priorities concludes: *The Niagara Parks Commissioners have recently defined their work [as] preservation, restoration, commemoration, beautification and attraction* (W-MCP7-1.154, Dec 31 1943). Elsewhere in the same document, McQuesten elaborates on his philosophy with regard to the importance of education:

The educational policy of the Niagara Parks Commissioners has been threefold. First, through the preservation of scenic beauty and the creation

Hon. T.B. McQuesten, KC
presenting bouquet of gladioli
to Margaret Anne Mather
on the occasion of
opening Mather Park

*of aesthetic values, they have cultivated a public appreciation of the
beautiful. Second, through the application of scientific gardening they have
created opportunities for the study of Horticulture and Botany notably in
the establishment of a school for apprentice gardeners. And third, through
the preservation of historic memories they have contributed in no small
measure to the development of patriotism and the highest qualities of
Canadian citizenship. The latter aspect is a somewhat unorthodox departure
form the usual conception of park planning and requires an explanation.
Throughout Ontario's Niagara Parks is perhaps concentrated more vital
history than in any similar area of North America. Every mile or so along
the Parkway from Lake Erie to Lake Ontario the traveller reaches the scene
of some past event which has influenced the destiny of this country. To mark
these sites, the Commissioners have encouraged, or themselves undertaken,
the erection of monuments and commemorative tablets. Furthermore they
have embarked recently upon a programme of historical restorations. The
policy of rebuilding important structures such as Fort George, Navy Hall, Fort
Erie and the William Lyon Mackenzie home, instead of merely preserving the
unintelligible ruins both contributed to the teaching of Canadian history and
the development of patriotism and high ideals.* (W-MCP7-1.154)

Today Mather Park plays host every year to the Friendship Festival in celebration of
the good relations between Canada and the USA since the War of 1812. The festival's
mission statement is to support and promote better relations between the two countnries,
along with economic development, tourism and cultural activities. In July 2012 the
Festival will commemorate 200 years of peace and friendship since the War of 1812.

Chapter 36

NORTHERN ONTARIO HIGHWAYS & BRIDGES

We are now closing the gap in the [Trans-Canada] highway across Ontario
from Long Lac [sic] to Hearst.
McQuesten to Broman, Sept 2 1941 (W9862g)

On April 29, 1936, the *Hamilton Spectator* reported that T.B. McQuesten received the portfolio of Northern Development. He was now in charge of the department with the largest budget in the provincial government. Northern Development also had the highest level of corruption and scandal of any department; consequently, highway and bridge construction had suffered delays and deferments for several years. Possibly Tom, in consultation with Hepburn, actually requested the portfolio. John Best comments, "McQuesten took over Northern Development partly to clean up the patronage and favouritism which had plagued operations from its inception" (Best 178). Given Tom's high standard of morality and ethics and his "straight arrow" approach to life, he very likely relished a chance to clean up the Department and would have taken on the portfolio with a certain enthusiasm. He immediately commenced internal reorganization, replacing slackers and grafters with individuals he could trust.

Thomas McQuesten had a great fondness for the north. As seen previously, he worked in a lumber camp on the Ottawa River for two summers when he was a student, and he articled in Elk Lake in the mining district before accepting a law position in Hamilton with James Chisholm. These experiences had allowed him to observe how poorly legal and government matters were handled in the North, and he knew that significant changes would have to be made if economic development and the growth of tourism were to take place.

While Tom was a young lawyer at Elk Lake, he wrote to Calvin to express his reservations about legal methods in the north:

> *I had a very interesting experience on the whole up north and it will be most*
> *useful to me. . . . Up there you had to rely on yourself as the bar of Elk Lake*
> *would not rank very high intellectually or legally or any other way. . . .*
> *In addition to this one gets into loose professional habits up there, it is the*
> *laziest way to work in the world. So that I thought I should not lose my*
> *opportunity to come down home, lest presently I should refuse to work again.*
> (W8212, Jul 15 1909)

When McQuesten had first assumed the Highways portfolio in 1934, both the federal and provincial governments were pouring monies into various works to mitigate the effects of the Depression. That year the *Hamilton Spectator* announced:

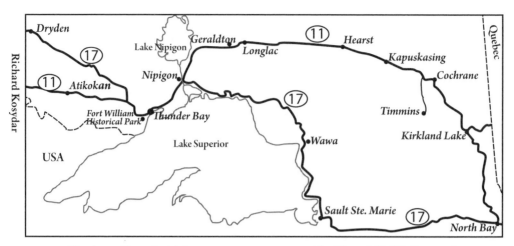

**Northern Ontario highways, most constructed by Hon. T.B. McQuesten's
Departments of Northern Development and Highways**

Ottawa Will Pay Large Share of Highway Works for Trans-Canada Highway.
The unemployment relief programs between the Dominion and Ontario and
Quebec will reach two provincial governments today for respective signatures.
Dominion to pay 50% of cost of Trans-Canada Highway work. (Oct 23 1934)

Newspapers subsequently carried reports of road progress in sections of the
north. McQuesten's journals of newspaper clippings at Whitehern contain hundreds
of notices for highway and bridge construction. Indeed, you can follow their
construction history by reading these notices, such as: "Call Due Soon for Bridge
Bids, for two spans near Peterboro on Highway 7 over Indian River, Otonabee River
and Trent Canal at East boundary of city. . . and Indian and Ouse River tenders" (*Daily
Commercial News*, Jan 11 1935); "50 Contracts on Road Work are Awarded and Named by
T.B. McQuesten" (*Toronto Globe*, Jun 27 1936). Some of the announcements were made
in the name of Deputy Minister of Highways R.M. Smith.

The Department of Northern Development was in charge of much of the expanded
construction work, which would provide employment for many, and it controlled
the distribution of continued relief monies to pay the newly employed workers. The
government relief programs allowed Tom to fulfill three major parts of his vision for
the north: to expand development; to provide employment for the poor; and to bring
proper legal measures into practice—all for which he had lobbied strenuously.

Shortly after Tom's appointment to Northern Development, the *Globe & Mail*
reported, "Early next week T.B. McQuesten, Minister of Highways and R.M. Smith,
Deputy Minister, will make a tour of the North in connection with new road plans . . .
to survey conditions in the North" (May 7, 1936). In September, the *Globe* made a
further announcement, with some humour:

North "Welcomes" McQuesten. In referring to the motor trip that T.B.
McQuesten is now making through Northern Ontario, the Timmins paper
expresses "good wishes" to the minister. But all the North will wish . . . that

rain will not fall too much when he is here and that he gets his jolly fill of the grittiest road dust. That he enjoys to the full the "washboard" effect . . . and that, in general, he has so many narrow escapes, so many bumps, so many annoyances, that he will fully realize the condition of the North's one road and feel in his heart and body that he must have it put into half-decent shape.

Several weeks later, the *Toronto Star* reported that, "The work on the Trans-Canada highway between Port Arthur and Winnipeg is to be continued this summer . . . still some sections to be finished" (Jul 21 1936). Since tourism was a major priority for McQuesten, he may have taken the opportunity while working on the highways in the northwest to visit Fort William and assist in the projected restoration of Old Fort William. He often included some restoration work in the Highways' budget.

In early 1937 an unidentified newspaper clipping states that McQuesten's intent was to open up the north for mining and tourism:

McQuesten declared a major part of work for the mine district. He would Modernize Old Roads. . . extending main routes will be carried out with the view to extending paved highway linking Sault Ste. Marie to Montreal and thus opening a vast tourist travel source from Michigan and the northern states. . . . Extending into Timmins and mining centres of the north. (Jan 20 1937)

The following year, the *Globe & Mail* carried a headline regarding Tom's work for the Gold Fields:

McQuesten Defends Road Program in North Before Trade Boards. He declared it would be a crime if the Gold Fields were not linked with the South by Good Modern Highways. He pointed to 400 miles of new road construction in the past two years in Northern Ontario and a great deal remained to be done.

Within a few years the section of Trans-Canada Highway 11 from North Bay through Temagami to Kirkland Lake in northeastern Ontario was in place and much of it paved, and the link to Timmins had been constructed.

New asphalt pavement on Hwy 11 north of North Bay, 1939
Photo courtesy of Ontario Ministry of Transportation

Hearst Gerldton Highway under construction 1941
(courtesy of Nipigon Historical Museum)

McQuesten built strategic arteries for the purpose of uniting widely separate regions of the north for resource development and tourism. One of his most striking achievements was completion of the Trans-Canada Highway link between Nipigon and Hearst via Longlac. This made it possible for vehicles to travel across Northern Ontario from Manitoba to Quebec, which stimulated tourism, allowed Northern Ontario's mining and forestry industries to flourish, and encouraged settlement.

Trans-Canada Highway 17 from Thunder Bay splits into two routes at Nipigon. One leads south to Sault Ste. Marie, while a northern branch (Highway 11) takes travellers to Hearst and points farther east. The two routes converge again at North Bay. The Nipigon-Hearst section of roadway was of the highest grade of highway construction, setting a standard used afterward in the construction of the Alaska Highway through Canada (Box 14-129). Construction costs on much of the northern highways proved to be high, given the engineering difficulties encountered with rocky terrain, bush conditions, and drainage.

Nipigon Bridge on Trans-Canada Highway
(courtesy Nipigon Historical Museum)

Opening ceremony of the Trans-Canada Highway Bridge over the Nipigon River,
Sept 7 1940 *(Photo by Everett, Courtesy of Nipigon Historical Museum)*

The community of Nipigon, located on the western shore of the Nipigon River, lies within the relatively narrow (60km) band of land between Lake Nipigon and Lake Superior at its northernmost point. Two bridges at the east end of town span the river, one a single-line railway bridge (seen at left in the photo above), and the other a two-lane road bridge. Canada's road network narrows down at this point to one highway, over one bridge. In 1937 the highway bridge opened the way for traffic to begin flowing over the Nipigon River, but the actual highway was not completed until 1940. The Nipigon Bridge and Highway 11 between Nipigon and Geraldton officially opened on September 7, 1940. Few people realize that to this day, all vehicles crossing Canada must traverse the highway bridge over the Nipigon River.

In 1941, Tom wrote to Matt Broman at the Niagara Parks Commission requesting that Broman inspect the progress of the Trans-Canada Highway: *I would like you to see the area from Port Arthur [Thunder Bay] east to Long Lac [sic], which we are now continuing by closing the gap in the highway across Ontario from*

Long Lac to Hearst (W9862g, Sept 2 1941). The completion of the road system between Longlac and Hearst finally joined northeastern and northwestern Ontario directly by highway. Upon completion of this vital link, the length of highway from Nipigon to Hearst was designated Trans-Canada Highway 11.

Opening of Trans-Canada Highway Bridge over Nipigon River.
Note people walking both ways. *(courtesy of Nipigon Historical Museum)*

Rest Areas, Northern Highway 17

In 1946, three years after McQuesten had left both the Highways and Northern Development portfolios, another associate wrote to inquire whether the highway between Sault Ste. Marie and North Bay had been completed. At the top of this letter, a note in Tom's hand—likely written in preparation for a reply—indicates that due to labour shortages some of the road work had not progressed, but that post-war work was planned: *1/2 done, nothing since I left. 1st road after war, labour impossible* (W-MCP7-1.091,n).

McQuesten constructed several other Northern Ontario highways and bridges during his tenure, some of which are enumerated in the list that follows. Notable among these are the bridge at Kapuskasing and the highway approaches and large bridge at Kenora over an arm of the Lake of the Woods in northwestern Ontario.

Kapuskasing Bridge Opening
T.B. McQuesten centre front holding white hat

**TRAVEL ONTARIO
ON THE
KING'S HIGHWAY**

Entrance to Huntsville

SOME OF MCQUESTEN'S NORTHERN ONTARIO HIGHWAYS & BRIDGES

HIGHWAYS:

-Highway from North Bay through Temagami to Kirkland Lake
-Highway and entrance to Timmins
-Highways from Timmins to mining centres of the north
-Highway, North Bay west to Sault Ste. Marie half completed;
 large stretches paved and graded
-Paved highways linking Sault Ste Marie to Ottawa (and hence Montreal)
-Trans-Canada Highway link from Hearst through Geraldton to mouth
 of Nipigon River, completed
-Trans-Canada highway between Port Arthur and Winnipeg
-Dual highway from Gananoque to Brockville

BRIDGES

-Large bridge at Kenora over an arm of Lake of the Woods
-Bridges at Longlac and Nipigon
-Bridge at Kapuskasing
-Bridge at Indian and Ouse River—completed in 1935
-Bridge at Peterboro, Hwy 7, over Indian River and Otonabee River
-Bridge at Trent Canal at East boundary of City of Peterboro
-Many smaller bridges

Second Channel Bridge, Kenora,
Ontario, Canada

Hwy 10
near
Gravenhurst

Chapter 37

RECONSTRUCTION OF FORTS

"I believe that [T.B. McQuesten and Ronald L. Way] were innovators
of heritage restoration in this country and this was the beginning
of the tourist industry as we now know it. Their contributions
laid the groundwork for how we interpret historic sites."

(Ron Ridley, Curator, Fort Henry, Jun 24 2009)[30]

War of 1812 Re-enactment, Fort Henry

Thomas McQuesten, as Chairman of the Niagara Parks Commission and
Minister of both Public Works and Highways, restored a number of historically
significant old forts in Ontario during the 1930s and 1940s. These restorations were
in keeping with Tom's strong sense of history, and his particular interest in the War
of 1812 and other historical conflicts that involved Canada and the U.S. McQuesten
felt that the forts in their derelict state were reminders of enmity and strife over the
ages, but could be reconstructed and beautified to emphasize the peace that had
been won through their sacrifices.

In 1936 Tom approached the federal government to request financial assistance for
the restoration of the old British forts in the Niagara area and Fort Henry at Kingston,
and the government agreed. His argument centred on the benefits to Canada from
increased tourism, which would soon repay the expenditure (Best 116). It is an irony
of history that these forts were originally designed to keep the American invaders out,
but the restorations were designed to induce them to come in as paying tourists.

---

[30] E-mail from Ron Ridley, Curator, Fort Henry National Historic Site, St. Lawrence Parks
Commission, Ontario (Jun 24 2009)

McQuesten had observed that many of the derelict forts built in the early nineteenth century were surrounded by large tracts of land, in locations near water. This would allow for the creation of pleasant park-like settings ideal for tourism. William Lyon Somerville, McQuesten's colleague and an avid student of history, was the architect of choice for most of these restorations, and his name appears on many of the architecture and engineering documents. The Dunington-Grubbs were the landscape architects of choice and did much of the landscape design.

The teaching of history was an important aspect of these projects. Not only the physical forts, but the lives of their inhabitants were to be reconstructed. Student volunteers in nineteenth-century British uniforms would provide authentic enactments of domestic and military activities in what are essentially outdoor, living history museums. A document, signed by M. T. Gray, General Manager of the Niagara Parks Commission and containing some handwritten notes and additions that are recognizable as being in McQuesten's hand, justifies and elaborates on this theme:

> *The existence of these restored buildings provides a means of showing students of history actual conditions as they existed at the time the events took place— much more forcibly than hours of reading. Restoration work is one of the prime duties of the Commission.* (W-MCP7-1.170, Feb 19 1944)

Some forts had been significantly modified through time, and deciding which version to rebuild became a judgment call. Authenticity was often impossible to achieve. McQuesten and Somerville would have weighed these decisions carefully, electing to include those elements that would attract students and the public on both sides of the border and would further the teaching of history. For instance, between 1832 and 1837, a second fort was built on the site of the first Fort Henry, and it is not the first fort, but the second which was rebuilt and stands today. Conversely, at Fort George, McQuesten and Somerville chose to reconstruct the first fort since it was the one that had opposed the Americans in the War of 1812.

It is difficult to know how many forts were either fully or partially restored by T.B. McQuesten in concert with the Niagara Parks Commission and Department of Highways. With regards to the Niagara area, however, an NPC document from late 1943 states, *Projects for the restoration of historic sites have occupied an important place in the work of the Niagara Parks Commission for almost a decade* (W-MCP7-1.154, Nov 10 1943).

FORT HENRY, KINGSTON, ONTARIO

FORT HENRY, minutes from downtown Kingston, Ontario, is centrally and strategically located between the cities of Montreal, Ottawa and Toronto. Here, Lake Ontario, the St. Lawrence River and the Rideau Canal meet.

Old Fort Henry was a nineteenth-century British military fortress that dates back to the War of 1812. It was used when border conflict occurred or was anticipated. The War of 1812 was the last of what could be deemed a war involving the border between the United States and its northern neighbour; however, serious tensions

Large Martello tower at Fort Henry
(Courtesy of Fort Henry National Site of Canada)

remained, and flared up from time to time afterwards. In 1816 for instance, strife ensued when the U.S. established high tariffs against British imports to protect American manufacturers and farmers. A naval arms race developed in the Great Lakes region, and several incidents occurred on the Great Lakes as the British exercised what they believed was their right to search U.S. ships.

In 1817, the U.S. War Department sent two expeditions to the south shore of Lake Superior to remove British flags and to establish U.S. influence in what was essentially "Indian country." While hostility remained on both sides for some time, the British and Americans were able to resolve their conflict and no war ensued. Britain and the United States were both liberal powers—one a constitutional monarchy, the other a republic. In 1818 the U.S. and Britain produced an agreement for disarmament on the Great Lakes. Each power was to have no more than four warships on the Great Lakes and no ship was to exceed 100 tons.

Fort Henry was rebuilt between 1832 and 1836 as part of a large-scale system of defense to protect the town of Kingston, the Royal Naval Dockyards on Point Frederick, and the entrance to the recently completed Rideau Canal. The Rebellion of Upper Canada in 1837-38 created some further hostilities between U.S. and Canadian interests, which persisted for a number of years.

During a period of heightened border tensions with the United States in 1846 to 1848, the fort was strengthened by the addition of four new large Martello towers— circular masonry towers so thick that they could withstand prolonged periods of cannon fire. Two smaller towers had been built as part of Old Fort Henry; all six survive today. Dry moats lead from the fort down to the St. Lawrence, ending at the large towers on the waterfront. The moats were intended to make it difficult for attacking forces to completely surround the fort.

Fort Henry was used by the British Army until 1870, when Queen Victoria's troops were pulled out of Canada. The Royal Canadian Horse Artillery, one of the first units in the newly formed Canadian Army, was based at the fort. During World War One the fort was used as an internment camp for political prisoners. After the war it no longer had value as a military base and was abandoned and allowed to deteriorate.

Work began on restoring the badly deteriorated structure in the 1930s as a make-work project funded by the Provincial and Federal governments during the Depression. More than a thousand labourers were employed for two years, but the key work of rebuilding some of the masonry structures such as the series of corbelled arches was done by experienced highly skilled masons. In a recent e-mail correspondence with Ron Ridley, curator of the Fort Henry Museum, Mr. Ridley comments on McQuesten's influence on who was hired for the reconstruction:

> The stone work was magnificent and required experienced stone masons, so they hired all the stone masons in the surrounding area to restore the fort. The family of one of those employees from Frid Construction has now donated some photos of the reconstruction to the Fort Henry archives.
>
> McQuesten appears to have used his influence to have Frid Construction from Hamilton appointed the contractor on the project and they used partial Hamilton and partial Kingston workers on the project, which was completed in an amazing two years. The project was massive as the Fort was in a terrible state of deterioration. The Fort was opened by Prime Minister Mackenzie King on 1st August 1938. (Jun 24, 2009)

To bring his restoration plans to fruition, McQuesten formed a close collaboration with Ronald L. Way, a recent graduate in history from Queen's University who had an

Restoration work, Fort Henry. Note damaged corbelled arches behind scaffolding.
Ronald L. Way is on the left. *(Photo courtesy of: Fort Henry National Site of Canada)*

Aerial view of restored Fort Henry

interest in military fortifications. Tom hired this talented young professional in 1936 to research the historical details of the fort. Besides restoring, as much as possible, the authentic feel of the buildings, Way was one of Canada's earliest innovators in the "living museum" approach to re-creating the world of 19th century military life in Ontario. He brought in students mostly from Queen's University, to be trained and drilled to a high standard and to perform precision military demonstrations. The lives of such civilians in the fort as schoolteachers and soldiers' wives were also represented.

Ronald Way went on to have an outstanding career as one of the country's finest restorers of historical sites. He worked on such sites as Upper Canada Village and the fortress of Louisbourg on Cape Breton Island. The challenge of achieving restorations with an authentic look and feel, given the limited resources available, was not trivial. Mr. Way's professional opinions were sought out for many projects in Canada and elsewhere. Again, McQuesten employed his tactic of seeking out the top individuals in the appropriate fields for his projects.

When World War II began one year after restoration work was completed, the Federal Government decided to use Fort Henry as a prisoner of war camp. McQuesten strongly advised against this in a memorandum (quoted here per Ron Ridley's e-mail of June 2009):

> I have absolutely no objection to the use of any property that is suitable for any war purpose—I cannot state that too strongly at the outset—but I know this property is not suitable. The buildings are vaulted and filled with earth and extremely unhealthy and it would be an outrage to house in them either troops or interned aliens. It was used for a short time by aliens in 1914,

but it was found to be unsuitable and they were sent to Kapuskasing. This experience should not have to be repeated.

I understand that now an engineer officer is going over the fort, with a view to heating it. Such a proposal is absurd. About one quarter of the rooms could be heated, the others cannot be. Please understand that I am not objecting to any sensible thing, but I suggest using this for the purpose outlined is not sensible and in the best interests of the administration. Very considerable patriotic interest is associated with the property and it might continue to be used to this end. The Province has a considerable collection in the Museum within the Fort. This, of course, would have to be removed entirely.

On behalf of this Province, may I request that consideration be given to a proposal that it be abandoned for war purposes, or for at least any such war purposes as involve the housing of troops or aliens on the premises. This Province has gladly put at the disposition of your Department many other of its facilities and resources but I do respectfully request that the present proposed uses for this property were abandoned.

Ronald Way made the same appeal to the Prime Minister but their requests were to no avail. Following the war, Fort Henry was reopened in 1948. T.B. McQuesten died on January 13, 1948 so he did not see the reopening of the fort. The Kingston *Whig Standard*, in an obituary statement, applauded McQuesten for his "persistent" efforts in its restoration:

[McQuesten] campaigned persistently to put an end to the policy of inaction that had allowed parts of the fort to crumble into ruin, and it was largely due to his efforts that the Federal Government agreed to restore Fort Henry, with the Ontario Government paying part of the cost. The fort then became the property of the Ontario Department of Highways, and its subsequent record of popularity as an historical monument testifies to the wisdom of Mr. McQuesten's judgment. When Fort Henry is again opened to the public, after serving the Federal Government during the war years, it would be fitting if due acknowledgement were made of Mr. McQuesten's part in having it restored to the public in the first place, after so many years of slow decay. (W-MCP7-1.266)

It appears that McQuesten was "forgotten" during both openings of Fort Henry, 1938 and 1948. Regarding the 1938 opening, Mackenzie King stated:

While very tired I felt more at ease at the dinner than I had felt in the afternoon gathering, and was able to say a few things which helped to compensate for what had been omitted in the afternoon speech. However, the place for them would have been at the Fort and at the time of the broadcast, particularly references to Mr. Way and Mr. McQuesten. (Mecredy 90)

Fort Henry has since been designated a National Historic Site. The cost of undoing the wartime modifications and restoring the structure to its pre-war condition cost almost as much as the original restorations.

**Painting of John Graves Simcoe arriving at Navy Hall
for the opening of Upper Canada's first parliament in 1792**
(Photo courtesy of Niagara Falls Public Library)

NIAGARA RIVER FORTS—FORT GEORGE AND OLD FORT ERIE

FORT GEORGE is located on the Niagara River where the river empties into Lake Ontario near Niagara-on-the-Lake. It was built by the British Army after the Jay Treaty (1796), at which time Britain agreed to withdraw from Fort Niagara just across the river on the American side. Named after John Jay, the American politician and statesmen who negotiated it, this treaty helped resolve numerous issues left over from the American Revolution. It resulted in ten years of peace and trade between the Americans and the British, during which the latter fought the French following the French Revolution. One issue that irked the Americans was the fact that some forts on American territory were still occupied by British troops well after the American War of Independence had ended. One of them was Fort Niagara, which had been granted to the United States in the Treaty of Paris in 1783, but remained in British hands for 13 years.

Fort George was built by Lieutenant-Governor Simcoe between 1796 and 1802 as a replacement for the loss of Fort Niagara. It became the headquarters for the British Army, the local militia and the Indian Department. The imposing new fort stood guard over transportation on the Niagara River and protected Navy Hall, a vital warehouse and wharf facility that was the site of Upper Canada's first provincial parliament in 1792. Navy Hall is a wooden structure encased within a stone structure that was used as a dining hall by officers from nearby Fort George.

Fort George quickly became the most important British post on the Niagara frontier, functioning as the major command post for the area. Six earth and log bastions were built and linked by earth walls and a dry ditch which surround the structure. Wooden poles twelve feet high were dug into the ground on these walls,

Original Stone Powder Magazine, Fort George
(photo courtesy Fort George)

creating a stockade similar to the forts of the wild west. Five stoutly constructed barracks, separate officers' quarters, storehouses, a kitchen, a guardhouse and a gunpowder magazine were built inside the enclosure. With the exception of the stone powder magazine, the buildings were constructed of wood.

Unfortunately the fort was within cannon range of Fort Niagara. During the War of 1812, American cannon badly damaged it before U.S. soldiers crossed the river in overwhelming numbers and captured the fort. The American forces then advanced down the Niagara Peninsula to Stoney Creek where they, in turn, were decisively defeated, and retreated back to the border.

In December of 1813, British forces reoccupied Fort George and, not to be outdone by the Americans, captured Fort Niagara and held it until the end of the war, then promptly returned it to the Americans. The fortifications at Fort George, now a wreck, were partially rebuilt. But by the 1820s they were allowed to deteriorate, as the location of the fort proved to be strategically indefensible. Hence Fort George was abandoned as a meaningful strong point.

A little over a century later, Thomas McQuesten worked with Somerville to reconstruct the fort. Work began in 1937 and was completed in 1940. Here again, considerable thought went into deciding which of the forts that had been built on the site would be reconstructed. McQuesten states in the 1943 annual NPC report:

Perhaps the most important decision connected with the restoration of Fort George was choice of the period in its history to be represented by its construction. The first fort had opposed the Americans in the war of 1812. There General Brock, the hero of Upper Canada, had his head-quarters [sic] and there

Fort George, Niagara-on-the-Lake, Ontario

Left: Fort George Barracks

(photos courtesy of Niagara Falls Public Library)

Below:
Fort GeorgeArtillery

he was buried after the Battle of Queenston Heights in 1812. The second Fort George, constructed by the Americans and afterwards garrisoned by the British for only a short time, was never attacked and has had few historical associations for Canadians. For these reasons, it was decided that Fort George might be best restored to its original state as built by the orders of Lieutenant-Governor Simcoe in 1796. (W-MCP7-1.154, Nov 10 1943)

For the restored Navy Hall, Matt Broman designed the gates, which were made by Fred Flatman in 1943. The dates on the gates, 1787 to 1937, represent an anniversary of 150 years. During wartime, metal was difficult to purchase and it was even more difficult to justify its use for purposes of art, so the gates were made of re-used historical

Restored Navy Hall dock,
Niagara River 1940
(Courtesy of Niagara Falls Public Library)

Restored Navy Hall, Fort George,
now a museum
(Courtesy of Niagara Falls Public Library)

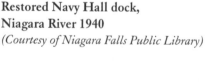

**Gates designed by Matt Broman
for restored Navy Hall,
made by Fred Flatman in 1943**
*(Courtesy of Niagara Falls
Public Library)*

materials. The maple leaves were forged from scrap and old spikes; the inner frame was fabricated from old park restaurant railings and tomb rails from the Drummond Hill Cemetery; the bands were forged from old Victoria Park railing and old spikes; and the figures were forged from an old piece of wagon tire (W-MCP7-1.145, Nov 10 1943). Flatman, as we have seen, was the metalworker/artist who made the Hendrie gates at RBG and the iron flowers in the Whitehern garden.

Restored Old Fort Erie

OLD FORT ERIE is situated at the opposite end of the Niagara River, where the river originates at Lake Erie. It was the first British fort to be constructed as part of a network of forts along the Great Lakes after the British won the Seven Years' War (British and French, 1756-63). The original fort, built in 1764, was located on the river's edge below the present restoration. For the next 50 years, Fort Erie served as a supply depot and as a port for ships transporting merchandise, troops and passengers to the Upper Great Lakes.

During the War of 1812 the fort was the site of a number of engagements. In 1813 it was briefly occupied by American forces who withdrew soon afterwards. In July 1814, defended by only a small number of British soldiers, the fort was once again captured, this time by 4,500 Americans. A determined British counterattack in August was a bloody failure with a large number of casualties, making this little fort the site of the bloodiest battle in Canadian history.

A few months later, with winter approaching and a lack of supplies, the Americans once again withdrew of their own accord, but only after blowing up the fort. The war ended in December. The damage to the fort was so complete that Lord Wellington reported thus, in fine British form, on what was left in 1825: ***The remains of an old fort, and a range of barracks perfectly in ruins and abandoned*** (W-MCP7-1.154, Nov 10 1943).

After the war the base was briefly occupied by the military but was soon permanently abandoned. Just after the American Civil War ended in 1866, a group of Fenians attempted to invade Canada in the cause of Ireland's independence from Britain. They briefly used the fort ruins as a temporary base but were quickly routed, retreating back across the river to the American side.

Old Fort Erie was rebuilt by the Niagara Parks Commission in 1937-39 under T.B. McQuesten with Somerville as the architect, and was jointly sponsored by the Provincial and Federal Governments. The fort was restored to the 1812-14 period, and officially reopened July 1, 1939. The objective was the reconstruction of the third fort as it stood in its most famous hour—the night of the British assault, August 14, 1814 (W-MCP7-1.154, Nov 10 1943). Today the fort is home to historical artefacts and re-enactments.

Restored Old Fort Erie, 1939
(Courtesy of Niagara Falls
Public Library)

Replica of Old Fort William near Thunder Bay

OLD FORT WILLIAM, THUNDER BAY

McQuesten's association with the restorations at Fort William is difficult to trace. He was involved in early plans for the reconstruction in the late 1930s and 1940s while building the Northern Ontario highway system that links Fort William (Thunder Bay), Nipigon, Geraldton, Longlac and Hearst. His Highways and Northern Development departments were connected with the early planning and restoration project for Fort William, and he helped to assemble period furniture, equipment, guns and other fittings for the reconstruction (Minnes 11).

A series of clippings from the *Times Journal* for 1938 and 1939, supplied to me by the Thunder Bay museum, indicate that the Dominion and Provincial Governments had some interest in backing the proposal to erect a replica of the Hudson's Bay Company Fort at Fort William. W.M. Babcock, a Minnesota archaeologist and museum curator, was hired for the job, and provided lectures and graphic stories of the founding of Fort William and the "romance of fur trading" (Aug 27, 29 1938). He described canoes of three tons capacity, loaded with furs and provisions that traveled up the lakes system from Montreal. Another clipping states: "The federal government, in connection with its program of expenditures for the relief of unemployment, has set aside the sum of $450,000 to assist in projects such as this" (Jun 11 1938). McQuesten administered the relief program in the Northern Highways portfolio and may have directed some of these monies to any costs incurred for the Fort William project.

A later clipping reads, "The Dominion government has been doing some historical reconstruction work at different places in the Dominion, through the Historical Sites and Monuments Board, and as Fort William was the fur-trading capital of Canada for half a century we believe some tangible evidence should be shown of its importance in Canada's historic past" (Jan 25 1939). And on Feb. 6, 1939:

> Aid Coming for Replica of Old Fort, Province Officials Will Co-operate in Proposed Scheme. Through the departments of highways and lands and forests, the Ontario Government will co-operate with Fort William and the Thunder Bay Historical Society in furthering the proposal to erect a replica of the fur-trading post from which this city developed.... The Ontario Highways department, from the standpoint of tourist traffic, is keenly interested in the plan to build here a fort and stockade similar to the original buildings that have vanished with the years. ... R.M. Smith, deputy minister of highways [under T.B. McQuesten], stated that reconstruction of old Fort Henry at Kingston, Ontario, multiplied tourist traffic to that region to a remarkable degree.

The discussions and planning came to an end with the coming of the Second World War. McQuesten resigned from the Highways portfolio in 1943, and he died in 1948. Another quarter of a century would elapse before any concrete action was taken at Fort William.

The actual reconstruction began in earnest in 1968 with an archaeological dig led by Lakehead University of what remained of the original site. In January 1971, Premier John Robarts announced that there would be a reconstruction of Fort William at a new location about 16 kilometres from the original site. The fort had closed in the 1880s and all of the original buildings were torn down; the site had since become an industrial area.

The new location was at Pointe de Meuron near the mouth of the Kaministiquia River. This site had historic links to the original Fort William, being used as an encampment by de Meuron mercenaries who helped Lord Selkirk of the Hudson Bay Company take over Fort William in August of 1816. On July 3, 1973, Queen Elizabeth II and Prince Philip officially opened Old Fort William Historical Park. Most of the buildings, however, were completed later during the 1970s.

McQuesten would have been interested in re-creating the settlement period, the battles, and the relationships of traders and aboriginals. The fur trade sent European trade goods and men into the interior of North America in search of the prized beaver pelt, valued because its properties made it ideal for the production of felt top hats, an essential fashion item for men in Europe. As the trade reached its peak in the late eighteenth and early nineteenth centuries, one of the largest and most powerful participants was the North West Company of Montreal. The fur trade grew so large and prosperous that the company amassed a great fortune from their ever-expanding territory. The Fort William post, at the half-way point between Montreal and the farther western posts, was the inland headquarters of the North West Company. The voyageurs could bring goods from the east and pelts from the west, meet at the headquarters, and make it home before winter.

Main gate and fortifications, *(courtesy)* **Old Fort William**

Reconstructed **OLD FORT WILLIAM** sits on 225 acres with 40 buildings which display the fur trade, heritage farming, medicine and crafts. During re-enactments the fictional conflicts reflect action from the Napoleonic Wars and the War of 1812, providing visitors with a close-up look at what period warfare was like during the early nineteenth century. At such times, Fort William Historical Park is awash with redcoats, bluecoats, militia, muskets, wall guns and cannons as re-enactors from the U.S. and Canada put on a colourful show. Smoke and fire abound as they demonstrate battle tactics from the early 19th century, with Fort William serving as the battlefield (www.fwhp.ca).

Chapter 38

OTHER HISTORICAL RESTORATIONS AND CONSTRUCTIONS

"McQuesten acted with characteristic stealth to rebuild Brant's home into a museum and park." (M.J.A.)

CHIEF JOSEPH BRANT MUSEUM, BURLINGTON

While constructing and improving highways around Hamilton and Burlington, McQuesten was determined to rebuild the home of Chief Joseph Brant before it was demolished. His proposal was voted down, but Tom felt so strongly about the historic value of Chief Joseph Brant and his house that he acted with characteristic stealth to rebuild Brant's home into a museum and park. He managed to absorb the restoration costs into his budget for the nearby QEW. It is impossible to say how many restorations Tom accomplished in this quiet way, or to what extent. He was resourceful, and history has justified his actions.

Joseph Brant Museum, Burlington, Ontario

Chief Joseph Brant (1742-1807), the Mohawk Chief Thayendanegea, was a legendary Mohawk warrior and diplomat admired for his courage and oratory. He inherited the status of Mohawk Chief from his father. He was also the Principal Chief of the Six Nations natives, a Christian missionary of the Anglican Church, and a Freemason. His Mohawk name, Thayendanegea, means "two sticks bound together in unified strength," a symbolism that Tom would have appreciated.

Brant served as a British military officer during the Seven Years' War and the American Revolution. With the help of the Iroquois, he fought for the British against the Americans. In 1777 a Treaty of Alliance was agreed upon between the British and the Iroquois, and Brant was acknowledged as War Chief of the Six Nations. After the war he led his people from the Ohio Territory to Upper Canada (now Ontario). In 1780 he was made a Captain in the British Army. For his service the Mohawk leader was also given a pension and 3,450 acres of land (1400h) at the head of Lake Ontario (Burlington).

Captain Joseph Brant (Thayendanegea)
Portrait painted by Gilbert Stuart, in the 1786
Collection of the Duke of Northumberland.
This is the portrait favoured by Brant's daughter;
it portrays Brant's sense of vision for his people.

On the occasion of Brant's trip to England to negotiate the role of the Iroquois Confederation of the Six Nations, a portrait was painted of Joseph Brant wearing the silver gorget (or piece of armour for the throat) presented to him by King George III.[31] Brant made a second trip to England in 1786 to gain assurances from the King of the rights of his people to regain what had been taken from them during the various wars.

In 1800, Brant built a house of cedar logs in Burlington; it was later covered by white frame siding. The building deteriorated over the years until Tom rebuilt it as a museum in 1937-38. Its doors opened as a one-room exhibit gallery in June 1942. Today the museum has more than 2,200 square feet of exhibit space and houses more than 10,000 artefacts, including such personal items as Brant's Masonic ring.

Brant sold off some of his land in Burlington. A parcel was purchased by the Brant Inn, which became a famous entertainment locale; and the Joseph Brant Hospital now sits on land formerly owned by Brant. The stained glass window in the hospital prayer room represents a native symbol for peace: The Tree of Peace.

BATTLEFIELD HOUSE AND PARK, STONEY CREEK

It is not known positively whether T.B. McQuesten participated in the restoration of Battlefield House and Park in Stoney Creek, even though it was near his home in Hamilton. Tom was a member of the Parks Board and Chairman of the Works Committee from 1922-47, but Battlefield House was privately owned by the Women's Wentworth Historical Society (WWHS), and did not come under his jurisdiction.

The Women's Wentworth Historical Society under Sara Calder was formed in 1899 as the result of a difference of opinion with the men in the society. The women had determined to build a monument to commemorate the decisive engagement of the War of 1812 on the grounds of the Gage family house, where the battle was fought; but the men wanted to build it at Smith's Knoll. The result was that the women formed their own society and two monuments were built.

In 1908 the federal government granted $5,000 to the WWHS toward their monument. Problems securing government funding caused construction delays throughout 1911. Work recommenced in 1912 when the Department of Militia and Defense guaranteed additional funds. The entire cost was approximately $12,000.[32]

---

[31] http://www.museumsofburlington.com/JBMuseum
[32] www.battlefieldhouse.ca/monument.asp

On the hundredth anniversary of the peace, the Women's Society opened the restored and refurbished house, the grounds around it, and the new monument, as Battlefield Park. It was here, on June 6, 1813, that the Battle of Stoney Creek took place. The dedication stone on the monument reads, in part:

> THEY WERE ENCAMPED IN THIS IMMEDIATE VICINITY WITH STAFF HEADQUARTERS IN THE GAGE FARM HOUSE, NOW MAINTAINED BY THE WOMENS WENTWORTH HISTORICAL SOCIETY THROUGH WHOSE REPRESENTATIONS AND UNDER WHOSE DIRECTION THIS MEMORIAL WAS BUILT.
>
> IN THE DEAD OF NIGHT THE BRITISH ADVANCED FROM BURLINGTON HEIGHTS AND SURPRISING THE ENEMY, PUT HIM TO CONFUSION. THIS IS HELD TO HAVE BEEN THE DECISIVE ENGAGEMENT IN THE WAR OF 1812-13.

It is a credit to the Gage family, who owned the property at the time of the War, that they took in the wounded with no regard for which side they were on. Battlefield House & Park, being the battlefield on which the peace was won, is an important site for commemoration of the War of 1812-13. A re-enactment of the decisive battle is held there every year in June.

Tom McQuesten became Minister of Highways and Chairman of the Niagara Parks Commission in 1934, and through these connections accomplished many historical restorations. When we understand the depth of Tom's interest in local history and the War of 1812, it is difficult to conceive that he would have ignored Battlefield House and Monument, especially since he employed ingenious measures to achieve other restorations such as the Joseph Brant Museum in 1937-38.

George Seibel writes: "the Niagara Parks Commission had taken an interest in Battlefield since 1924 with an annual grant of $1,000 changed to $800 annually in 1933" (276). These monies would have come under McQuesten's supervision when he served as Chairman of the Niagara Parks Commission and Minister of Highways

---

Some of McQuesten's Restorations and Reconstructions:

-Joseph Brant Museum, Burlington
-Battlefield House, Stoney Creek
-MacNab Street Presbyterian Church, Hamilton
-Brock's Monument, Queenston Heights near Fort George
-Home of William Lyon Mackenzie, Queenston

Some of McQuesten's Constructions:

-St. Thomas Psychiatric Hospital, Elgin County
-Construction of the Clifton Hill Memorial Arch at Niagara on the
  100th anniversary of the establishment of Responsible Government
-Queenston Heights Restaurant, Table Rock House, Refectory or Park
  Restaurant, Administration Building

(Left)
Battlefield Monument erected by the Women's Wentworth Historical Society, 1913

(Photos from Hamilton Public Library)

(Below) Battlefield House, Stoney Creek, restored 1980

and of Public Works in 1934-44, and may have been used for maintenance or restorations to Battlefield House, Monument and gardens. Wages at the time were often 15 to 20 cents per hour or even $1.00 per day, so the $800 would have paid for a great deal of labour.

In 1950, Howard Dunington-Grubb drew up plans for the grounds, but the WWHS was unable to raise the funds to implement them. Presumably the annual grant was being used for other purposes. Some records have been lost, so it is not known to what extent, if any, the plans may have been utilized at Battlefield Park. Had McQuesten lived and remained in his position beyond 1944, it is possible that the Dunington-Grubb plans (copies of which are kept at Battlefield House) might have been more fully implemented. Restoration planning is currently afoot to actualize Dunington-Grubb's vision (S. Ramsay, curator).

Major restorations took place after 1960 when the Federal and Provincial Governments combined to contribute $75,000 to the cost of acquiring the adjacent Smith property and restoring Battlefield Monument, House and gardens.

In 1962 the WWHS transferred the deed of the original Gage House to the Niagara Parks Commission (Seibel 276). Sara Calder and The Women's Wentworth Historical Society must be accorded a great deal of credit for their dedication to history and its preservation. The society disbanded in 1982. After Hamilton amalgamated with the surrounding communities on January 1, 2001, Battlefield House Museum & Park became a member of the Hamilton Civic Museums, and is now a National Historic Site.

MacNab Street Presbyterian Church

RESTORATION OF MACNAB STREET PRESBYTERIAN CHURCH

The McQuesten family regularly attended MacNab Street Presbyterian Church near Whitehern. Tom and his law partner, James Chisholm gave their time on the Board of Managers for many years. In 1934-35, T.B. McQuesten, with the help of Chisholm and W. L. Somerville, accomplished the renovation and restoration of the church.

John Best describes their contribution to the restoration: "[Tom and Chisholm] had organized the Gothic-revival restoration of the church interior in the 1930s, financing the project with a bequest from a client who had died without heir. . . . Both men had commissioned memorial stained glass as well" (185). The *Hamilton Herald* announced that a stained glass window was donated by T.B. McQuesten in "memory of Dr. Calvin McQuesten the grandfather, and one of the elders of the church" (Jan 10 1936). Tom's grandfather had donated funds to help build the church in Hamilton. Dr. McQuesten had been raised in the American Presbyterian Church in New Hampshire; therefore, MacNab Church had its roots in the American Presbyterian tradition. This is another connection with the U.S. and another reason why Tom worked so hard to ensure continued peace between the U.S. and Canada. He would have seen it as a Christian duty.

The *Herald* reported further that the old post office clock would be preserved and moved to MacNab Street Church, "arranged and donated by T.B. McQuesten" (Nov 2 1936). The stained glass windows in the church are "considered the finest example of Scottish stained glass in Canada" (Bailey, *Wee Kirks* 92).

Unfortunately, the TH&B railroad ran a track separating Whitehern from the church, which Tom and Noulan Cauchon attempted unsuccessfully to fight. Tom never forgave the railroad company, and devoted his efforts to the automobile, building roads and bridges.

In 1990, MacNab Street Presbyterian Church dedicated a yellow rose with an amber centre to the McQuesten family and their Whitehern garden. They named it the T.B. McQuesten Rose and presented seven rose bushes to Whitehern, one for each of the McQuesten children (Muriel died in infancy). Only the rose bushes at the church have survived. Plans are being made to reintroduce the McQuesten Rose to the Whitehern garden as part of the on-going restoration work, and to have it re-dedicated at Whitehern in 2011, the one-hundredth anniversary of Ruby's death. The rose would also be appropriate in the collections of Gage Park, RBG and the Niagara Rose gardens, since these gardens have grown and flourished as a result of Tom's vision and his key role in their development.

CONSTRUCTION OF ST. THOMAS PSYCHIATRIC HOSPITAL

T.B. McQuesten as Minister of Public Works, and W.L. Somerville, acknowledged as being one of Canada's leading architects, collaborated on the

building of the much-needed St. Thomas Psychiatric Hospital in Elgin County. Landscape plans were prepared by the Dunington-Grubbs in 1938. The project, completed in 1939 at a cost of $6,000,000, would have been important to Tom McQuesten's social conscience since several members of his family suffered from mental illness (see W2511 footnotes).

St Thomas Psychiatric Hospital

Initially the building was used as a temporary training centre for the Royal Canadian Air Force at the outbreak of the Second World War. In 1945 it opened as a hospital for the treatment of mental illness. It was the most modern and up-to-date hospital in the province of Ontario (Guelph McLaughlin Archives).

The hospital's *Encounter* publication echoes McQuesten's priorities regarding the therapeutic qualities of beauty: "Completed, the new hospital and grounds promise to be one of the points of interest in Western Ontario. Special attention is being given to the architectural design of the buildings and to the beautification of the grounds—

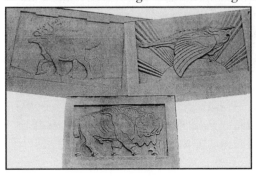

harmonious surroundings having been found to be very important in the treatment of mental illness." The main buildings are finished in stone, at

St Thomas Psychiatric Hospital bas relief sculptures in Canadian designs of elk heron and bison

McQuesten's precise recommendation, and display some of the Canadiana relief sculpture (featuring elk, bison, heron) that Somerville and McQuesten favoured. The hospital's Art Deco entrance is particularly impressive.

SIR ISAAC BROCK'S MONUMENT, QUEENSTON HEIGHTS

The present monument to Sir Isaac Brock, a hero of the War of 1812, was completed in 1856; its care was vested in the Niagara Parks' Commissioners in 1895. The 210-foot-high (64m) column has withstood storms and damage over the years. Being carefully repaired, it remains impressive. Maintenance of all military monuments and burial grounds at Niagara is the responsibility of the NPC (Way 209).

In 1941, "a tablet listing the members of the regular army, the Canadian militia and the Indian warriors killed in the Battle of Queenston Heights was attached to the memorial and unveiled in an impressive ceremony" (Way 207). The original inscription referred solely to Brock and his aide-de-camp, John Macdonell, who were both mortally wounded during battles of 1812.

Ronald Way also notes that the maintenance of all military monuments and burial grounds at Niagara is the responsibility of the Commissioners. This includes the monument commemorating Laura Secord's heroic journey of twenty miles on foot from Queenston to Beaver Dams to warn the British of an impending American attack. As a result of her action, Fitzgibbon captured 500 troops, 50 cavalry and 2 field-pieces. Drummond Hill Cemetery and Butler's cemetery and grounds have also undergone regular maintenance and preservation, and today many tourists visit these resting places of brave men and women of centuries past (Way 209). The magnificent gardens in these various locations receive regular planting and tending by Parks staff.

Sir Isaac Brock's Monument and Queenston Restaurant, Queenston Heights

RESTORATION OF WILLIAM LYON MACKENZIE'S HOUSE, QUEENSTON

William Lyon Mackenzie (1795-1861) was the leader of the Rebellion of Upper Canada which began in 1837. Nearly a century later (1936), T.B. McQuesten and

his associate, architect W.L. Somerville, undertook the restoration of the stone house at Queenston where Mackenzie lived from 1823 to 1824. This is where he began publishing his controversial paper, the *Colonial Advocate* and became known as a rebel. In his newspaper Mackenzie openly criticized the oligarchy of aristocratic families informally known as the Family Compact—a group of wealthy merchants who controlled the business and politics of the province and ensured that power remained within their small corrupt clique.

In 1828 Mackenzie won a seat in the 10th Parliament of Upper Canada (present-day Ontario). He immediately began agitating for reforms, gradually becoming something of a troublemaker. After years of ineffective struggle, he determined in the fall of 1837

William Lyon Mackenzie (1795-1861)

that violent rebellion would be necessary to effect change. With his reform leaders and some disaffected members of the Family Compact, Mackenzie called for an armed demonstration to take control of the government. After several delays and disappointments, Mackenzie managed to arm a group of reformers at Montgomery's Tavern in Toronto and they marched down Yonge Street.

While Mackenzie delayed, Col. Allan MacNab managed to recruit 1,000 loyal troops and on December 7, they marched on the rebels. In the ensuing Battle of Montgomery's Tavern, the Rebellion was quelled almost before it got started. Mackenzie's followers quickly surrendered after MacNab opened artillery fire, but Mackenzie escaped, and a proclamation offered a reward of one thousand pounds for his capture. MacNab was eventually knighted for his loyalty. Mackenzie is purported to have hidden in what became known as "Mackenzie's Cave" on the Sydenham Hill

above Dundas before he and other rebels were allowed to escape to the United States (Kaler, *The Dundas Connection*).

"Mackenzie's Cave"
Sydenham Hill, Dundas, Ontario
(photo courtesy of
Dundas Historical Museum)

Mackenzie went to Buffalo, N.Y. where, on December 13, 1837, he declared himself the head of a provisional government entitled the Republic of Canada. He then enlisted some Americans from the War of 1812 in a scheme to invade Upper Canada from Navy Island in the Niagara River. The American President, Martin Van Buren announced that participants would be prosecuted as criminals, and many of the volunteers returned home. On December 29, British troops and Canadian volunteers bombarded Navy Island, in the process destroying the *SS Caroline*, an American ship that was supplying Mackenzie's forces. Mackenzie was arrested in Buffalo but was released on bail; his American supporters grew disillusioned and withdrew from Navy Island. With the collapse of this scheme, Mackenzie settled in New York City in January 1838. Ever the reformer, he began editorializing on internal American politics and was soon embroiled in controversy again. Some rebels dedicated to the overthrow of British rule continued raids into Canada, using the U.S. as a base of operations until the raiding was decisively defeated, nearly a year after the Battle of Montgomery's Tavern.

In 1848 the Province of Canada was formed out of Upper and Lower Canada, and received responsible government. The reformers won in the next election, and in time the rebels of 1837 were granted amnesty. Mackenzie moved back to Toronto in May 1850 and resumed a career in politics.

It became evident over time that Mackenzie was never content with any form of government—British, Canadian or American—and always tried to reform the existing government wherever he was. History demonstrates that he was a radical and eccentric political reformer who was instrumental in breaking up the Family Compact. A controversial figure, he was both traitor and patriot. Later generations built on his reforms in forging Canadian institutions and establishing a national spirit of democracy, justice, and freedom from oppression.

Tom admired Mackenzie because he fought corruption and sought reforms along democratic lines. Tom also had a familial connection with the Mackenzie Rebellion in which his grandfather Dr. Calvin McQuesten, and cousin John Fisher, suffered hostility and danger in Hamilton because they were American (W-MCP4-6.193, quoted earlier).

Prime Minister William Lyon Mackenzie King (1874-1950), the grandson and namesake of William Lyon Mackenzie, was in office at the time of the restoration of Mackenzie's Queenston house. Mackenzie King

The Honourable William Lyon Mackenzie King
(Library & Archives Canada)

supported the project since it would enhance his grandfather's reputation and his own prestige. The site held special significance for King, as it was here that his father proposed to his mother, William Lyon Mackenzie's daughter. Tom arranged to further immortalize

Mackenzie in the proposed Clifton Gate Memorial Arch at Niagara Falls, which naturally pleased King and assisted McQuesten in gaining funding for restoration of the house.

In June 1938, the restored Mackenzie house became a museum, with a display of 500 years of printing technology that features one of the few original wooden presses remaining in the world. The museum was opened by Prime Minister Mackenzie King, who recorded the event

Mackenzie House and Printery with acacia trees, Queenston, Ontario

in his diary in typically devotional terms: "It was a deeply impressive sight. I felt I was on holy ground as I walked about where grandfather began his great battle for political liberty in Canada. The stone near the building carries the words The House of William Mackenzie. The Birthplace of Responsible Government in Canada."

Although McQuesten and King were on good terms at the time of the Mackenzie house unveiling, King as Prime Minister of Canada and Hepburn as Ontario Premier were particularly hostile to one another. They were in conflict over hydro rights that Hepburn wished to sell to Quebec, but that King refused to allow. King also had learned that Hepburn was planning an alliance against him with Quebec. Tom often had to tread a fine line between his premier and his prime minister. He was politically astute in choosing not to speak at the unveiling but, in King's words, "stood at the foot of the steps leaning against one of the large acacia trees," and left the speech-making to fellow commissioner Archie Haines (Best 128-29).

Hand Press used by William Lyon MacKenzie, now at his restored house in Queenston

(Ontario's Niagara Parks A History)

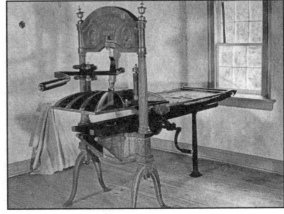

Chapter 39

CLIFTON GATE MEMORIAL ARCH, NIAGARA FALLS

"It would be hard to imagine any occasion could be of more historical significance.
I doubt, too, if ever beauty and history were combined as here today."
Prime Minister William Lyon Mackenzie King, 18 June 1938 (Best 129)

T.B. McQuesten and William Lyon Somerville, who shared similar political ideas
and ideals, collaborated on the design and execution of the Clifton Gate Memorial
Arch, built in 1938 at the entrance to the new Niagara Parkway in Niagara Falls. Four
bas-relief panels depict a nationalistic narrative of exploration, settlement, defence,
and the development of responsible government, including recognition of those who
participated one hundred years earlier in the 1837-38 Rebellion of Upper Canada.
One panel shows William Lyon Mackenzie presenting his Seventh Report to the
Upper Canada House of Assembly, in which he delivered the grievances Canadians
had experienced under the corrupt Family Compact.

**Clifton Gate Memorial Arch,
Niagara Falls, 1938**
(Demolished in 1968)
Note bas-relief sculptures on pillars

**Above: Bas-relief of Mackenzie
delivering grievances**

Tom also consulted with fellow Liberal William Lyon Mackenzie King, Prime
Minister of Canada at the time, on the design of the Clifton Gate Memorial Arch.
Needless to say, King was delighted with the plans to commemorate and vindicate his
grandfather and fellow rebels during the 1837-38 Rebellion. McQuesten requested

that the Prime Minister supply some Biblical passages appropriate for the dedication ceremony, which he did.

In their discussions, King expressed displeasure at Tom's plans to emphasize the Rebellion on this heroic monument: "I question in my mind the wisdom of associating responsible government too closely with the incident of the rebellion, since the real struggle had been going on years before." King suggested including, along with the names of rebels, the names of those whose "lives were lost upholding the Crown. They too were doing their duty . . . in support of King and country." This Tom did for him, although not quite with the exclusivity that King had anticipated.

**Clifton Gate Memorial Arch Dedication 1938
Prime Minister William Lyon Mackenzie King
and Hon. T.B. McQuesten**

T.B. McQuesten favoured some of Mackenzie's reforms, particularly those that were intent on the establishment of responsible government and the uprooting of patronage and corruption. The location of the Arch was intended as a symbolic recognition of the goals of the Rebellion and of the War of 1812, and of the peace

Dedication ceremonies for the Memorial Arch were held June 18, 1938 in Oakes Garden Theatre. Hon. T.B. McQuesten, Chairman of the Niagara Parks Commission is shown at the microphone. Honoured guests seated behind Mr. McQuesten include: second from the right, Sir William Mulock, Chief Justice of Ontario 1923-36; the Right Honourable William Lyon Mackenzie King, Prime Minister of Canada, who unveiled the Arch; Hon. C.D. Howe; William L. Houck M.L.A. for Niagara Falls Riding.

re-affirmed between Canada and the United States as a result. An inscription below the bas-relief panels reads:

This memorial was erected to honour the memory of the men and women
in this land throughout their generations who braved the wilderness,
maintained the settlements, performed the common task without praise or glory
and were the pioneers of political freedom and a system of responsible government
which became the cornerstone of the British Commonwealth of Nations.

Mackenzie King was invited by McQuesten to unveil the arch, and he wrote in his diary "accepted today an invitation . . . a significant fulfillment of God's Holy will." The unveiling took place on Saturday, June 18, 1938, the approximate hundredth anniversary of the end of the Rebellion of 1837-38. The event was triumphant for King, who stated, "my life has helped to mark, in no small part, the completion of Mackenzie's work." In his speech, King generously praised Tom and the Niagara Parks Commission: "It would be hard to imagine any occasion could be of more historical significance. I doubt, too, if ever beauty and history were combined as here today. We are assembled in what I believe to be the most beautiful spot in the world." (Best 127-29).

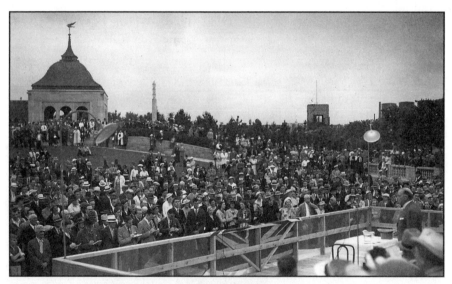

Mackenzie King (far right on stage) and crowd at Arch unveiling

The good relations between King and McQuesten did not last long. Once Mackenzie King was able to thoroughly examine the arch, he was shocked to find that along with the patriots' names were added those of raiders who had joined Mackenzie's struggle from the American side. Some were Yankees who attempted to turn the Canadian struggle for greater freedom into a revolution to set up a Republic of Upper Canada. Many of these had been executed as traitors. Nevertheless in Tom's view, they were also instrumental in bringing responsible government to Canada.

King was known for having a vindictive nature, and he remained angry with McQuesten for many years—an anger that would break out again during the Carillon controversy. His diary for that day complains of several other things, such as lack of promotion of the event, and the size of the arch: "a mere fifty feet in height was not monumental but merely ornamental, and not large enough for cars to pass through." The first complaint was not accurate, since radio stations had made many broadcasts. He also found the attendance inadequate since he had planned for a great national occasion, forgetting that the arch was a provincial project. A photograph from the event, however, shows a substantial crowd in attendance.

As a further affront to Mackenzie King, Ontario Premier Hepburn had his name inscribed on the arch near King's, and then declined to show up for the unveiling. This added to the already mutual animosity between the two which could break out with little provocation and now reached a new low.

**Carved Stone Medallion
of *HMS St. Lawrence*,
preserved in Toronto
near St. Lawrence market**

Thomas McQuesten managed to commemorate his own grandfather on the arch, which contained large medallions of two ships. One was the *HMS St. Lawrence*, the British ship on which Thomas Baker had served during the War of 1812. This powerful warship, the largest freshwater sailing vessel at the time, allowed the British to regain control of the Great Lakes in the War of 1812. The second ship, *The Griffin*, was that of the French explorer La Salle, who discovered Niagara Falls. The four large panels and the medallions were illustrated by C.W. Jefferys; the sculptor was Emanuel Hahn.

The art work, decorations and inscriptions were meant to be examined by pedestrians. When the time came to widen the road in 1968, no attempt was made to direct or move traffic around the arch, and it was demolished. By then Tom McQuesten had been dead for twenty years, and the last living member of the family— his brother, Calvin—died in 1968, leaving no one to speak for the preservation of the arch. However, some of the art work, the panels and the medallions were retrieved from the scrap yard, and have been preserved. The medallions are now on display in Toronto opposite the St. Lawrence Market on Front Street at Jarvis. The panel depicting William Lyon Mackenzie, along with some of the other panels, are displayed at the side of Mackenzie's Toronto house, which is now a museum.

**Side yard of Mackenzie House Museum
82 Bond St., Toronto**

Panel at left, Mackenzie delivering grievances to the Upper Canada
House of Assembly. Inscriptions are preserved on the wall at right.

Chapter 40

PARTISAN POLITICS AND McQUESTEN'S FORCED RESIGNATION

I resign herewith as Chairman and member of the Commission.
I understand the other members prefer to write you direct.

T.B.McQuesten, May 20 1944 (W-MCP7-1.150)

Although they were both Liberals, the strained relationship between Ontario Premier Mitchell Hepburn and Prime Minister William Lyon Mackenzie King continued to deteriorate in the late 1930s. In 1939 Hepburn severely criticized Mackenzie King for his insistence on accompanying King George VI and Queen Elizabeth during their tour across Canada: "Hepburn sees Mr. King's tour across Canada with Royalty as just a 'cheap publicity stunt.' I denounce it in no uncertain terms" (*Telegram*, Apr 27 1939). In 1940 Hepburn continued the attack: "Conduct Shameful declares Hepburn. Says King hogged the Royal Visit limelight" (*Telegram*, Jan 30 1940). King in turn was angry with Hepburn for a squabble over hydro rights. While the Prime Minister initially found Hepburn "promising," his opinion vacillated. He was not alone in this; even Hepburn's friends were concerned that his drinking and furious outbursts would create difficulties.

As the feuds deepened, Tom McQuesten found himself increasingly caught in the middle, like Ulysses between the proverbial Scylla and Charybdis, trying to anticipate and avoid a series of crises. For instance, Prime Minister Mackenzie King was severely criticized for his stand against conscription in Canada in World War II. Conversely, McQuesten and Hepburn believed that conscription and an all-out war effort was necessary. In January of 1940, Hepburn had declared in Parliament: "I stand firm in my statement that Mackenzie King has not done his duty to his country—never has and never

Hon. A.E. Matthews bows as he greets King George VI, May 22, 1939, Toronto

Premier Mitchell Hepburn and
Rt. Hon. Mackenzie King in background

will." He then read out a resolution, concluding with: "regrets by the House that the Federal Government at Ottawa has made so little effort to prosecute Canada's duty in the war in the vigorous manner the people of Canada desire to see." When Hepburn asked Robert Nixon to second the resolution and Nixon refused, Hepburn reportedly said to Tom, "Here, you are the President of the Liberal Association, second this" and when Tom obliged, King was infuriated (Best 141-2).

Hepburn, a Liberal, and Col. George A. Drew, Conservative Leader of the Opposition, joined in a "Fiery Attack on Mackenzie King in an outspoken charge against King's federal leadership in the National War Effort and a violent attack on the Prime Minister personally." The *Star* noted a revolt in the House: "Ten Liberals bolt Hepburn on war and thirty do not vote. Eighteen Conservatives line up with the Premier to censure Mr. King's policies . . . [and] the war record of Mr. King's administration at Ottawa. No mention of Mr. McQuesten on this" (Hamilton *Spectator*, Jan 19 1940). Obviously, McQuesten was attempting to avoid the cross-fire.

The rancor in Parliament continued into the following year. George Drew was particularly resentful of Premier Hepburn's failure, and that of his "lieutenant," Hon. T.B. McQuesten, to take their attacks on the King Government onto the previous spring's election platform. A few days later the *Star* carried the headline: "Hepburn and Drew in House Call Each Other Names . . . Verbal Slingshots" (Hamilton *Spectator*, Feb 19, 26 1941).

Despite the bad tempers in parliament, McQuesten attempted to continue his public works projects. Since highways were given preference in wartime, monies were made available for the Trans-Canada Highway. A railroad could be easily put out of commission by bombing, but roads and bridges were more easily repaired or circumvented. In March, 1941, the *Toronto Star* applauded McQuesten and his highway plans: "Highways are Indispensable Cogs in Canada's War Time Plans. The Department will spend more than fifteen million this year to extend the Queen Elizabeth from Niagara Falls to Fort Erie" (Mar 14 1941). At the same time, detractors criticized any beautification effort, since those funds could support the war effort. In answer to a Conservative question in parliament, it was disclosed that "grass on the QEW costs the province $58,862.95" (*Globe & Mail*, Mar 8 1941). Drew in particular was critical of the "sums spent refurbishing forts because the money spent on Fort Henry and Fort George could have purchased 48 fighter planes" (Best 153). In some cases, Thomas had to continue his restoration and beautification agenda covertly.

In 1942, Hepburn pushed his animosity for the Prime Minister too far and supported Mackenzie King's opponent in a Toronto by-election. King was politically much stronger than Hepburn. Both provincial and federal Liberal supporters thought the move an act of political suicide and called for Hepburn to step down. George Conant was designated interim Premier, and when a provincial Liberal leadership convention was held in May 1943, Hepburn finally tendered his resignation as leader, by telegram.

McQuesten made a very late entrance at the Ontario leadership convention. His platform was practical, stressing his successful leadership so far:

There will be no fanfare in my campaign; the times are too serious, the work ahead too important to the welfare of our people and our Party. In

conclusion, I offer you, ladies and gentlemen, my successful record in the posts of Minister of Highways, Municipal Affairs, Public Works; Chairman of the Niagara Parks Commission and Member of the Hydro Electric Commission of Ontario as concrete evidence that I have done these jobs well. From border to border of the Province there are visible improvements to further demonstrate my ability. I offer also my record as President of the Ontario Liberal Association and the way in which the Party was returned and retained in power and the manner in which we have held together and developed new strength and public prestige. (W-MCP7-1.264, Apr 17 1943)

T.B. McQuesten speaking

Tom did not receive the support he needed from Mackenzie King, who "begged off," doing nothing to help even though his own Liberal Party was in danger. It is likely that Tom's support of Hepburn cost him the votes he might have gained to eventually become party leader and premier himself. The Liberals lost 16 seats in 1943—the final tally of the popular vote showed the Conservatives with 37%, the CCF 32%, and the Liberals in third place at 31%. Robert Nixon was elected as the new party leader and Premier. Soon after, in the 1943 Ontario election, the Liberals under Nixon were routed, falling to third party status behind the Progressive Conservatives led by George Drew, and the Co-operative Commonwealth Federation (CCF).

Tom took some time off after his defeat in the election. When he returned, he

told a friend, "I was quite tired, and it took me a couple of months before I returned to the office . . . I started back at the office on the 1st of October. I find, after nine years very great changes in the firm's clients. Many have died or moved away. It will take more than a few months to re-establish my connections" (Best 174-75).

T.B. McQuesten speaking in 1940

PROGRESSIVE CONSERVATIVE GOVERNMENT IN ONTARIO

Progressive Conservative Premier George A. Drew, the 14th Premier of Ontario, was in office for the next five years (from August 17, 1943 to October 19, 1948), and

George Alexander Drew (1894-1973)
Premier of Ontario 1943-48

the Conservatives held Ontario for the next forty-two years. This, no doubt, is the major reason why Thomas McQuesten became the "Forgotten Builder." Partisan politicians tend to be biased in support of their own to the deliberate exclusion of others no matter how exemplary the record and status. By the time the Liberals returned to office with David Peterson (1985-90), so much time had elapsed that Tom McQuesten was easily forgotten.

It was not until 1988, when a Liberal Government reigned again, that the High Level Bridge was finally re-dedicated as the Thomas B. McQuesten High Level Bridge. After 1990, the Liberals would not be in office again until 2003 when Dalton McGuinty became Provincial Premier; he is now in his second term of office (2010).

Liberal Premier Hepburn had been swept to power in 1934 and T.B. along with him. McQuesten had a clear mandate to build and beautify under the Liberal Administration. He had been head of various Portfolios and Commissions and had accomplished much since that time. After the 1943 elections, Conservative Premier George Drew decided that the Liberal McQuesten should be replaced, in spite of Tom's tireless, selfless, exemplary work for Ontario.

Even before Drew was elected, he had begun a campaign of name-calling in the legislature. The *Globe & Mail* reported Drew's derision of McQuesten:

> Drew calls McQuesten 'Poo Bah' of Niagara [referring to the Gilbert & Sullivan comic opera, *The Mikado*]. The P.C. Leader told the Ontario Legislature yesterday that the Niagara Falls City Council had taken the proper course in trying to find out the limits of three government 'Commissions' in that city by sending telegrams to Premier George Conant [Liberal 1942-43] and the Minister of Highways, McQuesten himself. (Mar 31 1943)

Tom's election defeat in May 1943 immediately severed his connection with the Highways Department, but he still held his positions at Niagara. Tom sought legal advice to protect his position on the Niagara Bridge Commission, and received some assurance that the government could not interfere with that public position (Best 175).

Soon after the election, Drew began to put political pressure on T.B. McQuesten to curtail his construction and beautification agenda, which had flourished under the Liberals. The pressure initially took the form of criticism of some construction work as Drew began to find ways to fault Tom on several issues in the Niagara Parks.

He also demanded an audit of all of the commissioners, implying that some corrupt practices had taken place.

TOM'S FORCED RESIGNATION

A series of letters demonstrates the partisan nature of the chain of events that followed. Premier Drew obviously had to search for a reason to force a resignation from McQuesten. Drew began to "investigate" McQuesten's methods with a view to finding errors; the best that he could do was to criticize work on stone curbs in the park.

TO THE HON. T.B. MCQUESTEN K.C. from Premier George A. Drew (W-MCP7-1.146)
Whitehern, 41 Jackson Street West
Hamilton, Ontario

Office of
The Prime Minister & President of the Council
Toronto 2,
November 5, 1943

Dear Mr. McQuesten,

I have been intending for some time to have a talk with you about the Niagara Parks Commission and at your convenience would like to discuss the general situation there. In the meantime I thought I would convey my own views in regard to new construction.

When I was in Niagara Falls not long ago I noticed some work being done which I was told was for the purpose of putting in stone curbs in the park. It seems to me that anything but absolutely essential construction should be held in abeyance until the manpower situation eases. In fact, the holding back of such construction would seem to me to be part of our preparation for absorbing employment. I would ask that everything except actual maintenance construction should be stopped until we have a clear understanding of the necessity for the work and the part it will play in the general reconstruction programme.

While I am writing to you in regard to this matter I also want to explain that I have decided to have an independent audit of the various Commissions and I have arranged with Price Waterhouse and Company to conduct the audit of the Niagara Parks Commission. I believe this will help to start with a clear picture of the situation, and I would therefore ask that you give instructions to those in charge of the books of the Commission so that all the necessary records may be made available for this purpose.

Looking forward to seeing you at your early convenience, I am,
Yours Sincerely,
George A. Drew

In regards to Drew's complaint about the manpower situation, it was common knowledge that Tom always considered the employment situation and developed many work programs for the unemployed and for tradesmen. Three months later, Tom had Maxim T. Gray, the current General Manager of the Parks Commission, draw up a document titled *Post War Work* which also addresses its justification. This very thorough document appears to have combined the details of several discussions underway at the Niagara Parks Commission. The presentation of the document at this time, and its thoroughness, may well have been prompted by Drew's letter to

McQuesten. It also provides a justification for the restoration of forts that Drew had previously criticized. In several places the report notes that items have been under discussion for some time, which indicates that T.B. McQuesten had already planned ahead for this Post-War work (W-MCP7-1.170, Feb 19 1944).

There is little doubt that Drew would have been made aware of the *Post War Work* document, but he made no public response to it. This is not surprising since Tom was rigorously honest in his dealings. It is also not surprising that the auditors produced no stain on McQuesten's character or his honesty. The auditors declared their findings in March 1944 and, in spite of the time lapse of several months, they found no discrepancies in McQuesten's budget or bookkeeping. Tom expressed a desire to co-operate withDrew in every way, but Drew declined his offer.

After six months of searching, Drew could find no reason to have Tom dismissed, so in May 1944 he finally wrote to Tom with the only conclusion that he could muster, namely that Tom and the other members of the board should resign because they were not members of the Conservative Party.

TO HON. THOMAS B. MCQUESTEN, K.C. from Premier George Drew (W-MCP7-1.148)
Whitehern, 41 Jackson Street,
Hamilton, Ontario

Office of
The Prime Minister & President of the Council
Toronto 2,
May 4, 1944

Honorable T.B. McQuesten, K.C.
Chairman, Niagara Falls Parks Commission

My Dear Mr. McQuesten:
The Government has become impressed with the necessity for a continuous and direct contact with the Niagara Parks Commission, and has come to the conclusion that it is desirable that the Chairman of the Parks Commission become a member of the Government.

I wish to assure you that we appreciate the long years of service you have given to this work, and have been impressed with the desire you have indicated to co-operate in every way, but so many of the activities of the Commission are inseparably associated with the daily business of the Hydro Electric Power Commission and the Department of Highways that we believe you will recognize the advantage of having the Chairman sitting with us at our regular meetings.

For that reason I must suggest that the present members of the Board make it possible for us to carry out the reorganization which we believe to be necessary for the purpose of achieving closer collaboration between the various departments concerned.

Again, assuring you of our appreciation of your work and the desire you have shown to be of assistance, believe me,
Sincerely Yours,
George A. Drew.

T.B. McQuesten, in a very brief statement, promptly tendered his resignation as Chairman. Drew did not formally accept this until three months later.

TO PREMIER GEORGE DREW from T.B. McQuesten, Chairman of Niagara Parks Commission (W-MCP7-1.150)

Prime Minister for the Province of Ontario   Hamilton, Ontario
Parliament Buildings,   Whitehern, 41 Jackson St.
Toronto, Ontario   May 20, 1944

Dear Colonel Drew:
     Your letter of May 4th was read to the Commission today at its regular meeting. I resign herewith as Chairman and member of the Commission. I understand the other members prefer to write you direct.
     Faithfully yours,
     Chairman, T.B. McQuesten.

It is not known why Drew delayed three months in accepting McQuesten's resignation, but in August 1944, George Drew accepted the resignation with a somewhat insincere invitation that Tom continue to *offer any suggestions* based on his experience. This is a classic instance of political double-speak, since one can read the invitation as a sincere regret at losing such an effective Chairman, or as a way of reinforcing the fact that McQuesten was no longer officially connected with the Niagara Parks Commission:

TO THOMAS B. MCQUESTEN, K.C., from Col. George Drew, Progressive Conservative Premier of Ontario (W-MCP7-1.151)

Whitehern, 41 Jackson Street West,
Hamilton, Ontario

**Office of
The Prime Minister & President of the Council**
Toronto 2,
August 11, 1944

Dear Mr. McQuesten,
     In accepting your resignation as Chairman of the Niagara Parks Commission, I wish to express the appreciation of the Government of Ontario for the time you have given to this valuable public service.
     I hope that you will still feel free to offer any suggestions and to give us the value of your experience although not officially connected with the Niagara Parks Commission.
     As I already explained to you in an earlier letter, it was felt to be necessary for the efficient functioning of the Commission that the Chairman be a member of the Government.
     With kindest regards, believe me, yours very sincerely,
     George Drew

The time lapse between Drew's last two letters (more than three months) suggests that some negotiations took place between Drew and McQuesten. Drew's comment that he was *impressed with the desire you have indicated to co-operate in every way* indicates that Tom was attempting to negotiate a means by which he and his Commissioners could stay on even though they were members of the opposing party.

Two documents in the archive may have been the instruments of negotiation. The first is the *Niagara Parks Commission Annual Report for 1943* (W-MCP7-1.154,

Nov 10 1943), which gives a comprehensive overview of the history and policy of the Niagara Parks. Some of the projects that the Commission had accomplished to date are discussed, including various gardens, the River Road, the New Restaurant at Queenston Heights Park, the School for Apprentice Gardeners, Mather Park, and the restoration of Forts and of William Lyon Mackenzie's house. The second document, *Post War Work* (dated February 19, 1944), was pre-emptively prepared by Tom following Drew's election as Premier. The actual date of the end of the war was, of course, not yet known.

These are very impressive documents, and Drew might have been swayed to retain McQuesten and his Commissioners on a strictly non-partisan basis. The time lag suggests some deliberation on his part; however, Drew ultimately decided that all of the Liberal Commissioners must go and a new Progressive Conservative group be appointed.

With the advent of the new Progressive Conservative government, it must have come as a shock to Tom to be retired from his several portfolios. His portfolio as Minister of Highways, which he had held since 1934, ended in 1943; Minister of Public Works, 1934-37 & 1942-43, ended in the same year; and his role as Chairman of the Niagara Parks Commission since 1934 came to a conclusion in 1944.

Thus ended Tom's long and productive career with the Niagara Parks Commission—more than nine years. It was difficult for him to accept. Several analysts have observed that the Niagara Parks Commission has never had a Chairman as productive or as effective either before McQuesten or since.

TOM CONTINUES AS CHAIRMAN
OF THE NIAGARA FALLS BRIDGE COMMISSION

Although McQuesten's forced resignation came as a blow to him, he would not be idle for long. He continued as Chairman of the Niagara Falls Bridge

T.B. McQuesten, Chairman (back row, centre)
and fellow Niagara Falls Bridge Commissioners, 1943

Commission, and he and Somerville proceeded with the work on the Carillon tower. He also continued his work in Hamilton with the Board of Parks Management and RBG. Lands had been accumulated in 1929 and held for the purpose of a botanical garden, and plans had been quietly in the works for twenty years. Laking reveals that "A great deal had been accomplished towards the founding of a botanical garden before any public revelation of the fact" (11). The Rock Garden had been built as part of the northwest entrance project, and it was thriving; but the adjacent RBG and Cootes Paradise lands were yet to be fully developed. Tom also began to lobby council to commission a master plan in Town Planning, which they did, but it was the 1970s before it was incorporated into urban renewal plans (*DHB*4.190).

On May 15, 1944 McMaster University in Hamilton recognized T.B. McQuesten with an honourary LLD (*DHB*4.190). In June Tom's health began to fail, and he was laid up for a few months. His sister, Mary, notes in her journal that Tom "took a chill in June and he had not slept for weeks and he looks very tired." By late summer he had improved sufficiently to return to RBG and the Board of Parks Management (Best 179). He continued his work in City Planning and found that City Council was much more receptive this time, possibly due to the make-work opportunities. Tom also returned to his legal practice and became involved in such major projects as an assessment of the value of the steel industry in Hamilton for the Algoma Steel Co. (W-MCP7-1.212, Apr 23 1946).

**T.B. McQuesten at his desk,
Royal Botanical Gardens, 1940s**
Note: McQuesten's desk, with
      plaque, is still in use at RBG

Chapter 41

McQUESTEN'S RETURN TO ROYAL BOTANICAL GARDENS

RBG can never outlive the debt owing to him.
T.B. McQuesten is the very soul of a too-long-unsung leader in Ontario life.
Dr. Leslie Laking (W8703)

Shortly before Tom was forced to resign from the Niagara Parks Commission on May 20, 1944, he wrote a letter of recommendation for Matt Broman, probably in preparation for Broman's termination, should it come. Broman was not a Commissioner but he was a close associate of McQuesten's. Tom may have written several such letters for his close associates.

TO WHOM IT MAY CONCERN from T.B. McQuesten (W9865d)
May 16 1944

From: T.B. McQuesten.
Mr. K. Matt Broman, Boys School,
Niagara Parks Commission, Niagara Falls, Ontario.

TO WHOM IT MAY CONCERN

I do not hesitate to recommend him [Matt Broman] as a man of exceptional ability, foresight and energy. The work that he has done in developing the School and completely rehabilitating the parks and other properties of the Commission is of quite exceptional character. He has always had my full confidence and in my opinion he has deserved it. He has shown a competence and interest in the property and work of the Commission which could hardly be exceeded. He is a thoroughly well-trained gardener with a great knowledge of Botany, and a wide experience in parks developments and work all over the world. He has travelled widely and profited from what he has seen. I have great pleasure in recommending him as a loyal, conscientious, able and energetic man and landscape architect.

[Signed] *T.B. McQuesten,*
Chairman of the Niagara Parks Commission.

Matt Broman had begun his fine work with McQuesten in Hamilton in the late 1920s and early 1930s. Acting as Carl Borgstrom's "chief lieutenant," Broman did the original design work for the Rock Garden and the extensive planting along the full length of the northwest entrance to the city (Laking 25, 44-5). Best notes that Broman and Tom "had a long-standing friendship and collaboration dating back to

A young Matt Broman

Broman's supervision of the Rock Garden in Hamilton. His energy and imagination transformed a worked-out gravel pit into a spectacular sunken garden of international reputation" (Best 117).

From 1935 on, Broman worked with McQuesten at Niagara. On November 3, 1944 Tom wrote to him about the need for a school at RBG:

> *There is the greatest need too of quite an advanced teaching centre not only for garden work but for park executives, and this should include a very sound knowledge of gardening and administration. I think in subsequent courses it should go much beyond this for those who are ambitious to get training for large park administration.* (W9865j)

T.B. McQuesten (centre, front row) with the second graduating class of the NPC School of Horticulture, instructors, staff and several Commissioners
Matt Broman, wearing light-coloured suit and tie, is 2ⁿᵈ from left, 2ⁿᵈ row

It came as a shock when shortly afterward, Matt Broman was unceremoniously fired from the Niagara Parks, no doubt because of his loyalty to McQuesten. Tom wrote again to Broman to commiserate with him, and notified him of plans for his appointment to the staff of RBG:

TO MATT BROMAN from T.B. McQuesten (Excerpt, W9865i)
Queenston, Ontario   69 James St. South
                                                          Hamilton, Ontario
                                                          Dec 29 1944

Dear Matt,
  The turkey came yesterday in all its glory and I can assure you we are all ready to devour it on New Year's Day. I am only sorry you cannot share it with us. I also received the customary New Year's cigars which I will smoke in remembrance of past days and in expectation of better days to come.

We have all had an unsettling experience but this is life and we have to accept it and profit by it. I expected to take the fall but I never thought they would unseat you too! That is a piece of cold-blooded vindictiveness but you can rise above it!

As I told you over the telephone on Wednesday the City Council here put through my appointment for a three year term. We were waiting for this. My idea now is that our Commission will meet within the next week or so and take up your matter and we shall then get in touch with you.

I am anxious to get the Botanical Gardens work started and I think it should be possible this Spring, that is providing you can get men. Fred has not been able to get enough to keep up with the work, you might have some such men in view, but I would not make any arrangements until your own position is settled to your satisfaction. . . . I hope in a few months we will both be settled into some good course of development work and we can start again and forget what lies behind. . . .

Faithfully yours,
T.B. McQuesten

An extract from the Parks Board meeting of January 22nd, 1945 states that, "McQuesten brought up the matter of engaging Mr. Matthew Broman as Superintendent of the Royal Botanical Gardens at a salary of $3000. to be paid by the Royal Botanical Gardens" (W-MCP7-1.207). Broman was so dedicated to Tom and their shared vision that he already offered several years earlier to work with Tom on the RBG project gratis as a volunteer:

TO HON. T.B. MCQUESTEN K.C. from his associate Matt Broman (W9861u)

THE NIAGARA PARKS COMMISSION
Jan 27 1941

Hon. T.B. McQuesten,
Queen's Park, Toronto,

Dear Sir,
    I enclose with this letter a few notes which I have prepared, setting forth some ideas on RBG. I would appreciate any changes or additions you might care to suggest. Then, if feasible, have the corrected copy printed and presented to these people who might assist in getting this project started. Personally, I feel that even with a small start a good foundation might be laid.

For example, with a moderate grant, it would be possible to hire some labourers who could do the necessary cleaning up and plant some selections from our collection at the School Nursery. I shall be glad to devote all my spare time, gratis, to this scheme, and if the time comes when you feel that I can render greater service there I should be glad to do so.

I am very pleased with the progress that has been made at the [Niagara] School. The fine reputation which is being made by the students of this institution is already filling a real place in Canadian life.

Please advise me of any way in which I can be of further assistance.

Yours very respectfully,
Matt Broman

On the basis of Matt Broman's excellent work with the Niagara Parks School for Apprentice Gardeners, Tom recommended him for a position with RBG in Hamilton. Broman was happy to accept, and was the first appointee to RBG management staff. He was able to recruit experienced staff from his NPC school, and under his management as Superintendent, the institution and its school began to grow.

McQuesten and Broman purchased the Rock Chapel Lodge in 1945 as a headquarters for the RBG school. It was to be a professional school for senior park educators, managers and scientists in conjunction with nearby McMaster University. As such it required senior staff as professors, so designer Carl Borgstrom and palaeobotanist Dr. Norman W. Radforth, Head of the Botany Department at McMaster, were hired. Dr. Leslie Laking, a graduate of the Ontario Agricultural College with post-graduate training in botany at the University of Toronto, knew of Matt Broman's work on the early phase of the botanical garden project. Broman's presence on the management staff influenced Laking to accept the position of

Dr. Leslie Laking at RBG Laking Garden
(Photo from Hamilton Spectator, 1981)

Administrator of RBG Institute as "an opportunity indeed," despite the fact that the Institute had very little funding. In due course, Laking—who held the Kew Certificate from England—became Assistant Director and Horticulturalist (Laking 49).

T.B. McQuesten was the founder and first president of RBG. With Tom at the helm of the Parks Board, the institution thrived. Dr. Radforth was appointed its first Director in 1946. Dr. Laking took over as Director at a later date, serving until the early 1980s. Laking worked with McQuesten and Matt Broman from 1946 onward. He has the highest regard for Tom's vision, motives and integrity, and recalls his first impression of the man:

I learned of his dream to develop a fully functioning botanical garden which would do for the Hamilton area, the province and the nation, what Kew Gardens had done for Britain and the Commonwealth. He foresaw close association with centres of higher learning, particularly McMaster University. I witnessed his impatience to get on with the task, and his enormous pride in the magnificence of the lands that he and his Parks Board colleagues had assembled for this purpose. (Laking 5, 25-6)

Tom's close association with Broman is evident in a letter he wrote on January 2, 1946:

I hope the coming year will be a good year for all of us—which means of course, that we shall have limitless money to spend and freedom from all control. I am totally hopeful that as you get your feet planted and we are able to increase and improve our staff that our [RBG] undertakings will begin to take shape and the property will begin to commend itself to the public. I am grateful to you for all your interest and loyalty. In fact I do not know what we should do without you. (W9865l)

The original vision for RBG was conceived as a mixture of beautiful horticultural displays and protected natural forests and wetlands, and this continues to this day. With approximately 971 ha (2,400 acres) of property, RBG today is one of the largest such institutions in North America and certainly the largest in Canada; it is substantially larger than England's renowned Kew Gardens.

McQuesten and Broman were in agreement that the gardens at both Niagara and RBG should have an educational component. For RBG they added a children's garden and a centre for plant research. The Nature Interpretive Centre fulfills the Gardens' mission "to be a living museum which serves local, regional and global communities while developing and promoting public understanding of the relationship between the plant world, humanity and the rest of nature."[33]

While working for RBG, Tom continued to implement his vision at Niagara with the Rainbow Bridge Commission, but his battles with large political egos were not yet over. He would have yet another confrontation with a member of his own Liberal party—a member of very high standing and a formidable opponent, indeed: The Right Honourable, William Lyon Mackenzie King, Prime Minister of Canada.

McQuesten's eventual death in 1948 was a great loss to RBG. Dr. Leslie Laking knew T.B. McQuesten well, and he categorically asserts that, "RBG can never outlive the debt owing to him who was both founder and first president" (W8703, Feb 27 1948; Laking 66; W-MCP7-1.269, Jan16 1948).

MATT BROMAN'S LEGACY

That same year, the institution lost another valuable member when Matt Broman resigned to begin a consulting business in design and development. Broman would continue his legacy of beautification projects for another thirty years. In the course of his long career, he left his mark on many Hamilton parks (Laking 67). His accomplishments have been celebrated with a park, and with plaques in two separate locations in the city.

In 1980, the City of Hamilton dedicated a lookout park to Matt Broman on the edge of the escarpment at a curve in

**Knut Mattias (Matt) Broman
in the RBG rose garden, 1988**

(Photo from the Hamilton Spectator, in Special Collections, Hamilton Central Library)

---

[33] www.rbg.ca

Mountain Brow Blvd. where it intersects Mohawk Road. Appropriately for Broman, the park looks out on some of the city's most spectacular views to the north and east: King's Forest Park and Golf Course, Rosedale Park, Lake Ontario and, on a clear day, Toronto. A dedicatory bronze plaque set into a stone wall reads in part:

**In Recognition of the dedicated services of K.M. (Matt) Broman, Designer
and Landscape Architect, for The Corporation of the City of Hamilton 1935 – 1978.
The beautiful parks of this city are a lasting Testament
to the Skills and Talents of this modest man.**

Unfortunately, an oversight in the dates on the plaque does not give Broman full credit for his pioneering work in Hamilton on the design at the Rock Garden, the northwest entrance and RBG from 1928 onward. This illustrates just how easily credits can be forgotten, and how misinformation can be set in stone.

Ernest Seager (long-time secretary of the Hamilton Parks' Board) suggests Broman may have been so modest that some of his contributions to Hamilton have gone unheralded. At the time of Broman's retirement, however, the *Spectator* gave full credit to Broman for his earlier work: "Since 1928, when he oversaw the creation of RBG's rock garden and the city's western entrance, Mr. Broman has been a major influence on just about every piece of public garden in the city . . . the city's blood veins." Broman saw beyond partisan politics to a greater Canada, and recommended that "In every large park there should be a flagpole with a big Canadian flag. It gives you a feeling when you see the flag. You think; It's a beautiful country" (Jun 29 1978).

Two years after Broman's death, a second plaque was erected and dedicated by the Province of Ontario to commemorate the massive scope of Broman's vision and contribution (Laking 67). Located near the Thomas B. McQuesten High Level Bridge and the plaque to McQuesten, it is set into a large free-standing rock along RBG parkway:

THE BROMAN LANDS
Dedicated to
Founding Landscape Architect
Mattias (Matt) Broman
1895 - 1989
who shared his vision of this great
landscape

"The Broman Lands" refers to the "lands with which he was involved as a young man as part of the Borgstrom team in the development of the Northwestern Entrance to the City" (Laking 67). Broman's design for the northwest entrance was drawn up in 1928; hence his early work is acknowledged here. The proximity of Broman's plaque to McQuesten's is appropriate. They were very close associates who became lifelong friends, and they shared the same vision. In a detailed obituary tribute outlining many of Broman's parks and creations, Seager speaks eloquently of how closely Broman and Tom worked together: "Whatever McQuesten's mind conceived, Matt's skilled hand devised" (*Hamilton Spectator*, Jun 12 1989).

RBG TODAY

After T.B. McQuesten died in 1948, RBG under Laking's guidance continued to develop into the major entity it is today. RBG promotes itself as a living museum, a rare Carolinian forest, a Mediterranean Garden with orchids, a garden of herbs and curative plants, a wetland, and a wilderness and wildlife habitat; it also has one of the world's largest lilac collections. Its core programs are horticulture, education, conservation and research. It is Canada's first and only Royal Botanical Garden—a designation that Tom applied for and received in 1930, and which continues to protect the gardens in perpetuity. RBG is the country's largest botanical garden and one of its premier cultural, educational and scientific institutions. It offers extensive educational programs and serves as an outdoor laboratory for scientific research. This includes a strategy for conservation of Canada's biological diversity of rare and endangered native plant species, wild habitats and ecosystems.

RBG was declared a National Historic site on May 1, 1998 by Liberal Minister and Hamiltonian, Sheila Copps: "Minister of Canadian Heritage Sheila Copps today unveiled an Historic Sites and Monuments Board of Canada plaque officially recognizing the national historic and architectural significance of RBG. Among many dignitaries present at the ceremony were Michael Schwenger, President of the Board of RBG, and Dr. Leslie Laking, Director Emeritus."[34] The plaque is located in RBG's north colonnade where it is readily visible to the thousands of visitors who each year come to view the extensive collection of native and exotic plants, trees and flowers.

Over the years, McQuesten's contribution to RBG was almost totally forgotten. Dr. Laking sought to remedy the situation with the publication of his book, *love, sweat and soil: a History of RBG from 1930 to 1981* (2006). He refers to Thomas McQuesten as "the very soul of a too-long-unsung leader in Ontario life" (Laking 1).

Thomas Baker McQuesten, c.1920

---

[34] http://www/canadianheritage.gc.ca/newsroom

The plaque to T.B. McQuesten in the RBG Rock Garden

In 1976, McQuesten's secretary Jessie Yorston arranged for a bronze plaque to be erected in his honour in the Rock Garden:

THE ROCK GARDEN STANDS AS A MONUMENT
TO THE HON. THOMAS BAKER MCQUESTEN, Q.C., LL.D.
1880-1948
FOUNDER OF RBG

His foresight in acquiring lands for this great venture in the 1930's
while serving the Hamilton Board of Park Management and his wisdom
in procuring independent status for the Gardens, culminated in establishing
Royal Botanical Gardens, by statute of the Province of Ontario in 1941.
Erected in appreciation of the inspiration and leadership provided
by this great Canadian on behalf of grateful citizens of this area.
1976

Erected by the Ontario Heritage Foundation, Minister of Culture and Communication

Laking speaks of the event as "a bittersweet experience" and asks, "Why had it taken so long?" (Laking 123-24)

A few years ago, I quizzed a student interpreter at the Lilac Dell: "Who was the founder of RBG?" The response to my question was a negative shrug, and I was prompted to provide the answer in a five-minute lecture on the Gardens' origins. When I visited RBG's Lilac Festival last year and posed the same question to another young interpreter, I was delighted to hear her unhesitating reply: "Thomas Baker McQuesten."

Chapter 42

THE CARILLON CONTROVERSY

We will build a beautiful stone Bridge with a Carillon and Tower —
the finest in the world.

T.B.McQuesten, Jan 27 1938 (Box 14-122)

Carillon Tower at Niagara Falls, 1942
before installation of bells in 1945
(Photo courtesy of Niagara Falls
Bridge Commission)

The Rainbow Tower housing the Carillon is located at the Canadian entrance to the Rainbow International Bridge at Niagara Falls. The tower is 165 feet (50.3m) tall and houses a set of fifty-five tuned bells hung within, having a total weight of over 43 tons. The largest bell, called a **bourdon**, is 8 feet in diameter and 6.5 feet tall, weighing in at 10 tons. The smallest bell weighs less than 9 pounds and has a circumference of 5.75 inches. Work on the instrument was contracted in 1941 with John Taylor and Company, Bellfounders, Leicestershire, England; but manufacture of the bells had to be delayed until after the war. The Carillon was completed by June 16, 1947, when the bells were dedicated.

The music range of the Carillon at Niagara Falls is one of the broadest in the world. Although a bell sounds one note, there are five distinct tones in every carillon bell. The set of bells cost $48,000 to make. The instrument is controlled via a series

Fifty-five bells for the Niagara Carillon, two rows symmetrically placed c.1945

of 55 oak batons and 30 foot pedals. The first concert by the bells occurred on July 1, 1948,[35] nearly six months after T.B. McQuesten died.

William Lyon Somerville was hired as the architect for the Carillon Tower and the Rainbow Bridge plaza; Howard Dunington-Grubb was the landscape architect. Thomas McQuesten was responsible for the conception, planning and building of the Carillon Tower, and for the ordering of the bells and the inscription on the bourdon. Although the bells never did toll in concert for him, they "fore-tolled" Tom's political demise at the Niagara Bridge Commission and delivered the death knell of his career.

The largest bell bears a poem and an inscription to Winston Churchill and Franklin Delano Roosevelt, "Our Nation's Leaders" in the Second World War. King was incensed when he heard about this inscription, and demanded that Churchill's and Roosevelt's names be removed from the giant bell and his own name added. But Tom refused. Although a politician himself, he abhorred the monumental egos fuelled by politics, especially when they interfered and caused delays or stoppages in his work. The earlier animosity between King and McQuesten over the figures on the Clifton Gate Memorial Arch broke out again, and this time it was vicious.

The Whitehern archive contains three documents that pertain specifically to the Carillon and the giant bell. The first, dated December 12, 1941, is a copy of the original contract from John Taylor and Company, Bellfounders for the fifty-five bells; it is signed and witnessed by the proprietor of the firm and by three members of the Niagara Falls Bridge Commission. The second, dated June 19, 1942, is a copy

---

[35] Niagara Falls Bridge Commission (http://www.niagarafrontier.com/carillon.html)

of the amended contract from Taylor and Company, similarly signed and witnessed, postponing work on the bells until after the war (W-MCP7-1.027).

The third document, which is a carbon copy of a typewritten original, is somewhat of a mystery (Box 14-122, quoted below). The page number **(5)** at the top is immediately followed by precisely the same date and Commissioners' signatures which finalize the second bellfounders' contract:

June 19, 1942, signed by T.B. McQuesten, Chairman;
S.M. Johnson, Vice-Chairman; and C.E. Kaumeyer, Secretary,
witnessed by Mary V. Stuckey"

Mary Stuckey's name ends with a closed quotation mark ("). A line is drawn beneath the names. Text that clearly was written some years after the 1942 date, begins below this line and continues onto a second, unsigned page (6). All indications are that this third document was intended as a supplement to the two contracts; yet as its Whitehern reference number indicates, it was found in a different location in the archive, which is puzzling. The contracts themselves bear no page numbers; hence, in the absence of the third document's first four pages, its exact relationship with the contracts cannot be confirmed.

The text of the document constitutes an account of the Carillon controversy. Within the body of the text, the date of June 18, 1947 is used in the past tense, and a reference is made to T.B. McQuesten's death (which occurred in January of 1948). It is not known who wrote this account, but a few clues suggest that it may have

**Carillon Tower and beginning of Rainbow Bridge
seen from Oakes Garden Theatre c.1945
Note Clifton Gate Memorial Arch at centre right**

**William Lyon Mackenzie King, Franklin Roosevelt
and Winston Churchill, Quebec Conference, 1943**

been C. Ellison Kaumeyer, who was Secretary of the Bridge Commission at the time of signing on June 19, 1942, and who later became the Commission's General

**C. Ellison Kaumeyer General Manager
Niagara Falls Bridge Commission**

Manager. Kaumeyer had worked closely with T.B. McQuesten and had supported the latter's position to preserve the signatures on the giant bell. Conceivably Mary Stuckey, Kaumeyer's secretary from 1941 to 1972, was involved in its authorship.

The document relates in detail the events leading up to McQuesten's forced resignation from the Niagara Bridge Commission. When Tom refused to honour Prime Minister Mackenzie King's demands to change the inscription on the large bell, King was determined to have McQuesten terminated from the commission. The Prime Minister completely ignored the fact that removing the inscription would have ruined the bell's tone. He also ignored the fact that Churchill already knew about the inscription, and removing his name would have caused an international incident.

The following is a lengthy excerpt from the third Carillon document:

(5)

this nineteenth day of June Nineteen hundred and forty-two.

sgd.   T.B.McQuesten, CHAIRMAN
sgd.   S.M.Johnson, VICE-CHAIRMAN
sgd.   C.E.Kaumeyer, SECRETARY
(seal)

Witness to the Signatures of
T.B.McQuesten, C.E.Kaumeyer
and S.M.Johnson
sgd.   Mary V. Stuckey"

... The Bridge, the Tower and the Carillon were all Mr. McQuesten's idea. The day the Old Bridge went down, he had sent the Bridge Engineer from the Highways Department to watch it as they knew it was going to collapse, and that day he said in the presence of Mr. R.M. Smith, and myself [Kaumeyer? Stuckey?]: "We will build a beautiful stone Bridge with a Carillon and Tower - the finest in the world". Mr. R.M. Smith was the Deputy Minister [of Highways]. The year it was completed it was printed in "The Architectural Review" an English Magazine that the Niagara Bridge [Rainbow Bridge] was voted the finest in the world for that year, so he was not wrong.

There is cast on the great bell (20,000 lbs.) the following inscription:-

"CHURCHILL

Ev'n as a bird
Out of the fowler's snare
Escapes away
So is our soul set free:
Broke are their nets,
And thus escaped we
Therefore our help
Is in the Lord's Great Name
Who heaven and earth
By His great power did frame.
To God's Glory and in grateful memory of our Nations' Leaders ..
Winston Spencer Churchill
- and -
Franklin Delano Roosevelt"

The first part of this inscription is from the concluding lines of the 124th Psalm, Scottish Metrical Version.

Mr. Churchill has knowledge of this as he was sent photographs of same.

In June 1947, Mr. McQuesten gave the following Statement to the Newspapers:-

"I wish to dissociate myself from the action of the majority Members of the Niagara Bridge Commission in ordering the removal of the names of Mr. Winston Churchill and the late President Roosevelt from the inscription cast on the great bell (ten and a half tons) of the carillon. This action followed a long campaign in which at least three Ministers of the Government at Ottawa tampered with and put pressure upon Ontario Members of the Bridge Commission. Surely it is a most unbecoming thing that the name of the President of the United States to whom this country and the world owes so great a debt should be smudged out on the insistence of Members of the Government of Canada. Mr. Churchill and Mr. Roosevelt have thousands of friends in this Province. Their names are great names and should be treated with the utmost respect.

The Carillon was erected with the money of American bondholders. The record will show that the Bellfounders in England, when their advice was sought, could not guarantee that the operation of removing these names would not destroy the bell. The Commission's own Architect concurred in this, but so great was the pressure from Ottawa Ministers that this recommendation was disregarded.

The value of the carillon is in the order of $100,000. and the destruction of the great bell would be a very serious loss. The whole steel framework and bells would have to be taken out of the tower and the bell recast. It is improper that this should be forced upon the bondholders. Ottawa has contributed nothing to the whole project." [T.B. McQuesten]

Then on June 18th, 1947, Mr. McQuesten received the following telegram from George Drew:-

"This is to notify you that Order-in-Council has been passed terminating your appointment as a Member of Niagara Falls Bridge Commission effective Seventeenth June Nineteen forty seven stop you will receive letter enclosing copy of the Order.
D.R. Michener Provincial Secty Ontario."

The inscription still remains on the bells -

The man who attacked McQuesten in the Ottawa House was the Hon. Lionel Chevrier - a french Canadian - as to the inscription on the bells.

Mr. McQuesten became ill a few days after receiving the wire from George Drew and entered the Hospital the end of June [1947] where he remained for two months. In my heart I shall always feel that the Niagara Falls Bells killed Mr. McQuesten. He gave generously of his time and

> money for his expenses etc. and never at any time received anything from
> the Commission - not even gratitude. During the period of the nine years
> he served as Chairman of the Bridge Commission and Chairman of the
> Niagara Parks Commission and Hydro Commissioner he received no
> remuneration.
>
> Mr. McQuesten never heard the bells ring -
> Mr. McQuesten was awarded an Honorary Certificate from the Guild
> of Carillonneurs in North America for his interest in the art of the carillon.
> Apparently the Americans appreciated what he had done more than the
> Canadians.
>
> [No signature at bottom, no date except within the text (Box 14-122)]

The newspapers were scathing in their attack on King, and the *Globe & Mail* condemned the plan to erase the names. John Best reveals that other papers "continued to denounce tampering with the bell. The *Spectator* stated: the biggest carillon in the land is making Canada look pretty small" (188). CPAC, Canada's Cable Public Affairs Channel, states on its website that Mackenzie King was called a schemer, not a statesman, and Canadians remember him for his private eccentricities (www.CPAC. ca/The Prime Ministers).

Tom McQuesten received support for his position from the U.S. representatives of the Bridge Commission. They suggested their preference for a substitute inscription should Churchill's name be removed: *June 6th 1947, Discussed [?] with G.L. Lardi and he advised if any changes made in bell the inscription to the Unknown Soldier would be favoured by American representatives* (handwritten note, signed Kaumeyer; see W-MCP7-1.134).

King must have been aware that Churchill knew about the planned inscription. Churchill had visited Niagara in 1944 with his daughter, Mary, and had been made aware then of the plan for the bells, although they had not yet been manufactured. Obliterating Churchill's name after he knew of the plan would have constituted a grave insult to Britain.

Tom's intention had been to cement and celebrate the relationship between the two great powers, not to jeopardize it. The two powers had themselves been at war several times in the past, in particular the war of 1812. Tom found occasion many times during his years at Niagara to celebrate the peace achieved between Britain and America at the end of that war. The former battlefield had been transformed into a beautiful garden, and the Carillon would ring several times a day to remind the two great powers of the peace that had been won and was being perpetuated.

A little-known fact of profound importance to his dedication and good character is that Thomas McQuesten never received any remuneration for those many years as Chairman of the various commissions for which he laboured so tirelessly. As previously noted, he also refused to accept reimbursement for travel and auto

Rev. Calvin, Mary, Thomas and Hilda McQuesten c.1945

expenses. His sister, Mary, was disgusted with the government's treatment of Tom and wrote in her journal, "A man may kill himself and then be cast aside" (Best 177). Significantly, the Guild of Carillonneurs appreciated McQuesten's efforts to preserve the purity of the bells, while the Canadian political parties at the time would have disregarded both the sentiments connected with the inscription *and* the sanctity of the sound, for purely political reasons.

C.E. Kaumeyer was in collusion with Tom to prevent the inscription being removed, and even changed the locks on the Tower to ensure this. He sent a cryptic message to Tom on Bridge Commission stationery to inform him that he was securing the Carillon Tower and changing the locks and keys:

TO T.B. MCQUESTEN from C. Ellison Kaumeyer (W-MCP7-1.019)
69 James Street South,
Hamilton, Ontario

NIAGARA FALLS BRIDGE COMMISSION
RAINBOW BRIDGE
NIAGARA FALLS
September 7, 1945

Dear Mr. McQuesten:
For certain reasons I have found it necessary to lock the outer doors on the first floor of the Tower Building. I have ordered a Master Key to control all of the doors on

*the lower floor for each Commissioner and in the meantime until the keys are made I
have left a key with the Canadian Toll Collectors for your convenience.*
    Yours very truly,
    C. Ellison Kaumeyer, General Manager

Public access to the belfry was subsequently disallowed. Even news photographers
were not permitted to take pictures of the Carillon until 1975. This ban worked to
preserve the inscription until no political will against its existence remained. The bell
incident was a political fiasco, but the inscription was never removed and remains
intact to this day. T.B. McQuesten received a great deal of support for his position,
and Best quotes one of Tom's oldest friends, a judge in Muskoka, who wrote: "Well
if [Tom] gets that bell hung without King's name on it, he will not have lived in vain."
Furthermore, Best adds that "the *Globe & Mail* scorned King's wartime leadership
and praised Roosevelt and Churchill" (188).

The Carillon story illustrates Tom's fierce sense of moral integrity and his
defiance of any political authority that made unreasonable demands for purely
egotistical political reasons. By any analysis, Tom emerged triumphant, even though
the incident may have served to hasten his death. Some years later, his brother Calvin
found occasion to express directly to Premier Drew his own deep anger over Tom's
unjust treatment:

TO THE HON. GEORGE DREW from Rev. Calvin McQuesten (W7933)
House of Commons   Whitehern
Ottawa, Ontario, Canada   Hamilton, Ontario, Canada
                                    Oct 12 1951 Friday

Self-esteemed sir:
    *Yesterday I paid a visit to Niagara Falls, after a considerable interval, as I
have not had quite the same interest in it since you ousted my younger brother,
first from the chairmanship of the Niagara Parks Commission and then from the
Rainbow Bridge Commission. For I knew that the bright boys whom you appointed
to succeed my brother and his colleagues were not capable of adding anything to the
magnificent monuments which stand to my brother's memory in the Oakes Garden
Theatre and the splendid approach to the Rainbow Bridge which makes the United
States end of the bridge look like the mean corner on a back street, and I was afraid
that in their efforts to justify their appointment they might have made some horrible
"improvements."*
    *But my most gloomy periods of pessimism never pictured any so disastrous as the
spectacle I beheld when I went into the beautiful Garden Theatre (one of Dunington-
Grubb's noblest creations), eagerly anticipating the spectacle of the glorious
panorama of the combined American and Canadian Falls which takes the place of a
painted back-drop at the rear of the stage, and found the view of most of the Horse-
Shoe Falls blotted out by a blob of an advertising shack housing the Tourist Bureau of
the Ontario Government. I was simply horrified.*
    *Was it sheer stupidity for which your administration as Premier of Ontario was
so notorious? Or was it malice, a deliberate mutilation of one of the finest artistic
achievements promoted by my brother, a sort of defacing of one of the many fine*

monuments which perpetrate [sic] his memory? Perhaps you would enlighten the people of Ontario on this point.

It was very obvious that you disliked my brother; or you would not have seized upon so trivial an excuse to oust him from the chairmanship of the Canadian section of the Rainbow Bridge Commission, a piece of procedure which was not only illegal (as he was appointed for life) but an act of ingratitude which showed an utter lack of any sense of fair play in your substitute for an intelligent mind. For you were in a position to know, even better than I do, that except for him there never would have been a Rainbow Bridge owned by the people of Ontario and New York, so financed that it will soon be toll-free. Instead there would have been another bridge built and operated by the International Railway Company of Buffalo, which previous to the collapse of the Honeymoon bridge, was collecting tolls to the amount of half-a-million dollars a year on a million-dollar investment.

I feel sure that Mr. Leslie Frost, who has rehabilitated the ramshackle Conservative Government of Ontario with such conspicuous success, would never have done so contemptible a trick. But then he is a gentleman and a public servant with sound ethical principles and a sense of fair-play.

Perhaps I should not write in this strain to a poor political hack whose handsome facade gained him a prominence in public life for which he had neither the necessary ability nor the moral stamina essential to a sound statesman, and who is now down and out. The last Federal election left you down, and [you] will be out before the next election.

For according to the rules by which the Progressively Conservative party of Canada plays ball, it is not "three strikes and out." Instead of that, one failure to hit a home-run is sufficient to send a leader to the showers. You know this was what happened to Mr. Bracken and his predecessors.

Do you think you will receive any different treatment, when your defeat was the most sweeping on record? So, "Good-bye"!

Yours without any respect,
Calvin McQuesten

Calvin was not alone in these sentiments. Those in government who planned and executed Thomas B. McQuesten's demise never publicly recovered from their indefensible action and unscrupulous tactics. By contrast, the inscription on the Big Bell that appeared to be Tom's nemesis was in the end his triumph, for he emerged from the incident with his integrity and reputation intact.

Chapter 43

THOMAS B. MCQUESTEN'S VISION AND LEGACY

Thomas McQuesten is one of Canada's master builders.
No other politician has created so many good works for Canada.
Very few men can point to so many public benefits of enduring value.
Like Christopher Wren's, your monuments are beauty spots.

Rev. Ketchen, eulogy, Jan 17 1948 (W-MCP7-1.268)

Thomas B. McQuesten, 1935

Roland Barnsley ends his excellent book about T.B. McQuesten (1987) with a tribute to McQuesten's accomplishments from 1934 to 1943, and a regret that the government and the Niagara Parks Commission had neglected to properly acknowledge and celebrate McQuesten's contributions:

It has, regrettably, never been in the nature of Ontario's political parties to acknowledge the accomplishments of their political opponents in any meaningful way, no matter what their stature. This practice has been carried to extremes in the over 40-year span since McQuesten's death. In that interval, the Province has seen fit to honour the seventh and eighth chairmen of the Niagara Parks Commission [Charles Daley, James N. Allan, both Conservatives] but continues to ignore the sixth—McQuesten. It is time to accept the true worth of a great contributor to Ontario's growth, and in a manner appropriate to his contribution.

In fact the irony is the greatest in the case of the Niagara Parks Commission. It is this very agency that owes more to the McQuesten chairmanship than any other. . . . The very base of its fine reputation and growing revenues can be attributed to the developments and attractions conceived and executed by McQuesten. Others have questioned this anomaly. . . . It was the decision of the Commission that it did not wish to do anything further at this time. . . . [The commissioners finally decided] to hang a photo of all the past Chairmen. . . . They decorate a small private room adjacent to the Commission Board Room!

Barnsley concludes, "Perhaps this quiet, giant of a man will remain Ontario's Forgotten Builder—unless an ancient political bias and bureaucratic lethargy do not continue to obscure the man and his deeds" (61-63).

John Best's excellent book has, to a large extent, redeemed T.B. McQuesten's name. Ontario's commercial interests appreciated McQuesten much more than his fellow politicians. Evan Gray, president of the Ontario Board of Trade, summed up Tom's imagination and vision: [McQuesten has] "the imagination of a builder who sees the completed object before there is a line on paper and sees it complete and whole. More than that it is an artist's imagination because it sees beauty in the construction, sees it truly and builds it in. In short, it is the imagination of the lawyer-engineer-artist. I don't know any other like it" (Best 137).

TOM'S FINAL TOUR

John Best describes a rather forlorn final tour for Tom in December 1947, following the Carillon incident: "Before entering the hospital for the last time, he arranged to be driven to the Rock Garden. He was very weak and said but little. He merely sat on a park bench looking at the bare rocks and the evergreens, alone with his thoughts and memories" (Best 189).

Although Best's account may be accurate, a newspaper clipping relates a more poetically appropriate final trip for Tom to view his creations. This version may have originated with Tom's secretary, Jessie Yorston, as portions of it appear in her lengthy biography of T.B. McQuesten for the Biographical Encyclopedia of the World in New York (Box 14-129). In true folkloric fashion, the newspaper article begins, "They say. . .":

They say that just before he went to hospital Tom McQuesten had a last look at the things he had made possible for the people of his city.

He took a taxi and went the rounds and he must have known it was his sunset. There was the fine expanse of Gage Park now white in winter. And under the snow where people enter Hamilton from the west was the Rock Garden, which would again burst into gay summer bloom. Further along near McMaster he could think of the Botanical Gardens with all their classic beauty and peace—next summer would know them too.

He might have thought further of the great Way that stretched to the rushing Niagara—a Queen of England had given her name to it, and at the end of it the Rainbow Bridge, where Canadian and American voices would stir long memories of holiday hours and peace.

All his work—the work of a politician, a stern partisan if you like, but of a politician with an iron will and a heart as big as the happiness of people

Thomas Baker McQuesten

in his parks. All his works: with those many battles through a Legislature as Ontario Minister of Highways, defence on the hustings, bitterness, rebukes and worry. But in the end triumph; above all for his city, Hamilton.

To Tom McQuesten it was not a case of sectionalism or local pride. He loved Hamilton and the people in it. Surrounded by countless pictures and relics and reminders of its growth he stood for all that was best in the old and all that could be promised by the new. He wanted the best for his town, and that was one of the driving motives of his life.

In his last look around that day Tom McQuesten might well have said goodbye not to monuments, but to old friends. Echoes would come from far back, from loved and familiar places and landscapes. Then ahead there would be new and younger voices, picking up the threads of a city's proud and human growth; out of winter into summer. Just a little better for what Tom McQuesten had done for it. (W8267; newspaper unknown, Dec 23 1947)

Tom's sister, Hilda, shatters our illusions when we find that she had written along the edge of this clipping: "Imaginary, Tom was in his bed, H.B. McQ." No matter—as with all great heroes, this story will enter into the Hamilton mythology surrounding T.B. McQuesten. And if it did not occur just as described, it would certainly have transpired that way in Tom's imagination—and in ours.

Tom returned to the hospital on December 24 for surgery. "On the 5th of January as he lay in bed gravely ill, Calvin accepted Hamilton's Citizen of the Year award on Tom's behalf" (Best 189). Tom did not recover from his surgery but died on January 13, 1948. His cancer had spread, and it is reported that he died of intestinal and/or throat cancer.

Just before Tom's funeral, Calvin accepted, on Tom's behalf, a certificate of honorary membership in the Canadian Society of Landscape Architects and Town Planners for "outstanding service rendered the cause of landscape architecture." He was the only non-landscape architect to have received one. The certificate was presented by Carl O. Borgstrom and H. B. Dunington-Grubb (Minnes 9).

Although Tom was for many years the "Forgotten Builder," he is coming to be celebrated by those who know and appreciate how much he did for Canada, and how quietly and selflessly he laboured. The Hamilton Public Library honoured Thomas Baker McQuesten in 1986, when they inducted him into their Gallery of Distinction. In 1988, as we have seen, the High Level Bridge was rededicated and given his name; and nearby, the Ontario Heritage Foundation's memorial plaque acknowledging his numerous accomplishments was unveiled by Princess Margaret. Also, the city of Hamilton gave his name to the Upper Wentworth Street community park, and RBG named its amphitheatre the "McQuesten Theatre."

There can be no doubt that in the thirty-nine years that McQuesten held political office, he accomplished more for Hamilton, for Ontario than any other person or politician before or since. Chester S. Walters, former mayor of Hamilton and Deputy Provincial Treasurer, said of him, "Thomas Baker McQuesten was one of Canada's great men. He was the soul of honour" (Best 189).

T.B. McQuesten's estate verifies his honesty and his refusal to engage in any form of graft. His modest estate of $51,219.96 included his share of the house, Whitehern. His brother Calvin noted that Tom had to cash in some paid up life insurance to pay his income tax while he was Minister of Highways during the war. "Being head of the two biggest spending departments . . . Highways and Public Works, with an appropriation of $200,000,000 did not seem to put much money into his private pocket" (Best 191).

Tom had an iron will and a moral imperative to match. His remarkable vision never faltered even when his achievements were cut short by partisan politics. He was, indeed, a *Beaux-Arts* visionary and a Renaissance Master Builder.

One might say that Thomas Baker McQuesten's legacy was shaped by three separate, yet related visions. His mother, Mary Baker McQuesten, saw him as the only hope for restoring the McQuesten family's damaged honour and prestige; accordingly, she groomed him for this role, and devised the strategy by which the goal could be accomplished.

Tom's sister, Ruby Baker McQuesten believed in his potential to be a leader holding to the highest standard of moral integrity, who would accomplish much through a life of service in the political arena. She, his mentor and muse, hoped that he would be: *a man able to separate between good and evil. . . . and as a lawyer to distinguish that faint line between right and wrong. . . a man pure in politics . . . and so strong that he would keep above the tide of wrong-doing and stand firm and help up others* (W-MCP2-4.053, May 8 1905).

In a very real sense, Tom built upon and expanded both of their dreams to create his own unique vision for what he wished to accomplish. He believed that architecture, engineering and aesthetics must go hand in hand. Above all, he felt that in order to inspire and uplift the human spirit, beauty must be the guide; and he brought a continuity of artistic vision to all of his numerous, diverse projects.

Despite political pressure, Tom remained true to his vision of worthy City Beautiful and Social Gospel public undertakings. In so doing, he also attained Ruby's and his mother's visions for him. He had, indeed, achieved the restoration of the McQuesten name in honour, dignity, and prestige. His debt to Ruby had been honoured, and her prophetic vision fulfilled to the letter. He could come to his mother and to his sister Ruby, *with clean hands*. He died triumphantly—politically, professionally and personally—with his and his family's honour and integrity intact to the end.

Thomas Baker McQuesten in Whitehern Garden

Inscriptions on the McQuesten memorial
monument in Hamilton Cemetery
for Thomas (above) and Ruby (right)
(photos courtesy Richard Kosydar)

Although Ruby appears to have become the "Forgotten Sister," there is no doubt that she was a vital force in the development of Tom's character, as well as providing the only possible financial means for his education. Ruby's evocation of the image of a saviour in her letter of May 8 1905 would have appealed to Tom's religious and moral sense, and to his Presbyterian missionary zeal, but his innate modesty would have prevented his ever claiming it for himself.

The McQuestens were a deeply religious family, and if they felt some guilt at Ruby's sacrifice and death, they made reparation by sublimating their responsibility into creative and lasting works of beauty that have given Ruby's life and death, meaning and purpose. In many ways Tom was as selfless as Ruby had been. Forgoing any hopes of a personal life, he dedicated himself to public service, and never sought acclaim or fortune. Together Ruby, Tom and their mother, Mary, form a trinity of guardians of the McQuesten legacy today. They did not "go quietly into that good night"; they went triumphantly—and they have deserved their rest.

THE GREATEST GIFT

The gardens, Tom, are wonderful; so, too,
The Gage Park fountain and the Floral Clock,
The highways, bridges, golf courses and forts.
But what would you name as your finest gift?
Beloved Ruby sacrificed for you
And all the family, became the rock
Foundation for your future, the pure quartz
From which your grand achievements drew their lift.
What, then, stands as your greatest legacy?
Is it that you fulfilled her brilliancy?

G. W. Down (2008)

REPRESENTATIVE ACCOMPLISHMENTS
of Thomas B. McQuesten

Left and above:

Gage Park Fountain, Hamilton, Ontario

T.B. McQuesten, Hamilton Board of Parks Management, Chair of Works Committee

Architect: John M. Lyle; landscape architects: Dunington-Grubbs (1929)

The Sunken Garden, McMaster University, Hamilton, Ontario
T.B. McQuesten and Hamilton BPM
Landscape design and architects: Dunington-Grubbs (1929; razed 1972 for medical centre)

Victoria Park, Niagara Falls, Ontario
T.B. McQuesten as Chair of Niagara Parks Commission
Architect: W.L. Somerville; landscape design: Dunington-Grubbs
(Major improvements 1935-41)

Rainbow International Bridge and Oakes Garden Theatre, Niagara Falls, Ontario
T.B. McQuesten as Chair of Niagara Parks and Bridge Commissions
Landscape design: Dunington-Grubbs (1935-41)

Mather Memorial Arch, Mather Park, near Peace Bridge, Fort Erie, Ontario
T.B. McQuesten as Chair of NPC (Official opening, 1940)

Art Deco Landscape Design, Rainbow Gardens, Niagara Falls, Ontario
T.B. McQuesten as Chair of NPC
Architect: W.L. Somerville; landscape design: Dunington-Grubbs (1940)

Rock Garden, RBG, Hamilton, Ontario
T.B. McQuesten, Hamilton BPM, Chair of Works Committee
Landscape architects: Dunington-Grubbs, Carl Borgstrom and Matt Broman (1929-31)

Niagara Parks School of Horticulture, Niagara Falls, Ontario
T.B. McQuesten as Chair of NPC
Landscape design: Dunington-Grubbs; Matt Broman as first principal (founded 1936)

View of Niagara Falls from Oakes Garden Theatre
T.B. McQuesten as Chair of NPC
Architect: W.L. Somerville; landscape design: Dunington-Grubbs (1937)

The Japanese Garden, Oakes Garden Theatre
T.B. McQuesten as Chair of NPC
Architect: W.L. Somerville; landscape design: Dunington-Grubbs (1937)

Thomas B. McQuesten High Level Bridge, Hamilton, Ontario
T.B. McQuesten, Hamilton BPM, Chair of Works Committee
Architects: John M. Lyle and Noulan Cauchon; landscape design: Dunington-Grubbs (1929-32)

Sculpture Niches,
High Level Bridge
(empty since completion
of bridge, 1932)

Rainbow International Bridge, Niagara Falls, Ontario, open to traffic 1941

Rainbow Bridge, Niagara Falls, Ontario
T.B. McQuesten as Chair of NPC and Minister of Highways
Architect: W.L. Somerville (1938-41)

Above: *An early colour photograph*

The NIAGARA PARKWAY
from Fort Erie to Niagara-on-the-Lake
T.B. McQuesten as Chair of NPC
Architect: W.L. Somerville

The parkway was extended in 1936 with a total length of 35 miles
along the "Military Chain Reserve"

From battlefields to beauty

RAINBOW GARDENS,
Niagara Falls, Ontario
T.B. McQuesten as Chair of NPC
Landscape design and architects:
Dunington-Grubbs
(major improvements 1935-41)

Left:

Carillon Tower in the distance
T.B. McQuesten as Chair of NPC
Architect: W.L. Somerville (c. 1945)

Below:
Niagara Falls in the distance,
from the direction of the Tower

BLUE WATER BRIDGE, Sarnia, Ontario
T.B. McQuesten as Minister of Highways (1938)

The Blue Water Bridge was originally a single-span bridge
linking Sarnia with Port Huron, Michigan.
The bridge was twinned in the late 1990s, and constitutes
one of the busiest transportation arteries between the U.S. and Canada

**The original
Blue Water Bridge,
constructed in 1938**

Thomas B. McQuesten

THOUSAND ISLANDS BRIDGE, crossing the St. Lawrence River at Ivy Lea, Ontario

T.B. McQuesten as Minister of Highways (1938)

Fort George, Niagara-on-the-Lake, Ontario
T.B. McQuesten as Chair of NPC
Architect: W.L. Somerville with Ronald Way as consultant; landscape design: Dunington-Grubbs (1937-40)

Thomas B. McQuesten

Left:
Old Fort Erie,
Fort Erie, Ontario

Inset, below:
Military Guard
preparing for
re-enactment of
War of 1812,
Fort Henry,
Kingston, Ontario

Old Fort Erie and Fort Henry: T.B. McQuesten as Chair of NPC

Architect: W.L. Somerville with Ronald Way as consultant; landscape design: Dunington-Grubbs (Fort George 1937-40; Old Fort Erie 1937-39)

Mackenzie Printery & Newspaper Museum, Queenston, Ontario
T.B. McQuesten as Chair of NPC (Opened 1938)
Architect: W.L. Somerville

Below:
University Hall today

University Hall
in the 1930s

University Hall, McMaster University, Hamilton, Ontario
T.B. McQuesten and Hamilton BPM
Architect: W.L. Somerville; landscape design: Dunington-Grubbs (1931)

Above and right:
Lion Monument, QEW
Toronto, Ontario

T.B. McQuesten as
Minister of Highways

Sculptor: Frances Loring (1940)

Sculpture, Henley Bridge, St. Catharines, Ontario
T.B. McQuesten as Minister of Highways   Architect: W.L. Somerville (1939)

Tapestry presented to T.B. McQuesten c.1938-39,
as Minister of Highways
and president of the Canadian Good Roads Association

See photographs on pp. 206 & 223 for the tapestry's source of inspiration

BIBLIOGRAPHY

Whitehern Museum Archives. www.whitehern.ca. Mary J. Anderson, PhD and Janelle M. Baldwin, MA. All number references to letters and documents in the text are to this archive, and can be searched using the number shown in the text, or by a key word within the text.

Anderson, Mary J. *The Life Writings of Mary Baker McQuesten: Victorian Matriarch*. Waterloo: Wilfrid Laurier University Press, 2004.

Bailey, Thomas Melville, Rev. ed. *Wee Kirks and Stately Steeples: The Presbytery of Hamilton*. Burlington: Eagle Press, 1990.

——. *Dictionary of Hamilton Biography*. 4 vols. Hamilton: W.L. Griffin, 1981-99.

Barnsley, Roland. *Thomas B. McQuesten. The Canadians*. Markham: Fitzhenry & Whiteside, 1987.

Berketo, Paula, Niagara Parks Commission Study, 2000. www.niagaraparks.com.

——. Niagara Parks Annual Report, 1944. www.niagaraparks.com.

Best, John C. *Thomas Baker McQuesten: Public Works, Politics and Imagination*. Hamilton: Corinth Press, 1991.

——. *The Forgotten Builder*. Documentary for CHCH TV.

Bouchier, Nancy B. and Ken Cruikshank. "The War on the Squatters, 1920-1940: Hamilton's Boathouse Community and the Re-Creation of Recreation on Burlington Bay." *Labour/Le Travail* 51 (2003): 20 Oct. 2008. (http://www.historycooperative.org).

Boyanoski, Christine. *Loring and Wyle: Sculptors' Legacy*. Toronto: Art Gallery of Ontario, 1987.

Brackenridge, H. M. *History of the Late War between the United States & Great Britain, Comprising a Minute Account of the Various Military and Naval Operations*. 1854.

Cameron, Elspeth. *And Beauty Answers: The Life of Frances Loring and Florence Wyle*. Toronto: Cormorant Books, 2007.

Canadian Encyclopedia, The: ONLINE

Campbell, Marjorie Freeman. *Niagara: Hinge of the Golden Arc*. Toronto: Ryerson Press, 1958.

Carver, Humphrey. *Compassionate Landscapes*. Toronto: U. of T. Press, 1975.

Cauchon, Noulan. "Report on Mountain Highways of Hamilton, Ontario, 1919." (includes map).

Duffy, Dennis. *The Sideways March: Mackenzie King's Monumental Quest 1893-1940*. Ontario History ONLINE. http://www.accessmylibrary.com).

Dunlop, William. *Recollections of the War of 1812*. Toronto Historic Publishing, 1908.

Hamilton: City Planning Department, Hamilton, Ontario: 1919.

Hamilton, Robert D. *A Catalogue of the John M. Lyle Collection of Architectural Books*. Hamilton: Public Library.

Hunt, Geoffrey. Lyle, John, M. *Toward a Canadian Architecture*. Kingston: Agnes Etherington Art Centre, Queen's University, 1982

Kaler, John. *William Lyon Mackenzie: The Dundas Connection*. Dundas Valley Historical Society. (www.DundasHistory.ca).

Kilbourn, William M. *The Firebrand, William Lyon Mackenzie and the Rebellion in Upper Canada*. Toronto: Dundurn Press, 2008.

Laking, Leslie, Dr. *love, sweat and soil*. Hamilton: Royal Botanical Gardens Auxiliary, 2006.

Lewis, Paul E. *Niagara's Gorge Bridges: Marvels of Engineering*. St. Catharines: Looking Back Press, 2008.

Lyle John M. "Canadian Ornamentation Goes Native." *American Architect* (Dec 1931).

McArthur, Glenn. *A Progressive Traditionalist: John M. Lyle, Architect*. Toronto: Coach House, 2009.

Minnes, Georgina. *Whitehern Biographies*. Whitehern Museum, Hamilton: unpublished, 1999.

Newlands, T. J. *Wentworth Bygones*, No. 9, 1971. "The Parks of Hamilton." Head-of-the–Lake Historical Society, February 14, 1964. (Box 14-131).

Rogers, Richard. *Resurgence 207*, July 2001.

Seibel, George A. *Bridges Over the Niagara Gorge: Rainbow Bridge 50 years 1941-1991*. Niagara Falls Bridge Commission, 1991.

——. *Ontario's Niagara Parks - 100 years: a history*. 1985.

Somerville, W.L. "Planned Homes for our Munitions Workers." *Canadian Homes and Gardens 19*, 1 (January 1942): 11-13, 42.

——. "Planning Wartime Communities," *Canadian Homes and Gardens 21*, 1-2 (Feb. 1944): 38.

Stamp, Robert M. *QEW: Canada's First Superhighway*. Erin, Ontario: The Boston Mills Press, 1987.

——. *Bridging the Border: The Structures of Canadian-American Relations*. Toronto: Dundurn Press, 1992.

Way, Ronald L. *Ontario's Niagara Parks: A History*. Niagara Falls: The Niagara Parks Commission, 1960.

Yorston, Jessie. *Biographical Encyclopaedia of the World: "Thomas Baker McQuesten."* New York: 1949. (Box 14-129).

COLOUR PLATES:
PAINTINGS & PYROGRAPHY by Ruby B. McQuesten
(Research and captions by Julie Nash)

Colourplate 1. **Music** (After J.R. Seavey)

Colourplate 2. **Hand Holding a Scroll**

Colourplate 3. **Sepia Castor Plant Leaf**

Colourplate 4. **Charcoal Landscape with Ducks**

Colourplate 5. **White Stem Rose**

Colourplate 6. **Pink Stem Rose**

Colourplate 7. **Summer Strawberries**

Colourplate 8. **Pottery and Green Grapes**

Colourplate 9. **Autumn Maple**

Colourplate 10. **Afternoon Tea with Biscuits**

Colourplate 11. **Sailboat and Seagull Returning to Harbour**

Colourplate 12. **Sailboats and Five Windmills**

Colourplate 13. **Daffodils in a Ginger Pot**

Colourplate 14. **Early Winter**

Colourplate 15. **Poet's Daffodil**

Colourplate 16. **Pyrography box with Yellow Tulips**

Colourplate 17. **Pyrography tie rack with Irises**

Colourplate 18. **Grey Vase with Virginia Creeper**

Colourplate 19. **Bridging the River**

INDEX

Bolded page numbers refer to the photographs.

Please search the website (www.whitehern.ca) for possible further information.